William Faulkner

WITHDRAWN

William Faulkner

SIX DECADES OF CRITICISM

edited by LINDA WAGNER-MARTIN

Michigan State University Press, East Lansing

∞ The paper used in this publication meets the minimum requirements
of ANSI/NISO Z39.48-1992 (R 1997) (Permanence of Paper).

Michigan State University Press
East Lansing, Michigan 48823-5245

Printed and bound in the United States of America.

08   07   06   05   04   03   02   1   2   3   4   5   6   7   8   9   10

LIBRARY OF CONGRESS CATALOGING-IN-PUBLICATION DATA
William Faulkner : six decades of criticism / edited by Linda Wagner-Martin.
p. cm.
Includes biblographical references and index.
ISBN 0-87013-612-7 (alk. paper)
1. Faulkner, William, 1897–1962—Criticism and intepretation. I. Wagner-Martin, Linda.
PS3511.A86 Z9856955 2002
813'.52—dc21
2002006806

Cover design by Ariana Grabec-Dingman, Harriman, NY
Book design by Sharp Des!gns, Lansing, MI

Visit Michigan State University Press on the World Wide Web at *www.msupress.msu.edu*

Contents

Part III: *The Sound and the Fury* and *Absalom, Absalom!*, the Enduring Core

Part IV: Style, Humor, Genre, and Influence

Introduction

LINDA WAGNER-MARTIN

Few writers cast shadows as far-reaching as that of William Faulkner. Regardless of historical period, authors of novels and short stories seldom acquire the kind of prominence Faulkner has maintained throughout the twentieth century and now into the twenty-first. In a literary world generally quiet about the quixotic achievement of fame, Faulkner's name is the metaphoric equivalent of a crash of nearby thunder. Indeed, Michael Kreyling in his 1998 *Inventing Southern Literature* writes that getting out from under Faulkner's shadow is the pervasive dilemma of the coming century's literature.[1]

Perhaps such prominence is, in fact, not a dilemma. The world watches for standpoints, particularly at a century's end. If agreeing on the greatness of Faulkner's art can unify readers, scholars, critics and other writers, then that agreement serves as a touchstone for both a summary of twentieth century literature and a prediction of what writing in the twenty-first century might become. To describe Faulkner's art as universal is not merely a cliché.

As readers the world over have learned, a Faulkner novel is an experiential moment: one's life is marked by that reading. The intimacy of apprehending Faulkner's language and structures, and returning—sometimes repeatedly—to the work shapes the reader's taste for writing per se. Whether Faulkner's focus is the Civil War, or New Orleans in the 1920s, or World War I, the reader finds an immediacy, an urgency, in the fiction. In his superb 1994 biography of Faulkner, Richard Gray discusses the immediacy of the writer's universalizing tendency:

> Reading a Faulkner story, attending to its voices and agreeing with them . . . , we are involved in an activity that is vitally connected to what Faulkner was doing when writing it. We are engaging with other voices, other lives—including, above all, the voices and the life of the author—in terms of how we speak and who we are. We are being invited into a debate, a dialogue that requires a recognition of the living tissue of language that binds and separates us, as readers, characters and narrators: that asks us to assert, and also to honour, privacy. Autobiography *is* history, Faulkner realized. He wrote out of tensions that were his precisely because they were those of his special time and place.[2]

• • •

This collection is a modest attempt to chart the changes in the impact of Faulkner's great fiction. There is, of course, no other American writer whose art has changed the direction of all literature in English as Faulkner's has done from 1950 when he was awarded the Nobel Prize in Literature to the present. William Faulkner *is* the twentieth century novelist to be reckoned with: he must be studied, his greatness must be acknowledged, his influence must be allowed. In the reception of his work, which at times has been literally critical, there seems to be a new tone of appreciation, even of charity. It is as if the carping and stinginess of an earlier time in the scholarly assessment of Faulkner's oeuvre has given way to acceptance. The critic's stance has mellowed in the 1990s. The modern critic now chooses approaches that implicitly accept Faulkner's greatness and then employs strategies to show why his work is so affecting. Some of these strategies are themselves very new: one of the dimensions of Faulkner's greatness is that his chameleon-like work manages to remain contemporary. Consequently, it attracts readers who have been trained in comparatively new theoretical perspectives.

Twenty-five years ago, such was not the case. One of the best explanations of various shifts in Faulkner's critical reputation is John Duvall's description of the way that reputation moved out of the realm of Southern Agrarianism (which Duvall sees, rightly, as a phase of New Criticism). The changes in readers' reception of Faulkner's work, according to Duvall, has "not so much to do with Faulkner's texts as it does with the texts of Faulkner studies." The history of Faulkner criticism depended in part on Southern critics granting his work acceptance: not an easy role for people offended by much of his writing. As Duvall explains:

> Because influential Faulkner critics appropriated the paternal voice within Faulkner's texts, the scope of Faulkner's message about human relations often reduces to the play of acting males and acted-upon females. In short, a represented voice within Faulkner's texts becomes the prescriptive voice surrounding them. This interpretive paternalism buttresses a whole matrix of values regarding community, family, and gender. The paternalistic strain in Faulkner studies grows out of the social vision of Southern Agrarianism and goes much deeper than the particular criticism of any individual. The very questions asked about Faulkner's texts were originally framed within a discourse that consistently privileged 'community' and 'family.' As a result, conservative views of the relations between women and men shaped the Faulkner canon, trivializing the ideologically disruptive non-Yoknapatawpha material on the grounds that it is aesthetically inferior.[3]

Despite consistent praise for Faulkner's modernist writing, which reviewers from Evelyn Scott to Lillian Hellman and Conrad Aiken championed, Faulkner was traditionally viewed as the 'bad boy' of Southern writing. It was the work of Allen Tate, Robert Penn Warren, Donald Davidson, John Crowe Ransom, and Cleanth Brooks, then, to help readers understand the power of Faulkner's fiction as a highly conventional voicing of the complexity of the South. These critics read the Faulkner texts as heterosexual, male-centered, white, and Christian. Much of the ambiguity underlying Faulkner's strongest fiction was, thereby, lost. As Susan V. Donaldson points out about the Agrarian reaction to other Southern writers of the time, these critics "felt compelled to excoriate southern writers like Ellen Glasgow and James Branch Cabell" for their openness to the modern, but largely "'*because* they have a mixed thesis—, i.e., mixed of old Southern and Progress—*because* their intelligences are split into contradictory values.'" Donaldson quotes Tate's words in 1929—"'they are bad novelists'"—largely because they present opposing viewpoints. Tate continues, "'all great, or really good writers, must have a simply homogeneous sense of values, which incidentally are the kind of values we wish to restore.'"[4]

With this principle as their mantra, the Agrarians had difficulty even reading William Faulkner. They had already ejected African American writers and the less traditional (or more realistic, less genteel) white Southern novelists like Pulitzer Prize–winning T. S. Stribling from their covey of protected, values-centered Southern writers; and they accepted only a few women writers, the poet Laura Riding and Tate's wife, Caroline Gordon, into that company. But, despite their horror when William Faulkner's first few novels appeared (including the infamous *Sanctuary* in 1931), they responded to the obvious greatness of his art and devised ways to admit him into the Southern pantheon. (For example, in their readings of the offensive *Sanctuary*, the raped Mississippi coed, Temple Drake, became a symbol for the devastation of the South—figured as the embodied "Temple"—during and after the Civil War.) Robert Penn Warren's seminal essay on Faulkner, reprinted in his *Collected Essays,* 1958, and Cleanth Brooks' monumental *William Faulkner: The Yoknapatawpha Country,* 1963, became the acknowledged guides to reading Faulkner. In both of those works, the "homogeneous sense of values" Tate spoke of are discovered, emphasized, and touted: characters and themes in Faulkner's work that do not reinforce the Agrarians' moralistic readings are omitted from consideration.

It is partly because of this somewhat monolithic emphasis that, when deconstruction and feminist criticism arrived in the United States academic world, Faulkner's oeuvre was ripe for new kinds of explorations. Leaving aside Yoknapatawpha country, or at least recognizing that Faulkner's well-charted if imaginary location did not shelter all his characters and hardly presumed to stand for any world entire, critics found almost untouched many works to appreciate: *Soldiers' Pay, Mosquitoes, Pylon, If I Forget Thee, Jerusalem* (formerly titled *The Wild Palms*), *Intruder in the Dust, A Fable,* and many of the short stories (still ignored is Faulkner's role as great modernist short story writer). The result was an enormous shift in the definition, evaluation, and projection of Faulkner's intentions. What looking afresh at the Faulkner oeuvre, including, of course, the Yoknapatawpha novels, meant for these more recent discussions was a consistent interrogation of what the Agrarians had accepted as givens:

- that of course Quentin Compson honored his father's moral principles, cynical though they were;
- that the only power axis in Faulkner's world was drawn from one white man to another;
- that all of his African American characters were nostalgically stereotypical;
- that women characters existed only as foils for his men, or as prompts to spark action from the all-too-often passive Southern males;
- that the values of the South, and its attendant Christian philosophical base, were unquestioned in Faulkner's writing;
- that the customs of the South, regardless of time period, were stable and judicious;
- that the reasonable citizens of Faulkner's country were never plagued by guilt, sorrow, or irony, so that the role of memory in his writing was that of honoring the past, never questioning it.

Once critics began this widely-based interrogation,[5] it was only the sheer greatness of Faulkner's writing that enabled his work to maintain its prominence. In some ways, what readers thought they "knew" about Faulkner's texts changed so radically that the process of comprehending Faulkner required starting over, reading from the top once again. For instance, the controversy over Temple Drake's reasons for identifying a presumably innocent man as her rapist in *Sanctuary* took a radical turn when psychological information about the trauma of rape (the Stockholm syndrome) became public currency. Faulkner's character, then, could be seen as a seriously damaged woman, not a nymphomaniac who liked living in Miss Reba's Memphis whorehouse.

Deeper implications of the gendered power structure that enclosed Temple Drake, characteristic of the Southern middle class, led readers to see how stifling was the behavior of Temple's four brothers and her father, the judge, particularly as Faulkner emphasizes these characters at the end of the novel. New interest in the ineffectiveness of Horace Benbow, Lee Goodwin's attorney, the man whose portrait opened the novel and ran throughout it in sometimes strangely juxtaposed scenes, led readers to see how critical of the elite South—that culture as afraid to smell the shrimp as it was afraid to sully its daughters and its sisters—William Faulkner was. Education, a fine sensibility, and a willingness to ponder the deeper things in life were all traits that *kept* Benbow from doing his job. Benbow's training as a "good" Southern

man, replete with sexual frustration and the pride of being above social hierarchies, cost Goodwin his life. While *Sanctuary* is a novel about class and class
distinctions, it is surely also a text woven of gendered stories—power belonging to the male characters, whether they are bootleggers and murderers or
lawyers and judges, with women characters relegated to roles of sexual and
domestic servitude. In this example I am echoing the words of Anne
Goodwyn Jones and Susan V. Donaldson in their introduction to *Haunted
Bodies, Gender and Southern Texts,* which states that any contemporary evaluation of the South must bring into play "'a multiplicity of discourses' about
manhood and womanhood" and that "gender in the end may be as important an analytic category for making sense of the South as race itself traditionally has been acknowledged to be."[6]

Donald M. Kartiganer writes in his introduction to *Faulkner and Gender,
Proceedings from the 1994 Faulkner and Yoknapatawpha Conference* that gender
considerations are one of the strongest patterns in the 1990s emphasis on
cultural construction of texts, "the idea that reality is always already shaped
according to a dominant socio/political/ideological order, an order of language."[7] As he describes the evolution of gender approaches, correctly differ-
entiating between sex (the biological reality) and gender (the role, the
presentation, a learned response), Kartiganer points out that reading Faulkner
using Lacanian tools, considering the Symbolic Order and the Law(s) of the
Father, opens the body of work to strikingly new interpretations. Even though
I have grouped the first ten essays of this collection into two parts, titling the
first section "Recent Theoretical Approaches" and the second "Feminist,
Woman-Centered, and Sexualized Approaches," at base nearly all these essays
share a common interest in gender, if not—more directly—in the sexual.
Opening the book with these essays was the best way I could think of to
introduce today's reader to the fascinating ways available today of both
appreciating and studying the artistry of William Faulkner's works.

The essays in the first section have all been published in either 1998 or
1999: whether reading about the ways Faulkner chooses the food his characters identify with, or the manner in which World War I was continuously at
the imaginative heart of Faulkner's work (a topic to which, surprisingly, few
critics have attended), today's reader sees the way Faulkner's fictions overlap,
thread through each other to impart knowledge the reader cannot overlook.
These critics are all well-grounded in the Faulkner canon; they move easily
from discussion of one novel to a comment on another. Perhaps the mark of

the accomplished critic, regardless of that critic's age or experience, is such fullsome knowing of a body of work. The essays in the second section range from those published in the mid and late 1980s through Zender's essay from 1998. Each has had the benefit of a highly theoretical scaffolding, yet each is readable, concise, and text-centered.

The third section of essays—"*The Sound and the Fury* and *Absalom, Absalom!:* The Enduring Core"—reverses a reliance on theory, or at least modifies it. Whereas nearly all of the ten essays in the first two sections were published during the 1990s (indeed, five of them appeared during the decade's last three years), the seven essays which deal with these two central Faulkner works were published between 1971 and 1998. By providing a combined retrospective and contemporary view of Faulkner's own favorites, I hope to show how distinctive readings can be, even without a unifying theoretical perspective.

The fourth section of essays—"Style, Humor, Genre, and Influence"—reprints excellent essays (most published during the 1980s) that readers can benefit from knowing. This assemblage of work, like the book itself, is intended to be useful for all readers, regardless of their theoretical or political persuasion.

● ● ●

The history of this series of "decades" collections is itself interesting, and has been a part of my rationale for choosing the essays included here. When Lyle Blair, as director of the then Michigan State College Press, agreed to publish *William Faulkner: Two Decades of Criticism* for the leading modernist critic of the time, Frederick J. Hoffman and his protégé Olga Vickery, he was both honoring Faulkner and perceiving that this writer would become as important to the twentieth century as James Joyce had become somewhat earlier. *Two Decades* appeared in 1951; then Hoffman and Vickery prepared *William Faulkner: Three Decades of Criticism,* a collection that appeared in 1960 (from the Michigan State University Press) and remains frequently cited. The articles published in those first collections comprised a veritable pantheon of modernist criticism: Malcolm Cowley, George Marion O'Donnell, Conrad Aiken, Jean Paul Sartre, Warren Beck, Richard Chase, Richard Poirier, Ilse Dusoir Lind, Andrew Lytle, Walter J. Slatoff, Alfred Kazin, Ray B. West, Jr., Robert Penn Warren, and others.

After the deaths of both Vickery and Hoffman, Lyle asked me to assemble *William Faulkner: Four Decades of Criticism,* which was published in 1973. This collection followed the lead of the first two books and echoed Hoffman's description of the aims of the books—to be "of maximum usefulness" in their combining of "intelligent studies that settle some issues and raise others."[8]

In his introduction to *Two Decades,* Hoffman described the way critics of Faulkner's work were divided into two "camps"—the humanists and the leftists. Chary of general praise, the humanists feared that Faulkner's works might all fall into the pattern of "the cult of cruelty," a phrase coined by Alan Reynolds Thompson writing in *The Bookman* (1932), prompted by the publication of *Sanctuary.*[9] Hoffman's strategy in that first introduction was to prepare the reader for the variety of ways critics—even at that time—had studied Faulkner's works. By the time of *Three Decades,* when Faulkner's 1950 Nobel Prize had changed the tenor of commentary, Hoffman's introduction is much more positive, referring to Faulkner as "an acknowledged and established genius."[10]

My introduction to *Four Decades* (1973) continues these emphases and tries to list important works appearing since *Three Decades'* 1960 publication and, more importantly, since Faulkner's unexpected death in 1962. In that preface I predict the flood of criticism about to find its way to publication, which will make Faulkner the most studied American writer of the twentieth century. It is for reasons of this sheer quantity that the hiatus between 1973 and 2001—the publication years for *Four Decades* and *Six*—exists; in short, there has been no *William Faulkner: Five Decades of Criticism.* In some years during the 1980s, as many as fifteen books on Faulkner appeared. Even though the principle of selection for the "Decades" books was to choose among published essays rather than to use excerpts from books (in keeping with the aim of printing journal essays so that they would be accessible), this quantity of books suggests the proportionate quantity of essays. John Bassett, Faulkner's scrupulous bibliographer, notes in his introduction to *Faulkner in the Eighties,* his 1991 compendium of secondary criticism, that, while there have been "more than a hundred books on Faulkner in the last eight or nine years, not even counting the large project Garland has undertaken to publish volumes of Faulkner manuscripts and annotations . . . in many ways Faulkner commentary has been more diverse in the 1980s than in any other decade, a product partly of studies within newer critical frameworks."[11]

For a time, keeping track of the immense numbers of publications was almost beyond scholarly ability. But with the midpoint of the 1990s came the human tendency to look back at the century, and scholars wanted to categorize the work that had been done. (For instance, in 1995 M. Thomas Inge published his book *William Faulkner, The Contemporary Reviews,* an important collection of materials for readers and scholars.)

The impetus for *William Faulkner: Six Decades of Criticism* has been this move to organize the new, to give today's readers direction in their investigations of Faulkner's works—collectively and singly. This collection hopes to provide a set of perspectives different from those operative when the1951, 1960, and 1973 collections were assembled. To that end, I want to mention several books, published since the appearance of the 1973 volume, which made these striking changes in Faulkner criticism possible: these are the books that provided impetus for a turn in stance and comprehension for traditional (i.e., long-time) readers of Faulkner. Sometimes shocking during the first year or two after publication, these works nonetheless created the bodies of information and perspective that today inform many essays written by scholars old and young.

The first book to be acknowledged, paired as it often is with the Brooks' study mentioned at the start of this introduction, is Michael Millgate's 1966 *The Achievement of William Faulkner.* Perhaps because Millgate was a British critic, his even-handed assessment of Faulkner's novels, always stressing their craft and accomplishment, was immediately accepted. In 1975, John T. Irwin's much more controversial *Doubling and Incest/ Repetition and Revenge, A Speculative Reading of Faulkner* opened Faulkner criticism to the possible scope of psychoanalytic perspectives, cast as a long, unmediated personal essay without the usual trappings of academic scholarship. The reading experience, like the knowledge the book imparted, was unique. In 1983 Eric J. Sundquist began his work on Faulkner's pervasive attention to blackness, and the roles played by the African American characters in the fiction: *Faulkner: The House Divided* provided a rich weaving of historical and literary insights for scholars who wanted to get past the all-too-often-simplified dichotomies about Faulkner's texts criticism had urged. In 1990, Minrose C. Gwin's *The Feminine and Faulkner: Reading (Beyond) Sexual Difference* usurped the controversial role that Irwin's book had occupied for fifteen years. As she showed feminist theory's pertinence to Faulkner's writing, she gave readers invaluable information about ways of reading the novels. Partly because of Sundquist's and Gwin's accomplishment, in 1996 I was fortunate to edit *New Essays on*

Faulkner's Go Down, Moses, to which collection Gwin, Judith Sensibar, Judith Wittenberg, Thadious Davis and John T. Matthews contributed new work on this important and difficult novel. It is to two of these scholars—Sensibar and Davis—that this present collection of essays is dedicated.

Chapel Hill, North Carolina

<hr/>

NOTES

1. Michael Kreyling, *Inventing Southern Literature* (Jackson: University Press of Mississippi, 1998), xiv.

2. Richard Gray, *The Life of William Faulkner: A Critical Biography* (Oxford, Eng.: Blackwell Publishers, 1994), 372.

3. John N. Duvall, *Faulkner's Marginal Couple: Invisible, Outlaw, and Unspeakable Communities* (Austin: University of Texas Press, 1990), xii.

4. Susan V. Donaldson, "Gender, Race, and Allen Tate's Profession of Letters in the South," (quotations from a 12 December 1929 letter from Tate to Donald Davidson in *The Literary Correspondence of Donald Davidson and Allen Tate,* ed. John Tyree Fain and Thomas Daniel Young [Athens: University of Georgia Press, 1974], 245–46), in *Haunted Bodies, Gender and Southern Texts,* ed. Anne Goodwyn Jones and Susan V. Donaldson (Charlottesville: University Press of Virginia, 1997), 504.

5. Another important modernist writer whose work has been rejuvenated by the application of critical theories which are themselves younger than his work is Ernest Hemingway. The Hemingway of the 1990s—as studied through lenses psychoanalytic, deconstructionist, and feminist—is a very different author than the man labeled *macho* and *misogynist* at the time of his suicide in the 1960s. Changes in reading strategies gave critics and readers the means to move out from the biographical approaches that sometimes over simplified his art. For a series of essay collections that makes clear the effect of these changes, see my *Ernest Hemingway: Five Decades of Criticism* (1974); *Ernest Hemingway: Six Decades of Criticism* (1987); and *Ernest Hemingway: Seven Decades of Criticism* (1998), all published by Michigan State University Press.

6. Anne Goodwyn Jones and Susan V. Donaldson, "Introduction," *Haunted Bodies, Gender and Southern Texts,* 6, 16.

7. Donald M. Kartiganer, "Introduction," in *Faulkner and Gender* (Jackson: University Press of Mississippi, 1996), vii.

8. Frederick Hoffman, "Introduction," *William Faulkner: Two Decades of Criticism* (East Lansing: Michigan State College Press, 1951), v, vi.

9. Ibid., 2.

10. Frederick Hoffman, "Introduction," *William Faulkner: Three Decades of Criticism* (East Lansing: Michigan State University Press, 1960), vii.

11. John E. Bassett, *Faulkner in the Eighties: An Annotated Critical Bibliography* (Metuchen, N.J.: Scarecrow Press, 1991), vii.

PART I

Recent Theoretical
Approaches

"So I, Who Never Had a War . . .":
William Faulkner, War, and the Modern Imagination

DONALD M. KARTIGANER

So I, who had never had a sister and was fated to lose my daughter
in infancy, set out to make myself a beautiful and tragic little girl.

William Faulkner, "An Introduction to The Sound and the Fury"

There were three wars at work in the mind of William Faulkner: the American Civil War, World War I, and World War II. He did not fight in any of them, nor did he write about them, if by writing we mean an account, factual or fictional, of what occurs or is likely to occur during military engagement. They are all there—in novels, short stories, essays, and letters— and yet not there: wars fantasized as reckless adventure, wars recalled as part of a legendary past or foretold as apocalyptic future, wars that have paused and are about to begin again, but never the plausible, violent reality of actual battle.

With very few exceptions, war for Faulkner is an occasion for gesture, a decisive event that—in the fighting of it, in the telling and the fullest understanding of it—demands something other than concrete involvement: a figurative rather than a literal action, dramatic rather than strategic effect, the

---

Reprinted with permission from *Modern Fiction Studies* 44, no. 3 (1998): 619–45.

miming of battle. As for territory won or lost, casualties suffered or inflicted, prisoners captured, planes downed—these are not the purpose (although occasionally they are the result) of military action in Faulkner. What counts is the manner of engagement, however irrelevant to the war's ultimate outcome, which usually turns out to be of small importance. "What the devil were you folks fighting about, anyhow," asks Old Bayard of a Civil War veteran in *Flags in the Dust,* and Will Falls answers, "damned ef I ever did know" (252).

Surrounding Faulkner's accounts of his own experience in war and the portrayal of it in his fiction is a curious, in some ways unique, gathering of literary, regional, and biographical contexts: late nineteenth-century literary movements in France and great Britain; shifts in the American Southern cultural background, ranging from a paradox in turn-of-the-century Southern manners to the historical and psychological factors that were to contribute to the Southern Renaissance in the 1920s; and, finally, the specific crises of Faulkner's individual and family history. Together they comprise a series of modernist movements that pervade Faulkner's fiction, assuming a distinctive resonance in his treatment of the wars that preoccupy him throughout his career.[1]

Faulkner's introduction to literary modernism began under the tutelage of his fellow townsman, Phil Stone, in 1914 and continued more or less for over a dozen years. Unusually well read from the ancients to the modern poets, Stone supplied Faulkner with books and journals containing the work of the writers and theorists who were in the process of creating the modern age: Swinburne, Housman, Yeats, Pound and the Imagists, Eliot and Joyce, Frazer, Croce, Clive Bell.

Of particular importance to Faulkner as a poet—originally his preferred literary mode—were the French Symbolists, whom, like many of his British and American contemporaries, he probably first encountered in Arthur Symons's *The Symbolist Movement in Literature,* the 1919 edition of which also contained a large selection of poetry in English translation.[2] Here he could read not only the poems he would himself translate as some of his earliest published work, but also Symons's summary and interpretation of the theories lying behind French symbolism. Faulkner seems to have been particularly impressed by Symons's discussion of Mallarmé, which emphasized his commitment to the suggestiveness of allusion rather than to the detailed, realistic account of scene or situation:

to evoke, by some elaborate, instantaneous magic of language, without the formality of an after all impossible description. . . . Remember his principle: that to name is to destroy, to suggest is to create. Note, further, that he condemns the inclusion in verse of anything but, "for example, the horror of the forest, or the silent thunder afloat in the leaves; not the intrinsic, dense wood of the trees." (Symons 195–96)[3]

In 1955, during an interview at the Nagano seminar in Japan when he was asked to describe his "ideal woman," Faulkner responded, apparently recalling these lines of Mallarmé:

Well, I couldn't describe her by color of hair, color of eyes, because once she is described, then somehow she vanishes. That the ideal woman which is in every man's mind is evoked by a word or phrase or the shape of her wrist, her hand. . . . And every man has a different idea of what's beautiful. And it's best to take the gesture, the shadow of the branch, and let the mind [that is, the reader's mind] create the tree. (*Lion* 127–28)[4]

Reading elsewhere in Symons, Faulkner would have come across what would be regarded as some of the central statements of modern poetry: "Description is banished that beautiful things may be evoked, magically; the regular beat of verse is broken in order that words may fly, upon subtler wings" (Symons, 8), and this passage from Mallarmé: "I say: a flower! and out of the oblivion to which my voice consigns every contour . . . musically arises, idea, and exquisite, the one flower absent from all bouquets" (qtd. in Symons, 199).

Explicit here and in Symons's discussion generally is the sense of an alchemical magic and miraculism in symbolist poetry that the High Modernists, and especially their later New Critical interpreters, found compelling: part of what distinguished the language of poetry from the words of the tribe and the truths available to the more common uses of language.[5] A significant aspect of the current reappraisal of modernism is a reconsideration of the French Symbolists, Mallarmé in particular, which abandons magic, what Symons referred to as "that spiritulising of the word . . . that confidence in the eternal correspondences between the visible and the invisible universe, which Mallarmé taught (202–3). Such theorists as Michel Foucault and Julia Kristeva continue to regard the Symbolists—especially

Mallarmé—as responsible for what Kristeva terms a "revolution in poetic language," based on their quite secular attempt to reduce the control of established linguistic and social constraint over the word. The present emphasis is not on an Absolute or One, capable of being sounded by the poetic word, but rather on the notion that symbolist poetry restores to language a solidity, a corporeality that allows it to resist its role as a transparent vehicle of external meaning and achieve some degree of autonomous presence.

For Foucault, the upshot is nothing less than "the reappearance . . . of the living being of language," an unexpected reversal of the principle of "representation" that dominates ideas of language in the seventeenth and eighteenth centuries: "all language had value only as discourse. The art of language was a way of 'making a sign'—of simultaneously signifying something and arranging signs around that thing; an art of naming" (43). In the nineteenth century, by means of "suggestion" rather than precise naming, literature recovers for language a thickness of being that it had sacrificed to its representational function, giving up its own substantiality in order to transmit a significance not inherently its own. In its insistent remoteness from the materiality of "the intrinsic, dense wood of the trees," literature frees itself from a complete, totalizing sign system, within which the word is the passive servant of its referent. According to Foucault, literature "leads language back from grammar to the naked power of speech, and there it encounters the untamed, imperious being of words" (300). [6]

Kristeva's version of the Symbolist revolution focuses on Mallarmé's use of language so as to reveal more fully what she calls its semiotic force. The semiotic, an energy linked to Freudian primary processes and which exists prior to the formation of the subject, ultimately joins with the Lacanian "symbolic" (which functions virtually in opposite ways from the poetry of the Symbolist movement) to form "the *signifying process* that constitutes language" (*Revolution* 24). Within that union the semiotic, in its articulated form of a *chora*—an articulation Kristeva describes as "essentially mobile and extremely provisional" (*Revolution,* 7)—can assume a creative, revisionary role. While avoiding the psychosis that results from a total resistance to the formation of the Symbolic Order, the semiotic modality—particularly "in so-called poetic practice" (62)—can enact a transgression, a "breach" of the symbolic. Whatever its disruption of the socially, ideologically constrained order of the symbolic, however, the poetic "maintains a *signification*. . . . All its paths into, indeed valorizations of, pre-symbolic semiotic stases, not only require the ensured maintenance of this signification but also serve signification, even when they dislocate it" (65). The result is not the abandonment of meaning or that Symbolic Order which insists on it, but a renewal, a pluralization of meaning.

Central to Kristeva's focus on language—"meaning not as a sign-system but as a *signifying process*"—is her emphasis on a semiotic and symbolic in continual tension, energy at once released and articulated, "constrained by the social code yet not reducible to the language system" ("System," 28). The practice of signification involves "the acceptance of a symbolic law together with the transgression of that law for the purpose of renovating it" (28–29).

Language, in other words, because of the necessary relationship between the semiotic and the symbolic, remains an agent of possible revisionary signification within the context of the various constraints of grammar, society, and the paternal law. The transgressive nature of the semiotic, which Mallarmé invokes by his flight from precise naming to suggestion, has the power to renovate the symbolic; the semiotic remains possessed of what Kristeva calls a "negativity—drive-governed, but also social, political and historical—which rends and renews the social code" ("System," 33). Whatever the extremity of some of Mallarmé's lyrics, in which the word seems to strive for complete self-referentiality, in his theory, poetic language ultimately reengages the world. Poetry "remakes an entire word, new, unknown to the language, and as if magical, attains this isolation of speech" (Symons, 200); but, as *Crise de Verse*" continues, *"en meme temps que la réminiscence de l'objet nommé baigne dans une neuve atmosphère"* [at the same time the recollection of the object named bathes in a new atmosphere]" (Mallarmé, 368). Literature recreates the world of the real through the "suggestion" that has seemed to reject it.

The impact of Mallarmé and the French symbolists on Faulkner was to coincide with attitudes he derived from other sources. Chief among these were the historical, social, and psychological conditions that belonged to him by virtue of his birth and upbringing in the South at the beginning of the twentieth century.

In 1906, in *The Independent,* a New York weekly, there appeared an article by Mrs. L. H. Harris entitled "Southern Manners," exploring the role of dramatic gesture in the social behavior of contemporary white Southerners. Allusion, Harris insists, is the Southerners' central bodily and verbal currency, for they are caught, particularly the male, in the condition of being "himself and his favorite forefather at the same time" (322). [7] They inhabit "two characters . . . one which condemns us, more or less downtrodden by facts to the days of our own years, and one in which we tread a perpetual minuet of past glories" (321–22). The condition to which Harris refers is the familiar one of the post-Reconstruction, Southern white man, Lost-Cause ridden and suffering what Faulkner would later call, while describing Percy Grimm in *Light in August*, "The terrible tragedy of having been born not alone too late but not late enough to have escaped first hand knowledge of the lost time" (*Light*, 450).

The heart of Southern manners for Harris is the need to exist in the discrepancy between Southern past (or at least what Southerners take to be Southern past) and Southern present, a need that calls for theatrical gesture, the adoption of a "pose . . . [behind which] he sits and watches the effect of his own mannerisms with all the shrewdness of a dramatic critic. . . . [H]e feels the part, sees himself in the eyes of the other and enjoys the performance as much as if he were himself observing a good actor. And he is always a good actor; every Southern man and woman must be that" (Harris 322). In other words, the Southerner acts out, in full consciousness, a theatrical imitation of inherited social codes—with all the differences that theater requires. "[W]e carry our sword next to our manners, not literally, but figuratively— we have been compelled to substitute much that is figurative for what was once literal in our conduct" (322). And yet that "figurative" behavior must continue to convey the power of its former literal expression. 'Nothing is more offensive to Southern men," Harris continues, "than to intimate that every man-jack of them is not as dangerous today as when his favorite ancestor wore ruffles, knee buckles and a sword tied in his sash" (324). In the exchange of the literal and the figurative nothing need be lost; men must "preserve their honor" by practicing—and perhaps all the more perfectly for the empty scabbard at the hip—what Harris calls the "sword-point manner" (324). Mallarméan "suggestion" becomes a discipline of "gesture," in which the "intrinsic, dense wood" of violence is performed in bloodless pantomime.

The gesture need not be empty, a mere reference to another, more powerful form of behavior that is no longer feasible. Rather, it is a "new word," a revisionary act that accomplishes a comparable but not identical effect. Allusion has acquired a self-sufficiency beyond nostalgic representation: "Thus the Southern man continues to resent an insult with a challenge or a threat of one. But he never really fights a duel. It would be a scandal and an outrage for the friends of the prospective belligerents to allow them to go this far" (Harris, 323).

Harris's evocation of the Southerner who is "himself and his favorite forefather at the same time" captures on the social level the divided condition that Allen Tate, on the literary level, refers to decades later as a "double focus, a looking two ways" (*Memoirs,* 33). For Tate the double focus characterized the generations of Southern intellectuals of which Faulkner, born in 1897, was such a prominent member. "After the war the South again knew the world," Tate recalls in 1942, "but it had a memory of another war. With us, entering the world once more meant not the obliteration of the past but a heightened consciousness of it" (32–33). One of the two ways a Southerner looked was backward to the past of the Old South, which by 1900 had evolved into a complex mix of fact and myth. Young Southerners had come to regard it as an era of tranquility and elegance, an agrarian civilization of aristocratic refinement and high-mindedness, its slave economy either ignored or more or less justified by its alleged benevolence: all in all, an exemplary mode of existence which, moreover, had defended itself in the War between the States with extraordinary heroism and sacrifice.

The other way they looked was forward to a new freedom that was exhilarating precisely because it threatened everything that the previous age considered to be of lasting value. This was the modernist, urban, industrial, free-market world of intellectual as well as financial speculation, a world of universal questioning, fathered, in Paul Ricoeur's term, by the "masters of suspicion" (213)—Marx, Nietzsche, and Freud—and marked by a new order of economic, social, and aesthetic movements, all of which were determined, one way or the other, to, in Pound's phrase, "make it new."

For Faulkner's Southern generation the traditional and the modern clashed powerfully, even traumatically; the two perspectives not only looked in opposite directions, they looked at each other, and with equally subversive effect. On the one hand, under modernist probing, the Old South revealed its flaws: a glaring inequality among classes, the crude origins and highly questionable rise of the so-called planter "aristocracy," the squandering, irresponsible behavior of that planter class both in peacetime and in war, and a system of chattel slavery whose fundamental inhumanity was undeniable. On the other hand, to a traditional Southern perspective, modernism seemed to be, economically, the victory of Northern industry and its rampant

materialism, and culturally, a revolutionary stance without a program, one
that raised questions but gave few answers, exchanging a flawed but stable
order for chaos.

For Southern writers the competing visions of the Old South and the
modern world could become a fresh version of what Tate regarded as the most
harrowing, yet aesthetically fertile, historical examples of cultural conflict: the
clash of feudalism and the Reformation on the eve of the Elizabethan Age; and
the class of Puritanism and transcendental individualism on the eve of the
American Renaissance. At these moments, as with the Southern Renaissance
about to begin, there occurred what Tate called that "curious burst of intelligence that we get at a crossing of the ways" (*Essays*, 583).

The choice for the Southerner seemed to be either, on the one hand, a
single-minded commitment to the Old or New South—that is, a life of prin-
cipled yet impotent nostalgia or one of vital yet vulgar materialism—*or*, on
the other hand, clear-eyed acceptance of the conflict itself, that is, the double focus as the necessary stance of the fully aware individual. "Looking two
ways" could be a psychological torment, even a form of generational neuro-
sis: to harbor two utterly opposed ego ideals at the same time. And yet, as
Tate was keenly aware, it could also be the painful provocation for the most
comprehensive thinking and the greatest writing: "the perfect literary situation" (*Essays*, 292). The writer caught up in this conflict yearned for the past,
yet was morally troubled by it; embraced the excitement of the new, yet
feared it; was drawn in opposing directions and could resolve them, or at
least address them, more comprehensively in language than in life.

The Southern version of modernism thus contains a unique dialectic: not
merely the tension between old and new central to the language of any modernism, but one that compels the new, to a greater extent than usual, to
inscribe itself within the forms, the received conventions, of the old. One of
the results of that need, at least in the case of Faulkner, is to apply the
Mallarméan credo of suggestion and allusion to a kind of theatrical histori-
cism: a "gestural" mode of behavior and writing in which one's acts and one's
words define themselves as the repetition of an older cultural code still present, yet no longer viable—a code to be acknowledged, indeed faithfully performed, but as a form of allusion, in the half-parody of pantomime. However
faithful the performance, the effect is to rewrite the code so that gesture
becomes bodied with meanings its model never dreamed of, becomes the
new world, "unknown to the language," that alters everything.

• • •

War in Faulkner's life and fiction is one of his central points of entrance into this cultural and aesthetic network of gesture and indirection. The story of his war experiences—which is essentially the story of his imaginative reconstruction of those experiences—has been well told by his biographers, although perhaps not always with the humor that it deserves and may have been designed in part to elicit, or with awareness of that reconstruction as a kind of representative cultural text, one of the ways Faulkner had of being "himself and his favorite forefather at the same time." As a Southerner born in 1897, and as the great grandson of William C. Falkner, a decorated officer in the Civil War, Faulkner never ceased to regard war as a kind of quintessential experience for men, yet one that always seemed to have a strong aesthetic component: war as the epitome of Keatsian oxymoron, filled, as he would later put it in *Flags in the Dust,* with "glamorous fatality" and "needless and magnificent violence" (94).

As David Minter was the first to point out, Faulkner's inclination to theatricality took the form of his incessant role-playing. He presented himself to the world in a series of impersonations, variously playing the parts of the English Dandy, the bohemian poet, the town bum, the Southern aristocrat, the ex-bootlegger and gun-runner, the romantic suitor, the cynical father of illegitimate children, and eventually the hard-working farmer who happened to do some writing on the side. (See also Grimwood, 17–21.) But his greatest role, the one he played the longest and most consistently, and which represents his deepest personal involvement in the clash of Old South and modernist forces, is that of the World War I aviator. Within this masquerade Faulkner not only invoked the Southern nostalgia for heroic action; he also introduced, through comic exaggeration, an element of parody, as if he were at once reenacting and ridiculing the bold deeds that were a crucial part of the folklore surrounding the Civil War. That is to say, in performing verbally what was already a mythologized inheritance—claiming, of course, his poses were authentic—he also began the literary act of revising both the myth and its meaning; as Kristeva puts it, to "render . . . and renew . . . the social code" ("System," 33).

When the United States entered World War I in April 1917, Faulkner was not yet twenty years old, and, according to the Selective Service Act of May 1917, still not eligible to serve without his parents' permission. Subsequent events, however, indicate that Faulkner's ultimate failure to see active duty in the war was not merely the result of parental concern. Reading about the bizarre measures he and his partner in fantasy, Phil Stone, concocted in their attempts to get to "the show," one gets the impression that Faulkner's romantic requirements for war largely ruled out any actual involvement in it.

From the outset, Faulkner made it clear that he had no intention of merely enlisting in the army as a private. Apparently more important than his actual participation in the war was the manner of that participation; he wanted to go as his great grandfather had gone to the Civil War, as an officer, and even more, as an aviator. As eventually he would supply himself with a wholly apocryphal war record, Faulkner seems also to have fabricated tales even of his attempts to enlist as well as of his eventual experiences in pilot training school. Presumably concerned about minimum height and weight requirements, he claimed that before appearing at the United States Army's Signal Corps recruiting station he ate as many bananas and drank as much water as he could, on the grounds that the bananas, in combination with water, would swell, adding bulk to his relatively small stature. Evidently the stratagem didn't work, yet, according to Joseph Blotner, Army Air Service records contain no evidence that Faulkner ever tried to enlist, nor do they specify any height and weight requirements (60).

In 1918, having joined Phil Stone in New Haven, where the latter was at Yale working on his second law degree, both Faulkner and Stone decided to try for the British or Canadian services—Faulkner for the RAF, Stone for the Royal Artillery—by passing themselves off (quite unnecessarily) as Englishmen. They began to practice English accents and to assemble enough documentation of their British birth, Stone would later say, "to have put us in Leavenworth for the rest of our lives" (Snell, 107). Using a stolen notary public seal, Faulkner became a native of Finchley, in the county of Middlesex, born in 1898 rather than 1897, complete with a sterling character reference from someone named the Reverend Edward Twimberly-Thorndyke. Faulkner's new English mother, oddly enough, turned out to be living in, of all places, Oxford, Mississippi. Apparently Faulkner's family romance had its limits.

Despite his elaborate credentials, however—at least according to a story he told his younger brother John—when Faulkner finally presented himself at the RAF recruiting office on Fifth Avenue in New York, he was rejected as being too short; at which point, "Bill got mad and told them he was going to fly for someone and he guessed if they didn't need him the Germans would take him. They needed flyers too. He asked them the way to the German embassy"—whereupon the RAF recruiter, no doubt alarmed at the prospect of Faulkner on the opposing team, relented and accepted him as an applicant for flight training in the RAF-Canada (John Faulkner, 34–35).

Some of these pranks were ingenious, some were doubtless imaginary, and probably none was necessary—if Faulkner's intention were simply to get to the European front. Several Americans who would later write about the war, Hemingway and Dos Passos, of course, among them, volunteered for the Red Cross ambulance corps. A good deal closer to home was the experience of Faulkner's younger brother Jack, who, while Faulkner was bloating himself with bananas and inventing a hyphenated English vicar, quietly enlisted in the United States Marine Corps while still only eighteen years old. By September 1918 he was with American ground forces moving across France toward Germany; on November 1 he suffered serious leg and head wounds in the Argonne Forest, and eventually he returned, a decorated war hero (Murry C. Falkner, 91–101).

As for William Faulkner, he was a competent RAF cadet for the five months he spent in Canada while "the biggest thing that will happen in your lifetime" took place elsewhere (*Selected Letters*, 165–66).[8] He never got to Europe and it is virtually certain that he never flew a plane during his service, in fact may never have even been in a plane that was not sitting safely on the ground. But it hardly mattered. While in training, Faulkner began writing his parents of solo flights; of flying in such severe weather that "I came down the other day, so cold that I had to be lifted out of the machine, could scarcely stand" (*Thinking of Home*, 133). A month after the Armistice, having been "discharged in consequence of being Surplus to R.A.F. requirements (Not having suffered impairment since entry into the Service),"[9] Faulkner purchased a British officer's uniform, complete with overseas cap, Sam Browne belt, and wings on his tunic, and returned to Oxford, where he immediately began the process of turning himself into a comic folk hero of the skies.

There had been spectacular training-camp crashes, one of which ended with his plane inside a hangar, dangling from the rafters, with Faulkner drinking from a bottle of bourbon, while all three—the plane, Faulkner, and the bourbon—were upside down. He developed a limp and complained of headaches from a steel plate in his head (oddly imitating Jack's genuine wounds). Eventually he shifted the sites of his exploits to the European theater, where he claimed he crashed twice during aerial combat, once in France, once in Germany. By the time he was done, Faulkner had his war: the best of all wars, pure fiction.[10]

Faulkner's pose as a combat veteran continued through the 1930s and World War II. Although he took pains to see to it that Malcolm Cowley would delete his fantasized exploits from the Introduction to *The Portable Faulkner*, the fact is he never confessed the truth of his war experiences (Cowley, 82). The brief biography he supplied to *Forum* magazine, for example, which published "A Rose for Emily" in 1930, included this information: "War came. Liked British uniform. Got commission R.F.C., pilot. Crashed. Cost British gov't £2000. Quit. Cost British gov't $84.30. King said, 'Well done'" (*Selected Letters*, 47).

What was he doing, and why did he feel it necessary, or useful, to maintain the pose for a lifetime? He remained a player of roles, certainly; next to silence and indifference, it was his customary way of relating to the world. But the role of combat veteran was of a different order. Beginning with the apocryphal antics of his attempts to enlist, he gradually constructed an elaborate fable miming the war tales he had heard as a boy, the romantic quality of which he probably catches accurately in *Flags in the Dust*, in his description of Aunt Jenny's story of the death of her brother Bayard in 1862: "[A]s she grew older the tale itself grew richer and richer, taking on a mellow splendor like wine; until what had been a hair-brained prank of two heedless and reckless boys wild with their own youth, was become a gallant and finely tragical focal-point" (14). Over the years, in his life and fiction, the war experience Faulkner never had became a point of reference, a history he could call upon in order to impress a lover, wish a war-bound nephew well, console a friend in grief, or make a political or moral point.

On the one hand, all of this can be seen as Faulknerian gesture, comic yet complex versions of a willingness to adopt for his life what Mallarmé had advised for poetry, to turn from the mundane details of his reality to the "silent thunder" of his fantasies. On the other hand, Faulkner also realized, possibly through Symons's example of Mallarmé, that ultimately his life and language must replenish our vision of the world, not merely dismiss it. "The world," Symons writes, "which we can no longer believe in as the satisfying material object it was to our grandparents, becomes transfigured with a new light" (202).

Faulkner's warrior pose became a not quite reconciled meeting between emulation and parody, as if he were struggling to construct a gesture with a solidity of its own: an imaginary stance that yet casts a shadow, remakes the meaning of war from within an already intact Lost-Cause oral and literary tradition. Throughout Faulkner's creation of a war record, it is important to note, he never claimed to be a genuine hero, downing enemy planes, knocking out vital targets, saving lives. On the contrary, his tales celebrate the rashness of combat rather than its strategic aims, consisting of a series of extravagant comic episodes that belong more to the genre of the tall tale than to military history or realistic war fiction.

Faulkner "in war" is a man playing at being in war. In his play he invokes the stories he has heard of the Civil War, yet performs them, simultaneously, in the opposing modes of repetition and ridicule. He is honoring the combatants of that war through the flattery of imitation and yet also mocking the mythology that had attached itself to them. He confines his own deeds to comic flamboyance, in which courage is limited to the casualness—which is also the measure of the boldness—with which he confronts danger. Faulkner's war consists of zany theatrics, gallant pratfalls; gestures so empty of serious military content that they become at once farcical and heroic. Ultimately, this double-edged performance becomes the key to the wars he describes in his fiction, wars that reflect, with increasing complexity, the characteristic Southern conflict of "looking two ways."

Beyond the dual aims of imitation and parody, I suspect Faulkner believed that in some strange way he had successfully appropriated the war—not only as a civilian by eventually learning to fly but more by the sheer power of his imaginative empathy. There is a passage in *Absalom, Absalom!* which perhaps describes Faulkner's conviction that his war masquerade held a knowledge that transcended his lack of authentic experience. Quentin Compson, in his own Southern limbo of belatedness, envisions an episode from the war:

> It seemed to Quentin that he could actually see them; the ragged and starving troops without shoes, the gaunt powder-blackened faces looking backward over tattered shoulders, the glaring eyes in which burned some indomitable desperation of undefeat . . . he could see it; he might even have been there. Then he thought *No. If I had been there I could not have seen it this plain.* (154–55)

For Faulkner, even more than for Quentin—whose gestural existence cannot replace the heroic past denied him—the "real" war he had missed was an accident of time and circumstance that could hardly withstand the urgency of his need or the depth of his talent.

Faulkner's pose as combat veteran reaches its climax in two letters written during World War II. The first, written 3 April 1943, is to his nephew Jimmy Falkner, who was training as a pilot and would eventually see action in the Pacific. It combines some practical advice—if, given the source, of limited value—about foolhardiness and fear, with a by now characteristic paragraph of comic posturing that, under the circumstances, seems inappropriate at best:

> I would have liked for you to have had my dog-tag, R.A.F., but I lost it in Europe, in Germany. I think the Gestapo has it; I am very likely on their records right now as a dead British flying officer-spy.
>
> You will find something else, as you get along, which you will consider your luck. Flying men always do. I had one. I never found it again after my crack-up in '18. But it worked all right, as I am still alive. (*Selected Letters,* 170).

The second letter, written 1 July 1943, is not at all comic, and its implicit claim of veteran status sinks from inappropriateness to the level of indecency. He wrote the letter to Robert Haas, his former publisher, when Haas's son, a navel torpedo-bomber pilot, was killed in action:

> Bob, dear boy,
>
> Of course you don't want letters. They don't do any good. Besides, the sympathy is already yours without letters, from any friend, and some of the pride belongs to all the ex-airmen whom time has altered into grounded old men, and some of the grief is theirs too whose blood flies in this war. My nephew, 18, is about to be posted to carrier training. He will get it too. Then who knows? The blood of your fathers and the blood of mine side by side at the same long table in Valhalla, talking of glory and heroes, draining the cup and banging the empty pewter on the long board to fill again, holding two places for us maybe, not because we were heroes or not heroes, but because we loved them. (*Selected Letters* 175)

Faulkner does not quite claim to be among the "ex-airmen," but the possibility is surely open, and a letter three years earlier to Haas clearly implies it (*Selected Letters,* 125). Nor does he identify himself as hero or not-hero, but he will likely be at that long table in Valhalla, for all the world like one of his invented Sartorises, sharing the wine and talk of "glory and heroes." Was there no other prose available to him to console Haas for this terrible loss, except the fabulous language of his own self-aggrandizement? Is this bombast the sign of an astonishing insensitivity or of a shyness so deep it cannot express affection unarmed? Is he simply claiming their common blood—"the blood of your fathers and the blood of mine?" (Haas was Jewish, a fact that Faulkner had well in mind, as a letter written two days later indicates.) Or did he truly believe that he had so mastered the gestures of war that his failure to experience it hardly mattered—that he could say, with at least the authority of Quentin Compson, *"No. If I had been there I could not have seen it this plain"?* Indeed, did he believe that if he had been there, he could not have more genuinely fought it?

· · ·

The move from biography to fiction is always perilous, especially when so much of the biography is also fiction. In Faulkner's case one link between the two is that war, as the violent engagement of armies or individual soldiers in what we take to be a plausible account of combat, is not only missing from the life but also rarely occurs in the fiction, virtually never in the novels (Gresset, 15–16). And like his general public stance, so often characterized by impersonation, Faulkner's fictional wars are steeped in gesture.

Flags in the Dust (the original novel from which *Sartoris* was extracted and published in 1929) provides vivid scenes of both the Civil War and World War I, yet invariably they focus on acts of pure individual recklessness, as irrelevant to war as Faulkner's tales of his own experiences. Aunt Jenny's account of her brother's absurdly gallant ride behind enemy lines in order to capture a supply of anchovies from a Union officers' commissary tent—resulting in his being shot in the back by a cook—replicates itself three generations later in World War I, with Johnny Sartoris's foolish or drunken insistence on engaging in grossly uneven aerial combat with a German fighter plane. This scene, as his brother Bayard narrates it, concludes with Johnny climbing out onto the wing of his burning plane: "Then he thumbed his nose at me like he always was doing and flipped his hand at the Hun [who had just riddled his plane with bullets] and kicked his machine out of the way and jumped"

(280). Such heroics signify a war essentially without pain, without blood or shattered bone, and unblemished by any mention of a cause to justify the loss of life. Their supposed glory lies in their very pointlessness: "deaths of needless and magnificent violence" (94).

In Bayard's memory, the war is a cosmic event, of gods who continue their glorious dying eternally, their exploits surviving whatever motives may have once driven them: "[H]e fell to talking of the war. Not of combat, but rather of a life peopled by young men like fallen angels, and of a meteoric violence like that of fallen angels, beyond heaven or hell and partaking of both: doomed immortality and immortal doom" (*Flags*, 133).

Much of the problem with this early novel lies with its erratic tone. The novel vies between, without adequately controlling, a celebration of Old South heroics and a criticism of their irrelevance. Certainly the war scenes Bayard and Aunt Jenny narrate are both characterized by the absence of any sense of the abiding gap between the gesture and its material core. This is not a case, as Edmund Wilson put it in his early discussion of symbolism, of "metaphors detached from their subjects" (21), but of metaphors that have no subjects at all. The manner of Johnny's death does not so much remake its subject—the violence of war—or reveal its hidden truth, as simply ignore it.

A possible consequence is the collapse of Tate's double focus or Harris's subtle distinction between the literal and figurative versions of an action. *Flags in the Dust* may be an example of the Southern text that avoids the tension of "looking two ways" by committing itself wholly to a nostalgic rehearsal of an already mythologized past: gesture is all there is. Johnny's repetition of Sartoris's bravado is thus empty of the ironies of the interval between "himself and his favorite ancestor" because there is no difference between them. In Kristevan terms, gesture here is absent of the tensions of which any genuine "signifying *practice*" is made, absent of "the moment of transgression" of the Symbolic Order ("System," 29). As a result, the possibly unintended point of the novel may be that Sartoris's gesture has no meaning: it rests, as Mr. Compson says in *The Sound and the Fury*, "symmetrical above the flesh" (177).

One of the major differences between *Flags in the Dust* and *Light in August* is the latter's deep and consistent probing of a mind determined to see the virtue of war as rooted in its remoteness from any object whatsoever, a version of Kant's "purposiveness without purpose" (77). The death of Hightower's grandfather, following the burning of the Union storage depot in

Jefferson, becomes *for Hightower* the height of superfluous gesture—and this is its beauty. Its status as such does not necessarily lie in the grandfather's behavior but rather in the grandson's reading of it. The point of that reading is to recreate war as a substitution of art for life, and then use it as a model and justification for present behavior. Hightower's obsession with his own vision of his grandfather's death is an instance of Lost-Cause nostalgia perfectly aware of, indeed priding itself on, its irrelevance.

The raid on the Jefferson stores—based on General Earl Van Dorn's raid on Holly Springs in 1862, although placed by Hightower in 1865—was by no means a mere gesture, but an extremely effective military action.[11] Hightower's refusal to acknowledge this—like his shifting of the date to a point in time when any Southern triumph could be little more than gesture—betrays his preference for the act unmarked by strategic significant: "A handful of men . . . performing with the grim levity of schoolboys a prank so foolhardy that the troops who had opposed them for four years did not believe that even they would have attempted it. . . . Boys. Because this. This beautiful" (*Light,* 483).

Consistency being as inconsequential as fact, Hightower is not bothered by the contrary versions he has heard of his grandfather's death. In one, the grandfather is shot from his horse during the raid itself; in the other he is killed, following the raid, stealing chickens. Hightower prefers the second story (without acknowledging the contradiction) precisely because of its implausibility and its pointlessness.

> They didn't know who fired the shot. . . . It may have been a woman, likely enough the wife of a Confederate soldier. I like to think so. It's fine so. Any soldier can be killed by the enemy in the heat of battle, by a weapon approved by the arbiters and rulemakers of warfare. Or by a woman in a bedroom. But not with a shotgun, a fowling piece, in a henhouse. (*Light,* 485)

Crucial to Hightower is the fact that his own commitment to untruth becomes a dismissal of reality commensurate with, perhaps surpassing, the act itself (which may not have occurred): "And I believe. I know. It's too fine to doubt. It's too fine, too simple, ever to have been invented by white thinking. A negro might have invented it. And if Cinthy did, I still believe. Because even fact cannot stand with it" (484).

The Unvanquished is a major transitional text in Faulkner's treatment of war. To be sure, the Civil War scenes of the novel are predictably far-fetched, focusing on John Sartoris's boundless capacity to outwit superior Yankee forces—although his skill hardly results in any significant victories. In one episode, he escapes capture on his own front porch through the ruse of pretending to be a demented old man; in another, with the help of two teenage boys, his son and a slave, he disarms and disrobes an encampment of sixty Yankee soldiers, without losing—or killing—a man.

The concluding story, however, "An Odor of Verbena," written in 1937, seriously alters Faulkner's understanding of the possibilities of gesture. Not a war story, "An Odor of Verbena" nevertheless climaxes in a duel in which gesture not only replaces violence, it appropriates its power—and yet without sacrificing its own metaphoric nature. Bayard Sartoris (grandfather of Johnny's brother Bayard in *Flags in the Dust*) is determined to confront the killer of his father, John Sartoris, yet he refuses to repeat literally his boyhood act during the Civil War of vengeance against the profiteer Grumby, which would be the behavior consistent with the prevailing social code. Instead, Bayard enters Redmond's office without a weapon, his unarmed presence figuring the armed, his refusal of violence becoming its theatrical equivalent. So skillful is Bayard's performance that he compels Redmond to participate in the play: Redmond misses twice with his pistol and then leaves town—the literal succumbing to the power of gesture.

What has happened is that allusion has taken on body; Bayard's unarmed stance simulates the armed, enfolds itself within the established code in order to transgress it. He remains within the classic Southern paradox of "himself and his favorite forefather at the same time," yet also writes Mallarmé's new work *("un mot total, neuf, étranger à la langue" (Oeuvres,* 368) ["an entire word, new, unknown to the language" (Symons, 200)]). Redmond, like Bayard, may also be ready to forego violence; note that when Redmond raises his pistol, Bayard thinks, "I could see the foreshortened slant of the barrel and I knew it would miss me" (*Unvanquished,* 248). Yet when Redmond realizes that Bayard has no gun at all, not even in order to miss intentionally, he becomes aware of a new sign and is shaken by its revisionary power. He rises "with a convulsive motion . . . one arm extended as though he couldn't see and the other hand resting on the desk as if he couldn't stand along . . . he blundered along the wall and passed me and reached the door and went through it" (249).[12]

Upon returning home, Bayard receives the same confirmation (and scolding) from Aunt Jenny that would have come from his literal violence: "'So you had a perfectly splendid Saturday afternoon, didn't you? Tell me about it.' . . . [A]nd suddenly the tears sprang and streamed down her face . . . 'Oh, damn you Sartorises! . . . Damn you! Damn you!'" (254–54). Aunt Jenny, accustomed to earlier forms of Sartoris bravado, is unable (or unwilling) to draw any distinction between pure gesture and gesture complicated with moral cause. Perhaps her anguish is justified, given the genuine risk Bayard has taken. Even in its revised form, the duel betrays Faulkner's continued attachment to the old bravado, which allows Bayard to retain the approval of the community, even as he violates—or at least seriously revises—one of its most cherished conventions.

● ● ●

Following *The Unvanquished,* Faulkner's representation of war shifts again. Not only does he still avoid any attempt to portray war in terms of credible military action, but also he begins to eliminate battle scenes of any sort. He takes us to a point that is virtually outside time, poised within an expanded prelude to a war or a period of delay—war figured as a fantasy of postponement, as about to happen or be prevented from happening, as imminent, portentous, yet almost magically forestalled, like a film image suddenly frozen on the screen.

In *Intruder in the Dust,* a memorable speech (by Gavin Stevens, spoken to his nephew Chick Mallison) invokes the moment before the tide-turning battle of the Civil War:

> For every Southern boy fourteen years old, not once but whenever he wants it, there is the instant when it's still not yet two oclock on that July afternoon in 1863, the brigades are in position behind the rail fence, the guns are laid and ready in the woods and the furled flags are already loosened to break out and Pickett himself with his long oiled ringlets and his hat in one hand probably and his sword in the other looking up the hill waiting for Longstreet to give the word and it's all in the balance, it hasn't happened yet, it hasn't even begun yet. . . . (194)

Hovering above the long-settled outcome is an abiding potentiality. Knowing and fully registering the disastrous ending, "every Southern boy fourteen years old" can yet recover the exhilaration and hope that must have preceded, can harbor the double vision that gathers its power of possible reversal from the very battle it holds back:

[I]t not only hasn't begun yet but there is still time for it not to begin against that position and those circumstances . . . yet it's going to begin, we all know that, we have come too far with too much at stake and that moment doesn't need even a fourteen-year-old boy to think *This time. Maybe this time* with all this much to lose and all this much to gain. (194–95)

With *A Fable*, Faulkner's massive World War I novel, deferral moves beyond even the complexities of Southern memory. At its center is the moral act of soldiers bringing war to a halt by refusing to mount an attack. But that deferral, despite the three-day peace that descends on the front as a result, is also no more (and no less) than gesture designed to accomplish nothing, altering neither the inevitable resumption of war nor its enduring necessity. Gesture is the refrain of *A Fable*, appropriated by those who would continue the war—and the status quo it protects—as much as by those who stop it. Thus the particular engagement halted by the mutiny was itself purely gestural, an attack calculated to fail, the regiment to be sacrificed to an undisclosed military expediency. Moreover, the second mutiny of the novel, the one inspired by the model of the first, only succeeds in bringing to a climax, and terminating, the three days of peace.

Led by the Sentry, the Runner, and the Reverend Sutterfield, a British battalion climbs out of the trenches, and begins to run, weaponless, across the battlefield, towards a unit of German soldiers which has also emerged, unarmed:

[T]he two of them running toward each other now, empty-handed, approaching until he could see, distinguish the individual faces but still all one face, one expression, and then he knew suddenly that his too looked like that, all of them did: tentative, amazed, defenseless, and then he heard the voices too and knew that his was one also—a thin murmuring sound rising into the incredible silence like a chirping of lost birds, forlorn and defenseless too. (*Fable*, 321)

But the mutiny is doomed, the men of both forces merely running toward the artillery barrages that have already been launched from both sides: "[A]nd then he knew what the other thing was even before the frantic uprush of the rockets from behind the two wires, German and British too" (321).

Of the practical pointlessness of this second mutiny the runner at least is aware. The generals of both sides, anticipating the plan, have colluded to prevent it from spreading: "Then they will shoot at us, both of them, their side and ours too—put a barrage down on all of us. They'll have to. There wont be anything else for them to do" (313). Such is the gestural quality of the action of the whole novel: the hope of men "to have done with it, be finished with it, quit of it" (317); of the Corporal to overthrow the war culture over which the Old General, the Corporal's father, presides; or, for that matter, of the Old General to tempt his son away from his martyrdom—they are all acts whose meaning has nothing to do with their realization in the world, or even the expectation of it.

And yet *A Fable* builds its theme of the irrelevant act into a vision of a potentiality that never subsides, that maintains the power of possibility even though completion is inconceivable. Faulkner accomplishes this by bringing together something of the magical quality that Symons identified in the French Symbolists—"that confidence in the eternal correspondences between the visible and the invisible universe" (203)—and the metaphysical mystery inherent in the Christian story he has chosen as the narrative core of the novel; the gesture that redeems even as it awaits fulfillment. In Karl Löwith's description of the event of Incarnation, "Invisibly, history has fundamentally changed; visibly, it is still the same . . . the time is already fulfilled and yet not consummated. . . . [E]verything is 'already' what it is 'not yet'" (Löwith, 188).

If *A Fable* contains a tragic view opposite to that of the New Testament— the recognition that potential and actual redemption will never coincide—it also contains the hope implicit to the fact that they will never relax their tension: "[W]e are two articulations," the Old General says to the Corporal, "two inimical conditions . . . I champion of this mundane earth . . . you champion of an esoteric realm of man's baseless hope and his infinite capacity— no: passion—for unfact" (*Fable*, 347–48). Fact and gesture, father and son, law and mutiny, Symbolic and semiotic, "the intrinsic, dense wood of the trees" and "the silent thunder afloat in the leaves"—Faulkner balances them against each other, confirming an essential tension of his career, in this novel unwilling to advance them beyond a static equilibrium.

For the fullest account of the theme of gesture (and much else) I conclude with Faulkner's greatest novel, *Absalom, Absalom!*. War in *Absalom, Absalom!* is generally peripheral to the main action: the rise of Thomas Sutpen and the ultimate destruction of his family, and the retelling of that history by four narrators in the present. Yet the novel's climactic scene takes place in an encampment of Confederate soldiers, shortly before the end of the war, when the outcome is inevitable.

Quentin and Shreve, still talking in their freezing Harvard dormitory, create the scene—the action of which has less factual support than any other in the novel—and in doing so reach the greatest point of intimacy with each other and with the two men whom they have recreated as brothers: "Because now neither of them was there. They were both in Carolina and the time was forty-six years ago, and it was not even four now but compounded still further, since now both of them were Henry Sutpen and both of them were Bon . . ." (280).

For the setting, they have chosen central North Carolina in 1865, where two warring armies have also come together, on the eve of the end of their four years of battle. Invisible but for the camp fires, the combatants are close enough to begin to talk across the coming doom that divides and unifies them:

> [T]he two picket lines so close that each could hear the challenge of the other's officers passing from post to post and dying away; and when gone, the voice, invisible, cautious, not loud yet carrying:
>   Hey, Reb.
>   Yah
>   Where you fellers going?
>   Richmond
>   So are we. Why not wait for us?
>   We air. (280–81)

The tragedy of scene and setting is that all the talking can only lead to one end: for Quentin and Shreve, it is their final interpretation that Charles Bon is part black and therefore had to die; for the armies it is the culmination of the war in the South's total defeat. And yet, as Faulkner freezes the entire scene of some seven pages in the italics of the possible, there is a sense of fact faltering before the imaginary. As long as Quentin and Shreve keep recreating the past, they remain virtual brothers inventing the brotherhood of Henry and Bon. As long as the interpretive play lasts, metaphor will disarm reality; words rob time of its destiny. As long as the soldiers around the fires keep talking, the war will not come down.

It is as if Faulkner were holding back the war, holding back history, holding back the murder whose meaning he wants to explore forever, in the artist's delusion that, supremely rendered, the real will give way to gesture, the body to the imaginative power—as if what Symons called the Symbolist desire to "evade the old bondage of exteriority" (8) could achieve its complete reversal.

Within the scene the great cultural conflict of Faulkner's life and work receives its most intense depiction. Here, at the edge of ultimate defeat, is the pinnacle of Old South heroism—"*Why not wait for us? We air*"—that provided Faulkner's generation with its most daunting challenge; and yet here also emerges the novel's grandest example of modernist imaginative intervention. The narrators too late for the war nevertheless strive to explain it, join themselves to the past by bringing to bear on it meanings only the present can dare to take hold of. They take the leap no teller of the story, no actor in the story, has ever made: that the destruction of the Sutpen family, the destruction of the South, is a tragedy of race: the white man murders the black man who is his brother.

The majesty of the Symbolist dream so central to Faulkner's literary development found uncanny resonance in the Southern contexts central to his life: a war that ended more than thirty years before his birth, the war of his own time he could not experience while keeping his double consciousness intact. His response was the imaginative power that at once reflects the real and rewrites it through the gesture that, almost magically, unfolds reality's unknown possibility: demonstrating in "failed" novel after novel just how dangerous he was, how much the prose gestures of his life and his writing could perfect "the sword-point manner" that enabled him not only to possess but also to revise the reality he had only missed in ordinary time: "*No. If I had been there I could not have seen it this plain.*"

NOTES

1. See Gresset for a list of Faulkner's novels and stories (approximately twenty-five) that concern themselves with war.

2. See Kreiswirth, whose examination of Faulkner's translations of Verlaine provides convincing

evidence that Faulkner consulted the 1919 edition of *The Symbolist Movement*—certainly by 1920 when the translations were published.

3. Symons's quotations are from *"Sur l'Evolution litteraire,"* an 1891 interview, and *"Crise de vers,"* written 1886–1896, first published in full in 1897. Throughout this essay I use Symons's translations of Mallarmé's prose, since they are very likely the ones with which Faulkner was familiar.

4. See Minter (283n. 21) for a comment on the similarity of Faulkner's statement to Mallarmé.

5. See Kermode's chapter on Symons, which emphasizes the element of the occult in symbolism: "Symbols are, simply, images with this essential magical power" (Kermode, 112).

6. See the discussion of Foucault in Bürger, 48–54.

7. For further discussion of Harris, see Banta, 208–9.

8. The quote is actually Faulkner's comment in a letter to his stepson Malcolm A. Franklin (5 December 1942), complimenting him on his desire to enlist in the service.

9. I am grateful to Panthea Reid, who provided me with a copy of Faulkner's discharge papers. Under the category "Casualties, Wounds, Campaigns, Medals, Clasps, Decorations, Mentions, etc." the papers bear the stamp "NIL."

10. See Anderson's story, "A Meeting South," based on Faulkner's supposed war injuries (103–21).

11. Combined with an action by Nathan Bedford Forrest, Van Dorn's raid on Holly Springs forced Grant—his supply lines cut—to delay his advance on Vicksburg. See McPherson, 578.

12. See the discussion of this scene in Hinkle and McCoy, 205. There is a similar scene in *Absalom, Absalom!,* when Sutpen "subdues" the Haitian natives: "[H]e just put the musket down and had someone unbar the door and then bar it behind him, and walked out into the darkness and subdued them, maybe by yelling louder, maybe by standing, bearing more than they believed any bones and flesh could or should" (204–5).

WORKS CITED

Anderson, Sherwood. "A Meeting South." In *Sherwood Anderson's Notebook,* 103–21. New York: Boni & Liveright.

Banta, Martha. "The Razor, the Pistol, and the Ideology of Race Etiquette." *Faulkner and Ideology,* edited by Donald M. Kartiganer and Ann J. Abadie, 172–216. Jackson: University Press of Mississippi, 1995.

Blotner, Joseph. *Faulkner: A Biography.* New York: Random House, 1984.

Bürger, Peter. *The Decline of Modernism,* translated by Nicholas Walker. University Park: Pennsylvania State University Press, 1992.

Cowley, Malcolm. *The Faulkner-Cowley File: Letters and Memories, 1944–1962.* New York: Viking, 1966.

Falkner, Murry C. *The Falkners of Mississippi: A Memoir.* Baton Rouge: Louisiana State University Press, 1967.

Faulkner, John. *My Brother Bill: An Affectionate Reminiscence.* New York: Trident, 1963.

Faulkner, William. *Absalom, Absalom!. The Corrected Text.* 1936. Reprint, New York: Vintage, 1990.

———. *A Fable.* New York: Random House, 1954.

———. *Flags in the Dust.* 1973. Reprint edited by Douglas Day. New York: Vintage, 1974.

———. *Intruder in the Dust.* New York: Random House, 1948.

———. *Light in August. The Corrected Text.* 1932. Reprint, New York: Vintage, 1990.

———. *Lion in the Garden: Interviews with William Faulkner 1926–1962,* edited by James B. Meriwether and Michael Millgate. New York: Random House, 1968.

———. *Selected Letters of William Faulkner,* edited by Joseph Blotner. New York: Random House, 1977.

———. *Thinking of Home: William Faulkner's Letters to His Mother and Father, 1918–1925,* edited by James G. Watson. New York: Norton, 1992.

———. *The Sound and the Fury. The Corrected Text.* 1929. Reprint, New York: Vintage, 1990.

———. *The Unvanquished. The Corrected Text.* 1938. Reprint, New York: Vintage, 1991.

Foucault, Michel. *The Order of Things: An Archaeology of the Human Sciences.* 1966. Reprint, New York: Vintage, 1973.

Gresset, Michel, "Faulkner's War with Wars." In *Faulkner and History,* edited by Javier Coy and Michel Gresset. Salamanca: Ediciones Universidad de Salamanca, 1986.

Grimwood, Michael. *Heart in Conflict: Faulkner's Struggles with Vocation.* Athens: University of Georgia Press, 1987.

Harris, L. H. "Southern Manners." *The Independent* 9 August 1906:321–25.

Hinkle, James, and Robert McCoy. *Reading Faulkner: The Unvanquished.* Jackson: University Press of Mississippi, 1995.

Kant, Immanuel. *Kritik of Judgment.* 1790. Reprint translated by J. H. Bernard. London: Macmillan, 1892.

Kermode, Frank. *Romantic Image.* New York: Vintage, 1964.

Kristeva, Julia. *Revolution in Poetic Language,* translated by Margaret Waller. New York: Columbia University Press, 1984.

———. "The System and the Speaking Subject." In *The Kristeva Reader,* edited by Toril Moi, 25–33. New York: Columbia University Press, 1986.

Kreiswirth, Martin. "Faulkner as Translator: His Versions of Verlaine." *Mississippi Quarterly* 30 (1977): 429–32.

Löwith, Karl. *Meaning in History.* Chicago: University of Chicago Press, 1949.

Mallarmé, Stephane. *Oeuvres Completes,* edited by Henri Mondor and G. Jean-Aubry. Paris: Gallimard, 1945.

McPherson, James M. *Battle Cry of Freedom: The Civil War Era.* New York: Oxford University Press, 1988.

Minter, David. *William Faulkner: His Life and Work.* Baltimore: Johns Hopkins University Press, 1980.

Ricoeur, Paul. *The Philosophy of Paul Ricoeur: An Anthology of His Work,* edited by Charles E. Reagan and David Steward. Boston: Beacon, 1978.

Snell, Susan. *Phil Stone of Oxford: A Vicarious Life.* Athens: University of Georgia Press, 1991.

Symons, Arthur. *The Symbolist Movement in Literature.* New York: Dutton, 1919.

Tate, Allen. *Essays for Four Decades.* New York: William Morrow, 1970.

———. *Memoirs and Opinions, 1926–1974.* Chicago: Swallow, 1975.

Wilson, Edmund. *Axel's Castle: A Study in the Imaginative Literature of 1870 to 1930.* New York: Scribner's, 1931.

Unquiet Ghosts: Memory and Determinism in Faulkner

LEE ANNE FENNELL

Faulkner's fictional world is easily recognized as a "land haunted by memory" (Gray 231). Yet despite the pervasive influence of memory in Faulkner's novels, too little attention has been given to memory's over-arching role in elucidating such distinctively Faulknerian elements as disordered time, preoccupation with the past, the influence of the dead, and, most importantly, determinism. It is memory, with its disregard for chronological time and its idiosyncratic and highly personal chains of association, that pulls pieces of the past into the present, resurrects the dead, and remakes family history. And it is memory, the subjective and selective construction of a private past, that ultimately dooms Faulkner's characters to fates that in retrospect appear unavoidable.

In this article, I explore the central and unifying role of memory in Faulkner's work, drawing material from several of the novels. I begin by

Reprinted with permission from *The Southern Literary Journal* 31, no. 2 (1999): 35–49.

considering the scope and function of memory in the narratives, with particular emphasis on memory's role in directing the flow of time and appropriating the past. Next, I discuss memory's role in creating the sense of fate, doom, and determinism with which Faulkner's work is suffused. I conclude my analysis by discussing the price that memory exacts in the form of grief, and the power of memory to transcend death and loss.

Memory provides a useful template for understanding the disorderd time sequences found in Faulkner's work. Time collapses for Faulkner's people: the past is conflated with the present, the dead share narrative space with the living, and childhood traumas lie just beneath the skin of the present moment. Likewise, memory itself eschews chronological time, and often can "create the impression of an internal chronological disorder" as "[i]mages overlay each other, yield, intermingle, and pile on one another" (Ferrarotti, 31). Through such chronological disorder, the past in Faulkner's novels is experienced as a "detemporalized unit" accessible only "through a succession of plunges" (Pouillon, 82–83). As Jean-Paul Sartre explains in his seminal article on Faulknerian time, memory follows patterns set by the heart rather than by the clock; the most important pieces of the past, rather than those that are merely most recent, are placed closest to the surface of the consciousness: "We must not believe that the present event, after it has gone, becomes the most immediate of our memories. The shift of time can submerge it at the bottom of memory or leave it on the surface. Only its own intrinsic value and its relevance to our lives can determine its level" (228–29). Sartre analogizes the disruption caused by memory to an airplane's encounter with sudden rough air pockets, an analogy considerably more apt than his better-known image of a man facing backwards in a convertible as it proceeds through chronological time (228). As Sartre himself emphasizes, the idea of a linear progression in time (regardless of which way one is facing) is completely alien to the operation of memory. Faulkner's characters do not gain psychological distance from past events as they move forward through time; not only do certain memories leap out again and again regardless of the temporal distance traversed, such memories can at times completely arrest all forward motion.

Of course, even those memories lying closest to the surface of consciousness may remain inaccessible in the absence of triggering stimuli. Remembered events may lie dormant for years and then emerge suddenly and vividly in response to a particular sensory impression or chain of associations. It is this interaction with present experience that makes memory such a powerful, intrusive, and insistent force in the lives of many of Faulkner's characters. This contextual feature of the operation of memory is laid bare in *The Sound and the Fury* (1929), in which Faulkner traces the interior life of the mentally retarded Benjy, a character who not only lacks the cognitive apparatus to resist the constant intrusion of memory into the flow of present sense impressions, but cannot even identify the intrusions *as* memory. In deed, "the Compson grounds become a simple analogue for the memory" as "every site of Benjy's domain opens immediate access to all of the moments that have ever occurred there" (Matthews 65).

It is also significant that memory never merely rearranges recorded episodes from the past in the manner of one rearranging bits of film footage. Memory is creative, continually interpreting, selecting, and transforming the past to make it serve one's present needs; its content is subjective, fluid, fallible, and highly personal. As Franco Ferrarotti explains, "[m]emory works on a trace, reconstructs the general picture, a gestalt form, from the unsteady outline of a blurred footprint" (109). The notion of memory as personal reconstruction is perhaps most vividly illustrated in *Absalom, Absalom!* (1936), in which the saga of Thomas Sutpen shifts and blurs as various narrators attempt to recreate the story. Significantly, the "blurred footprint" upon which memory works does not consist of rationally ordered thought. As Miss Rosa explains in *Absalom, Absalom!*, the "substance of remembering" is "sense, sight, smell: the muscles with which we see and hear and feel—not mind, not thought," recognizing too that "its resultant sum is usually incorrect and false and worthy only of the name of dream" (143). Linked as it is to its bearer's emotions, mental states, and sensory impressions, memory cannot provide an objective replay of events. Yet as an often-quoted passage from *Light in August* (1932) suggests, it is both more primal and more tenacious than rational knowledge: "Memory believes before knowing remembers. Believes longer than recollects, longer than knowing even wonders" (104).

The slippery and contingent nature of memory may make it a poor substitute for an objective record of events, but these same features permit it to play an integral role in the formation of personality. It is largely through memory's process of selectivity and reconstruction of the past that one's identity is formed. In an important sense "we are what we remember we were" (Ferrarotti, 6). Faulkner himself seemed to believe that an individual could not be separated from his past as carried forward in memory:

No man is himself, he is the sum of his past. There is no such thing really as was because the past is. It is part of every man, every woman, and every moment. All of his or her ancestry, background is all a part of himself and herself at any moment. And so a man, a character in a story at any moment of action is not just himself as he is then, he is all that made him. (*Faulkner in the University*, 84)

Faulkner's comments also point to another characteristic of memory—its historical scope. Faulkner's novels are steeped in the past, often reaching back many generations through the exercise of memory. Memory always encompasses far more than what one personally remembers; it also draws in and appropriates the important stories of the family and the community to which one has been exposed. For example, in "Was" in *Go Down, Moses,* the reader is introduced to Isaac McCaslin and then told a story which was "not something he had participated in or even remembered except from the hearing, the listening, come to him through and from his cousin McCaslin" (4). As such memories are appropriated and made personal, they gain a vividness and immediacy that can rival present events. In "The Old People," the boy Ike McCaslin listens to old stories told by Sam Fathers until "those old times would cease to be old times and would become a part of the boy's present, not only as if they had happened yesterday but as if they were still happening, the men who walked through them actually walking in breath and air and casting an actual shadow on the earth they had not quitted" (171).

Such family and community memories are passed down not only through language, but also through an unconscious or preconscious process of absorption. This phenomenon is quite evident in *Absalom, Absalom!,* in which Quentin struggles to reconstruct a story which occurred decades before he was born, relying not only on spoken retellings, but also on memories acquired as if by osmosis. In recalling a conversation with his father about Thomas Sutpen, Quentin explains that it was not necessary to listen "because you knew it all already, had learned, absorbed it already without the medium of speech somehow from having been born and living beside it, with it, as children will and do; so that what your father was saying did not tell you anything so much as it struck, word by word, the resonant strings of remembering" (212–13). At times, something akin to a Jungian collective unconscious seems to be at work.[1] In "The Bear," Ike McCaslin recognizes that the bear "had run in his listening and loomed in his dreams since before he could remember and . . . therefore must have existed in the listening and dreams of his cousin and

Major de Spain and even old General Compson before they began to remember in their turn" (200–1). In similar fashion, Ike "inherits" the harsh unrecorded facts of his ancestry, just "as Noah's grandchildren had inherited the Flood although they had not been there to see the deluge" (289).

Yet memories are never simply transmitted from mind to mind through the generations like an object passed from hand to hand. Instead, each act of recalling and retelling transforms, interprets, selects, and reshapes the remembered material; each act of listening (or absorbing) reshapes the material anew.[2] Thus, in *Flags in the Dust,* young Bayard Sartoris is exposed not to the bare factual story of his great-granduncle's violent and foolish death, but to Miss Jenny's incessant and highly glamorized retellings of the tale. Young Bayard's own perception of the story is, in turn, influenced by the memory of his twin brother's violent death (Rollyson, 19). A similar process is at work in *Absalom, Absalom!,* in which each of the multiple narrations and interpretations reveals personal biases, belief systems, and obsessions (Waggoner, 176–82). It is in this manner, as Quentin observes, that past events continue to have repercussions in the present:

> Maybe nothing ever happens once and is finished. Maybe happen is never once but like ripples maybe on water after the pebble sinks, the ripples moving on, spreading, the pool attached by a narrow umbilical water-cord to the next pool which the first pool feeds, has fed, did feed, let this second pool contain a different temperature of water, a different molecularity of having seen, felt, remembered, reflect in a different tone the unchanging sky, it doesn't matter. (*Absalom,* 261)

Flags in the Dust demonstrates that a family's collective memory is transmitted intergenerationally not only through the telling of self-contained "stories," but also through the myths that the family weaves out of the raw material of recalled events. The uses to which individual narratives are put and the connections that are constructed between them are central to such mythmaking. Miss Jenny, for example, bases not only her own identity but that of the entire Sartoris clan on the reckless and violent manner in which her brothers, Colonel John Sartoris and Bayard Sartoris, lived and (more importantly) died. What evolves from her storytelling (and that of others in the community, such as old man Falls) is a myth of Sartoris that transcends the individual doings of the dead and sweeps down through the generations to influence the living. An even more insidious process of family mythmaking can be discerned in *The Sound and the Fury,* in which Caddy and Quentin come to view themselves as "cursed" (196).

Just as storytelling can extend memory beyond the life of the individual participants, so too can the written language. In many ways, the written word acts as a proxy for human memory, capable of transcending mortality and speaking across the generations, yet subject to the same problems of interpretation and fallibility that spoken memories exhibit. This theme is explored in "The Bear," in which the old ledger entries must be deciphered in order to reconstruct past events. Likewise, in *Absalom, Absalom!* Miss Rosa alludes to writing as a way of preserving memory when, in telling Quentin the story of Thomas Sutpen, she comments, "maybe some day you will remember this and write about it" (9–10). The transcendent power of the written word is also hinted at in *The Sound and the Fury* when Dilsey explains to Caddy that her name will remain Dilsey "when they's long forgot me" because "[I]t'll be in the Book, honey . . . Writ out" (71). It appears that Faulkner viewed his own work, and that of all literature, as a similar attempt to transcend oblivion and forgetting:

> I think that a writer wants to make something that he knows that a hundred or two hundred or five hundred, a thousand years later will make people feel what they feel when they read Homer, or read Dickens or Balzac, Tolstoy. . . . [H]e knows he has a short span of life, that the day will come when he must pass through the wall of oblivion, and he wants to leave a scratch on that wall—Kilroy was here— that somebody a hundred, a thousand years later will see. (*Faulkner in the University,* 61)

Because of its power to carry the past forward and make sense out of it, memory is a formidable creative force. But memory can also thwart and hinder; it can paralyze or inflict unimaginable pain. And, for Faulkner's characters at least, it has the power to eclipse future prospects entirely and condemn its victims to seemingly predetermined fates. A statement by Olga Vickery helps to pinpoint the problem: "Though man's measurement of time is logical, his comprehension of it depends not only on reason, but on memory and hope. The former defines his past, while the latter anticipates his future" (193). What is missing from Faulknerian time is not memory, but the concept of hope which would make contemplation of the future possible (Magny, 69; Sartre, 231–32).

In short, memory in Faulkner's work has the power to doom. Faulkner's novels are permeated with doom and determinism.[3] His characters are "irretrievably choked by fate" (Pouillon, 79); they appear as pawns moved by a cosmic Player, debtors called to account by a ruthless Creditor, or helpless subjects waiting for their destinies to be tumbled out by an indifferent dice-man.[4] It is not surprising that Faulkner's characters are often conceptualized as doomed and volitionless, "blind marionettes of Destiny, chessmen in the hands of the supreme Player" (Coindreau, 32). These images are chilling, suggestive of an omnipotent power that views human beings as mere playthings to be toyed with and cast aside when they become tiresome. But while Faulkner's characters frequently seem powerless to elude their destinies, a close reading of the novels suggests that this is due not so much to malevolent cosmic forces of fate, but to the almost hypnotic force of memory. If a Faulkner character is a plaything, he is, in the words of André Breton, "above all the plaything of his memory" (11). Of course, the fact that Faulkner's characters are victims of an "inner fatality" rather than external forces does not in any way dissipate the feeling of doom that hangs over the works (Pouillon, 85–86). Jean Pouillon is unmistakably correct in asserting that "Faulkner has no intention of presenting his reader with a theory of fatality. Rather, he wants to communicate to us those very impressions that strangle his characters . . ." (86). As readers, we are required to feel the doom that oppresses Faulkner's characters, to experience it ourselves with the imaginative empathy that great literature is capable of eliciting (Sheppard, 151). Far from reducing Faulkner's determinism to mere "psychological causes" and thereby emasculating it, as Pouillon warns (86), recognizing the role of memory in creating a sense of doom deepens empathy. It also makes the works more compelling. It is far more interesting to participate empathetically as a character struggles in the web of memory than it is to witness the predetermined downfall of a violitionless puppet.

At times, the machinations of memory seem to grant controlling power to persons long dead, filling the narrative landscape with ghosts that often upstage living persons (Gray, 231; Sowder, 98–99). As *Light in August*'s Byron Bunch puts it, "It's the dead ones that lay quiet in one place and don't try to hold him that [a man] cant escape from" (65). The influence of the dead is quite apparent in *Flags in the Dust,* a novel which is set in the shadows cast by Colonel John Sartoris and his reckless brother Bayard, and which concludes in a dusk "peopled with ghosts of glamorous and old disastrous things"

(432). The Sartoris home is haunted by "a legion of ghosts," and suffused with a family myth that destines all male Sartorises to die "deaths of needless and magnificent violence" (84). So powerful is the pull of memory and the force of family myth-making in *Flags* that it is easy to agree with André Bleikasten that "the living are shown to be the helpless hostages of the dead" (34).

But it is not the dead themselves that hold the living captive in *Flags*; rather, it is the ghosts that memory conjures in the minds of the living. To be sure, young Bayard Sartoris appears doomed throughout the novel as he pursues a self-destructive pattern of dangerous and pointless behavior; the reader is no more surprised than Miss Jenny when he finally dies in a virtually suicidal attempt to fly an experimental airplane. But young Bayard is not doomed by the family name he carries, as Miss Jenny believes, but rather by the impact of the family myth on a mind already obsessed and guilt-ridden over another memory—that of his twin brother's death in combat (Rollyson, 19). That genetics and family name alone are insufficient to fix unalterably the destinies of Sartoris men is demonstrated by the life of Old Bayard Sartoris, who lives into old age before dying of heart failure. In *The Unvanquished* (1938), we learn that Old Bayard (then in his youth) was confronted with all the weight of the Sartoris legend when his father, Colonel John Sartoris, was killed. Upon learning of his father's death, one of Bayard's first thoughts was the realization that he was now "The Sartoris" (247). Yet despite the pressure of his family name, Bayard acted against community expectations by refusing to violently avenge his father's death. This suggests that even a Sartoris, one of the "pawns shaped too late and to an old dead pattern" (*Flags*, 433), is capable of an act of free will.

The ghosts of the past, as reconstructed by memory, also hold sway in *Light in August*. As Eileen T. Bender observes, "the persistent force of memory drives each of the major characters, functioning like fate in this multi-leveled drama" (5). While the novel contains an intriguing plot involving present actions, "the significance of these present actions is to be found in the past, and the bulk of the novel actually consists of retrospective accounts of that antecedent action" (Slatoff, 174). For example, the entire life of the fallen clergyman Gail Hightower is dominated by a glamorously transformed image of his grandfather's death, a death that actually occurred during the decidedly unheroic act of raiding a henhouse: "It was as if he couldn't get religion and that galloping cavalry and his dead grandfather shot from the galloping horse untangled from each other, even in the pulpit. And that he could not untangle them in his private life, at home either, perhaps" (53). Near the end of the book, Hightower seems to understand at last the nature of the spell cast by memory and to accept personal responsibility for its devastating consequences, recognizing that "[a]fter all, there must be some things for which God cannot be accused by man and held responsible" (42) (see Slatoff, 191).

Joe Christmas never reaches such a realization; he remains bound by the force of memory until the moment of his death. The importance of memory in sealing Joe's fate becomes evident early in the book, when the narrative lapses into an extended flashback to Joe's childhood and youth that runs for over four chapters and occupies almost one-quarter of the novel. In this flashback, the reader gains access to the most tenacious and destructive of Joe's memories and finds the roots of his self-loathing and lack of racial identity. Because he cannot escape the force of these early memories, Joe aggressively seeks to fulfill the prophecy he is convinced they contain by flaunting his possibly mixed blood. He finally accomplishes his fate, with the help of Joanna Burden, a woman caught up in her own family legacy,[5] and Percy Grimm, a young man doomed by the memory of a war in which he was too young to participate (394).

Joe is not doomed by a society that refuses to accept him, as is sometimes asserted (e.g., Connolly, 41–44); he is doomed because he cannot distance himself from the child that he was (or, rather, the child which "memory believes" he was). Thus, he dares society, in the strongest terms at his disposal, to carry out the punishment he has been expecting since that long-ago day he stole toothpaste from the orphanage dietician. He receives this punishment at last, in a shocking scene that itself bears witness to memory's tenacity: "They are not to lose it, in whatever peaceful valleys, beside whatever placid and reassuring streams of old age, in the mirroring faces of whatever children they will contemplate old disasters and newer hopes" (407).

Nor is Joe Christmas doomed by the objectively bad events that occur during his childhood and youth. Although clearly traumatic, none of these events, viewed objectively, is of such crushing magnitude as to make free action utterly impossible. It is only when Joe's memory transforms these past events into inescapable obsessions that he becomes truly doomed by them. That such obsessiveness is not the inevitable result of objectively bad events is demonstrated by Lena Grove, a character to whom fate could hardly have been less kind. In the first few pages of *Light in August,* Lena's past is recounted: at the age of twelve, Lena nurses both her mother and her father through their final illnesses; she loses them both during the same summer. She then goes to live with an older brother whom she does not even remember, and spends the next eight years doing all of the housework and cooking for his family, including singlehandedly caring for his innumerable children and his continually pregnant wife. When she is about to be literally crowded out of the home (she is sharing a lean-to room with three of her brother's children), she takes up with Lucas Burch, promptly becomes pregnant, and is just as promptly abandoned (3–5). But far from obsessively reliving these events, Lena merely says, "that's just my luck," and moves on (5).

As I Lay Dying (1930) offers a completely different perspective on the power wielded by the dead through the force of memory. The Bundrens' ten-day odyssey through floods and fire with a rapidly deteriorating corpse is motivated by a promise exacted by Addie Bundren prior to her death. This remembered promise, which carries with it the memory of Addie's own strong will, has the force of inescapable obligation for the Bundren family. Even when circumstances make the continuation of their ghastly journey almost unthinkable, the shiftless Anse pushes onward towards the Jefferson burial he remembers promising his wife, speaking as if she were still alive: "I give her my promise. Her mind is set on it" (109) (see Galanos, 6). Although Addie's memory is powerful enough to drive the family through seemingly endless travails, it seems to release its grip once she has at last been buried, perhaps proving Richard Gray's point about the relatively greater ability of Faulkner's "farm people" to escape the past (235). The family moves on, with Anse sporting new teeth and a new wife. Only Darl is unable to move forward; his efforts to obliterate the evidence of the past by setting fire to a barn result in his commitment to an asylum.

Absalom, Absalom! is centrally concerned with the work of memory. The novel's only present action involves the reconstruction of the story of Thomas Sutpen and his son Charles Bon, both of whom have been dead for more than forty years at the time the novel begins. Thomas Sutpen, in turn, is driven and ultimately doomed by a very specific childhood memory—the memory of being turned away from the front door of a plantation house. Bon's downfall is likewise linked to his preoccupation with the past and his attempt to recover the memory of his lost father. Miss Rosa and Mr. Compson each show themselves to be strongly bound to their own personal conceptions of the past as they relate their versions of the story of Sutpen's life to

Quentin. Quentin and Shreve, in turn, become obsessed with reconstructing these past events. Such an obsession with the past comes naturally to Quentin, who is described as "a barracks filled with stubborn back-looking ghosts" (12), yet the process of reconstructing the Sutpen story is as treacherous for Quentin as it is mesmerizing (Dunne, 64). The work of memory culminates in Quentin and Shreve's cold dormitory room, where the highly personal meaning Quentin draws from the reconstructed story leaves him panting in the dark as he recalls a South he can neither forget nor disavow (*Absalom* 378). Shreve's comments on Charles Bon's childhood departure from Haiti apply with equal force to Quentin's relationship with the South:

> You were not supposed to know when and why you left but only that you had escaped, that whatever power had created the place for you to hate it had likewise got you away from the place so you could hate it good and never forgive it . . . that you were to thank God you didn't remember anything about it yet at the same time you were not to, maybe dared not to, ever forget it. (298)

But the influence of the memory of Sutpen is still not finished; it presumably continues to work on Quentin's mind, interweaving itself with Quentin's own troubling memories of Caddy as he moves closer and closer to suicide.

When we next see Quentin, in *The Sound and the Fury*, he is inescapably caught in memory's stranglehold and has already decided to kill himself. His thoughts on his last day are heavily dominated by memories of his sister Caddy; he is unable to keep his mind in the present moment for more than brief intervals before succumbing to memory's intrusion again.[6] Quentin is torn apart by grief over his sister, and his mind runs in grooved channels as he wanders aimlessly around Cambridge. He recalls past scenes over and over, examining them from every angle, as if to extract a final measure of torment from each one. Although the reader is made privy to Quentin's thoughts for only that final day, it is clear that Quentin has been agonizing over these same remembered sequences for months.

At least one critic has suggested that Quentin's suicide was a "creative act" undertaken to ensure that he would never forget his sister, citing Mr. Compson's statement that "you cannot bear to think that someday it will no longer hurt you like this" (*Sound,* 220) (Matthews, 79–82, 86). But suicide obliterates both memory and pain; it is the ultimate act of forgetting. As an act of negation, it has no creative power (except insofar as it creates troubling

and painful images in the minds and memories of those left behind).
Moreover, a review of Quentin's thoughts on his last day strongly suggests
that his suicide was prompted not by the prospect of forgetting, but by the
agony of constantly remembering. A more consistent reading of Quentin's
conversation with his father would be that Quentin's agitated mind could
not even conceive of the possibility that his current pain was only, as his
father cynically put it, "a temporary state of mind" (*Sound,* 220). Quentin
interrupts his father's fatalistic monologue with the single word "temporary"
four times after this flippant characterization, and one can almost hear the
outrage and incredulity building with each repetition (220–21). Quentin is
taking issue with the word; it may make sense to his father's alcohol-
benumbed mind, but it is nonsensical to one who, like Quentin, is locked in
an endless cycle of obsessive self-torment.

Benjy also suffers from the pain of Caddy's memory, although he lacks
the understanding and volition even to contemplate the possibility of ending that pain. For Benjy, remembering Caddy is agony, for it points up the
inescapable fact of her absence and his own irremediable loss. Because memory is always predicated on "the unavailability of [its] object" (Matthews, 69),
memory which has as its object a beloved and absent person is always an
exercise in grief. Benjy grieves inconsolably for Caddy throughout the novel
as the wound of her absence is reopened again and again by the force of
memory. It is important to recognize that grief, like all forms of memory,
exists in the remembering mind at the present moment. While it is common
to think of a person consumed by grief as "living in the past," this is not quite
true. Instead, a grieving person is painfully rooted in a present which no
longer contains the absent loved one. Memory looks to the past to measure
the magnitude of the present loss, but the past does not exist as an independent "place" to which one may retreat (or from which one may escape).
This is the point Faulkner was making when he said: "If *was* existed there
would be no grief or sorrow" (qtd in Meriwether and Millgate, 255).

Memory as grief is also an important theme in *Go Down, Moses,* as John
T. Matthews has emphasized (212–73). In "Pantaloon in Black," Rider struggles with, and is ultimately defeated by, the memory of his recently deceased
wife. After the funeral, he insists on returning to the house he had shared
with her, ignoring the advice of one already familiar with the power wielded
by the newly dead: 'You dont wants ter go back dar. She be wawkin yit" (136).
There, he is confronted with the stifling weight of memory; he finds the

entire six months of married life they had spent there "now crammed and crowded into one instant of time until there was no space left for air to breathe" (139–40). Raw with anguish, he gets drunk and commits murder, yet still cannot dull the pain of his wife's memory. In the last glimpse we are given of him before he is taken away and hanged by a vigilante group, he lies pinned to the floor of the jail, saying "Hit look lack Ah just cant quit thinking. Look lack Ah just cant quit" (159).

Despite all the pain that memory causes, Faulkner suggests that the prospect of forgetting is far worse. As Wilbourne comes to realize in *The Wild Palms* (1939), memory can only exist as long as there is someone alive to do the remembering; otherwise "it wouldn't know it was memory" and "wouldn't know what it was it remembered" (265). Thus memory provides a reason to endure, a reason to sustain "the old frail eradicable meat" in which memory resides (265). Death can obliterate one individual's memory—"when she became not then half of memory became not" (273)—but as long as someone remains alive to remember, there is still something held back from death. It is this capacity of memory that binds the boy Ike McCaslin to the man Sam Fathers in "The Old People," so "that the man would continue to live past the boy's seventy years and then eighty years, long after the man himself had entered the earth as chiefs and kings entered it" (*Go Down, Moses,* 165). In "The Bear," Ike McCaslin comes to understand the role of memory in transcending his own mortality: "he would marry someday and they too would own for their brief while that brief unsubstanced glory which inherently of itself cannot last and hence why glory: and they would, might, carry even the remembrance of it into the time when flesh no longer talks to flesh because memory at least does last" (326).

But if memory is a hedge against mortality and forgetting, it also exacts a price—the agonizing grief that the acknowledgment of loss entails. Wilbourne accepts the bargain: "Between grief and nothing I will take grief" (*Wild Palms,* 273). Likewise, in *The Hamlet* (1940) the widower Jack Houston returns to the house that he had shared with his wife (albeit without the furniture he had purchased for her) despite the grief this evokes. His retreat into the old house he had occupied during his bachelorhood proved unbearable, for "there, he lost everything, not only peace but even fibred and durable grief for despair to set its teeth into" (215). As McCaslin Edmonds puts it, "even suffering and grieving is better than nothing" (*Go Down, Moses,* 186). But McCaslin recognizes that there is always another choice: "you don't have to continue to bear what you believe is suffering; you can always choose to stop that, put an end to that" (186). This is exactly what Quentin Compson does; finding the price of memory too high, he drowns himself and extinguishes the memories he alone held of his beautiful, lost sister.

NOTES

1. For a discussion of Jung's work in this area, see Shelburne (28–34).

2. An analogous process is responsible for the evolving and often indeterminate meaning of myths, as Mary Douglas explains in her discussion of the work of Claude Levi-Strauss (5–56).

3. This point has been well noted by critics (e.g., Connolly; Baker).

4. For a discussion of the prevalence and significance of game imagery in Faulkner, see Rinaldi.

5. For a discussion of the influence of this legacy, see Sichi (73–75).

6. Of the 130 pages contained in the "Quentin" section, only 39 take place wholly in the present moment.

WORKS CITED

Baker, Carlos, "William Faulkner: the Doomed and the Damned." In *The Young Rebel in American Literature,* edited by Carl Bode, 145–169. London: William Heinemann Ltd., 1959.

Bender, Eileen T. "Faulkner as Surrealist: The Persistence of Memory in *Light in August." Southern Literary Journal* 18, no. 8 (1985): 3–12.

Bleikasten, André. *The Ink of Melancholy: Faulkner's Novels from* The Sound and the Fury *to* Light in August. Bloomington: Indiana University Press, 1990.

Breton, André. *Manifestoes of Surrealism,* translated by Richard Seaver and Helen R. Lane. Ann Arbor: University of Michigan Press, 1972.

Coindreau, Maurice Edgar. "Preface to *Light in August."* In *The Time of William Faulkner; a French View of Modern American Fiction,* edited and translated by George McMillan Reeves, 31–40. Columbia: University of South Carolina Press, 1971.

Connolly, Thomas E. "Fate and 'the Agony of will': Determinism in Some Works of William Faulkner." In *Essays on Determinism in American Literature,* edited by Sydney J. Krause, 36–52. Kent, Ohio: Kent Sate University Press, 1964.

Douglas, Mary. "The Meaning of Myth." In *The Structural Study of Myth and Totemism,* edited by Edmund Leach, 49–69. London: Tavistock Publications Ltd., 1967.

Dunne, Robert. *"Absalom, Absalom!* and the Ripple-Effect of the Past." *University of Mississippi Studies in English* 10 (1992): 56–66.

Faulkner, William. *Absalom, Absalom!.* New York: Modern Library College Edition, 1936.

———. *As I Lay Dying.* New York: Vintage Books, 1964.

———. *Faulkner in the University: Class Conferences at the University of Virginia, 1957–1958,* edited by Frederick L. Gwynn and Joseph L. Blotner. Charlottesville: University of Virginia Press, 1959.

———. *Flags in the Dust,* edited by Douglas Day. New York: Vintage Books, 1974.

———. *Go Down, Moses.* New York: Vintage Books, 1973.

———. *The Hamlet.* New York: Vintage Books, 1956.

———. *If I Forget Thee, Jerusalem [The Wild Palms].* New York: Vintage International, 1995.

———. *Light in August.* New York: Modern Library College Edition, 1932.

———. *The Sound and the Fury.* New York: Vintage Books, 1946.

———. *The Unvanquished.* New York: Vintage Books. 1966.

Ferrarotti, Franco. *Time, Memory, and Society.* New York: Greenwood Press, 1990.

Galanos, Jorgos. "The Metaphoricity of Memory in Faulkner's *As I Lay Dying." The Faulkner Journal* 5, no. 2 (1990): 3–13.

Gray, Richard. *The Literature of Memory: Modern Writers of the American South.* Baltimore: Johns Hopkins University Press, 1977.

Magny, Claude-Edmonde. "Faulkner or Theological Inversion." In *Faulkner: A Collection of Critical Essays,* edited by Robert Penn Warren, 66–78. Englewood Cliffs, N.J.: Prentice Hall, Inc., 1966.

Matthews, John T. *The Play of Faulkner's Language.* Ithaca: Cornell University Press, 1972.

Meriwether, James B., and Michael Millgate, eds. *Lion in the Garden: Interviews with William Faulkner 1926–1962.* New York: Random House, 1968.

Pouillon, Jean. "Time and Destiny in Faulkner." In *Faulkner: A Collection of Critical Essays,* edited by Robert Penn Warren, 79–86. Englewood Cliffs, N.J.: Prentice-Hall, Inc., 1966.

Rinaldi, Nicholas M. "Game Imagery and Game-Consciousness in Faulkner's Fiction." *Twentieth Century Literature* 10 (1964): 108–18.

Rollyson, Carl. E. Jr. *Uses of the Past in the Novels of William Faulkner.* Ann Arbor: UMI Research Press, 1984.

Sartre, Jean-Paul. "Time in Faulkner: *The Sound and the Fury."* In *William Faulkner: Three Decades of Criticism,* edited by Frederick J. Hoffman and Olga W. Vickery, translated by Martine Darmon, 228–29. East Lansing: Michigan State University Press, 1960.

Shelburne, Walter A. *Mythos and Logos in the Thought of Carl Jung.* Albany: State University of New York Press, 1988.

Sheppard, Anne. *Aesthetics: An Introduction to the Philosophy of Art.* Oxford: Oxford University Press, 1987.

Sichi, Edward Jr. "Faulkner's Joe Christmas: 'Memory Believes Before Knowing Remembers.'" *Cithara*

8 (1979): 73–75.

Slatoff, Walter J. *Quest for Failure: A Study of William Faulkner.* Ithaca: Cornell University Press, 1960.

Sowder, William J. *Existential-Phenomenological Readings on Faulkner.* Conway: University of Central Arkansas, 1991.

Vickery, Olga W. "Faulkner and the Contours of Time." *Georgia Review* 12 (1958): 192–201.

Waggoner, Hyatt. "Past as Present: *Absalom, Absalom!*" In *Faulkner: A Collection of Critical Essays,* edited by Robert Penn Warren, 175–85. Englewood Cliffs, N.J.: Prentice-Hall, Inc., 1966.

"He was getting it involved with himself": Identity and Reflexivity in William Faulkner's *Light in August* and *Absalom, Absalom!*

HELEN LYNNE SUGARMAN

In both *Light in August* and *Absalom, Absalom!*, William Faulkner presents a world in which twentieth-century perceptions of identities and social roles are radically altered. Detailed readings of the two novels will show that the fear of cultural or economic difference which was so prominent in the South of Faulkner's novels can be viewed as a reflection of the massive social reordering that occurred directly after the Civil War. In the South of *Absalom, Absalom!* and *Light in August,* the South in which the different social and economic roles of the races and classes were strictly prescribed and which was emerging from the defeat of the Civil War, difference of any kind acquired an even more charged meaning than it had before the war.

After the Emancipation Proclamation was issued, the relationships between blacks and whites were no longer legally mandated. According to Elizabeth Fox-Genovese, in spite of the fact that blacks were considered equal

Reprinted with permission from *The Southern Quarterly* 36, no. 2 (1998): 95–109.

to whites under the law, whites' deeply ingrained ideas about racial hierarchies did not change (66).[1] At that point, perhaps because the legal issues surrounding racial relationships were radically altered, the socioeconomic status of many of the less affluent whites was severely affected as well. Michael Goldfield, following the arguments of Theodore Allen, finds the origins of the racial issue in the seventeenth century, when the rebellions of both black and white laborers highlighted the need for a "social buffer" with which affluent people could impose some sort of control over the laboring population (117). Before this time, it was uncommon for people to think in terms of race, but rather in terms of economics; in fact, there were both black and white slaves and indentured servants.

In "The Color of Politics in the United States," Goldfield attributes the poor whites' racial prejudice to what he views as the economic manipulation inflicted on them by the wealthy. Instead of encouraging a more economically feasible alliance with blacks, he argues, upper-class whites manipulated their less affluent counterparts into a significantly less beneficial alliance with themselves.[2] Such an alliance, based solely on racial origin, naturally benefited no one but the affluent whites. It seems, however, that the issues of race and class in the South cannot be so neatly separated. A truer version of the post–Civil War realignment might contain elements of both the race hatred that older critics like W. J. Cash foreground as well as the economic issues that more recent critics like Goldfield view as central.[3]

Taking such arguments into consideration, I would suggest that after the Emancipation Proclamation new realities forced the white upper class to reassess the identities and social roles of those whom they had formerly held in bondage. More importantly they had to remodel their own identities and social roles as well. Now that they no longer officially held a legal and economic advantage, were they essentially the same as their former slaves? Both *Light in August* and *Absalom, Absalom!* bring forth such questions.

In *Light in August*, Joe Christmas must decide to what extent he can reorder himself to fit his assessment of the expectations of Jefferson's white-dominated society. *Absalom, Absalom!*, on the other hand, is centrally concerned with the inability of Jefferson's townspeople to successfully negotiate what they see as the constant distortion of social convention represented by the outsider Thomas Sutpen and his "grand design."

Joe Christmas, believing that he is of mixed parentage, finds himself incapable of functioning successfully within either white or black society.

Consequently, a central concern in *Light in August* is the process by which Joe refuses to embrace either culture. As a result of this refusal, he ultimately kills his white mistress, Joanna Burden.[4] The novel is permeated with imagery illustrating Joe's vacillation between the two worlds. It appears that Joe's unclear understanding of what society expects of him encourages him to reject all socially determined moral codes. However, even though he rejects society's rules, the community still holds him accountable to these same rules, killing him and then castrating him.[5] I would suggest that part of the reason for the town's violent reaction to him is that they had once treated him as one of themselves. Consequently, once the townspeople realize that Joe Christmas is not who they think he is, they begin to question their own identities and self-perceptions.

Ralph Watkins argues that the prevailing fear in the South at this time was a fear of mulattoes, rather than a fear of blacks (13). Because blacks were considered an "inferior and distinct *species,"* Joe's racial ambiguity has two implications for the people of Jefferson (Watkins, 13 emphasis added). First, the town's uncertainty about Joe's place in society reflects the murkiness of their own social positions. Their unwillingness to accept that ambiguity becomes more understandable when Joe's unclear identity also forces them to question their fundamental status as human beings. For, following the pre-vailing argument of the time, if one believed that blacks were truly a differ-ent species, then the racially specific definition of a human being is no longer valid. If, as the townspeople realize, the way a person looks and the roles that person fulfills are not a guarantee of racial identity, then in the final analysis there is no way of knowing with any certainty what anyone's identity is.

Through a similar process, although economic rather than racial issues are emphasized, the wealthy people of Jefferson are forced to reassess their per-ceptions of their own economic identities. Because Thomas Sutpen was not born into Jefferson's elite, the town's reluctant toleration of him results in *Absalom, Absalom!*'s narrators holding him more than usually accountable to their subtle local norms and mores. This question of accountability is directly parallel to Joe Christmas's experience in *Light in August.* Joe could not suc-cessfully function in either black or white society, but he is accountable to both, while Sutpen, as an outsider, must reconcile both his past and present lives to the townspeople's satisfaction if he is to be truly accepted in Jefferson.

It may be helpful to compare Sutpen's experience upon arriving in Jefferson with Joe Christmas's oscillation between the black and the white worlds. After his early life in an orphanage, Joe is raised as a white boy, complete with an unsuccessful sexual initiation by a black girl. It is not, however, the success or failure of the sexual encounter that is important here, but the fact that Joe's intended participation in it underscores his position as a white boy, identifying him as the powerful one in future racial relationships. In this encounter, Joe goes to the shed, intending to copulate with the black girl, with whom "one of the older boys had arranged" the experience (146). Significantly, the girl is never identified; rather, she is referred to only as "the negro girl" and then later only as an odor: "He could not move at once, standing there, smelling the woman, smelling the negro all at once; enclosed by the womanshenegro and the haste . . ." (147).

Even sixty-five years after the Civil War, black women were still considered to be objects whose sole purpose for existence was to affirm the masculinity of young white boys. This inability to conceive of non-whites as human is described in *Absalom, Absalom!:*

> girls of [Henry's] own class interdict and inaccessible and . . . hence only the slave
> girls [were accessible to a young white boy] . . . and the young man rides up and
> beckons the watching overseer and says Send me Juno or Missylena or Chlory and
> then rides off into the trees and waits. (87)

In this sense, interracial relationships are no different in *Light in August* than they were during the antebellum years of *Absalom, Absalom!*.

In the same way that Joe Christmas must struggle to formulate a racial identity for himself in the 1920s, Thomas Sutpen struggled for social and economic identity nearly one hundred years earlier. Having been born in the mountains of Virginia, Sutpen is "innocent":

> He didn't even know that there was a country all divided and fixed and neat with
> a people living on it all divided and fixed and neat because of what color their
> skins happened to be and what they happened to own. (179)

The process by which he discovers this innocence and conceives his "grand design" is reconstructed by Quentin Compson from the story told him by his father (who heard it from his father, General Compson, who supposedly heard it from Sutpen himself). It is significant that Sutpen himself never speaks; his enforced silence ensures that the narrators' reconstructed view of him is the only access to him that Faulkner's readers receive.

Because the townspeople do not know Sutpen's past, they cannot understand him. Consequently, they attempt to interpret Sutpen and his actions in terms of their understanding of identity and social roles. Although the steps he takes towards establishing himself do not appear outwardly unconventional, the town's inability to comprehend him encourages the narrators who reconstruct his story to view him antagonistically. For example, Sutpen arrives in Jefferson in 1933 after repudiating his first wife because he had discovered that "she was not and could never be, through no fault of her own, adjunctive or incremental to the design I had in mind . . ." (194). He has left her because she is of mixed race, and though her background might not be a debilitating social problem for him in Haiti, it is not conducive to his intentions in Mississippi. The language attributed to Sutpen is important here, as it implies that his racism does not result from a morality which unilaterally prohibits interracial unions; rather, Sutpen's racism appears to result solely from his wife's racial background, which would hinder him in completing his "design." That Sutpen's racism does not stem from the same source as the townspeople's only exacerbates their inability to comprehend Sutpen's actions, and therefore further increases their hostility.

In spite of his apparent discomfort with interracial unions, Sutpen nonetheless establishes his family in Jefferson by fathering both black and white children, much as other plantation owners must have done.[6] Sutpen's first daughter Clytie is born to one of the slave women he brings with him to Jefferson; his son Henry and second daughter Judith are born to his second wife Ellen.

There is almost no unmediated evidence for either Thomas Sutpen's social background or for Joe Christmas's racial background, which may partially account for the townspeople's confusion and hostility towards both men. In *Absalom, Absalom!*, Thomas Sutpen's voice is buried under layers of narrative reconstruction and cannot speak for itself, and in *Light in August*, Joe's comment to his girlfriend Bobbie is the only time Joe himself acknowledges what he believes his background to be: "I think I got some nigger blood in me . . . *I don't know.* I think I have" (184, emphasis added). However, since Joe has been encouraged to "pass" for white for most of his life, he has had a sort of entrée into white society, but once society begins to question his identity that door is closed. Ralph Watkins argues convincingly that the danger that Christmas represents to society in Jefferson exists because Joe has done two things. First, he has "crosse[d] the threshold between white and black, and his existence brings together what should, in a racist society, be wholly separate" (13). Because Christmas cannot be definitely labeled, his ambiguity has the potential to destroy the social fabric of Jefferson, which is dependent on clear-cut racial categories.

In light of that potential, Lucas Burch's reaction to the sheriff's questioning after Joanna's house burns down is representative of a much greater social fear—if the townspeople cannot determine with any certainty who Christmas is, then perhaps they cannot be sure about themselves either. According to Byron Bunch, Lucas Burch becomes more and more desperate to receive the $1,000 reward, so he finally plays his trump card:

> Like if he had knowed that if it come to a pinch, this would save him, even if it was almost worse for a white man to admit what he would have to admit than to be accused of the murder itself. "That's right. . . . Go on. Accuse me. Accuse the white man that's trying to help you with what he knows. Accuse the white man and let the nigger go free. Accuse the white man and let the nigger run." (91)

"It's like he knew he had them then," Byron continues. "Like *nothing they could believe he had done would be as bad as what he could tell that somebody else had done"* (91, emphasis added). The same social complicity illustrated by Byron's comment can be found in Mr. Compson's description of the town's reaction to Sutpen's wagonload of furniture. The town had by that point accepted Sutpen's presence on some level, and some of the men of Jefferson appear to be friendly enough with him to address him informally. However, when he returns with the furniture he buys on Mr. Coldfield's credit, Mr. Compson tells Quentin:

> [H]is position had subtly changed . . . the affront was born of the town's realization that he was getting involved with himself; that whatever the felony which produced the mahogany and crystal, he was forcing the town to compound it. (33)

That Mr. Coldfield—who appears to serve as a sort of moral barometer for the people of Jefferson—was involved in Sutpen's actions raises the question of whether others in Jefferson might do the same. Consequently, the townspeople must rethink their own relationship to and their potential involvement with Sutpen. This necessity makes them distinctly uncomfortable.

Similarly, when Sutpen plans and executes his "grand design" according to the values of the mountain society in which he was raised, the townspeople are equally confused. In the mountains (according to Quentin and Shreve's reconstruction), people owned no more than they needed; the concept of ownership for the sheer pleasure of possessing a thing was foreign to him: "nobody had any more . . . than you did because everybody had just what he was strong enough or energetic enough to take and keep . . ." (179). The town's hostility at this point illustrates the extent to which Sutpen's actions have subverted the townspeople's conventional expectations.

In an essay entitled "'How can a black man ask?' Race and Self-Representation in Faulkner's Later Fiction," Theresa M. Towner argues that

> the explosive power of the underclass lies in its willingness to say what the gentlemen would prefer not to, and that power finds its clearest expression in the power of the male members of the class to hold the gentlemen hostage to racial and sexual violence. (7)

Although Towner is referring to *The Reivers* and *Sanctuary,* Thomas Sutpen seems to serve a similar function in *Absalom, Absalom!:* first, Sutpen's decision to leave Haiti and to fulfill his "grand design" in Jefferson is directly related to the fact that his first wife was of mixed race. Second, I would argue that Sutpen's betrayal of his first wife functions as economic rape (in this sense, equating economics with sexual violence). Third, and most obvious to the townspeople, Thomas Sutpen's refusal to acknowledge conventional racial barriers—Clytie's central position in Sutpen's household and his fighting with his slaves, for example—defies the norms and mores of Jefferson's affluent society. These three instances are clear articulations of what "gentlemen would prefer not to [say]" and the townspeople's inability to ignore them is representative of the power Towner finds in the underclass. Therefore, regardless of how well Sutpen appears to follow Jefferson's mores, the townspeople will never be able to accept him; he has too much potential to destroy their rigid class and racial demarcations.

The implications of such a conflict between value systems are clearly illustrated by Rosa Coldfield's relationship with Clytie. Trained from childhood to view Clytie as a slave, Rosa is uncomfortable with Clytie's apparent status in the Sutpen household. She assumes that her relations with Clytie will follow traditional mistress/slave patterns.

Rosa's expectations, however, are shattered on the day that Henry kills Bon. That day, Rosa is called to Sutpen's Hundred, where Clytie meets her. Clytie attempts to stop Rosa from running up the stairs, an act to which, as a slave, she has no right, but as an person concerned for the welfare of her family it is natural that she attempt to protect Rosa from what is upstairs. Rosa does not realize the extent of her discomfort with Clytie's refusal to acknowledge the rigid hierarchies of adult racial relationships until Clytie touches her:

> but let flesh touch with flesh, and watch the fall of all the eggshell shibboleth of caste and color too . . . I remember how as we stood there joined by that volitionless (yes: it too sentient victim just as she and I were) hand, I cried perhaps not aloud, not with words . . .—"And you too? And you too, *sister, sister?*" (112, emphasis added)

Rosa ultimately refuses to accept Clytie's sisterhood, but she is forced to reassess first their relationship and then her own complicity in society's racial hierarchy.

Unlike Rosa at this moment, Emily Miller Budick places the issue of slaves' humanity within a larger cultural context, viewing slavery itself as an even greater moral abomination than simply refusing to acknowledge the humanity of others:

> The statement that slave owners did not see their slaves as human beings conceals what is most profoundly horrific about slavery; that many slave owners did see their slaves as human beings and still denied them fundamental human rights. (116)

Rosa's inability to call Clytie, to verbally recognize their common humanity, prevents her from ever being able to understand the egalitarian values behind Sutpen's design.[7] As a result, Rosa never accepts what she views as Sutpen's perversion of convention, and her narrative becomes simply one more representative voice of the townspeople.

A similar, though less extreme, process occurs in *Light in August* when Joe Christmas shows up for work at the mill. Not surprisingly, the novel's first real discussion of him focuses on his strangeness; when he first arrives the mill workers think he is a foreigner (29). The reader is left to infer his background from the narrator's description of Joe's "dark, insufferable face" (20) and one worker's comment that "that's a pretty risky look for a man to wear on his face in public . . . he might forget and use it somewhere where somebody won't like it" (28). The full impact of the workers' discussion does not become clear until later, as James Snead argues in *"Light in August* and the Rhetorics of Racial Division": "[Joe is] a man destined to break all the semiotic codes of society. . . . Insofar as Joe Christmas . . . cannot signify any one thing, [he] must finally question the very possibility of unitary significance" (156–57). I would take Snead's argument a step further and suggest that not only does Joe himself break all semiotic codes, but in so doing, he forces the townspeople to once again question their own "unitary significance."

Because Joe is uncertain about his racial background, he cannot be sure exactly how to project himself. In the novel, the town becomes progressively more fearful and hateful as it becomes more strongly convinced that Joe is indeed black—suggesting once again their fear that Joe's unclear identity may reflect their own equally unclear status. Because society has treated Joe as a white man, although he is not part of it, he must conform to white society's morality codes. Joe's anger comes, in part, not only from his uncertainty about his identity, but from society projecting onto him its anger at what it interprets as his willful deception.

Ironically, it is when Joe attacks his foster-father, a man who has consistently refused to acknowledge Joe's individuality, that the question of his mixed background is strongly emphasized.[8] After Joe attacks McEachern, Bobbie says to him, "Bastard! Son of a bitch! Getting me into a jam that always treated you like you were a white man! A white man!" (204). The emphasis on Joe's race is significant because it illustrates the extent to which he subverts social convention. Before the attacks on McEachern, Bobbie was a prostitute and Joe was her (white) client; now, his coming to her for shelter implicates her on both personal and professional levels. In light of her personal involvement, then, Joe's background becomes important to her. Her concern also forces Joe to question himself once again.

Clearly, in spite of Bobbie's condemnation, Joe still views himself as a white man. His belief is tenuous enough that during his fifteen-year absence from Jefferson, he alternates between living as a white man and living as a black man: "he had once tricked or teased white men into calling him a negro in order to fight them or be beaten; now he fought the negro who called him white" (212). In a last-ditch hope for resolution, he actively assumes the identity of a black man and tries to convince himself that he no longer wants any part of his "white" background. He finds it difficult to reach any sort of resolution:

> At night he would lie . . . in bed . . . with each suspiration trying to expel from himself the white blood and white thinking and being. And all the while the odor he was trying to make his own would *whiten* and tauten. (212, emphasis added)

In *Absalom, Absalom!*, Sutpen's arrival in Jefferson appears to provoke in the townspeople an ambivalence similar to that felt by Joe Christmas. At the beginning of chapter 2, an anonymous narrator describes the event:

> the other men sitting with their feet on the railing of the Holston House gallery looked up and there the stranger was . . . face and horse that none of them had ever seen before, name that none of them had ever heard, and origin and purpose which some of them were never to learn. (24)

An unwillingness on the part of the townspeople to accept Sutpen into Jefferson's symbolic order can be traced directly to their lack of knowledge about him—Sutpen has no past that they can trace. Their hesitation directly parallels the sheriff's reaction to Lucas Burch's telling him about Joe's background in *Light in August*. In both instances, people feel that there is something odd—and disconcertingly familiar—about both Sutpen and Joe, but they are unable to decide what it is, and indecision makes them hostile. Though both men's actions appear conventional—Sutpen builds a house and starts a family, while Joe works at the mill—the townspeople's ambivalence belies the outward ordinariness of Sutpen's and Christmas's actions. As a result, the narrators must question the extent of their own complicity in both men's actions.

The town's view of Sutpen's relationship with his slaves provides yet another example of the way in which his actions subvert Jefferson's norms. Sutpen and his slaves communicate in French (although the townspeople do not recognize it as such) which fuels Rosa Coldfield's suspicion that Sutpen is a demon not governed by the laws of mortal human beings. The slaves themselves are not discernibly different from any others, but are initially another source of fear. Whenever Sutpen's slaves appear in the novel, they are described as "wild negroes," fighting among themselves or with Sutpen, "as if their skins should have been . . . covered with fur" (21).

As a descendant of these slaves, Clytie is described by Rosa as an alien being, the inheritor of both Sutpen's unresolved place in Jefferson's symbolic order and the town's suspicion of its own complicity in whatever evil forces they believe Sutpen represents. Clytie's sisterly relationship with Sutpen's white daughter Judith clearly disturbs the townspeople:

> the face without sex or age because it had never possessed either: the same sphinx
> face which she had been born with, which had looked down from the loft that
> night beside Judith's and which she still wears now at seventy-four. (109)

One reason for this discomfort may be that while the townspeople clearly distinguish between themselves as white people and the black slaves as chattel, Sutpen does not draw the same distinction. He works along with the slaves to build his house and occasionally participates with them in the fights he stages to entertain his guests. Perhaps even more important, Sutpen acknowledges Charles Bon as his son, even though he is aware of Bon's racial background (78).[9]

Sutpen's refusal to follow the role prescribed for him as the master of Sutpen's Hundred thwarts the townspeople's interpretive mechanisms. There is nothing out of the ordinary in Sutpen's having slaves, but it is unexpected that he should relate to them as he does. In this way, the conventions of the master/slave relationship are subverted, particularly for Rosa, who is outraged at what she believes is Sutpen's lack of respect for her sister's place in Jefferson society and the implicit equation of whites and blacks that she feels his actions imply:

> down there in the stable a hollow square of faces in the lantern light, the white
> faces on three sides, the black ones on the fourth, and . . . Ellen seeing not the
> two black beasts she had expected to see but instead a white one and a black one,
> both naked to the waist and gouging at one another's eyes as if their skins should
> not only have been the same color but should have been covered with fur too. . . .
> (20–21)

In fact, neither Sutpen's relationship with his slaves nor the town's interpretation of his relationship with Clytie would have been unusual in
Mississippi during the 1930s. F. N. Boney points out that social status was not
fixed in stone, and Cleanth Brooks suggests that it was not unheard of for
someone to move from a log cabin to social prominence.[10] The fluidity of the
class structure appears to have resulted in a very strong, almost obsessive
need to draw clear racial and class distinctions. The idea of a rigid social hierarchy based on race or socioeconomic status is not new and, I suggest,
Faulkner would argue that these standards were important because in order
to overcome the need for such distinctions, we must first formulate racial and
economic identities. Only then can we begin to create a language with which
to discuss changing that hierarchy.

NOTES

1. See also Ayers, 132–59 and Cash, 177.

2. Ayers in *The Promise of the New South* and Cash in *The Mind of the South* provide a more comprehensive discussion of such actions.

3. See the work of David Roediger, especially *The Ages of Whiteness: Race and the Making of the
   American Working Class* and *Towards the Abolition of Whiteness: Essays on Race, Politics, and
   Working Class History,* for further discussion of these issues.

4. John N. Duvall argues persuasively for a reconsideration of our use of the word "murder" to
   describe Joe's actions. Two ideas are particularly important: first, that Joanna attempts to kill
   him before he kills her, and second, that in using the word "murder," we are implicating ourselves in the racist ideology of both the textual community of Jefferson and the interpretive
   community of readers and critics.

5. Interestingly, Eric Sundquist places the blame for Joe's actions on Joanna. Sundquist attempts
   to tie the "dependent crises of blood and sexuality" to Joe's later life, stating that Joe's belief
   in his mixed ancestry is the vehicle "through which the twisted passion of Joanna Burden will
   be released, and for which he will in the end be killed and castrated" (81). This comment
   implies that Joe should not be held accountable for his actions.

6. Although there do not appear to be any accurate statistics regarding interracial liaison, Cash,
   Wyatt-Brown, and Persons discuss the issue.

7. "Egalitarian" in this case does not imply "democratic." Rather, it refers to the fact that in for-
   mulating his "grand design," Sutpen does not appear to the townspeople to place the same

emphasis on race as they do.

8. It has never been established whether or not Joe kills McEachern. Even critics as well known as Cleanth Brooks and Eric Sundquist refuse to commit themselves.

9. Sutpen's acknowledgment does not imply that he is happy about the discovery.

10. For further discussion of this point, see Cash, *The Mind of the South;* see also J. Wayne Flynt's introductory essay to the section entitled "Social Class" in *The Encyclopedia of Southern Culture.*

WORKS CITED

Ayers, Edward. *The Promise of the New South.* Oxford: Oxford University Press, 1992.

Boney, F.N. "The Middle Class." In *The Encyclopedia of Southern Culture,* 1440–1. Chapel Hill: University of North Carolina Press, 1989.

Budick, Emily Miller. *Engendering Romance.* New Haven: Yale University Press, 1994.

Cash, W.J. *The Mind of the South,* 1941. Reprint, New York: Knopf, 1991.

Duvall, John N. *Faulkner's Marginal Couple: Invisible, Outlaw, and Unspeakable Communities.* Austin: University of Texas Press, 1990.

Faulkner, William. *Absalom, Absalom!* 1941. Reprint, New York: Random, 1990.

———. *Light in August.* 1932. Reprint, New York: Vintage, 1972.

Flynt, J. Wayne. "Social Class." In *The Encyclopedia of Southern Culture,* 1383–90. Chapel Hill: University of North Carolina Press, 1989.

Fox-Genovese, Elizabeth. "The Anxiety of History: The Southern Confrontation With Modernity. *Southern Cultures* 1, no. 1 (1994): 65–82.

Goldfield, Michael. "The Color of Politics in the United States: White Supremacy as the Main Explanation for the Peculiarities of American Politics from Colonial Times to the Present." In *The Bounds of Race: Perspectives on Hegemony and Resistance,* edited by Dominick LaCapra, 104–33. Ithaca: Cornell University Press, 1991.

Parsons, C.G. "An Inside View of Slavery: or a Tour Among the Planters." In *Voices of the Old South,* edited by Alan Gallay, 287–91. Athens: University of Georgia Press, 1994.

Roediger, David R. *The Wages of Whiteness: Race and the Making of the American Working Class.* New York: Verso, 1991.

———. *Towards the Abolition of Whiteness: Essays on Race, Politics, and Working Class History.* New York: Verso, 1994.

Snead, James. *"Light in August* and the Rhetorics of Racial Division." In *Faulkner and Race: Faulkner and Yoknapatawpha, 1986,* edited by Doreen Fowler and Ann J. Abadie, 157–70. Jackson: University Press of Mississippi, 1987.

Sundquist, Eric J. *Faulkner: The House Divided.* Baltimore: Johns Hopkins University Press, 1983.

Towner, Theresa M. "'How can a black man ask?' Race and Self-Representation in Faulkner's Later Fiction." *Faulkner Journal* 10, no. 2 (1995): 3–21.

Watkins, Ralph. "'It was like I was the woman and she was the man': Boundaries, Portals, and Pollution in *Light in August*." *Southern Literary Journal* 26 no. 2 (1994): 11–25.

Wyatt-Brown, Bertram. *Honor and Violence in the Old South*. New York: Oxford University Press, 1986.

"Like a lady I et":
Faulkner, Food, and Femininity

CHRISTINA JARVIS

As Lilian Furst observes in *Disorderly Eaters: Texts in Self-Empowerment,* eating practices "as every anthropologist realizes, [are among] the activities most highly conditioned by the culture in which they are sited" (93). With the rise of dieting and a startling increase in the number of reported eating disorder cases in the second half of the twentieth century, many feminist scholars have sought to examine the complex cultural factors that have enabled these trends.[1] Expanding on the insights made by writers like Susie Ohrbach and Kim Chernin, feminist philosopher Susan Bordo has reappropriated Foucauldian genealogical methods to read female bodies—especially the anorexic's—not only as gendered texts of culture, but as "practical, direct loci for social control" (Bordo, 165).

Employing Bordo's insights and other recent work on food and eating in twentieth-century American culture, I would like to examine the socially

Reprinted with permission from *Southern Quarterly* 37, no. 2 (1999): 105–17.

encoded gender norms in Faulkner's representations of eating and feeding. Despite the fact that food and eating appear frequently in Faulkner's fiction, surprisingly little critical work has addressed this topic. The articles which do investigate representations of eating/not eating, Pamela Boker's "'*How can he be so not hungry?*': Fetishism, Anorexia, and the Disavowal of the Cultural 'I' in *Light in August*," Thomas Morrisey's "Food Imagery in Faulkner's *Light in August*," and Marilyn Chandler's "Food and Eating in *Light in August*," center their analyses around one novel, focusing on Joe Christmas's rejection of culturally imposed identities through his refusal to eat.[2] Perhaps because we have been so culturally conditioned to associate women with domestic roles, as the preparers of food and providers of nourishment, readers of Faulkner easily dismiss Cora Tull's worries about her cakes in *As I Lay Dying* or Mrs. Varner's intruding presence in the kitchen in *The Hamlet* as mere background detail. I will argue, however, that an exploration of Faulkner's women's complex relationships to food can potentially reveal new insights into several of his female (and male) characters. This essay will investigate the ways in which characters in *Sanctuary* and *Light in August* both simultaneously reject and adhere to social gender norms for eating/feeding others. Specifically, I will examine how Ruby's, Temple's, Joe's and Lena's complex relationships with food respectively reinscribe or reconfigure cultural constructions of femininity.

In a novel like *Sanctuary*, where "the focus is primarily on what happens to, in, and between bodies" (Bleikasten, 18), representations of food and eating logically occupy an important role in the text. Faulkner sets up this focus in the first chapter of the novel with his depiction of Ruby in the kitchen at the Old Frenchman place. The novel's early descriptions of Ruby and her cooking, in fact, strategically establish a series of complex norms against which we can later read Temple's actions.

In *Perfection Salad: Women and Cooking at the Turn of the Century*, Laura Shapiro suggests that cooking magazines, advertisements, cooking columns in newspapers, and other popular culture sources contributed to the idea that early twentieth-century women were supposed to derive pleasure from feeding others, not themselves. She notes that "too much evidence of an overt fondness for food would have made women appear gross and unfeminine" (73). In *Sanctuary*, we see these cultural gender norms clearly in place. Although Ruby resents cooking for "crimps and spungs and feebs" (8) and getting her water from a distant spring, she is certainly accustomed to her "proper" domestic role. Faulkner opens chapter 2 with a description of Ruby in the process of feeding "her" men:

> Watching her, Benbow did not see her look at him as she set the platter on the table and stood for a moment with that veiled look with which women make a final survey of the table, and went and stopped above an open packing case in a corner of the room and took from it another plate and knife and fork, which she set before Benbow with a kind of abrupt yet unhurried finality. . . . When the meal was over . . . the woman cleared the table and carried the dishes to the kitchen. She set them on the table and went to the box behind the stove and she stood over it for a time. Then she returned and put her own supper on a plate and sat down to the table and ate. (9–10)

As this passage indicates, Ruby is not only adept at her role as server/cook, she is a "natural." Reduced to the title "the woman" throughout many of the opening passages at the Old Frenchman place, Ruby seems to be fulfilling her "natural" function—as mother and care provider for men.[3] She keeps her appetite, which functions both literally and metaphorically, under control, eating in seclusion. As Bordo suggests, "the social control of female hunger operates a practical 'discipline' (to use Foucault's term) that train female bodies in the knowledge of their limits and possibilities" (130).

Whether through her domestic duties or through her efforts to help Lee with his legal troubles, Ruby demonstrates this self internalization of limiting female gender roles repeatedly in the novel. Her reactions to Horace, for example, reflect her inability to view women outside of the limiting Madonna/whore binary. One of her first assessments of Horace is that his women folk "don't make him eat right" (13). And earlier, she remarks to herself, "He better get on to where he's going, where his women folk can take care of him" (11). These comments, in conjunction with her request for "an orange stick" (14), reflect that Ruby is hardly capable of imagining women outside of their "useful" roles to men.[4] When Horace asks what he can send her from Jefferson, "something [she] might need" (14), Ruby can only imagine herself as someone who deals with "dishwater and washing" (14). As Deborah Clarke observes in *Robbing the Mother: Women in Faulkner*, Ruby, "accepting female sexuality as defining her power and position, uses it for men's benefits rather than her own and now lives in poverty and monogamy rather than in luxury and promiscuity" (56). Horace reinforces this idea in his explanations to Narcissa: "she's out there, doing a nigger's work, that's owned diamonds and automobiles too in her day, and bought them with a harder currency than cash" (62). Like her literal appetite, which is satisfied in private, curtailed, and controlled by prescribed gender roles, Ruby's metaphorical appetite for luxuries and independence has also been suppressed. Though Faulkner does not offer an explicit indictment of these limiting gender roles, Ruby's "proper" adherence to these roles results in disaster for herself and, indirectly, for Temple. Instead of enjoying the wealth and independence offered her through prostitution, Ruby's "proper" behavior reduces her to a subservient role—one which ultimately proves unsuccessful in restraining Lee and contributes to the couple's later difficulties.[5]

Gender coding concerning food and eating are present not only in the divergent depictions between Ruby feeding the men and feeding herself, but also in the actual food that is consumed. According to Shapiro, in the early twentieth century, certain foods were clearly gendered: "menus planned for women always emphasized sweet, ethereal foods, some of them almost imperceptible as nourishment . . . the dinners planned for men were mighty, sometimes blatant, symbols of maleness" (101–2). She further notes, "Affecting the languor and the wandering appetite they associated with femininity, girls of all social classes would refuse meat in favor of pastries and bread" (101). Almost impossible to overlook, the narrator mentions the meat that Ruby is preparing at least three times in the opening kitchen scene and seven times during Ruby's conversation with Temple while preparing dinner in chapter 6. While descriptions of "the spluttering of frying meat on the stove" (32) undoubtedly heighten the gothic effects of the novel, they also emphasize the maleness of the Old Frenchman place and the meals there. (Faulkner may, of course, also be ironically highlighting several of the characters'— especially Popeye's—failed masculinity.) Although the novel never specifies what Ruby eats at the Old Frenchman's place, the narrator does mention that she prepares a separate dinner for herself, possibly suggesting that she does not partake of the meat she prepares for the men. Temple's refusals of meat, however, are more explicit. At Miss Reba's whorehouse, Temple rejects a thick steak, opting instead for a strip of potato, which she took up "gingerly in her fingers and ate" (89).[6]

Significantly, the two places in the novel at which eating is most frequently represented, the Old Frenchman place and Miss Reba's whorehouse, are also the locations of the novel's sexual encounters. The focus on male appetite, particularly on male consumption of flesh (meat), seemingly suggests that physical appetite can also be read metaphorically as sexual appetite; these metaphorical dimensions of eating are, of course, underscored by Popeye's vicarious satiation of his sexual appetite via Red and the corncob. Given the strong associations between eating and sex, then, it is appropriate that Ruby, now "wife" and mother, refrain from displaying an appetite that might threaten the novel's patriarchal order. Further, Temple's many refusals to eat—particularly meat—when viewed metaphorically in terms of sexual appetite complicate claims that "Temple's life has been oriented toward sexual promiscuity" (78), that she is a nymphomaniac or siren.

Both contributing to and deriving from these "Victorian" gender codes for male/female appetite, however, is a more fundamental philosophical conception of the body. According to Bordo, the "classical" mind/body dualism, which promotes "male activity and female passivity . . . has been one of the most historically powerful dualities that inform Western ideologies of gender" (11–12). From Aristotle to Hegel to current popular culture and advertisements, various discourses have marked "female" bodies not only as passive, but also as more material than "male" bodies. In *Sanctuary,* we witness numerous repudiations of the female body through Temple's violations, Horace's vomiting, and, more subtly, through the conversations and thoughts of different characters.

Appropriately enough, Popeye is the first character to show disdain for female bodies that take up too much space or that eat too much. In the opening kitchen scene at the Old Frenchman place, Popeye informs Ruby: "'You're getting fat here. Laying off in the country. I wont tell them on Manuel Street.' The woman turned, the fork in her hand. 'You bastard,' she said." (9). Arguably, Ruby's hostile response to Popeye stems from his reminders of her former life as a prostitute, but it may also be linked to a self consciousness about her weight. Having recently given birth and working to curb her appetites, Ruby would quite logically resent the remark. Popeye's comment, which links Ruby's weight gain to her decreased sexual activity, also serves to establish associations between thin, active bodies like Temple's and sexual desirability.

Later in the novel, while at Miss Reba's house, Temple recalls a conversation that she and her peers had while "dressing for a dance" (86) which reinforces this idea. After noting another girls' "short legs" (86) (and her apparently plumper figure), Temple remembers:

> The worst of all said boys thought all girls were ugly except when they are dressed . . . they said How do you know? And Temple thought of her backed up against the dressing table and the rest of them in a circle with their combed hair and their shoulders smelling of scented soap and the light powder in the air and their eyes like knives until you could almost watch her flesh where the eyes were touching it, and her eyes in her ugly face courageous and frightened and daring, and they all saying, How do you know? until she told them and held up her hand and swore she had. That was when the youngest one turned and ran out of the room. She locked herself in the bath and they could hear her being sick. (86)

This passage establishes, through the youngest girl's vomiting, both a fear or revilement of sexuality and a disdain for the too fleshy female body. Her vomiting therefore might be two-fold: an expression of anxiety and an attempt to purge her own body of excessive flesh. Further, the first girl's comment about male preference for clothed or contained female bodies coupled with Temple's focus on the girl's "short legs" and her readily visible flesh seemingly indicates that these women have self-internalized complex gender ideologies about eating and their bodies.

With all these gender norms controlling women's appetites and bodies, it is hardly surprising that Temple displays many symptoms of anorexia nervosa. Although other critics have noted her flapper-like qualities, her boyish figure, and her inability to eat, no one has specifically examined how her apparent anorexia may function within the larger context of *Sanctuary*. Critics like David Williams have often focused on the symbolism of Temple's body, ignoring the literally inscribed messages that her body offers as a cultural text of gender. In "The Profaned Temple," Williams observes,

> the thinness of her body itself suggests, in psychic terms, her destructive character; the fullness and massiveness of the nourishing good mother, closely identified with earth, is entirely absent from the portrait of Temple. It might appear that she is constitutionally disposed toward the person of the destroying goddess. (99–100)

Like numerous earlier critics, Williams analyzes Temple's symbolic body and the negative sexuality which (he and others argue) Temple represents in

Sanctuary. While more recent criticism has focused on her literal (as well as symbolic) body, much of this work has considered Temple's body only to the extent that it casts her as victim.[7] Largely in an effort to free her from decades of misogynist criticism, recent articles have focused more explicitly on the numerous rapes and bodily violations. Although important and insightful, these studies focus perhaps too much on "Temple's position as victim . . . as a woman deprived of agency and will" (Boon, 34–35). I contend that an understanding of Temple's anorexic symptoms further complicates the critical binary which reads her as tease or victim. Her anorexia serves both as a reinscription and protest of cultural gender constructions; in many ways, Temple's refusals to eat can be read as attempts to formulate a type of agency or control.

Read against contemporary academic and medical descriptions of the anorexic, Temple's behavior and body easily categorize her as such. Throughout the novel, she is frequently described in terms of her extreme thinness and boyish body. Upon her arrival at the Old Frenchman place, Tommy immediately focuses on Temple's thin frame: "'She's a right tall gal, too,' he said. 'With them skinny legs of hern. How much she weigh?'" (5). Later that same evening, the narrator describes her: "She looked quite small, her very attitude an outrage to muscle and tissue of more than seventeen and more compatible with eight or ten" (41); "long legged, thin armed, with high small buttocks—a small childish figure no longer quite a child, not yet quite a woman" (52). These comments, along with descriptions of Temple's "matchlike" figure and "her waist shaped slender and urgent" (19), call attention not only her extreme thinness, but to her specifically non-feminine body. As Bordo suggests, the anorexic's desire for thinness is more than an extreme embodiment of cultural norms advocating slenderness for women, it is also a statement about the gender/power axis which pervades a wide range of social discourses. Bordo argues that there are two levels of gendered meaning associated with anorexia: "One has to do with the fear and disdain for traditional female roles and social limitations. The other has to do, more profoundly, with a deep fear of 'the Female,' with all its nightmarish archetypal associations of voracious hangers and sexual instability" (155). We recognize in Temple this complex relation of both adherence to and rejection of her prescribed social roles. On the one hand, she rejects the male control that her father, brothers, and school officials exert over her; in this respect, she acts like other 1920s flappers, who through their denial of a feminine body, attempted to pursue "a new freedom and daring that demanded a carefree, boyish style" (Bordo, 163). Simultaneously, however, Temple's attempts to starve her female body, reducing it to a "boyish" one, also function in a very practical sense as she endeavors to stave off Popeye's (and others') sexual advances.

While Temple's comments reveal that she has not eaten for some time before she enters the Old Frenchman place, we must also note that she refuses to eat anything the entire time she is there. Furst observes that "eating, like noneating, is a tool for power both over oneself and over one's surroundings. The individual, especially when forced into a coercive situation of any sort, can exercise control and a measure of choice by the mode and amount of food ingested" (4). Upon her arrival at the Old Frenchman place, Temple registers her discomfort: "'I don't want to go there,' she said. 'You go on and get the car,' she told the man" (26). Her subsequent refusals to eat, despite her extreme hunger, might be interpreted as attempts to control her situation.

Temple's repeated references to her hunger also serve to align her further with the anorexic. Bordo's assertion that "anorexic women are as obsessed with their hunger as they are with being slim" (146) certainly rings true in Temple's case. The narrator informs us that upon first entering Ruby's kitchen, she "stood on tiptoe, listening, thinking I'm hungry. I haven't eaten all day" (31). Minutes later, she remarks to Ruby, "And so we hadn't eaten and we stopped at Dumfries and he went into the restaurant but I was too worried to eat" (33). That evening when Ruby offers her supper, Temple refuses food, despite her acute awareness of her hunger: "'Go on and eat. Nobody's going to hurt you.' 'I'm not hungry. I haven't eaten today. I'm not hungry at all.'" (38) The following morning, Temple again refuses food, taking only coffee: "I'm not hungry. I haven't eaten in two days, but I'm not hungry. Isn't that funny? I haven't eaten in . . ." (52). From these and other passages, we witness both Temple's obsession with her hunger, and her desire to control it. Temple's repeated disavowals of hunger function not only as an attempt to express "masculine" qualities of "self-control, determination, cool, emotional discipline, mastery and so on," but also as an attempt to rid herself of "the social and sexual vulnerability involved in having a female body" (Bordo, 171, 177).

Although the rape scene is never actually narrated in the novel, the story Temple tells Horace clearly shows that she was by no means "asking for it" as earlier critics have claimed.[8] Her descriptions, in fact, are remarkably similar to anorexics' perceptions of their bodies and sexuality. According to Bordo, "as her body begins to lose its traditional feminine curves, its breasts and hips and rounded stomach, begins to feel and look more like a spare, lanky male body, [the anorexic] begins to feel untouchable, out of reach of hurt" (178). In her story narrated to Horace, Temple verbalizes the figurative attempts to deny her sexuality that accompany her literal denials by not eating. As Diane Roberts suggests, Temple's story is "an attempt to take control through the making of her own fiction" (*Southern Womanhood,* 125). Temple creates this fiction both through spoken language and the language of her body.

In her conversation with Horace at Miss Reba's Temple finally verbalizes her desire to transform literally her gender, to become the boy whose name she already possesses.[9] Describing the Saturday night before the rape, Temple explains:

> I was looking at my legs and I'd try to make like I was a boy. I was thinking if I just was a boy and then I tried to make myself into one by thinking. . . . So I'd hold my eyes tight shut and say Now I am. I am now. I'd look at my legs and I'd think about how much I had done for them. I'd think about how many dances I had taken them to—crazy, like that. Because I thought how much I'd done for them, and now they'd gotten me into this. So I'd think about praying to be changed into a boy. (122–23)

Temple's descriptions of her body in this passage are rather telling. Like the anorexic, Temple experiences her body "as alien and outside" (Bordo, 147). Similar to an earlier passage where "she stood and watched herself run out of her body" (53), her narration here reflects a desire for a disembodied female self. She blames her female sexuality/body for her hardships; it is the feminine pair of legs, the one which goes to dances, that she claims have "gotten me into this" (123). Temple, frequently described as running or in motion at the Old Frenchman place, also focuses on the work that she has done for her body—the exercise (and not eating) that has made it lean and boyish. Despite all her efforts to transform her body into a boy's, she is nonetheless limited biologically to a female body. Thus, she must turn to linguistic play and fantasy to deny her unwanted female body.

After narrating her initial desire to become a boy, Temple describes the range of alternative identities that she imagines. She visualizes herself dead in a coffin, as a forty-five-year-old teacher with "iron-gray hair and spectacles" (124), and as an "old man, with a long white beard" (124). It is not until she imagines the literal transformation of her genitals, however, that she can go to sleep. Temple describes the "successful" transformation:

> Then I thought about being a man, and as soon as I thought it, it happened. It made a kind of plopping sound, like blowing a little rubber tube wrong-side outward . . . I could feel it, and I lay right still to keep from laughing at how surprised he was going to be. (124)

As Clark observes, "What is most outrageous about this outrageous process is that it can be said to work; Temple gets through the night without being physically penetrated" (65). Nonetheless, the passage highlights Temple's biological limitations; having a boyish body simply is not enough to stave off Popeye's attack. Like other anorexics, she learns that her experience of power "is, of course, deeply and dangerously illusory. To reshape one's body into a male body is not to put on male power and privilege" (Bordo, 179). She experiences this reality through her brutal rape with a corncob and during Popeye's vicarious violations committed via Red.

Although her attempts to erase her female sexuality fail at the Old Frenchman place, Temple continues her efforts to control her situation through other refusals to eat. Perhaps still associating eating with her violated body, she eats infrequently at Miss Reba's, often taking only gin for supper. When she first arrives at the Memphis brothel, we are told that "when she looked at the food she found she was not hungry at all, didn't even want to look at it" (89). Apart from her first night there, Temple apparently only consumes gin and smokes cigarettes.[10] Interestingly enough, her obsession with hunger and her body are de-emphasized after her initial violation. She seems to realize that she must adopt other strategies if she hopes to escape Popeye's terror.

Aided by her massive alcoholic consumption, Temple adopts a strategy of mimicry in an effort to free herself from Popeye's control. Often noted for her "parrotlike" responses throughout the novel, she attempts to reinscribe other female gender constructions in order to placate Popeye and to win Red, who Temple sees as one of her only vehicles for escape. As Ulf Kirchdorfer notes, "Temple may have learned the melodramatic sexual talk she uses on Popeye and Red from cheap gangster stories" (52). Given her apparent anorexia, these efforts to take various gender norms to an extreme are not surprising. Her efforts to become a vamp, though practical in her situation, are ridiculous. With her skinny, boyish body, she falls short of the voluptuous female temptress figure. Instead, her sexuality is described as frightening, almost inhuman: "When he touched her she sprang like a bow, hurling herself upon him, her mouth gaped and ugly like that of a dying fish" (135).

Quite clearly, Temple's anorexia and later behavior in the novel are not easily interpreted matters. Like the anorexic, Temple makes her body a site of struggle within and resistance to cultural norms of femininity. Her body offers an "indictment of a culture that disdains and suppresses female hunger, makes women ashamed of their appetites and need, and demands women's constant work on the transformation of their bodies" (Bordo, 176).[11] Yet despite her embodied protest and struggles to exert "male" control, she is still raped and ultimately forced to adopt other limiting gender roles, relying on masculine protection. While Temple's agency is certainly limited by the gender ideologies which shape the novel, we must nonetheless acknowledge her endeavors to reinscribe her biologically and culturally imposed identity. In this respect, reading Temple's anorexia and its various embodied protests, complicates earlier critical discussions which cast her as either vamp or victim.

Published shortly after the 1931 edition of *Sanctuary, Light in August* bears some rather interesting similarities to Faulkner's sixth novel both in terms of its focus on individuals resisting social gender norms and its attention to both "natural" and culturally inscribed bodies. As Judith Bryant Wittenberg suggests,

> *Light in August* contains, for a Faulkner novel—and perhaps for any novel written by a man in the early twentieth century—an unusual number of references to physiological processes such as menstruation, childbirth, and menopause, and these facts of feminine physicality are related to the more complicated presence of the Female. (119)

With such a focus on bodies and their various processes, it is hardly surprising that Faulkner also includes significant descriptions of food and eating in the novel. An examination of the complex roles that food and eating/not eating play in *Light in August* reveals a fuller understanding of the culturally imposed gender and racial identities against which many of the characters in the novel struggle.

Though ostensibly polar opposites in terms of class, character, and social position, Joe Christmas and Temple Drake both possess unusual relationships with food. Both probably anorexic, both conscious of the realization that "something is going to happen to me," Temple and Joe view their refusals of food as ways to repudiate the feminine and to gain control over threatening situations. While Temple's anorexic protests are extremely gender focused, Joe's relate to both race and gender.

From Byron's initial descriptions of him in chapter 2, we see Joe not only as "rootless" (27) and foreign, but also as a man who does not eat. Reflecting on Joe's appearance, Byron notes, "His face was gaunt, the flesh a level dead parchment color. Not the skin: the flesh itself, as though the skull had been molded in a still and deadly regularity and then baked in a fierce oven" (30). After discovering Joe's poverty, the reason "he had had no lunch with him either yesterday or today" (30), Byron offers him his own lunch. Joe, who "had lived on cigarettes for two or three days now" (31), refuses saying, "I ain't hungry. Keep your muck" (31). His later failures to eat with the other men at the plant and his suppressed appetite function not only to place him as an outsider with the community, but also as a means to demonstrate his discomfort with prescribed gender norms. 'Men are *supposed* to have hearty, even voracious, appetites. It is a mark of the manly to eat spontaneously and expansively" (Bordo, 108). When depicted eating, however, Joe usually eats modestly and by himself; his appetite—his taste for things "sweet and sticky" (112) like the toothpaste and coconut pie—is more easily culturally coded as feminine.[12]

As other critics have noted, Joe's troubling relations with food, female sexuality, and racial identity begin with his experiences at the orphanage. Hiding behind a curtain in the dietitian's room "among delicate shoes and suspended soft womangarments" (112), Joe inadvertently witnesses her sexual encounter with the young doctor. Exposed after vomiting up the toothpaste he has consumed, he is reprimanded: "Spying on me! You little nigger bastard!" (114). Thus, as Clarke suggests, "Vomiting, femininity, and blackness are intertwined for Joe, who associates race and gender not just with each other but with physical revulsion" (105). Significantly, Joe's relationship with food is also disturbed; he has been rejected and reviled by the dietitian, the woman whom he associates most clearly with food:

> to eating, food, the dining room, the ceremony of eating at the wooden forms,
> coming now and then into his vision without impacting at all except as something

of a pleasing association and pleasing in herself to look at—young, a little full-bodied, smooth, pink-and-white, making his mind think of the dining room, making his mouth think of something sweet and sticky to eat. (112)

Understanding his early associations of food with the dietitian helps us to read his later refusals of food as disavowals of the feminine, or more specifically the maternal.[13] Later in the novel, Joe rejects the food of his adopted mother, Mrs. McEachern, violently overturning a tray of food at one point. Clearly associating his adopted mother with "the dishes she would prepare for him" (157), as the woman who "insisted on his eating" (158), he begins to view his not eating as a vehicle to sever his connections with "the woman: that soft kindness which he believed himself victim of" (158). Like the anorexic, he realizes that his "disorderly eating can thus represent . . . a means for [him] to attain a kind of domination" (Furst, 6) over his mother, and later, over female sexuality.

Joe's disorderly eating surfaces once again in his relationship with Joanna.[14] Although he associates the food on Joanna's table that first night with his childhood, he consumes the subsequent meals she prepares for him because he can disassociate the food from the preparer—from the woman he sees by stealth at night. As the narrator explains, if Joe "saw her by day at all, it would be on Saturday afternoon or Sunday when he would come to the house for the food which she would prepare for him and leave up on the kitchen table. Now and then she would come to the kitchen, though she would never stay while he ate" (220). Additionally, he recognizes Joanna's "masculine" qualities during their sexual encounters: "There was no feminine vacillation, no coyness of obvious desire. . . . It was as if he struggled physically with another man" (222), further disassociating her food from that prepared by earlier "maternal" figures. It is not until Joe decides that he has "made her a woman at last" (223) that his troubling relationship with food reemerges. Directly following this incident, Joe reverts back to former behavior, rejecting food and the feminine principle he associates with it: "The next day he lay again all day on his cot in the cabin. He ate nothing; he did not even go to the kitchen to see if she had left food for him" (223).

Ultimately Joe *does* go to the kitchen, where he confronts his anxieties about both femininity and racial identity. Viewing the food Joanna has left for him as dishes *"Set out for the nigger. For the nigger"* (224), he repeats his childhood actions, hurling the food at the wall. After throwing three different dishes, he thinks, *"This is fun. Why didn't I think of this before?* Woman's muck" (25). Once again, Joe attempts to use food (specifically his rejection of it) as a vehicle to exert control over a situation that he otherwise could not control. Unsure of his parentage and racial identity, he can disavow his possible black blood as well as his connection to the maternal by throwing away the "woman's muck." Further, he does not eat for the three days following this incident; like the anorexic, he hopes to control his identity by mastering his hunger.

Joe's most obvious attempts to achieve mastery over his situations through his control over hunger, however, occur during his flight from Jefferson. On the lam after killing Joanna, he is now faced not only with reminders of his ambiguous racial identity (present in the "negro dishes, negro food" [317]), but also with a clear threat to his life. Because he can draw on help from neither the white nor the black community, he realizes that his situation is dangerously out of control. He thus turns to what he can con-trol—his hunger:

> He thought of eating all the time, imagining dishes, food. He would think of that meal set out for him on the kitchen table three years ago and he would live again through the deliberate backswinging of his arms as he hurled the dishes into the wall. . . . Then one day he was no longer hungry. It came sudden and peaceful. He felt cool, quiet. Yet he knew that he had to eat. . . . It was not with food that he was obsessed now, but with the necessity to eat. (316)

Recalling his earlier behavior in Joanna's kitchen allows Joe to confront his various anxieties; by disavowing his appetite, he seems to become master of his body. Nonetheless, although no longer hungry, he is still obsessed with food, still subject to his body's demands for nourishment.

Significantly, just prior to his decision to go to Mottstown, Joe has an epiphany: "suddenly the true answer comes to him. He feels dry and light. 'I don't have to eat anymore,' he thinks. 'That's what it is.'" (320). He has reached what for many anorexics is the ultimate goal—the point at which they "don't need to eat at all" (Bordo, 146). Described as feeling "dry and light," Joe seems to have renounced his body, his fleshly self. At last, he real-izes that it was not food that he needed to master, but his own body. With his parchment colored skin, his body is the inscribed surface upon which oth-ers have written his cultural identity. Like Temple, who attempts to reject her biologically and culturally imposed gender identity, Joe seeks to remove the body which threatens his attempts to control his identity. His "lightness" seems to suggest that, like the spirit in classical dualist axis, he has transcended the confining body. Joe can now give himself up to the authorities because his "body is experienced as *alien,* as the not-self, the not-me" (Bordo, 144); it is separate from his "real" self.

Although both Joe's and Temple's anorexia can be read as bodily protests against their biological and cultural identities, their resistances to these identities have very different results. Temple, in "employing the language of femininity to protest the conditions of the female world" (Bordo, 177), inadvertently helps to reproduce rather than transform restrictive cultural gender norms. Although she reinscribes these norms, taking her "feminine" appetite and role as vamp to an extreme, her agency remains limited because she works within prescribed boundaries. Joe's protests, however, are more culturally disruptive. By adopting a "feminine" language of protest,[15] he is able to help deconstruct some of the cultural identity categories that he is resisting. His anorexia and sexual relations with women code him as both "male," through his oedipal separations from the mother, and "female," through his rejection of symbolic language in favor of a bodily, semiotic language/protest. Ultimately, though, Faulkner seems to suggest that rejections of the physical body are not adequate means by which to transform any cultural categories— gender or racial. Despite their desires to transcend their bodies, both Temple and Joe suffer horrendous bodily harm; neither is triumphant at the end of either novel.

Through the character of Lena Grove, Faulkner reminds us that one can challenge cultural gender norms while still celebrating bodily experience. Beginning with the image of the nine-months' pregnant Lena and ending with her comment, "My, my. A body does get around" (480), she strategically figures into the novel as both mother and a transgressor of cultural identity norms. Clarke argues that Lena's role as storyteller, as "a creator of fictions" (96), breaks down the distinction which associates men with figurative language and women with literal discourse. Further, Clarke notes that Lena's fictions indicate "that she has the figurative capability to live outside of her body as well as the procreative ability within that body. By recasting her world as more interesting, more romantic, she integrates the figurative and literal" (97). Closely linked to her transgressions into the "male" realm of figurative discourse through storytelling are Lena's literal/bodily transgressions of gender norms. One of Faulkner's few women to display a healthy appetite and be shown eating, Lena offers a more positive alternative to Joe's and Temple's cultural protestations.[16]

From Lena's own reflections, we see that she understands what constitutes a "feminine" appetite. While waiting for a ride to Jefferson at Varner's store, she recounts her earlier experiences at the Armstid house:

> She is remembering breakfast, thinking how she can enter the store this moment and buy cheese and crackers and even sardines if she likes. At Armstid's she had had but a cup of coffee and a piece of cornbread: nothing more though Armstid pressed her. "I et polite," . . ."Like a lady I et. Like a lady traveling. But now I can buy sardines too if I so wish." (23)

Although she denies herself physically at breakfast, Lena does not deny herself imaginatively. Despite her class and the fact that the Armstids fed her out of charity, she transforms the experience into one of her many fantasies. She not only sees herself as a lady, almost a house guest, but also creatively turns the piece of cornbread into that "decorous morsel of strange bread" (23). Unlike Temple, Ruby, or Faulkner's other women who have a seemingly troubled relationship with food, Lena does not; she displays no guilt about her appetite or thoughts of food, imagining it instead as enabling substance.[17]

As we observe shortly after this scene, Lena gratifies herself with actual food as well as with her stories. After purchasing cheese and crackers and sardines, she sensuously surrenders herself to these delicacies on the wagon ride to Jefferson. No longer concerned with suppressing her appetite in front of others, "she begins to eat." (26):

> She eats slowly, steadily, sucking the rich sardine oil from her fingers with slow and complete relish. Then she stops, not abruptly, yet with utter completeness, her jaw stilled in the midchewing, a bitten cracker in her hand and her face lowered a little and her eyes blank, as if she were listening to something far away or so near as to be inside her. . . . "It's twins at least," she says to herself, without lip movement, without sound. Then the spasm passes. She eats again. (26)

This passage highlights not only Lena's hearty appetite but also her comfort with and awareness of her body. As we can see from the very first (and seemingly most important) question she asks the driver, "Will we get there before dinner time?" (24), and her behavior during the ride, she possesses a healthy, unabashed relationship with food—one quite unlike Joe Christmas's.

Lena arrives in Jefferson "before dinner time" and meets up with yet another generous host. Shortly after reaching Byron's boarding house, she again gratifies her appetite with another satisfying meal: "Lena ate heartily again, with that grave and hearty decorum, almost going to sleep in her plate before she had finished" (80). Although Mrs. Beard feeds Lena "after [the men] have all et" (80), allowing her more freedom to indulge in the repast than the presence of the male boarders might permit, her appetite and her willingness to satisfy it exceeds normal social boundaries. Her obvious enjoyment of the food and her comfort with her pregnant body represent an interesting transgression from the "Victorian novel's 'representational taboo' against depicting women eating" (Bordo, 183). As a potential mother, she is supposed to feed others, not herself; instead, she rejects the social mechanisms of control that attempt to train her in the knowledge of her limitations. She gives in not only to her literal appetites, but to her figurative ones as well—she travels, creates stories, and moves about somewhat freely in "masculine" space, albeit under male protection.

This is not to say, though, that Lena completely rejects standard female gender roles or fails in her maternal duties to feed her baby. On the contrary, she nourishes her new son generously. As we learn from the image of her in the cabin with "the child at breast" (385) and the salesman's story, Lena freely provides ample sustenance: "the baby hadn't never stopped eating, that had been eating now for about ten miles, like one of these dining cars on the train" (480). In contrast to the novel's other eating, feeding relationships, Lena seems to have passed on her own hearty appetite and healthy relationship to food.

This ability to provide sustenance physically also differs remarkably from Ruby's efforts as a mother. From the narrator's careful observations (59, 154–55), we see that Ruby, apparently exhausted from her duties at the Old Frenchman place and her restrained appetite, can only bottle-feed her baby. As a result of the mothers' varying physical abilities to care for their children, Lena's child with its strong lungs and insatiable appetite has far more hope for survival than the quiet, pale Goodwin baby, who, Temple observes, "is going to die" (37). Lena's hearty appetite and relationship with food, then, can be interpreted as a positive response to cultural gender roles as she both adheres to and transgresses them.

Although, as Clarke contends, Lena is not that "threatening to the community on account of her class and marital status" (99), she does offer notable challenges to several social gender norms. These challenges are registered by Armstid almost immediately after he meets up with Lena. Commenting on her ability to "walk the public country . . . without shame," Armstid concludes: "right then and there is where she secedes from the woman race and species and spends the balance of their life trying to get joined up with the man race. That's why they dip snuff and smoke and want to vote." (12) While the novel offers no evidence of Lena's desire to disrupt gender norms in these particular ways, the slippage created as male characters in the novel constantly misread her thoughts and actions attests to her abilities to disrupt various gender constructions. As the narrator repeatedly reminds us, "she is not thinking about [Lucas] and the approaching crisis" (23); instead, she focuses on satisfying her desires to eat, to travel, to move freely in (male) public space. In a novel about individuals renegotiating their identities within the community and culture at large, Lena offers not only a more positive alternative to Joe's violence, but also a reminder that we must not forget the body as we struggle against culturally imposed identities.

Both *Sanctuary* and *Light in August* exhibit "Faulkner's ability to understand and portray women [and men] struggling with the limitations imposed upon them by a restrictive Southern society" (Wittenberg, 103). By exploring Faulkner's depictions of food and eating in both novels, we can see just how pervasive some of these "disciplining" mechanisms of social control are. Nevertheless, we can also locate in these depictions of food and eating important sites of resistance for reinscribing and reinterpreting cultural gender and racial norms.

NOTES

I wish to thank Deborah Clarke for reading various drafts of this essay and for offering her time, comments, and suggestions.

1. I do not mean to imply that eating disorders like anorexia nervosa are a late twentieth-century phenomenon. Although not as widespread or widely studied, eating disorders in the late nineteenth century and early twentieth century clearly existed and were tied to the same sorts

of cultural gender norms that influence modern cases. As Joan Jacob Brumberg has noted, "cultural pressure on women to control their appetite" really begins in the late nineteenth century, with the early decades of the twentieth century marking the first best selling weight-control books marketed specifically to women (374, 376).

2. Although Chandler does focus on Joe Christmas, her general argument is broader. Considering *Light in August,* she writes, "The grotesque and unnatural uses of food, the emphasis on the connection of food with filth, the transformation of nourishment into excrement, function as analogues for the grotesque and unnatural uses of religion, sexual relations and social customs which fail to nourish, sicken and kill the human spirit" (93). Morrisey's 1978 essay likewise interprets food imagery in *Light in August* as Faulkner's vehicle for commenting on various characters' relations to the "life cycle" and depicting "the inevitably tragic consequences of reliance on [certain] philosophical or religious stances" (41). While these readings of *Light in August*'s food imagery offer some valuable insights into the novel's larger themes and structure, they tend to ignore the complex gender codings of food and eating as well as the potential agency that food consumption/rejection offers individual characters.

3. Adhering to this role, however, does not make Ruby a good mother; placing her baby in a box behind the stove hardly constitutes loving maternal care.

4. Ruby's past employment as a prostitute—especially when she "made money to get [Lee] out of prison" (37)—certainly contributes to this belief as well.

5. Although Lee does not physically assault Temple, his terrorization of her prior to her rape in the barn no doubt contributes to her willingness to perjure herself.

6. Ultimately Temple does eat part of the steak, perhaps comforted by thoughts "of her father and brothers at home" (99). For the most part, however, she rejects more hearty forms of sustenance. Earlier in the novel we see her take a bite of the sandwich that Popeye gives her in the car on the way to Memphis. But after this bite, she "ceased chewing and opened her mouth . . . she sat motionless, gazing straight at him, her mouth open and the half chewed mass of bread and meat lying on her tongue." (80). This passage seems to suggest that Temple refuses not only nourishment, but food that might associate her with a sexual appetite.

7. This trend in criticism can be seen in the following works: Kevin Boon's "Temple Defiled: The Brainwashing of Temple Drake in Faulkner's *Sanctuary,*" Diane Luce Cox's "A Measure of Innocence: *Sanctuary*'s Temple Drake," Laura Tanner's "Reading Rape: *Sanctuary* and *The Women of Brewster Place,*" and Diane Roberts's "Ravished Belles: Stories of Rape and Resistance in *Flags in the Dust* and *Sanctuary,*" Also worth noting is Linda Dunleavy's 1996 article, "*Sanctuary,* Sexual Difference, and the Problem of Rape," which attempts to move Temple criticism beyond the victim/vamp dichotomy by examining sexual difference and the novel's "social structures of power" (171); nonetheless, like previous critics, Dunleavy also fails to grant Temple any agency within the novel's existing gender/power structures.

8. Both Kevin Boon and Diane Luce Cox succinctly present summaries of such earlier readings of Temple's behavior.

9. After telling Minnie her name, Minnie responds, "you got a boy's name, aint you?" (83). Also worth noting is the make-up of Temple's family; growing up in an all male environment may have contributed to her negative perceptions of her body and sexuality.

10. Considering cigarette advertising campaigns of the time, Temple's smoking habit might be interpreted as another weight loss strategy. Stressing that "overweight must be avoided," Lucky Strike ads promised women the slim figures of 1920s actresses if they would "reach for a *Lucky* instead of a sweet." Temple, of course, carries this behavior to an extreme, substituting cigarettes and the empty calories of gin for all nourishment.

11. I am not suggesting that Temple is fully self conscious of her bodily protest—many anorexics are not.

12. An important exception to this, however, occurs in the middle of chapter 7. After dumping the tray of food brought to him by Mrs. McEachern, Joe "rose from the bed and went and knelt in the corner as he had not knelt on the rug, and above the outraged food kneeling, with his hands ate, like a savage dog" (146). His behavior here may function as a rejection not only of mothering but also of McEachern's attempts to impose a socialized, religiously based identity upon him.

13. Employing the writings of Kristeva, both Pamela Boker and Deborah Clarke offer more thorough analyses of this idea in their treatments of Joe Christmas.

14. For a more complete discussion of the complex role that food plays in Joe and Joanna's relationship see Boker's and Chandler's articles on this topic.

15. While not an exclusively female eating disorder, anorexia nervosa is usually coded "feminine" because over ninety percent of all anorexics are female.

16. In *The Hamlet*, Eula is also often depicted eating. Because she is represented primarily as a type of fertility goddess and described in more sensual terms, her appetite seems to function largely as a metaphor for her presumed sexual appetite.

17. This may, in part, be due to Lena's status as a paradoxically asexual character. Although pregnant and often seen by critics as a type of fertility goddess, the narrator describes her as "young, pleasant faced, candid, friendly, alert" (9) and "serene, peaceful" (20)—hardly terms that would construct her as an overtly sexual being. Byron, in fact, is so convinced of Lena's asexuality that it is only after she gives birth that he admits "that she is not a virgin" (380).

WORKS CITED

Bleikasten, André. "Terror and Nausea: Bodies in *Sanctuary.*" *Faulkner Journal* 1, no. 1 (1985): 17–29.

Boker, Pamela, "'How can he be so nothungry?' Fetishism, Anorexia, and the Disavowal of the Cultural 'I' in *Light in August.*" *Faulkner Journal* 7, nos. 1–2 (1992): 175–91.

Boon, Kevin. "Temple Defiled: The Brainwashing of Temple Drake in Faulkner's *Sanctuary.*" *Faulkner Journal* 6, no. 2 (1991): 33–50.

Bordo, Susan. *Unbearable Weight: Feminism, Western Culture and the Body.* Los Angeles: University of California Press, 1993.

Brumberg, Joan Jacobs. "Fasting Girls: The Emerging Ideal of Slenderness in American Culture." In *Women's America: Refocusing the Past,* edited by Linda Kerber and Jane Sherron De Hart, 4th ed., 374–82. New York: Oxford U Press, 1995.

Chandler, Marilyn. "Food and Eating in *Light in August.*" *Notes on Mississippi Writers* 18, no. 2 (1986): 91–101.

Clarke, Deborah. *Robbing the Mother: Women in Faulkner.* Jackson: University Press of Mississippi, 1994.

Cox, Diane Luce. "A Measure of Innocence: *Sanctuary*'s Temple Drake." *Mississippi Quarterly* 9, no. 3 (1986): 301–24.

Dunleavy, Linda. *"Sanctuary,* Sexual Difference and the Problem of Rape." *Studies in American Fiction* 24, no. 2 (1986): 171–91.

Faulkner, William. *As I Lay Dying.* 1930. New York: Vintage/Random, 1990.

———. *The Hamlet.* 1940. Reprint, New York: Vintage/Random, 1964.

———. *Light in August.* 1932. Reprint, New York: Vintage/Random, 1972.

———. *Sanctuary* and *Requiem for a Nun.* 1931. Reprint, New York: Signet, 1958.

Furst, Lilian. "Introduction." *Disorderly Eaters: Texts in Self-Empowerment,* edited by Lilian Furst and Peter Graham, 1–9. University Park: Penn State University Press, 1992.

Kirchdorfer, Ulf. *"Sanctuary:* Temple as Parrot." *Faulkner Journal* 6, no. 2 (1991): 51–54.

Morrissey, Thomas J. "Food Imagery in Faulkner's *Light in August.*" *Nassau Review* 3, no. 4 (1978): 41–49.

Page, Sally R. *Faulkner's Women: Characterization and Meaning.* DeLand, Fla.: Evertt/Edward's, 1973.

Roberts, Diane. *Faulkner and Southern Womanhood.* Athens: University of Georgia Press, 1994.

———. "Ravished Belles: Stories of Rape and Resistance in *Flags in the Dust* and *Sanctuary,*" *Faulkner Journal* 4, no. 1–2 (1988–89): 21–35.

Shapiro, Laura. *Perfection Salad: Women and Cooking at the Turn of the Century.* New York: Farrar, 1986.

Tanner, Laura. "Reading Rape: *Sanctuary* and *The Women of Brewster Place.*" *American Literature* 62:4 (1990): 559–82.

"We Know our *Luckies*. That's How We Stay Slender." Lucky Strike Advertisement. *Collier's* 19
    January 1929, 37.

Williams, David. "The Profaned Temple." In *Twentieth Century Interpretations of Sanctuary: A
    Collection of Critical Essays*, edited by J. Douglas Canfield, 93–107. Englewood Cliffs, N.J.:
    Prentice, 1982.

Wittenberg, Judith Bryant. "The Women of *Light in August*." In *New Essays on Light in August*, edited
    by Michael Millgate, 103–22. New York: Cambridge University Press, 1987.

PART II

Feminist, Woman-Centered, and Sexualized Approaches

The Abjection of Addie and Other Myths of the Maternal in *As I Lay Dying*

DIANA YORK BLAINE

In many ways William Faulkner's *As I Lay Dying* exemplifies what Susan Cole has called the paradox of mourning.[1] Cole argues that ritual tragedies reveal both reverence and revulsion towards the newly dead person, becoming "performance[s] of ambivalence on behalf of an absent present" (Cole, 1). Certainly few works of literature manifest such unambiguous ambivalence towards a later clan member as Faulkner's novel does; the Bundren children's obsession with their mother continues even as her increasingly repulsive corpse rots more each day. Despite this repulsiveness, they appear unable to separate themselves from her either physically or psychically. But there is a crucial difference between *As I Lay Dying* and the majority of dramatic tragedies—Cole notes that ritual acts of mourning almost always involve a fallen father or father-figure, and that the "canon of tragic drama, on the whole, concentrates on the experience of male protagonists." Neither father

Reprinted with permission from *Mississippi Quarterly* 47, no. 3 (1994), 419–39.

nor fallen king, Addie Bundren nevertheless takes center stage in Faulkner's mutant modern version of the traditional patriarchal tragedy, leaving us to wonder why this average, impoverished and unhappy farmer's wife has been so promoted, and what impact, if any, the presence of the mother in the place of the father has on the degree of ambivalence enacted in the text.

Certainly there is no paucity of critical interpretations willing to substitute Addie for the king, the father, or even the Christ figure, without pausing to consider the manifold ramifications of such potentially redemptive readings. More than one critic compares Addie, via the fish dinner, to the main course in a totemic meal, the type of meal traditionally ingested to insure the continued protection of the sons by their dead father. And interpreting Addie's character through a combination of Christian and classical symbolism, Patrick Samway speculates that "we have an intimation in the fish image that she will be resurrected on the last day."[2] Even readings that follow less explicitly patriarchal religious blueprints locate a source of comfort in Addie's passing, as does Patricia McKee's: "All phenomena change here, in relation to others. And because change is always and everywhere present, losses—and gains—are absorbed into the experience of the novel without being denied or made up for, and without seeming alien or negative."[3] Despite the improbability of it, McKee seems to ask us to find permanence in the loss of the mother.

Granting Addie's (absent) presence the power of grounding meaning, as each of these types of interpretations ultimately does, obfuscates the profound differences between Faulkner's text, one which places a woman in the paramount position of power, and those phallogocentric texts, like but certainly not limited to the Bible, which rely upon the central informing presence of the paternal and the marginality and subjectivity of the maternal. Simply swapping Addie for Jesus, or Laius, or the elder Hamlet, sidesteps several key issues. Women historically have not, in literature or out of it, occupied powerful symbolic positions with the same frequency as men, nor can powerful women exercise their authority without attracting overtly negative criticism.[4] And even though Faulkner apparently felt it was appropriate to grant the mother such power, to portray her in a traditionally masculine position, he also felt it necessary to kill her off without leaving behind an intact matriarchy to carry on her reign, to reify her authority. Instead we see woman as symbol of power eclipsed as she ascends, her putative centrality undermined by the symbolic system that subsumes her abject corpse into the ground at the end. So other than being allowed symbolic status, as nominal head of the family, or at least as an irreplaceable individual in the lives of her children, she functions, a direct descendent of Eve, as the agent of chaos and representative of death in yet another Western text. This contrasts markedly with the masculine line of generation, the patriarchal system, that remains in place at the end of *Hamlet* or Sophocles's *Oedipus Rex.* What is so dangerous about the representation of maternal power that, once conjured, it must always already be repressed? Furthermore, if this type of force so threatens the symbolic order that it can only be depicted when denuded, why attempt to represent it at all?

Contemplating potential answers to these questions helps to reveal previously unexamined ways in which *As I Lay Dying* operates as contemporary, not traditional, fiction, and highlights the significant differences between the classical world of tragedy as Susan Cole defines it and Faulkner's postmodern one. For what André Bleikasten calls a "timeless fable" seems actually to be rooted very much in the twentieth century, its plot and its form a reaction not only to the instability occasioned by death itself but to the radical instability of the traditional institutions of the culture in which that death takes place. In fact, what Cole describes as the uncontrollable, dangerous liminal realm into which the deceased passes in classical mourning rituals seems to mirror the marginalized transitional landscape the *living* Bundrens inhabit. Nothing is what it seems, the traditional narratives of patriarchal power have been usurped, and in their place a problematized figure of the maternal holds brief and uneasy sway.

Hamlet's epistemological concerns over what to believe or whom to trust differ markedly from the ontological instability occasioned by Faulkner's text, a text in which the boundaries between being and not being are challenged by both its use of shifting narratives and its theme of death in life. What the privileged and royal inhabitants of Elsinore feared was rotten in the state of Denmark—intrigue, murder and corruption of the human variety—at least takes place on a stable playing field, with recognizable political, social and familial systems remaining relatively intact. This realism contrasts markedly with the physical and figuratively decay which pervades the lives of the impoverished denizens of Faulkner's bleak Mississippi scrub country. And unlike in *Hamlet,* this decay is not limited to the setting or morality of the story, nor is it limited to the reality of the economic and spiritual poverty of the existence of poor farmers in post–Civil War America. Hamlet's confusion over appearance and reality, a plot device for Shakespeare, extends in Faulkner's text to the very shape of the narrative itself; the latter author's deliberately confusing stream-of-consciousness monologues resist the reader's desire for recognizable discourse even as they destroy the possibility of comprehending clearly the "real" events of the plot. And just as the ontological musings of whether "to be or not to be" in *Hamlet* take for granted the possibility of "being" something comprehensible and not merely the fragmented figment of a character, Shakespeare's highly figurative language invites interpretation whereas Faulkner's dissociated monologues seem to mock it. Death in *Hamlet* represents a clear break with life, one half of a starkly defined dichotomy whose line is blurred only by the disruptive yet contained presence of the father's ghost, a ghost who comes out of that "undiscovered country from whose bourn / No traveler returns" not to problematize the status of death but to further the plot. Addie, on the other hand, smears death all over the narrative, making it impossible to discern presence from absence in any cogent way. She speaks after she's already decomposed, she remains a literal presence for almost the entire length of the novel, she goes away without leaving; in short, her character resists the now seemingly secondary concern over whether "to be or not to be" by foregrounding the issue of what it means "to be" in the first place.

In *Over Her Dead Body,* Elisabeth Bronfen documents the long history of textual representations of dead women, concentrating on the well-documented Victorian obsession with them, and in her argument she interprets the ubiquitous appearance of the feminine corpse as part of an ingrained and long-standing cultural association of women with alterity and death, the "materiality-maternity-morality matrix." Focusing particularly on nineteenth-century visual art and literature, she argues that both "femininity and death cause a disorder to stability, mark moments of ambivalence, disruption or duplicity, and their eradication produces a recuperation of order, a return to stability."[5] Certainly Faulkner's Addie follows this paradigm: we watch her disrupt the text in life and in death, until finally and with surprisingly little fanfare she is swallowed up into the seemingly seamless earth and unceremoniously replaced. Yet there exists a crucial difference, at least in degree, between Addie's tenacious corpse, refusing to go softly into that dark night, and the multitude of tubercular, pale waifs who populate—perhaps *mortify* would be a better term—the paintings and fictions of the Victorians. Picture Millais' Ophelia, all weedy and wan, looking positively thankful for the attention. The last thing this figure would want to do would be to manifest any unbecoming authority, and so she remains apparently satisfied with her role as contained irruption, denuded enigma. No need to despair when you look upon her, ye mighty, for the Other is clearly not you. Ophelia's womanly alterity is contained in this visual depiction just as the textual Ophelia is contained by paternal prohibition at first and insanity at last. But while Addie also functions as wasted corpse, her soma stubbornly resists closure, and perhaps even more shocking, she manifests autonomous desires in the text. Not mere representation of object nor semiotic irruption, Addie symbolizes and speaks. In this way she cannot be interpreted simply as another instance of our culture's documented obsession with silencing death and women, but as a postmodern permutation of it. The abyss opened up by her corpse will not easily be filled by Anse's remarriage, and in this sense, the novel forces us to assess the changing dynamics of gender in the twentieth century. Now, more than ever, the maternal is seen as both locus of meaning and yawning maw, or perhaps as the indeterminacy that gets repressed and reduced by meaning. André Bleikasten emphasizes this link between postmodernism, indeterminacy and the maternal in *The Ink of Melancholy:*

> Faulkner seems on the threshold of postmodernist freeplay. Real power, social and aesthetic, resides in the authority of the one who confers names, the modern Adam who is Oedipus' double. But there are substantial reservations in Faulkner: the cavalier displacement of the mother fails to erase Addie Bundren's hold on our readerly consciousness. It is she who affirms for us the consequences of symbolic authority on the body of experience, in feelings of pleasure and pain.[6]

In the modern world, it seems, we can no longer merely contain the maternal by naming it, by repressing it with a weakened symbolic structure, and so are left with a post-modern indeterminacy.

It is important to note that opening up such a line of investigation into the novel's profound ontological instability and corresponding ambivalence about the mother precludes a number of critical commonplaces regarding *As I Lay Dying*. First of all, the many supposed moments of comic relief cannot surpass the oppressive despair of the characters and their joyless, meaningless lives. Anyone who has taught this novel to undergraduates knows that they do not think it is very funny, and while quite willing to laugh heartily at the black comedy of something like Flannery O'Connor's "Good Country

People," they find this text extremely disconcerting for any number of (good) reasons. The prolonged and agonizing death and burial of Addie, coupled with her complicated representation as mother, monster, victim and victimizer, profoundly disturbs these first readers, and, if we subscribe unquestioningly to the standard criticism, leaves us in the rather unsupportable position of trying to convince students that what seems horrible to them is actually quite humorous, and that all they need to do is study the text in a more sophisticated way to appreciate its true impact. The alternative approach is to renegotiate our own reaction to the text, refusing to accept the overly intellectualized, and possibly patriarchal, idea that much of the book's content generates laughs. Undergraduates may not be the best judges of literature, of course, but free from the influence of a (possibly) overdetermined critical canon that has grown up around this novel, their fresher responses deserve consideration.

Indeed, one of the surprising things about critical reaction to *As I Lay Dying* is this apparent ability to deny that the very matter of this text about a woman's death is, in fact, a woman's death. The title makes us aware that the book's central (or decentered) focus is death and dying, and soon after starting to read we know it is about the death of the mother, but most critical ink is spilled not on considering what this means, but on issues of heroism, humor and aesthetics. Elisabeth Bronfen argues that we are "culturally blind to the ubiquity of representations of feminine death" precisely because they are so obvious, and because our focus is simultaneously drawn to the author "who guides the spectator's view of the depicted object" (3–5). Faulkner's guiding hand could hardly be more apparent in this novel as he frustrates our desire to read a comprehensible story; he pushes us away by providing no context, guides us in by placing us square in the psyche of each character, throws us off the trail by forcing us to reconstruct the events as best we can—in short, he dazzles with an array of literary tricks worthy of P. T. Barnum. The result is that far from empathizing with the dying woman, we are, like Dewey Dell, too preoccupied to notice what is taking place literally under our noses, and must focus instead upon the male author, the authority, who is in charge of our experience and emotions. As she lies dying, Faulkner keeps writing, and his Modernist virtuosity not only stabilizes the maternal semiotic irruption but steals sympathy and attention from the Mother even though it is her story that generates the text just as the text generates her story.

Feminist critic Judith Fetterley suggests that women defy their years of academic acculturation into a patriarchal literary canon that repeatedly presents the male perspective as equivalent to universal experience, accomplishing this by learning to "resist" as they read, especially as they read texts written by men that portray women in stereotypically negative ways.[7] Resisting a reading of this novel as funny frees us from having to accept that the behaviors or assumptions of an abhorrent character like Anse are funny. What can we feel but contempt for this man who is too cheap to call a doctor for his dying wife, too lazy to pitch in with the hard work necessary for running a farm? Yet according to some critics Anse not only brings much of the perceived humor into the text but is perhaps the "most touching victim" in the narrative.[8] Economic victimization may be one thing, but contemptuous uncaring behavior towards family members within the context of that economic victimization is quite another, leaving me forced to wonder to what degree responses to Anse, sympathetic or risible, might be dictated by gender. Could a woman find Anse the "most touching victim" in this tale? Can women laugh along with men over a book that asserts man's uncompromising symbolic and actual authority over woman even when the man is as reprehensible as Anse?

Along these same lines I am forced to wonder how many women readers of the text are struck by the speciousness of yet another critical commonplace, the "heroic" majesty of Cash's obsessive carpentering. While making his mother's coffin within her hearing and for a prolonged period allegedly brings this dying woman relief, Cash could just as well be indicted for insensitivity and boorishness. The ceaseless sound of the saw chases down the other family members, a few of whom are openly critical of Cash's protracted efforts. After all, he is making her not a stereo cabinet but a coffin made necessary by the cancer her indefensible husband ignored until it is now eating away relentlessly at her wasted body. The scant evidence Faulkner gives us that Addie supports this spectacle of coffin creation occurs when she raises herself up to watch Cash work with "neither . . . censure nor approbation."[9] That leaves us with only Anse's occasional assertions that this elaborately designed and executed coffin conforms with Addie's wishes, and considering what we know of Addie's alienated and hateful feelings towards Anse, his reliability on this important matter is suspect at best. This critical fascination with the mastery of Cash's ability is clearly a phallocentric one, as if putting the mess that is Addie in a perfectly formed box can somehow subsume the horror and alterity of the feminine into a comprehensible and orderly (male-authored) symbolic structure.

William Rossky's description of Dewey Dell as "a highly comic figure" seems to emerge from a similarly male perspective.[10] Can women readers forget the gravity of the situation in which this character finds herself? Can women ignore the desperation of a young girl who, with no one to confide in, is forced to seek an illegal abortion? Are we entirely comfortable with Faulkner's depiction of her as bovine bearer of seed? In the same breath that Rossky asks us to laugh at Dewey Dell he informs us that she, and all of these Bundrens of "limited" vision," are ultimately heroes—so we are laughing at them then, or with them? Perhaps Rossky wants to read these characters as quaint throwbacks to a time when life appeared to have meaning because they do fulfill their pact to the dead mother, personal material motivations aside, and so in some sense seem connected to the world of the traditional mourning ritual that Susan Cole describes. As I have suggested, however, the differences between their world and the classical one loom larger than the similarities, and so readings of the novel must take into account the events of a history even more modern than that of Cervantes.

John T. Matthews's Marxist reading does just that by applying Adorno's aesthetic theories to the novel and arguing that a "sediment of reality" plays off of "replicas and substitutes" in the art of the modern world, or "the Machine Age," in Matthews's terminology. The commodification of culture has profoundly altered our relationships to one another and to the image, he believes, and Faulkner's fiction serves as proof that the twentieth century consists of a series of aesthetic sleights of hand: we are constantly forced to accept these replicas and substitutes in lieu of "the real thing" (Matthews, 91). Paradoxically he believes that the novel manages to stay in touch with "the sediment of reality it frames and forms"—a surprising bit of nostalgia on his part when you consider the pervasive sense of confusion in the novel and the world it represents. Not only are the events unclear and represented via subjective narrative perspectives, but the characters' relationships to one another and indeed their very psychology remain mysterious, open only to speculation. These are not grounded, centered characters peopling a linear plotline, and it seems that far from presenting art as simulacrum of life, this novel suggests that life as we know it is linguistically constructed as well.

In attempting to account for the existence of *As I Lay Dying* at the particular point in literary history from which it emerged, Matthews interprets it as a failed brand of the new Modernism, one incapable of "resisting and transmuting the forces of modernization and commodification" (90) because it is too pat, too seamless. By reintegrating the "story of misery" into a "tragicomic narrative of aesthetic virtuosity," Matthews believes, Faulkner presents us with a type of compensation for disillusionment, albeit an artificial one, and permits us to ignore the "empirical reality," which is the evil of mechanization. But this focus on mechanization and technology prevents Matthews from considering the ways in which the novel fairly bleeds desperation and horror—aesthetic virtuosity is simply not enough to staunch the flow of psychological bile emanating from *As I Lay Dying*, and it is this single-minded interest in the "image" that generates his odd description of Anse as "perhaps the most touching victim" in the text. Matthews seems to have missed the fact that the text signifies over, and because of, the dead body of a woman, or perhaps he does not see this death to be as significant as the "death" of true craftsmanship in the face of mechanization, a death that makes Cash's personal care over the coffin so heroic. And he seems to be ignoring much else about the book when he argues that the text appears "seamless," at least for those of us interested in understanding the characters' murky psychology.

In fact, viewed from a psychological perspective rather than a Marxist one, the bifurcation Matthews delineates between the novel and "empirical reality" can be attributed to radical changes in the way modern human beings shape and interpret their lives. Like Matthews's version, this reading requires a recognition of the influence of industrialism and capitalism, but it also requires that we acknowledge the impact on Western culture of the decentering of other traditional metanarratives besides these economic ones including those regarding religion, science, politics and psychology. From this perspective, the experiment that is *As I Lay Dying* seems less a coping mechanism than a manifestation of previously repressed psychic energies, energies once contained and controlled by pervasive mythologies regarding how the world functioned and where we fit in it.

Julia Kristeva accounts for the fragmented form of avant-garde poetry in a similar way. Freed from the constraints of religious oppression, the Symbolists, according to Kristeva, constructed poems shot through with psychic pulsions, bodily drives, and pre-rational impulses. While her early *Revolution in Poetic Language* takes an approbative, down-with-society type of stance that may seem inappropriately anarchistic to Americans approaching an uncertain twenty-first century, the ideas contained within *Revolution in Poetic Language* nevertheless seem highly relevant to movements in Faulkner's novel.

One needn't look far into the landscape of Faulkner's text to see the Ozymandias-like ruins of the traditional metanarratives. Even Nietzsche would marvel at the way the Christian God is done away with here; the most "authentic" religious figure is Cora Tull, a soulless and hypocritical harpy, and the "official" man of God the adulterous and spineless Whitfield. Nature isn't just read in tooth and claw; it's represented by lurking, humanoid vultures come to pick our flesh. Science and medicine are shams, their promises of omniscience undelivered, and their representatives either unscrupulous, like the boys in the pharmacy, or ailing themselves, like the "pussel-gutted" Peabody. The American government and the attendant American dream seem farther away than Jefferson to the country Bundrens, their scant evidence found only in the encroaching roads and certain taxes. And finally, and perhaps most profoundly, human beings, no longer Enlightenment bastions of individuality and humanism, prove to be complicated and interrelated linguistic constructions; neither fish nor fowl, these inexplicable, unknowable organisms are definitely dis-integrated. Darwin's fantasy of an evolutionary *Telos,* the same one Tennyson clung to in his elegy to Arthur Henry Hallam, dissolves in the dust of Jefferson, mocked by the image of the mindless Bundrens munching bananas, their moronic mien an insult to apes.

Nor should we forget, as most critics seem to, that this book is set after the demoralizing years of World War One. Darl was even there, we know, because Paris is where he procured the pornographic picture of the beast with two backs, yet no critical interpretations of the novel consider or discuss this crucial point. Before America and Europe experienced World War, what William Rossky describes as "the insanity" was still under wraps—dreams were alive, myths were under attack but intact, the Victorians dug in for the long haul. Then, as Pound notes, when we lost the best of them for an old bitch gone in the teeth, we lost more than just young men—many finally lost hope in Western civilization as the highest representation of human culture, and I think this loss is central to *As I Lay Dying.* In a way World War One was irrefutable truth that our benign patriarchs were not necessarily capable of making everything right, that in fact they might not be as benign as we had believed, and that a patriarchal America could very well be a dangerous place in which to reside. Just ask Darl. He'd seen with his own eyes the horror of a war that used mustard gas, and yet (the euphemistically termed) "shell shock" is never considered as a contributing factor to his nervous breakdown.

With these larger issues in mind, Addie's central position in the text becomes even more intriguing. Is she there to replace a fallen Fatherland? After all, to return to your mother, to run to mama, is the most comforting thing to do in times of uncertainty. Yet Faulkner's novel unearths her power in untraditional and experimental ways. Inscribing Addie as pre-Oedipal force, Faulkner shows her suspicious of language, interested in the corporeal over the intellectual, and consumed with and by the process of mothering— the very face of the abject. But, in her function as fallen epic hero, she also inhabits the position of the symbolic paternal signifier and this complicates her role as the representative of materiality-maternity-morality. Unlike the nineteenth-century dead heroine, Addie resists interpretation as a presumably realistic, stereotypically passive woman as she introduces into the text thoughts and desires traditionally associated with the masculine. In other words, as these gender stereotypes crumble, representations of women can and will become increasingly "real": female characters can be speaking subjects as well as viewed objects, as Addie is (briefly) permitted to be here, talking realistically about previously taboo subjects, including the consideration of pregnancy as a kind of physical and pyschical violation and of motherhood as an excruciatingly complicated state.[11] And yet Faulkner's text still adheres to fundamental Western culture associations of women with death and illness—in breaking ground, *As I Lay Dying* quickly moves to cover it back up.

Just who is this enigmatic woman ensconced at the center of Faulkner's tragedy? One son, Darl, calls her "Addie Bundren," this formality a symptom of his early inability to cathect with his mother, an inability which has left him vulnerable to psychosis. Another son, Jewel, fantasizes about heroically protecting her, in knight-in-shining-armor fashion, by "rolling rocks down the hill" at the faces of those people who have come to gather at her deathbed. Dewey Dell barely thinks of her at all, even as she is about to repeat her mother's enslavement to procreation, perhaps too terrified to acknowledge what the loss of her mother really means, and desperate at this point for help from the world of men. To Vardaman, notoriously, Addie is a fish. Clearly no one version of Addie exists in the novel and, except for her one opportunity to speak for herself, she is constructed by each person's perceptions.

In Cora Tull's opinion Addie is damned and unmaternal, figuratively blinded by her lack of "the eternal and the everlasting salvation and grace." While we might tend to ignore the importance of this pesky persona, annoyed with her hypocrisy and self-righteousness, Cora's position as foil to Addie should not be underestimated—in her character we see normative behaviors for women and mothers represented, unappealing as these may be. Addie's presumed refusal to bend to the will of her society, as reflected in Cora Tull's sanctimonious disapproval, certainly contributes to her position as sacrificial victim in the text. Addie will pay with her life for her willfulness, just as James's Daisy Miller does when she dies of the malaria caught strolling late at night in the Roman catacombs with a man. Both of these characters die from physical pathology, but their vulnerability is occasioned by a refusal to behave according to social norms.

Of course, even though Addie pays with her life for manifesting antisocial behavior, Cora Tull's "version" of Addie as "not a true mother" is no more apt than the versions held by her children or anyone else in the text. For Addie *has,* in fact, sacrificed her autonomy already by taking on the socially sanctioned roles of wife and mother. Yet we are so uncomfortable with her unbecoming admissions about the burdens of motherhood and living in loveless marriages that she is branded as strident at best and evil at worst. Even critics fall into this trap. Writing on *As I Lay Dying,* Jan Bakker, for example, explains that even though Addie "is domineering and assertive, she remains an intensely feminine woman in that she ultimately only trusts the concrete and through her physical body tries to gain a hold on reality."[12] A number of interesting assumptions operate in Bakker's statement, but perhaps the most surprising is his description of her as "domineering and assertive." Exactly what has she asserted? Her right to toil ceaselessly until death for a man she does not love and a family she cannot connect with? The implicit criticism here of her inappropriate emotional independence seems directly related to the cultural myth of the endlessly sacrificing mother, one devoid of either desire or identity save as they relate to the needs of her family. Anse, of course, is the real monster, refusing to work lest he sweat himself to death, while Addie kept the farm going and raised the children, but she alone is open to this sort of attack, this accusation that simply having desires renders her "domineering and assertive."

Bakker's attempt to mitigate his criticism by describing Addie as "intensely feminine" doesn't help much either. First of all, this sexist assumption that assertiveness is somehow unfeminine, as if women should not manifest any will, is surprising to find in an article written in 1980. And remember, after all, that this is not Katherine in *The Taming of the Shrew* under consideration here, but a hard-working, hard-scramble and largely silent farm wife. The few conversations recounted involving Addie show her to be uninterested in hypocrisy à la Cora Tull and insistent that her dead body be taken back to Jefferson. Other than that, it seems that she pretty much played her part as household servant and field hand, so the use of the term "domineering" seems inaccurate and unfair. After all, a truly "domineering" wife would have had Anse sweating.

Second, we need to challenge the idea that to be feminine, or I think what Bakker really means is to be female, is to trust only the "concrete" and manifest reality only through the "physical body." This assumption comes close to those same sexist Aristotelian oppositions relegating woman to the side of the natural, the physical and the illogical, and handily preventing her access to the rational, cultural or spiritual. Children traditionally come from the body of the woman following sexual union with a man, and so women are associated, consciously and unconsciously, directly with the physical. By extension woman has come to represent death and illness in Western mythology and been prohibited historically from access to the intellectual, as if bearing children precludes thinking, and as if the man's seminal contributions to the creation of life is in some way less culpable or crucial than woman's ovular one. The notion that mothers may have a closer relationship to the infant child insofar as women have traditionally been the primary care givers is not what is under dispute here, nor is the concept that the infant relationship to the maternal body is a primal one. The problem lies in the assumption that the maternal body in some way totalizes the woman in question, defining her as solely soma, incapable of independent identity or intellect. To say Addie is "intensely feminine" because she distrusts abstraction is to say that she, and all women, can only hope to feel "like a wet seed wild in the hot blind earth" (64).[13]

Far from having only physical interests, Addie actually introduces into the text some crucial (and abstract) questions about the nature of family relationships, the social order and the role of women. Like the protagonist of Gilman's *The Yellow Wallpaper*, Addie wants intellectual and creative fulfillment apart from the banalities of mothering and wifing. Addie detests her grimy charges when she is forced to be a teacher, but because teaching was seen as an extension of mothering it was a socially acceptable, if personally abhorrent, career for her until she was lucky enough to be "rescued" by some man who could "provide" for her economically. This is clearly Anse's attraction—he has a farm, and a house, and can offer her an alternate destiny—for she has very few options. In fact this is why *both* of the Mrs. Bundrens in the text marry Anse. The much-maligned duck-shaped woman who closes the book is undoubtedly just as desperate and economically dependent as Addie, needing not only income but the social approbation that comes from being a married woman. For it is not the reality of Anse that matters in this connection, but his position in the patriarchy. He can bestow his name, take a wife, and thereby grant social status to an otherwise dangerously unattached female. Anse is certainly *not* a victim, touching or otherwise, but an undeserving beneficiary of the sexist social order.

Addie's mistrust of language actually springs from her suspicions about the motives of those who have constructed words to try to embody concepts that they want to make into reality: "I knew that motherhood was invented by someone who had to have a word for it because the ones that had the children didn't care whether there was a word for it or not" (171–72). The concept of "motherhood," Addie astutely senses, describes not the personal, individual act of bearing children, but its social, symbolic and public ramifications. The etymologies of the term in the OED, which stress the beatific, religious aspects of motherhood or the shame that should be felt by all women who do not become fulfilled through the act, reveal this social emphasis. In fact one Miss Mulock, writing in 1875, even goes so far as to say that "The mere fact of bringing eight or ten children into the world does not in the least imply true motherhood." "True motherhood" here obviously defines something other than the act of bearing children, as if all women, regardless of economic circumstance, must become irreproachable as soon as they give birth, and must be sure that their emotional experience closely matches the socially sanctioned one; in other words, they need to disappear as individual subjects and become defined only in relation to serving others. Clearly Mrs. Tull and Miss Mulock would have seen eye to eye on these issues, but what *would* their word be for that woman who bore a "mere" eight or ten children? Probably "not a true mother," the exact phrase that Cora Tull uses to damn Addie (172).

Yet if Addie was "not a true mother," how do we explain her family's intense attachments to her? For intense they are, whether displaced, as in

Jewel's case, or sublimated, as in the distracted Dewey Dell's. Every member of her family capable of deep emotional relationships has one with her (I'm excepting Anse for obvious reasons). We know that she is the most important figure in their lives, not just because the book spins out from her centrifugally, but because each child's identity is profoundly related to his or her relationship to the mother. And yet as a society we constantly refuse to recognize this crucial dynamic; perhaps as a legacy of Freud, we look to and value the Oedipal struggle as having the most profound impact on the child's emerging subjectivity. The role of the mother is seen traditionally as useful only in its nurturing aspects, as if somehow the child is helped along with food and diapers toward the important Oedipal phase without forming any psychic attachment before this time.

Faulkner's novel seems to recognize the weight of the pre-Oedipal stage in groundbreaking ways, even as it also makes sure to bury the primal mother at the last second before the unleashed powers of the unrepressed can blaze out and destroy the patriarchy completely. I want to be very careful here to distinguish the sexist association of women with death because they can bear children from a consideration of the primal pre-Oedipal association of the infant with the maternal. First of all, just as the patriarchy does not refer necessarily to individual men—plenty of women partake in patriarchal power structures—the maternal does not necessarily refer to women. Rather it is the relationship between the infant body and that of the primary care giver, whoever this may be, and, even more importantly for my considerations here, the mature adult's unconscious memory of that infantile pre-linguistic time of somatic completeness.

So while it is valid and indeed essential to consider the pre-linguistic stages of development as well as the post-, it is not valid to take the next (sexist) step of saying that women belong on the side of the material in a binary opposition. Female subjects must enter into language just as males must, and while childbirth is certainly a psychic challenge to the mother's discrete identity (a subject left largely undiscussed in literature until the advent of Modernism), adult women's identities are no more or less linguistically constructed than men's. When Addie tells us that "motherhood" was made up by someone who hadn't undergone the experience, she is not so much discounting the role of language as challenging the current definition as a patriarchal one. And when she *does* note the impossibility of saying exactly what you mean in a discursive system not grounded by the *Logos,* in a system where each word is "just a shape to fill a lack" (172), her proto-Lacanian observation says more about the original lost object than it does about women's presumed earthiness.

Part of the reason that words like "motherhood" do not match the experience of women is that they were not written by them. A patriarchal culture which represents the most famous mother as a virgin clearly does not validate the real experience of women, women like Addie, who keep a family together in spite of the emotional damage wrought upon them when they find that the reality of their lives does not match the cultural myths they have grown up with. Addie's designated roles as teacher, wife, and mother did not speak to her desire to be free, free like "the wild geese going north" (170); paradoxically, freedom for her could only come through marriage to a male member of the community, and her courtship with Anse reflects the gross economic elements of the transaction:

> "They tell me you've got a house and a good farm. And you live there alone, doing for yourself, do you?" He just looked at me, turning the hat in his hands. "A new house," I said. "Are you going to get married?"
>
>   And he said again, holding his eyes to mine: "That's what I come to see you about." (171)

Addie knows that to change her situation she must take this man, this uneducated, poorly groomed man who slumps. In time she will find that the word "love," like the word "motherhood," doesn't describe her nuptial experience with Anse. How could it? He is beneath her in every way, yet has the legal right to treat her as a brood mare, and does exactly that. And marriage, far from being a partnership, is presented to her as a "duty," a duty she fulfills by staying with him in spite of her hatred. There can be no "love" in Addie's life of economic dependence and servitude.

Rather than considering her "intensely feminine" then, as Bakker does, because she distrusts the empty, meaningless phrases used to prescribe experiences rather than describe them, we need to recognize the vast disjunction between what Addie feels and what language says. Because language, as part of our symbolic system, seeks to control experience, it must attempt to expel anything that does not fit within the acceptable limits of our mortal consciousness. Language allows us to construct the illusion of a transcendent identity, of a discrete subjectivity, separate from any hint of the materiality that threatens this fantasy of immortality. Kristeva's discussion of abjection addresses both the attempt to construct this illusion and the impossibility of doing it successfully, assailed as we are by reminders of our status as material objects. Hard as we may try to construct discrete identities through linguistic systems, the unsuccessfully repressed memory of our pre-Oedipal, pre-linguistic positionality creeps in to attack the effort. But because Western culture values an immortal, transcendent identity over one recognized as messily finite and material, we have to expel this reminder of our finite physicality at all costs, and the costs have been to women, who have been used to represent the physical in all its negative aspects.[14]

And so we have in *As I Lay Dying* both Addie's frustration at the sterility of language, drained as it is of somatic connection, *and* her representation as abject mother, come to threaten our transcendent patriarchal subjectivity. For this novel obviously connects the maternal with illness and death; after all, the ultimate representational objection is the corpse, and Addie spends the majority of the narrative physically rotting, being followed by buzzards and offending the community. She threatens our sense of self, and in this way the novel breaks no new ground but adheres to the documented commonplace of the dead woman in literature. Our need to contain death, to totalize its instability, is made possible by representing it as woman, already the locus of alterity in our culture: "What makes the death of a woman so impressive is . . . her position in culture as the unfamiliar Other, like death recuperable in the form of an image" (Bronfen, 92). So Faulkner attempts to present the aestheticized, palatable image of death in his exit in order to contribute to the communal effort to expel it.

But without the traditional tools available, the modern author will not be able to do as effective a job as earlier artists could. From the very start it is apparent that his attempt to contain experience via language will not take a traditional route; his text is famously experimental. We may account for this experiment by considering the semiotic irruption of the abject Addie, made possible by the instability of what Lyotard has called our *grand récits*, our metanarratives. In the face of the tottering paternal signifier, the maternal, associated with the feminine, physicality and death, cuts across the smooth surface of our discourse, disrupting it, dislocating it, and confusing our attempts to signify. Isn't that exactly what Faulkner's text does? It signifies confusedly. For example, Cash spends one entire chapter listing by number the reasons he made the coffin on the bevel. While clearly stating his case, this artificial monologue confuses the reader: Are we to believe that Cash thinks in this bizarre fashion? Should we trust the quasi-rational tone of the logic of his list when part of it involves such pseudo-science as "the animal magnetism of a dead body"? Or should we recognize this monologue as yet another attempt to contain that "dead body," that semiotic attack on the symbolic, by cramming it into a very self-consciously rational linguistic structure?

It is not only such strange constructions that are confusing in the novel. From the very outset even the pronouns are used to confuse us, as when Cora Tull tells us that "the quilt is drawn up to her chin, hot as it is," without having told us yet who *she* is, or when Addie conflates the wild geese and her students by moving abruptly from one to another:

> Sometimes I thought that I could not bear it, lying in bed at night, with the wild geese going north and their honking coming faint and high and wild out of the wild darkness, and during the day it would seem as though I couldn't wait for the last one to go so I could go down to the spring. (170)

Insofar as much of the novel, if not all, refuses our attempts to construct a pat, comprehensible linear narrative, it reflects what Kristeva terms semiotic irruption, or the appearance of the pre-Oedipal in the post-Oedipal. Like the avant-garde poets that Kristeva concentrates on, Faulkner seems to be writing from a different place than, say, Milton, a place less constrained by the rational, less explained by the cultural, and this (other) place is associated by psychoanalysis with the time of maternal fusion. I hope it is clear by now that one need not be a woman to have an understanding of or an access to the pre-linguistic. It is not dictated by adult gender, but is an experience universal to infants. In fact, if men are indeed forced to construct a more rigidly independent sense of subjectivity than women, as Carol Gilligan has suggested,[15] then it follows that their "break" with patriarchal discourse would be all the more abrupt, all the more apparent even, and this notion would help us to account for the extremes of Faulkner's *oeuvre*.

The implication that language is in some way drained of primal energies except when cut free from rigid signification and allowed to express the inexplicable must understandably be associated with the infant's maternal relationship, the original connection to a body not your own that rocks you and sings to you and babbles with you. But to make the connection between this pre-rational period and women as agents of death is disturbing, and it is a connection that is made explicit in *As I Lay Dying*. As much as this text validates the woman's importance in the development of the child's identity, it presents this as terrifying as well, and relies on the same old negative stereotypes of women as sexually inconstant and morally dangerous. By displacing onto the maternal our fear of death we are prohibited from benefiting from a recognition of both the importance of the pre-Oedipal maternal and the post-symbolic Mother, and so we find ourselves in this text as a cultural impasse, conflicted by our need for stabilizing metaphors yet prohibited from using the idea of the maternal in any positive, conscious way. Hence the heightened sense of ambiguity towards the dead woman felt by both the family and the readers of the novel; much more than an empty paternal signifier being buried in a ritualized way in order to ensure continuation of the clan, Addie also represents both our need to connect with the maternal, to partake of its *jouissance,* and the fact that this connection threatens identity as it is constructed in our culture.

One of the many ways that Addie is associated with death includes her strange admission that she's never had any living relatives. Apparently she comes out of death, including a dead mother we must assume, and moves into death following her illness, with life only the opportunity "to get ready to stay dead a long time" (169). Because it is her father who told her this we know that he was in fact alive during her lifetime, but still she tells Anse she has never had "any other kind" of relatives but dead ones (171). This "dead" father represents the dead paternal signifier, unable to generate meaning for her just as Anse is unable to generate meaning, and we can now begin to understand why Addie likens words to orphans, "fumbling at the deeds" (174). Like an orphan herself, cut off from connection with the living yet made to create life, Addie is unable to make a connection between the word and the deed. Yet insofar as it is the dis-position of her dead body that generates the narrative, the novel uses Addie's abject corpse to mediate between language and soma just as it uses her abject corpse to mediate between life and death.

Bronfen notes that traditionally Western literature either speaks "of," "to," or "for" dead women, confirming their status as Other, as outside of the text, and hence the author writes from a male subject position (395). Bronfen argues that writing from a female subject position permits the placement of the dead woman at the center of the text, and in that way the text is "speaking her" instead of "to," "for," or "of" her, and she goes on to discuss a number of modern women authors who do this, including Plath, Sexton and Atwood. Despite the author's gender in this case, I think we need to consider Faulkner's novel as in certain ways speaking from what Bronfen identifies as a female subject position. Certainly Addie is at the center of the text, including nominally; the title informs us that this is *her* story, and it is her corpse that holds the narrative together even as it disintegrates. While the novel treats her in certain ways as the objectification of death, as I've noted, it also attempts to "speak her," to give voice to Addie not only in the literal sense but also through the interminacy of the monologues of each of the characters. The multiplicity, the non-linear form, the unstable language all contribute to an attempt to "speak" something outside the symbolic, something not constructed exclusively through our always already repressive linguistic system. Through reading the novel, we discover that Addie's unsettling experience is to some degree ours; in this way the text assimilates what has been traditionally expelled, the material-maternal-mortal matrix.

NOTES

1. Susan Cole, *The Absent One: Mourning Ritual, Tragedy, and the Performance of Ambivalence* (University Park: Pennsylvania State University Press, 1985).

2. Patrick Samway, S.J. "Addie's Continued Presence in Faulkner's *As I Lay Dying*," in *Southern Literature and Literary Theory*, ed. Jefferson Humphries (Athens: University of Georgia Press, 1990), 295.

3. Patricia McKee, "*As I Lay Dying:* Experience in Passing," *South Atlantic Quarterly* 90 (summer 1991), 588.

4. Cora Tull attacks Addie's "femininity" on just such grounds.

5. Elisabeth Bronfen. *Over Her Dead Body: Death, Femininity and the Aesthetic* (New York: Routledge, 1992), xii.

6. André Bleikasten, *The Ink of Melancholy: Faulkner's Novels from "The Sound and the Fury" to "Light in August"* (Bloomington: Indiana University Press, 1990), 152.

7. Judith Fetterley, *The Resisting Reader: A Feminist Approach to American Fiction* (Bloomington: Indiana University Press, 1978).

8. John T. Matthews, "*As I Lay Dying* in the Machine Age," *Boundary 2*, 19 (spring 1992): 92.

9. William Faulkner, *As I Lay Dying* (New York: Vintage Books, 1990), 48.

10. William Rossky, *"As I Lay Dying:* The Insane World," *Texas Studies in Literature and Language* 4 (spring 1962): 92.

11. A "project" really begun, it seems to me, by Charlotte Perkins Gilman in her previously silenced "Yellow Wallpaper" and continued today in texts such as Toni Morrison's *Beloved* and Marge Piercy's *Woman on the Edge of Time.*

12. Jan Bakker, *"As I Lay Dying* Reconsidered," in *Modern Critical Views: William Faulkner,* ed. Harold Bloom (New York: Chelsea House Publishers, 1986), 230.

13. The research by Carol Gilligan and others that suggests that women have more permeable ego boundaries than men, making men more comfortable with independence and women with intimacy, seems to be a related phenomenon, but one that certainly does not preclude women's access to the intellectual or "rational."

14. Cf. the prohibitions against menstruating women in Leviticus.

15. See Gilligan's *In a Different Voice: Psychological Theory and Women's Development* (Cambridge: Harvard University Press, 1982).

A Measure of Innocence:
Sanctuary's Temple Drake

DIANNE LUCE COX

The charges that have been leveled against Temple Drake of Faulkner's *Sanctuary* since its publication in 1931 are often astonishing both in their substance and in the subjective involvement betrayed in these accusations. She is said to be a man-devouring nymphomaniac, a murderess, a pathological liar, a whore, a siren, a snare for innocent men, a psychopath, a masochist; depraved, sluttish, frigid, promiscuous; evidence of Faulkner's hatred of women and his premarital performance anxiety. It has been written of Temple that "She wants Popeye to assault her; she tells the sordid tale to Horace Benbow . . . 'with actual pride.' She could escape from the Memphis house, but she doesn't because she loves life there. She could save Goodwin's life. She does not because she has no compassion whatsoever." [1] And elsewhere: "Subconsciously, she desires to be raped at the Goodwin place. She stays in the Memphis bordello to rebel against her father and the accepted

Reprinted with permission from *Mississippi Quarterly* 39, no. 3 (1986): 301–24.

moral code. She testifies against Lee Goodwin, among other reasons, merely to perform another sinful act. . . . The only character who senses Temple's unhealthy state of mind is Horace Benbow. . . ."[2] And similarly: "In the events to follow: the rape, the sojourn in the Memphis brothel, in the trial of the innocent Godwin [*sic*], she is a driven helpless creature, progressively degenerate. At last she causes the death of an innocent man by refusing to bear witness. She has nothing against him; it is just that she has no capacity for responding to moral stimuli."[3]

These are judgments about a character who herself suffers the most outrageous betrayals and violations in the course of the novel.

Though the character of Temple drawn in *Sanctuary*—young, irresponsible, playing at life—is not in many ways admirable or likeable, Faulkner asks us to read her story with pity for what she suffers, much as one reads the story of Darl Bundren or Joe Christmas. The initiation into evil, the realities of death, destruction, and injustice, that Temple undergoes, and her reactions to the progressive phases of that initiation are treated realistically but not unsympathetically.

Though there have been judicious readings of the book, too, many of them ultimately dismiss Temple as one who succumbs without a struggle to sexual and moral corruption. The prevailing view seems to be that if she is a victim, she was a victim waiting for Popeye to happen to her. Much of the hostility critics have directed toward Temple seems to result from their accepting Horace Benbow's view of her. It is important to keep in mind, as Warren Beck's perceptive analysis of Faulkner's techniques and achievement in *Sanctuary* has noted, that this novel is Horace's story, and its depiction of events and characters is colored by his sexual obsessions even in omnisciently narrated scenes where he is present.[4] His desire for justice is genuine, but his view of Temple is deeply biased because he is himself a deeply ambivalent character: "He stands . . . as an anxiously striving champion of human rights and security for Goodwin and the woman and child, but also as self-hypnotized victim of a veiled but tolerated lust."[5] But in counterpoint to Horace's perspective, we are also provided several other points of view of differing degrees of reliability, including those of the omniscient narrator in scenes when Horace is not present, of Temple herself, and of Ruby, who witnesses portions of Temple's ordeal at the Old Frenchman's Place. It is helpful, I think, to read *Sanctuary* (and all of Faulkner's novels) as one reads *The Sound and the Fury* and *As I Lay Dying*—with a careful use of each narrative perspective as a touchstone for the reliability of the others and as a supplement to the evidence supplied in the others.

Further, if we are to understand Temple Drake, we must not approach her as we do the "opaque" Popeye. [6] While the enigma of evil is at the center of *Sanctuary* in the figure of Popeye, the other characters are usually given plausible motivations for their actions, even their evil ones. Thus, before we conclude with the self-castigating Temple of *Requiem for a Nun* that she merely "liked evil," or with many critics that the novel provides inadequate evidence of her motives for perjury, [7] we should proceed on the assumption that Faulkner is sufficiently in control of his creation to know why Temple lies—just as he knows why Horace fails to take her from the Memphis brothel and why he fails to cross-examine her—and that therefore he has probably provided sufficient evidence of these motivations, though in his typically indirect manner. In fact, if we proceed from this assumption, we find quite a bit of evidence about the actions of Popeye, Temple, Narcissa Sartoris, Eustace Graham, Clarence Snopes, Judge Drake and the Memphis lawyer in the few days before the opening of Lee Goodwin's trial that has direct bearing on Temple's motivation for perjuring herself.

At the opening of the novel Temple, like her counterpart Horace Benbow, is an innocent. She is the only daughter of her respectable father, Judge Drake, and the sister of four protective older brothers, one of whom has threatened to beat her if he finds that she has been in the company of a drunken man. [8] She has been raised in a household of men in which her experience has been strictly limited, but where she has apparently been given instruction about the danger that exists in the world and about the need to avoid the appearance of contamination by it at all costs (much as Horace Benbow instructs his stepdaughter Little Belle not to soil her slippers by forming acquaintances with college boys she meets on trains) (15). Apparently Temple is restive in this sheltered environment, because when she goes away to college at Oxford, she sets about doing whatever she can get away with to broaden her experience. She is not very imaginative about these opportunities, but she does sneak out of the dorm at night to go riding with the town boys who have cars, dating them on weeknights and reserving the weekends for the college boys.

However, she is not very practiced at breaking rules, and she gets herself into trouble of two kinds. Most immediate is her being put on probation by the school. But in addition, she angers several of her acquaintances with her lack of restraint and judgment—especially the town boy, Doc, who is jealous of her attentions to them, and that "Virginia gentleman," Gowan Stevens, who sees her name written on a lavatory wall.

Temple is pretty and popular, and she relies on her attractiveness to secure the dates she wants, and also to help her placate the various competitors for her attentions. But she is not entirely successful at this last, partly because she is, in her relations with the boys, an opportunist. "[C]ool, predatory and discreet" (32), she apparently cares little for any of them, and as a virgin, too, she is little troubled by the sexual arousal they must deal with. Nevertheless, they are a necessary adjunct to her social life: the fins and wings of her existence. Temple knows how to act only through men—and, in addition, only through men who accept the conventions of her social world. But she is no different from her peers in this. Except for some whom Temple does not understand, they measure their self-worth by the standards of popularity and the amount of "damage" they can do to boys without losing their respectability. When Temple thinks of the girls' shared preparation for the school dances, she thinks with pity of the ugly girl who swears she has lost her virginity, sacrificing her reputation to affirm her attractiveness (181–82).

Thus, when Temple willfully jumps off the train[9] to join Gowan and finds that he has broken the cardinal rule that one does not drink heavily in the presence of a lady (his discovery of her name on the lavatory wall having raised doubts in his mind that she is a lady), she is at a loss for a course of action. The logical thing for her to do is to take the next train back to Oxford, but after a look at the dingy train station and the overalled men watching her (31), she instinctively chooses the drunken Gowan as one who will, she believes, honor his obligation as a gentleman to protect her. She has no confidence in her ability to deal with the country folk at the train station, she opts for one of her own class, passively putting herself in his hands (though as the day proceeds she becomes less hopeful that she will extricate her from this very compromising situation).

Temple's fear of the overalled men at the train station prepares for her reaction when Gowan drives the car headlong into the felled tree obstructing the entrance to the Old Frenchman's Place. She accepts the impact without a sound, seeing, as she is thrown violently from the car, the gangster Popeye and the half-wit Tommy, armed with a shotgun, emerge from the roadside foliage:

She scrambled to her feet, her head reverted, and saw them step into the road. . . . Still running her bones turned to water and she fell flat on her face, still running. (44)

This running with head reverted characterizes much of Temple's behavior while at the Old Frenchman's Place. Like Isabella of *Measure for Measure,* though there are important differences, Temple recognizes evil; she fears it, tries to escape it, but is not unwilling to face it.[10] Paradoxically, though, this is because in her childish innocence she doesn't quite believe in it. Like Horace and Gowan, she believes that the things she fears don't really happen. And given her background, there is some justification for Temple's inability to believe in a violent, unjust world. Sheltered as she has been, she has no experiential basis for such belief. She has always been admonished to preserve respectability, but not especially to avoid evil. It is as if her social class alone will protect her from that. Indeed, she seems to think that evil resides only in other social classes and perhaps even that it is only a matter of social class—like having a different set of manners. She tells Ruby, "'Things like that don't happen. Do they? They're just like other people. You're just like other people. With a little baby. And besides, my father's a ju-judge. The gu-governor comes to our house to e-eat'" (64). She repeatedly uses the incantation "My father's a judge" in the face of danger at the Old Frenchman's Place—and her gradual discovery that it is an impotent talisman parallels her acceptance of the reality of evil. So while Temple's primary emotion at the Old Frenchman's Place is fear, it is mixed with a strange denial that evil can touch her; and both are manifested in a childish sort of assertiveness that might best be called whistling in the wind.

Contrary to seeking violation, from the moment that Temple arrives at the bootlegger's camp where she is so out of her element she begins looking for sanctuary, and this search lasts until the end of the novel. In this world Temple is an infant, and her desire for protection is nowhere more painfully obvious than when she takes an army canteen, a vessel suggesting her absent mother but endowed with the protective aspects of the father, to bed with her, or when she projects her fear on Ruby's baby, mothering it to console herself: "'Now, now; Temple's got it. . . . I'm not afraid'" (64). She looks in turn to each of the others first to help her get back to her dormitory and then just to remove her from the growing danger; but except for Tommy each not only refuses her protection but adds to her fear. Though Ruby has stressed that she must leave before dark, Gowan knows Popeye carries a pistol and refuses to ask him for transportation. When Temple takes the initiative in her jaunty, collegiate style, attempting a winning smile that is transmuted into a "cringing grimace" (57) by her fear, Popeye sees through her naïve coquetry and responds, "'Make your whore lay off of me, Jack'" (58). By reflex Gowan objects, and encouraged by her assumption that she has a gentlemanly ally after all, Temple retorts saucily, "'What river did you fall in with that suit on? Do you have to shave it off at night?'" Appalled, Gowan hurries her away and then goes in search of more alcohol, and Temple realizes that her protector is himself terrified of Popeye. At this point she panics, sinking down tearfully into a corner next to a rifle, an ambiguous image of masculine strength and potential protection, but as it anticipates Popeye's pistol, also of threat.

Temple's inexperience and self-centeredness make a failure of her attempt to enlist Ruby's aid, too. Temple's story of her father and brothers' political power and her thoughtless social condescension anger Ruby and prompt her to lecture Temple on her lack of self-reliance and to upbraid her for her failure to carry her own weight in life—truths of which the events of the day have made Temple increasingly aware. What's more, Ruby realizes that Temple's obvious fear of sexual violation is arousing to the men there, and her compassion for the girl is stifled by her own fear that their reactions to Temple will disrupt the life with Lee that she has purchased at great cost, prostituting herself to get him released from jail for murdering another man in a fight over a Filipino woman (68).

Most of Temple's actions are ill-judged and counterproductive. She is, as Ruby calls her, a "little gutless fool" (70).[11] She envies and wonders at Ruby's ability to cope with these frightening men without really understanding what gives Ruby her assurance. The immediate lesson of Ruby's story of her own courage in trying to save the life of her lover Frank and of Frank's courage in standing up to her father and his rifle is mostly lost on Temple. However, she listens attentively enough to Ruby's tale to learn the dubious lesson that to earn the protection of a "real man" one must be a "real woman," or sexually active. Ruby's account of her father's killing Frank and calling her a whore (67) may lead Temple to recognize more clearly that before that the repressive man—the father—is a captor who would enforce innocence by denying sexual experience and love, and to conclude that the cost of gaining love and protection may be losing respectability. Later on, in the scene at the roadhouse, Temple will imitate Ruby and draw on some of these lessons in her attempt to escape Popeye. Here the story only serves to convince her of her powerlessness because she recognizes the truth of Ruby's criticisms of her. Ruby's perceptiveness about Horace and Temple and her loyalty to Lee should not blind us to the fact that she fails Temple just as surely as do the men in this novel. The frightened girl looks to her for comfort and advice, but the older woman's selfish concerns lead her to deny any human sympathy with Temple and to humiliate her for the fear she exhibits. Her response to Temple is exactly as she tells Horace it was: "I've lived my life without any help from people of your sort; what right have you got to look to me for help?" (195–96). Ruby would use people according to their deserts, but as Hamlet reminds us (II. ii.), under the application of that philosophy how shall she herself escape whipping when she needs help from Temple?

Temple hasn't the courage to walk away partly because she continues to hope that she will get away with this venture—that she will get back to Oxford in time for one of her friends to sneak her into the dorm. She fears violation, but she also fears the consequences of breaking her social code, of being caught being indiscreet, of suffering a lapse in respectability; and all her life this, not violence, has been the most immediate danger. So, terrified though she is of the men who are gradually becoming more threatening, she removes her dress and carefully folds it before going to bed, lest it appear rumpled when she returns to the safety of the campus (83). There can be no doubt of the sincerity of her fear of rape, given the fantasies she reports having that night of turning into a boy or wearing a chastity belt, and given her loss of consciousness when Popeye puts his hand into her underwear. Her version of the story is corroborated in large part by the omniscient narration of the same scene. Why, then, does she fluff out her hair and powder her nose before lying down in the bed (83–84), an action that has been cited as evidence that she is subconsciously preparing for a desired sexual encounter?[12] It is plausible that she does this precisely because she fears an intrusion from the men. Her preparations for bed are, on the one hand, a kind of denial; the primping is a habit, and going through these motions reassures her that it is still an orderly world. On the other hand, Temple sees her beauty as her only tool with which to control men; even in her frightened fantasies she does not think of rebuffing them by turning ugly.

The rigidity of Temple's thinking is equally clear during her abduction from Frenchman's Bend to Memphis. She has been brutally raped, has witnessed a murder, and has been subtly threatened with a pistol herself. She rides passively with Popeye as she had with Gowan, but this should not be construed as an affirmation of her rape or a desire to go with Popeye. The girl has suffered a series of traumas. The countryside passes her seemingly blind eyes until Temple subconsciously notices the lush spring flora and sees in it a reflection of her recent experience:

> It had been a lavender spring. The fruit trees, the white ones, had been in small leaf when the blooms matured; they had never attained that brilliant whiteness of last spring, and the dogwood had come into full bloom after the leaf also. . . . But lilac and wisteria and redbud, even the shabby heaven-trees, had never been finer, fulgent, with a burning scent. . . . The bougainvillea against the veranda would be large as basketballs and lightly poised as balloons, and looking vacantly and stupidly at the rushing roadside Temple began to scream. (164)

With a new knowledge of the evil her father and brothers have been sheltering her from while warning her only against the appearance of evil, teaching her to be discreet but not how to live in a world that contains evil, Temple now perceives that evil invading even her garden at home. She has shown every indication of wanting life and experience—of chafing under the watchful protection of her male kin. Now that she has experienced a violent sexual initiation into evil and can no longer deny its existence, she is horrified at it.

However, Temple's initiation is not accomplished in a single lesson. She is still naïve enough to assume that now that she has lost her virginity—presumably the worst fate her family has warned her of—the ordeal is over. Thus she does not attempt to escape from Popeye because she believes he is driving her to a town where he will release her, and when they arrive in Dumfries she begins "to look about, like one waking from sleep. 'Not here!' she said. 'I cant—'" (166). Her fear of compromising appearances again controls her behavior. It is terrible to be raped but equally terrible to have it known. When Popeye leaves the car to get food and Temple sees an acquaintance, she disobeys Popeye's instructions to stay in the car and hides around the corner of a building lest the boy recognize her and see the blood still running down her legs. She ought to understand her situation when Popeye approaches her threateningly, his right hand freed to reach the pistol in his pocket,[13] but she doesn't. It is only when Popeye hands her a sandwich, a gesture of nurturance, and takes the road toward Memphis, that she comprehends he means to keep her:

> Again, the bitten sandwich in her hand, she ceased chewing and opened her mouth in that round, hopeless expression of a child; again his hand left the wheel and gripped the back of her neck and she sat motionless, gazing straight at him. . . . (168–69)

In the brothel, Temple's violation continues, and still she finds no help either from older women or from men. Probably willfully, and because she doesn't suspect his impotence, Reba does not recognize that Popeye has kidnapped Temple. She keeps referring to Temple as his "girl" and tells her that she is lucky Popeye is such a free spender. Still, in her shock, Temple is slow to understand the terms of her imprisonment. Popeye has told her he'll buy her a new coat (168), but when Reba tells her they'll shop for new clothes tomorrow, Temple thinks despairingly that she has only two dollars (187). But she understands well enough that she is a prisoner and that her keepers repeatedly violate her privacy. Temple's fear is now numbed because she believes the worst has already happened to her, but she writhes in anguish as Minnie and Reba ruthlessly expose her shame—taking her knickers to wash them, discussing the blood, checking the arrangement of the towels around her loins.

Given the first opportunity, Temple locks Reba and Minnie out of her room, and she is reluctant to admit the doctor. That she finally does so suggests that she hopes a professional man—someone like her father—will help her to escape. But Reba will not leave them alone, so she has no opportunity to ask him to rescue her. Further, Dr. Quinn is a coarse, insensitive man who reaches toward her with "a thick, white hand bearing a masonic ring, haired over with fine reddish fuzz to the second knuckle-joints" (179). The violations both of the night before the rape, when Popeye touches her, and of the rape itself are about to be re-enacted, and so, "Lying on her back, her legs close together, she began to cry, hopelessly and passively, like a child in a dentist's waiting-room" (179). After suffering these repeated attacks upon her helplessness and innocence, Temple is disoriented, wrenched by time and experience out of the orderly garden created for her by her father and brothers; and her view of life temporarily takes on a dark sensibility (ironically heightened by gin) of which she has not previously been capable:

She watched the final light condense into the clock face, and the dial change from a round orifice in the darkness to a disc suspended in nothingness, the original chaos, and change in turn to a crystal ball holding in its still and cryptic depths the ordered chaos of the intricate and shadowy world upon whose scarred flanks the old wounds whirl onward at dizzy speed into darkness lurking with new disasters. (180–81)

By the time that Horace Benbow learns of Temple's whereabouts, she has been there nearly three weeks. He has heard part of her story from Ruby already, and so he fears what he will hear from Temple because he is not certain he can bear it. Even before he meets Temple, Horace has begun to associate her with his step-daughter, Little Belle. What he thinks he fears for both girls is their exposure to irresponsible young men like Gowan Stevens and through them to evil, but what he really fears is that they may be impervious to evil, that they may be able to survive it. Indeed, in his nausea at his relationship with his pampered, twice-married wife, Belle, and his manipulating sister, Narcissa, Horace is prepared to believe that all women of his social class are thoroughly corrupt though they hide behind a façade of respectability. But his disgust at respectable women is largely a projection of his lustful feelings for his step-daughter, Little Belle, whose experience with college boys he would like to curtail but whom he compulsively watches in the grape arbor (i.e., garden) in a manner that Faulkner tellingly pairs with Popeye's watching Temple and Red, who "looked like a college boy" (283). His jealously over Little Bell's emerging sexuality leads him to project the guilt for his own lust onto her and onto Temple. Temple's story of her night of terror at the Old Frenchman's Place will excite in Horace, who fortifies himself with a drink, "'A big one'" (254), just before listening to it, a hallucination in which the two girls merge in the photograph of Little Belle, and through some action of his own "the small face seemed to swoon in a voluptuous languor, blurring still more, fading, leaving upon his eye a soft and fading aftermath of invitation and voluptuous promise and secret affirmation like a scent itself" (267–68). He vomits as he imagines Temple/Bell's violation, his body position suggesting that he himself is the violator: "he . . . leaned upon his braced arms while the shucks set up a terrific uproar beneath her thighs." However, the truth revealed in this hallucination is something Horace must deny, so he spends a good deal of energy inwardly railing at the hypocrisy of women. This is why he is so interested in Ruby: because he thinks that she, with her frank sexuality and capacity for loyalty, is categorically different from the "chaste" women he knows.

Horace arrives in Memphis well prepared to believe that Temple is there because she wants to be, and expecting—even hoping—to be shocked at her. Nothing Reba tells him beforehand would lead him to think differently. She even refers to Temple as one of "my girls" (253). Again, as with the doctor, Temple is ashamed to face Benbow. He is a lawyer as are two of her brothers, and he is of her social class. But she agrees to see him, and again it is likely that she hopes he will take her away from Popeye. But again, Miss Reba quietly insists on staying in the room and hearing their conversation. Having agreed to see Horace, then, Temple hides under the covers until he and Reba explain that they want her to testify on Lee's behalf. Then she suddenly emerges from them utterly shamelessly and with a "black antagonism" directed at Horace. This is because he has unwittingly made it perfectly clear what he thinks of her, while professing to know how she feels:

> "I just want to know what really happened. You wont commit yourself. I know that you didn't do it. I'll promise before you tell me a thing that you wont have to testify in Court unless they are going to hang him without it. I know how you feel. I wouldn't bother you if the man's life were not at stake." (255)

What Horace doesn't offer speaks volumes. For Temple there is to be no sanctuary in the law. Reba has made it even clearer, assuring her that Popeye will not be arrested and that they'll still be together. When she adds, "'The lawyer'll take care of you'" (256), Temple thrusts back the covers demanding a drink. (She has been given a lot of alcohol at Miss Reba's both to make her feel better and to control her.) If nice-girl-turned-whore is what Horace wants, that's what she'll give him, and with a vengeance. The two innocents face each other, he punishing her for his disillusionment with women, she punishing him for her betrayal by men. She gives Horace only one hint that all is not as he thinks, but predictably he fails to perceive it. When Horace repeats that she needn't tell Popeye's location, she protests, "'don't think I'm afraid to tell. . . . I'll tell it anywhere. Don't think I'm afraid'" (257). But of course she is afraid of Popeye, and she skillfully avoids telling Horace anything that would incriminate her kidnapper because she sees that Horace will not protect her from him. Horace misinterprets even her anxious attention to her auditors' reactions. He sees that she is trying to affect them, "looking from him to Miss Reba with quick, darting glances like a dog driving two cattle along a lane" (259), but he cannot see that her behavior is prompted by fear of reprisal from Popeye were she to reveal anything. Instead he ascribes it to feminine vanity: "She went on like that, in one of those bright, chatty monologues which women can carry on when they realise that they have the center of the stage; suddenly Horace realised that she was recounting the experience with actual pride, a sort of naïve and impersonal vanity, as though she were making it up" (258–59).

Reba apparently is moved by the recounting of Temple's night of terror, for she tells Horace as he leaves, "'I wish you'd get her down there and not let her come back. . . . She'll be dead, or in the asylum in a year, way him and her go on up there in that room. . . . She wasn't born for this kind of life'" (264–65). But Horace refuses to feel compassion for Temple, thinking, "Better for her if she were dead tonight. . . . For me, too" (265). That is, he thinks he would be better off if Temple were dead. He thinks he can't bear to see this symbol of innocence exposed. But subconsciously he desires her violation and yet cannot admit that he takes a secret relish in it, so in that way, too, he would be better off—safer from his own intolerable desires—if she were dead. He leaves her in the brothel to serve his own purposes, both his conscious and unconscious ones. He certainly knows that were he to remove her Popeye would kill Goodwin—and possibly Temple, too—and that even if Popeye didn't kill her, Temple's respectable father would very likely prevent her from testifying. It is a fact that Temple is more accessible to him as a witness right where she is, under Popeye's "protection" rather than Judge Drake's.

Abandoned by Horace as by Gowan, Temple casts the next man she has access to in the role of her savior. We learn that Popeye has brought her a lover for four consecutive days. The most apparent reason for this is that Popeye wants to achieve sexual gratification through voyeurism, since he cannot do it in any other way. But both impotence and rape are often motivated by hostility. Like Horace and many other men in this novel, Popeye is attracted by Temple's immaturity, by her provocative innocence, and he wants to see it (literally) violated. Red, like the corncob, is Popeye's instrument in this repeated rape. But Popeye may also want to do the violation. At the Old Frenchman's Place, he is aroused to imitate Van's abusive behavior the night before Temple's rape. Having entered the room just in time to see Van rip open the raincoat she is wearing and be torn away from her by

Goodwin, Popeye approaches her himself: "His right hand lay in his coat pocket. Beneath the raincoat on Temple's breast Tommy could see the movement of the other hand, communicating a shadow of movement to the coat" (87–88). It may be that Popeye's decision to bring Red to Temple is motivated by his hope that he can visually "learn" the potency to act out his hostility. Certainly he chooses in Red someone who is known to be sexually potent. If Red awakens Temple's sexuality without sufficiently awakening Popeye's potency, Popeye must be doubly frustrated by his experiment. He apparently decides it is a poor idea, and Red comes to Temple no longer.

But this brief relationship has been enough to demonstrate to the naïve Temple the difference between Popeye and a "real man." In her innocence she not only reverts to the law of the college dance floor and expects that her preference for Red will make Popeye retire in dudgeon, but also she assumes that Popeye's sexual impotence means he is less potent in other matters than she had thought—that this discovery makes him less a power to be reckoned with. She finds the courage, with the help of more gin, to steal out to arrange to meet Red, but ironically she cannot find it within herself to use that same opportunity to leave Memphis. She still fears Popeye enough to think that she needs a man to take her away from him, and she hopes that Red can do so. When she returns, in gloating repudiation but highly agitated, she tears all of the clothes Popeye has bought her out of the closet, flinging them on the floor, followed by bottles of perfume (270). Then she extracts the only one of these dresses she thinks she will ever wear again and hangs it up (274). But later that evening when Temple dresses for her "date" and sneaks out, she finds Popeye waiting for her.

The confidence born of her discovery of Popeye's impotence and her knowledge that he has left his pistol in her room stays with her only until she realizes that Popeye is carrying another pistol (280–81) and that he means to kill Red, whom he now sees as a threat to his possession of Temple and thus to his impunity for the murder of Tommy. Then all her attentions are turned to averting the disaster. As at the Old Frenchman's Place, she is again filled with terror, and she tries to placate the men she must control. But now she has learned what sex is and what, for Popeye, Red, and women of their class, sexual behavior is. She is still the scared college girl grinning in abasement, but now the gestures are different ones. Caressing him and whispering, she tries to vamp Popeye into turning over his pistol—even stroking him seductively: "'Give it to me,' she whispered. 'Daddy. Daddy.'" But then she abruptly stops in confusion and revulsion, saying "'I forgot . . . ; I didn't mean . . .'" (284), undoing in a moment her attempt at allurement by implicitly referring to his impotence.

Temple's language here and her taunting Popeye that Red is a "better man" (278) indicate that she associates the pistol-carrying Popeye with Ruby's shotgun-wielding father and probably with her own possessive father, the judge. In certain ways the events at the Grotto re-enact details of Ruby's story about her lover Frank, and at some level of consciousness Temple must recognize the analogies because she acts on them. When she realizes that Popeye intends to kill Red, she tries, like Ruby, to give Red a chance to escape. She offers to return to Miss Reba's, but Popeye rejects her efforts to placate him. When she sees Red enter the roadhouse, she urges Popeye to dance, frantically manipulating him to keep his back to Red. But Red, like Frank, does not run, and he asks her to dance. Again like Ruby, she tries to send him away, refusing the dance.

Her fear leads her to drink heavily; she becomes disoriented, and a sense of intense bereavement overcomes her, accompanied by desire. As with Laverne in Faulkner's novel *Pylon,* Temple's fear of loss triggers a desire for intimacy,[14] and when she can speak to Red alone for a moment, she flings herself on him, demanding that they escape together immediately and declaring that she's "on fire" (289). It is important to distinguish between Temple's ugly and exaggerated behavior here and her feelings. The narrator tells us that she feels both grief and desire, and that is reasonable and understandable. But an unselfconscious passion that could make Temple writhe and gape like a "dying fish" (287) is simply not consistent with her vanity and immaturity. Furthermore, it is patently incredible that, after being brutally raped once and made love to under the randy eye of an abductor a total of four separate times, now inebriated and wrung with terror and exhaustion, Temple or anyone could generate quite this kind of urgent passion. Rather, it seems logical that Temple is pathetically trying to arouse passion in Red, to reach him through "sexual" behavior to get him to take her away in spite of Popeye and his goons. This is perfectly consistent with her earlier behavior with men; it's just that now she has overt sexual tactics in her repertoire. Once she leaves Red in the room, she is no longer described as manifesting or feeling any desire.

Further, Temple's use of sexual manipulation is also related to her memory of Ruby's story of Frank. Red's continued presence is grounds for Temple's hope that he, like Frank, might have enough will and courage to take her away from "Daddy." But to arouse him to be a "real man" she feels she must be a "real woman." Her behavior mimics what she imagines Ruby's sexual behavior to be. She is playing out Ruby's romantic illusion of the courageous lovers, but her naiveté makes her behavior a parody of adult sexuality. Moreover, she forgets that Frank's courage, like Tommy's, counted for nothing in the face of a loaded gun and remembers only the courage to defy Ruby's father that her sexual love had inspired in Frank. Temple needs a man with the courage to defy Popeye. She certainly doesn't want Red to die; she wants him to live to defeat Popeye and rescue her. But once again Temple's tactics fail. Red has not run because he does not know of Popeye's intent to kill him until Temple herself tells him at the same moment that she tries to arouse him (288). Despite her telling him repeatedly that he is a man, Red is afraid of Popeye and is not aroused by Temple's grotesque attempt at seduction. Possessing neither Tommy's mental limitations nor Frank's love, Red is unmanned by Popeye, and he chooses the reverse of Frank's course; he sends Temple away, hoping that Popeye will ignore the incident. Popeye does not. So Temple is left with yet another failure to find a protector, she has seen yet another instance of Popeye's murderous intent, and she has acted in such a way that she might expect him to retaliate violently against her. Through a turn of events, though, she is given a chance to ransom herself from his custody, and she takes it.

Popeye kills Red on June 17.[15] On the day following Horace's interview with Temple,[16] Narcissa has told the ambitious and unscrupulous district attorney that Clarence Snopes gave Horace some information that caused him to go to Memphis. He'll have to find out why for himself, she says (317–18). Presumably, then, Graham has contacted a lawyer in Memphis to take care of the investigation because on the 18th, two days before court opens,[17] Clarence is in Oxford bitterly complaining that while he was in Jackson selling information to a certain judge, he had the same information beaten out of him by a "Memphis jew lawyer" (320). The information, of course, is that Horace knows Temple is a witness to Tommy's murder and that both Horace and Judge Drake now know where Temple is. The evidence of the courtroom scene suggests the following. The Memphis lawyer has underworld connections (he is probably the same Memphis lawyer who attempts to defend Popeye when he is arrested for murder in Alabama in the last chapter), and he warns Popeye—probably as early as the 17th, before Red is killed, thus giving Popeye additional motivation for that murder. Then the lawyer negotiates a three-way arrangement to satisfy Popeye, Graham and Judge Drake. Temple disappears from the night of Red's death (322) until she appears in court.[18] It seems likely that some time between the 18th and the 20th, Popeye or his henchmen turn her over to the Memphis lawyer and Eustace Graham, who coach her on her testimony just as Horace coaches Ruby on the night of the 20th (325). If Temple does as they instruct her and testifies that Lee Goodwin raped her and killed Tommy, then she will be free to leave with her father and brothers. If she does not perjure herself convincingly, clearing Popeye of the murder and pre-empting any later charges against him for the rape, he will be waiting for her outside the courtroom. Temple must choose to save herself or to save Lee, who has been too afraid of Popeye to testify in his own behalf.

On June 21, Temple arrives in court in a new, stylish black dress, probably purchased by Graham (342), and is called as a witness by the district attorney, not by Horace Benbow, who has allowed her to be sworn in as his witness (339) but does not call her to testify because he has promised not to question her unless he thinks they will execute Lee without her testimony (255). With the Memphis lawyer there to observe her behavior (338), and her father and brothers there expecting her to be returned to them after her testimony, she testifies as though drugged and with the parrot-like answers apparently taught her by Graham, who skillfully phrases his questions so that she can answer in a single word and insists that she not run ahead of him to tell anything in her own way. During her entire testimony, Temple compulsively watches the back of the room, both before and after her father arrives, and she never looks at Judge Drake until he takes her from the witness stand. Her intent, distracted gaze, mirroring Lee Goodwin's gazing at the narrow window in his cell through which he expects Popeye to shoot him, is evidence of her continued fear of Popeye and his gun. Even when the Court releases her to go back to the protection of her father and brothers, she cringes in fear at the doorway until all five men close in a tight bodyguard around her and force her to move outside with them (347–48). Temple's dropping of the platinum bag Popeye had given her[19] and her father's kicking it out of their way are the only signs of defiance they make toward Popeye. Judge Drake's gesture implies not only his awareness of the bag's significance but also that he is cooperating with Popeye's plan though he is disgusted at having to. Temple's perjury and public humiliation are the ransom she and her father are required to pay. Now that it is over and Popeye is out of danger, the judge can afford to show his feelings even in the presence of the Memphis lawyer, who does not watch them but gazes "dreamily" out the window through which he might have given a sign if all had not gone as planned (348).

The testimony about the rape and the well-timed interruption of the court proceedings by Judge Drake are both calculated to prevent Horace's cross-examination of Temple. Graham has evoked such a strong feeling of sympathy for her and her father in the courtroom that Horace stands to lose more than he can gain by insisting that she stand cross-examination. The day before, he himself had assured Lee that their case was won because Graham was "'reduced to trying to impugn the character of your witness [Ruby]'" (324). Had he called Temple as his own witness and questioned her first, he would have avoided testimony about the rape because he thinks that she liked whatever Popeye did to her, and he himself can't bear to expose the evil he projects on her. The only objection he raises during Graham's questioning of Temple (though the Court expresses surprise that there are no objections to the district attorney's incendiary questions) is to Graham's statement to Temple about her whereabouts after Tommy's death: "'You were in hiding, then, because something had happened to you and you dared not—'"(343). Horace objects, then, when Graham leads the witness to reveal her rape and when he realizes that Goodwin is to be accused of that, too. As the testimony continues along these lines, he has nothing further to say. Graham moves Temple quickly to naming Goodwin as the murderer/rapist, and Horace knows he has been defeated.

Furthermore, it is likely that Temple's testimony shakes Horace's faith in Ruby and Lee and thus in himself. Temple's version of the events surrounding Tommy's death is as plausible as Ruby's. Horace has believed from the start that Temple wanted to be in Memphis while never fully believing that she had been raped. Now he must consider the possibility that Goodwin raped her and that she has been hiding from him and from her shame. Of Horace's four informants, Lee will tell him nothing, Ruby and Reba do not know the facts of the rape, and Temple herself makes only one ambiguous reference to it.[20] If this daughter of respectable society will testify publicly to having been raped by Goodwin, a man who has been convicted previously of murdering a man over a woman other than Ruby (Horace has learned this only the night before; 331–34), how can Horace prove even to himself that

Temple is not telling the truth? Surely Horace is confronted with the truth about himself here: that he has been willing to believe Ruby and to condemn Temple just because the one is so different and the other so like his respectable womenfolk against whom he harbors intense anger. Horace is not prepared to cross-examine Temple because he has never been objective enough to consider alternative explanations of the evidence—to anticipate, as any good trial lawyer should do, the case that could be made for the opposing side. Indeed, he has been too personally involved to follow Narcissa's quite practical advice that he hire a better criminal defense lawyer for Goodwin, rejecting that advice partly because it comes from his sister, who wants him, he thinks, to put appearances before justice, and partly because this case has become his personal crusade not so much to get justice for Lee as to champion the lowly, loyal, pure-of-heart womanhood that Ruby symbolizes for him, the idealized woman that he wishes to possess, a woman who will repeatedly sacrifice herself for her man no matter how self-indulgent his desires or how wayward his behavior. (One wonders if this is not why Horace chose to marry "somebody else's wife" [17]: to possess a woman who would make that sacrifice to his desires. Once possessed, however, Belle reveals herself to be a "real" woman in quite another sense than Ruby means, and Horace is inordinately disgusted at her flawed nature.) Horace is not the best criminal lawyer, but he is an intelligent man. He cannot escape the recognition, however quickly denied, that his idealization of Ruby and his condemnation of Temple have contributed to the conviction of Lee Goodwin. He has been too self-blinded, he does not know enough, to cross-examine Temple effectively.

Temple does, then, actively participate in the killing of Lee Goodwin, an act which involves the direct or indirect complicity of almost every major character in the novel and of the community as a whole. His lynching is part of the well-laid plan. He must die immediately both to lay to rest the question of who killed Tommy and as punishment for Ruby's earlier testimony implicating Popeye. This is partly why Temple is made to testify to her rape as well as to the murder. Graham uses that testimony to incite the mob, suggesting the precise means by which Goodwin is to be killed: "'this is no longer a matter for the hangman, but for a bonfire of gasoline'" (340). Again, though hardly an admirable or imaginative response to evil, Temple's behavior is perfectly understandable. She implicates Lee under great duress, fearing for her own life. More than anything else, she wants to escape Popeye, and everything she has tried for six weeks has failed: everyone she has turned to has failed her. Now Popeye and the law and her father and brothers are giving her an opportunity to free herself and helping her to take advantage of it. It is not evidence of a liking for evil that she does so. But, as is often demonstrated in this book immaturity, the confusion of social respectability with moral responsibility, lack of self-knowledge, lack of human empathy—all of the failings of flawed humanity—will suffice as evil's tools.[21] Or with only a slight shifting of perspective does Faulkner not also ask us to see the enigmatic and impotent Popeye as the tool, the nightmare shape embodying the concerted impulses toward evil exhibited by all of the novel's characters, the self-righteous Horace and Ruby included?

Temple survives her exposure to evil, as Horace fears she will. At the end of the novel, both have returned to their ironic sanctuaries of home and family, but Horace is a defeated man. With his failure to vanquish evil in the courtroom, he simply gives up and returns to Belle and Little Belle, over whom he hovers even more protectively, having learned nothing that allows him to establish a healthier acceptance of reality. In another closing chapter, Popeye demonstrates a comparable desire for retreat from the emptiness of his life, and he finds it in death; but Temple survives.[22] She is not happy in the sanctuary chosen for her by her father, sitting "sullen and discontented and sad" (379) in the Luxembourg Gardens. But she should not be. She has exchanged a brief life of evil with Popeye for the death-in-life with her father. Her gazing with discontent on the gardens in the embrace of the season of rain and death seems a slightly optimistic note. One cannot withdraw from life to remain in an artificial garden of innocence forever. It may be that Temple is anxious to get on with life; she is ready for another season.

NOTES

1. Lewis P. Simpson, "Isaac McCaslin and Temple Drake: The Fall of the New World Man," in *Nine Essays in Modern Literature,* ed. Donald E. Stanford (Baton Rouge: Louisiana State University Press, 1965), 100.

2. James R. Cypher, "The Tangled Sexuality of Temple Drake," *American Imago* 19 (fall 192): 249.

3. R. F. Haugh, "Faulkner's Corrupt Temple," *English Studies in Africa* 4 (1961): 9.

4. "Realist and Regionalist," in *Faulkner* (Madison: University of Wisconsin Press, 1976), 222–25.

5. Beck, 230. However, Beck's study, which has relatively little to say of Temple, sees her as "grossly lecherous" (226) and morally irresponsible.

6. This is Beck's apt description of Popeye and Flem Snopes, characters who are "unamenable to evocation through instancings of their consciousness in progress and [who] must be realized at some remove, by what they do and say and by others' overt and subjective response to them" (208).

7. The most thorough of several attempts to deal with the evidence is by Cleanth Brooks, *William Faulkner: The Yoknapatawpha Country* (New Haven: Yale University Press, 1963), 121–27, but even he misses some relevant details and concludes that some questions can't be answered.

8. *Sanctuary* (New York: Jonathan Cape & Harrison Smith, 1931), 63. All further references to this novel are noted in the text.

9. Like that of Conrad's *Lord Jim*, Temple's is an untested innocence; her "fall" from that innocence is emblematized in a leap.

10. Michael Millgate has pointed out that the title, themes, and some details of setting in *Sanctuary* may derive from Shakespeare's *Measure for Measure* (*The Achievement of William Faulkner* [New York: Random House, 1966], 120–21). I think the parallels are even more extensive than those he details. For instance, Isabella's predicament points to the paradox that to maintain one's innocence, one must be sufficiently knowledgeable to recognize and avoid evil. Horace paraphrases but fails to follow this principle when he tells Ruby, "'Damn it, don't you know that putting yourself in the position for disaster is the surest way in the world to bring it about? Hasn't your own experience shown you that?'" (327).

    Further, Horace's willingness to cast blame on the women who tempt him, his hypocrisy, his self-righteousness, his very lack of the self-knowledge required for acting with moral responsibility make him the central Angelo-figure in *Sanctuary*. Like Shakespeare's Angelo, like Milton's Satan, like Melville's Claggart, Horace (and perhaps Popeye) wants to see innocence defiled because he believes that it is corruptible and therefore already corrupt. Actions in defense of innocence provoke these characters' desire to violate it. Consider the conversation of Temple and her classmates about the effect of modesty on the sexual desires of men. One girl, in a childish revision of Biblical myth, asserts that "the Snake had been seeing Eve for several days and never noticed her until Adam made her put on a fig leaf" (181). In her naiveté, Temple rejects the truth of this because the girl who asserts it is physically unattractive. Had she accepted it, she might have anticipated the effect her own fear would have on the men at the bootlegger's camp. Again like Angelo, Horace cannot acknowledge his rapacious desires. Repressed, they nevertheless do their work as Angelo's do theirs. At the end of both works, both men return to women whom they had set aside, Horace to his wife, Angelo to his betrothed. For both, this return is punishment for their inability to recognize their own corruption in time to act with moral responsibility.

11. Ruby also calls Horace a "poor, scared fool" (18), emphasizing Faulkner's pairing of these "innocent" intruders into the world of evil epitomized, as Beck says, by Popeye.

12. See, for instance, Robert L. Mason, "A Defense of Faulkner's *Sanctuary,*" *Georgia Review* 21 (winter 1967): 430–38. This question is also addressed by Elisabeth Muhlenfeld, "Bewildered Witness: Temple Drake in *Sanctuary,*" *Faulkner Journal* 1 (spring 1986): 43–45. On this point, and other questions about Temple's behavior at the Old Frenchman's Place, Muhlenfeld's conclusions are compatible with mine. Though I disagree with her argument that Temple perjures herself primarily because Lee's persecution of her and indifference to her suffering make him a convenient choice on which to place blame, Muhlenfeld makes a strong case that Lee is the foremost object of her fear. Certainly this, together with her knowledge that Lee has a criminal record, may allow Temple to rationalize her decision to save herself at his expense.

13. "When he [Popeye] saw the car it was empty. He stopped ten feet away and changed the sandwich to his left hand. . . . The mechanic . . . saw him and jerked his thumb toward the corner of the building" (167) Popeye's purpose in freeing his right hand is clarified by repeated references to his concealed pistol and his placing his hand in his right pocket when he wants to assert his control in the scenes at the Old Frenchman's Place. See, for example, pp. 87–88.

14. (New York: Harrison Smith and Robert Haas, 1935), 193–96. See also Joseph McElrath's helpful interpretation of this scene in *"Pylon:* The Portrait of a Lady," *Mississippi Quarterly* 27 (summer 1974): 285–88.

15. "It was on the night of June 17 . . . when Red had been killed" (361).

16. At the beginning of the chapter relating Narcissa's betrayal of Horace, he sees Clarence Snopes, who had followed him to Miss Reba's, warned him of her high prices, and tried to get him to spend the night at a Negro whorehouse (248–250; 252); Snopes tells Horace, "'Too bad I missed you last night . . . I could have took you to a place most folks don't know about'" (313–14). "later in the morning" Horace sees Narcissa disappear near the entrance to Graham's law offices, but he does not think to look for her there (314).

17. "The trial was set for the twentieth of June" (321). Faulkner also specifies this date on page 318. Clarence's complaint occurs "Two days before it opened" (319).

18. Temple is taken from the roadhouse by Popeye's henchmen (290; 361). "On the night of the nineteenth [Horace] telephoned [Reba]. . . ."

    "'They're gone,' she said. 'Both of them. Don't you read no papers? . . . I don't know nuttin about them . . .'" (332).

19. The platinum bag is described and mentioned several times as Temple prepares to meet Red on June 17. See pages 271, 273, 276.

20. Temple tells Horace that when she feared violation at the Old Frenchman's Place, she imagined wearing a chastity belt, which she has heard about but never seen. She says, "'I was

thinking maybe it would have long sharp spikes on it and he wouldn't know it until too late and I'd jab it . . . all the way through him and I'd think about the blood running on me. . . . I didn't know it was going to be just the other way . . .'" (261). Though Temple's language hints that she was raped, she never asserts it unequivocally, and as if frightened that she has nearly done so, she abruptly asks for a drink and changes the subject.

21. Conversely, in *Measure for Measure,* the nearly inhuman Isabella refuses to commit an evil act even to save her brother's life; and the Law, in the person of the disguised Duke, works behind the scenes as a force for justice and morality. But the issues are not simple in Shakespeare's dark comedy either: in choosing to preserve her chastity rather than her brother's life, Isabella, like Temple, shows herself willing to sacrifice the life of another in order to spare herself.

22. Warren Beck emphasizes the passivity of all three characters in the closing chapters, which he finds a triumphal tonal conclusion to the book, except for the interpolation of the naturalistic account of Popeye's past. I agree with Beck, but find in Temple's restiveness under the protection of her father a less acquiescent and defeated withdrawal from life than those of Horace and Popeye.

"All That Matters Is That I Wrote the Letters": Discourse, Discipline, and Difference in *Requiem for a Nun*

KELLY LYNCH REAMES

In *Requiem for a Nun* (1951), William Faulkner undertakes what has been construed as the feminism of many women novelists; asking how women whose lives have been made into social narratives can counteract those narratives and reclaim their own subjectivities, or, put another way, how two disempowered women can change their lives through language.[1] Returning to the story of Temple Drake, whose brutal rape, abduction, and imprisonment in the Memphis brothel are the subject of *Sanctuary* (1931), Faulkner links Temple's story to that of Nancy Mannigoe, the African-American prostitute in "That Evening Sun" (1931). Eight years after the events of *Sanctuary*, Nancy is employed as a nanny by Temple and Gowan Stevens, and the dramatic portion of the novel opens with Nancy's sentencing for murdering their baby daughter. Both Temple and Nancy, renowned "whores" in the local lore, try to maintain their subjectivities despite the public narratives

Reprinted with permission from *The Faulkner Journal* 14, no. 1 (1998): 31–52.

that constrain their identities. By situating these women in the judicial system, Faulkner makes explicit the effect of these repressive cultural narratives on their lives.[2] As the women try to reclaim their stories from those with legal and cultural power, they use different strategies because of their disparate social positions. Class and racial privilege give Temple access to social power that is denied Nancy. Using her identity as Mrs. Gowan Stevens, Temple tries to manipulate the interpretations of her life story in order to control her fate and free Nancy. With far less access to power, Nancy protects her subjectivity by refusing to acknowledge others' power over her, as when she refuses to respond to the judge before he pronounces a sentence of death by hanging in the first dramatic scene. She thereby parodies the judicial system.[3] Both women's strategies for counteracting the narratives of public identity fail. But their relationship, which arises out of their similar experiences of misogynist violence and which their class and racial differences would ordinarily preclude, offers a potential source of resistance that is more powerful than either woman's singular efforts. Despite their ultimate separation and failure, the novel thus suggests that women's alliance across racial and class differences empowers their resistance and is a necessary precursor to social change.

Temple's strategies for freeing Nancy literally and herself figuratively are determined by public identity narratives. The sexual transgression forced upon her has rendered her "unfit" for the role of the chaste, pedestalled wife, and public discourse has divided her identity into two separate characters, Temple Drake and Mrs. Gowan Stevens. The language and narrative surrounding sexual acts in her past have come to constitute her identity as Temple Drake, whereas her "redeemed"-through-marriage identity as Mrs. Gowan Stevens demands that those sexual facts never be spoken. She is well aware of discourse's power to constrain women within their roles by punishing deviation with verbal or written gossip. In a mocking tone, she reveals to the Governor how humor exacerbated the trauma of her rape and imprisonment.

> You remember Temple: the all-Mississippi debutante whose finishing school was the Memphis sporting house? About eight years ago, remember? Not that anyone, certainly not the sovereign state of Mississippi's first paid servant, need be reminded of that, provided they could read newspapers eight years ago or were kin to somebody who could read eight years ago or even had a friend who could or even just hear or even just remember or just believe the worst or even just hope for it. (551)

As a part of legend, Temple is herself already a text that is interpreted—often, as she points out, by those who desire the most lurid story. Her story speaks to a common female experience within patriarchal society: that of the woman labeled "whore." While her experience is extreme, it reflects the psychological violence enacted upon women by a culture that defines them as virgins, wed mothers, or whores.

Temple's reaction to her predicament is to try to control her public identity by anticipating other people's interpretations of her behavior and then presenting a public self that leads to an interpretation she prefers. She admits to Stevens, for example, that she played the role of the "bereaved mother" at the trial (527). In this sense, public narratives, having split her identity into Mrs. Gowan Stevens and Temple Drake, have created her tendency to speak of both in the third person.[4] She herself attempts to suppress Temple Drake, preferring to perform Mrs. Gowan Stevens, the identity she feels she can control. This bifurcation leads to several verbal conflicts with Gavin, her uncle by marriage and Nancy's lawyer, who insists that she *is* Temple Drake, as when she returns from California to try to save Nancy:

> STEVENS. Yet you invented the coincidence [that brought her back from CA].
> TEMPLE. Mrs. Gowan Stevens did.
> STEVENS. Temple Drake did. Mrs. Gowen Stevens is not even fighting in this class. This is Temple Drake's.
> TEMPLE. Temple Drake is dead.
> STEVENS. The past is never dead. It's not even past. (535)[5]

Temple wants to control her name because she believes her identity as Mrs. Gowan Stevens can exorcise her past.[6]

Temple cannot completely control her identity, however, even by cleaving to her Mrs. Gowan Stevens persona, because she cannot control all the discourses surrounding her. Her past continues to circulate in public conceptions of her identity, regardless of the persona she adopts or how faithfully she executes her role. Since her rape and brothel imprisonment became public knowledge through Goodwin's trial in *Sanctuary,* her sexual past functions as an "open secret" as Eve Kosofsky Sedgwick describes it. Sedgwick maintains that the secrecy of the closet has specific meanings for homosexual identity: "Vibrantly resonant as the image of the closet is for many modern oppressions, it is indicative for homophobia in a way it cannot be for other oppressions" (75). Nevertheless, I want to suggest that the structural effects of the open secret implicate Temple as well, particularly because sexual acts have been made a constituent part of her identity and because of the transgressive, and therefore threatening and disruptive, nature of those acts. The rape, the bondage, and the brothel lend to Temple's past the aura of the illicit, which is powerful because it suggests the existence of further illicit details that are not publicly known. A "whore's" identity, as Sedgwick states of homosexual identity, exists in an atmosphere of "crystallizing intuitions or convictions . . . [with] their own power-circuits of silent contempt, silent blackmail, silent glamorization, silent complication" (80). Furthermore, the details of Temple's past, especially the time spent in the brothel, act as what Sedgwick terms a "pathogenic secret," which carries with it "the consciousness of a potential for serious injury that is likely to go in both directions [to revealer and revealed-to]" (80). The weight of this secret has been hurting Temple and Gowan and has the potential to do more harm if revealed—in other words, if Temple "outs" herself by verbalizing the details of her sexual experiences. Again, borrowing from Sedgwick,

> The double-edged potential for injury in the scene of coming out . . . results partly from the fact that the erotic identity of the person who receives the disclosure is apt also to be implicated in, hence, perturbed by it. This is true first and generally because erotic identity, of all things, is never to be circumscribed simply as itself, can never not be relational, is never to be perceived or known by anyone outside of the structure of transference and countertransference. (81)

Here one thinks of Gowan, who, by his Uncle Gavin's arrangement, sits silently hidden in the governor's chambers as Temple confesses; he is more or less responsible for Temple's ordeal and has expressed doubt that he is Bucky's biological father.

What is the secret, beyond the public assumption of lurid details, that has such explosive and destructive potential, even for Temple and Gowan, the two most intimately involved in the past events and their repercussions? The most transgressive, most taboo element of Temple's experience in *Sanctuary,* because it is the most forbidden, is her open expression of insatiable sexual desire for Red. In *Requiem,* that desire is contained in the letters she wrote him; thus her sexuality is explicitly connected to the act of writing. Initially posed by the letters, the threat soon becomes the possibility that

Temple will choose a life in which she can again openly express her sexuality. Pervasive cultural fear of unrestrained female sexuality operates much as the homophobia Sedgwick discusses, making it especially problematic for Temple to integrate past and present, public and private, into a coherent subject position from which to speak and act.

Temple's struggle to regain control of her narrative is expressed mainly through her conflict with Gavin over how the story will be told. Although Gavin insists his goal is the "truth" and making Temple tell it, he constantly interrupts her and creates parts of her story himself. Temple rebukes Gavin for his desire to control her story. When he treats its narration as a game—"Wait. Let me play too"—she "bitterly" responds, "You too. So wise too. Why can't you believe in truth? At least that I'm trying to tell it. At least trying now to tell it" (558). Silenced by all the retellings of her story by others, Temple resents the appropriation of her story by the man who coerced her into telling it. The nature of the truth that Gavin derives from his role as Temple's confessor must make us question his motivation. Foucault's description of the confessor's role indicates the extent of this power, which may itself be Gavin's chief reward:

> the revelation of the confession had to be coupled with the decipherment of what it said. The one who listened was not simply the forgiving master, the judge who condemned or acquitted; he was the master of truth. His was a hermeneutic function. With regard to the confession, his power was not only to demand it before it was made, or decide what was to follow after it, but also to constitute a discourse of truth on the basis of its decipherment.

Furthermore, Foucault's comments on the purpose served by confession help illustrate what may be Gavin's more hidden motive: "It is in the confession that truth and sex are joined, through the obligatory and exhaustive expression of an individual secret. *But this time it is truth that serves as a medium for sex and its manifestations*" (*History of Sexuality,* 61; emphasis mine). Gavin wants to force sex into discourse. He, too, wants the lurid details of Temple's past to be spoken, whether to hear them, to know all of them, to see others hear them in his presence, or just to make Temple say them for the suffering that is accorded such redemptive value throughout the novel, for, as Foucault argues, in the confession "investigation and punishment become mixed" (*Discipline and Punish,* 41).

In contrast to Gavin's ostensible desire for an existential freedom that can be achieved through language, Temple focuses on the practical, social effects of language and tries to get Gavin to do so as well. She wants to save Nancy and believes legal discourse can affect that. She wants to say the necessary words that will get Gavin to create the necessary paperwork: "All we need is an affidavit. That she is crazy. Has been for years" (528). Despite the fact that Gavin tells her they cannot save Nancy, Temple persists: "what you will need will be facts, papers, documents, sworn to, incontrovertible, that no other lawyer trained or untrained either can punch holes in, find any flaw in" (533). Her desperation to save Nancy, for which she tells Gavin she "will do anything, *any*thing" (532), is what makes her vulnerable to Gavin's power, to his demand for her confession. She keeps asking him, "How much will I have to tell?" (538). She resists resurrecting Temple Drake, realizing that to submit to Gavin's demand for confession requires her to accept the rape as a meaning that both defines and emanates her from essential identity. To believe that the rape resulted from something within her would be to accept that the rape was her fault—to say she "wanted it." Temple mocks Gavin's purported purpose—the truth: "For no better reason than that. Just to get it told, breathed aloud, into words, sound. . . . Why blink your own rhetoric? Why don't you go on and tell me it's for the good of my soul—if I have one?" (533). Nevertheless, perhaps compelled by what Foucault has shown as the pervasive demand within individuals to turn sex into discourse, she comes to need to tell her story, even after it is clear that she cannot prevent Nancy's execution. She tells the governor, "I've got to say it all, or I wouldn't be here. But unless I can still believe that you might say yes [that he will save Nancy], I don't see how I can" (559).

Temple's need to save Nancy is in fact her need to save herself, their identities and destinies have become enmeshed.[7] As Temple Drake and Mrs. Gowan Stevens, she inhabits both ends of the oppositional definition of woman. She is committed to performing the Mrs. Gowan Stevens social identity, which disciplines her subjectivity and by definition precludes her sexuality. Nancy enables Temple to maintain another subjectivity, one that allows her sexuality—is, in fact defined by it. That subjectivity seems to promise more freedom because it seems to be less normalized. Resistance, however, is an inevitable component of any power relation and is often contained by the dominant system.[8] This alternative, seemingly resistant identity, then, is just as normalized as the Mrs. Gowan Stevens identity, at least to the extent that being Temple Drake means inhabiting the identity defined by all the lurid stories. Temple's alternative subjectivity has been co-opted by the label "whore": discourse exercises power, making her the site of her own discipline. The label "whore" thus serves as an ontological category, making her essential identity out of a sexual act or acts presumed to have been done to or by her, and thereby determining the range of her possible actions.

Forms of resistance are given a specifically female history in the prose sections of the novel. The women in these sections, who contextualize Temple and Nancy culturally and historically, establish a women's culture that both resists and informs the dominant culture. The repetition of the Southern women's refusal to accept defeat by the North as the outcome of the Civil War becomes a refrain and emphasizes this heritage of resistance: "only the undefeated undefeatable women, vulnerable only to death, resisted, endured, irreconcilable" (629). Women are, in fact, a counter-force, "reversed and irrevocably reverted against the whole moving unanimity of panorama" (633). Their legacy of resistance survives them, and their characteristic description eventually becomes a trait of the town's inhabitants, who become "the irreconcilable Jeffersonians and Yoknapatawphians" (642). Subsumed by the larger culture, however, the legacy is reduced or normalized into class distinctions and social forms: "at last even the last old sapless indomitable unvanquished widow or maiden aunt had died and the old deathless Lost Cause had become a faded (though still select) social club or caste, or form of behavior when you remembered to observe it" (638).

Sites of resistance, women nevertheless remain within the roles society ascribes to them. The Southern middle-class white woman's role is represented by Cecilia Farmer, who is described first as the prison turnkey's daughter, "a frail anemic girl with narrow workless hands lacking even the strength to milk a cow," and then as a part of the prison structure: "the old tough logs . . . were now the bower framing a window in which mused hour after hour and day and month and year, the frail blonde girl" (626, 627). Cecilia is framed by both the window and her father's home, which is literally the prison.[9] She is also framed by her cultural role, that of the Southern daughter, placed on the pedestal, who waits, passively and silently, to be carried off and married by a man. Her cultural role is analogous to that of the socially elite Temple Drake.

Cecilia's only autonomous act is "inscribing at some moment the fragile and indelible signature of her mediation in one of the panes of it (the window): her frail and workless name, scratched by a diamond ring in her frail and workless hand, and the date: *Cecilia Farmer April 16th 1861* (627). While her name is described as "paradoxical and significantless" (629), the act of writing it is not. Importantly, Cecilia achieves this act with an object of female inheritance, "her grandmother's diamond ring" (629), which, paradoxically, symbolizes the cultural exchange of women. Her signature is her assertion of her existence, and through it she writes herself into town legend and makes herself a central figure.[10] Faulkner thus places special emphasis on women's written language as an assertion of subjectivity and a potential means of achieving power. Writing is a private act that allows women to express a subjectivity other than that mandated by the public narrative of their role in society.

Cecilia's signature sets the stage for the love letters Temple wrote to Red after their enforced liaisons while she was held prisoner in the Memphis brothel. These letters, creative acts through which she maintained her subjectivity, enable Temple to imagine an identity that is not socially mandated. Through the letters, Temple achieved what Hélène Cixous theorizes in "The Laugh of the Medusa": "by writing her self, woman will return to the body which has been more than confiscated from her, which has been turned into the uncanny stranger on display" (880). At the time Temple wrote them, they were a means of controlling her situation by writing the narrative of her relationship with Red. Created out of her sexuality, which she has suppressed to some extent in order to enact the socially defined role of Mrs. Gowan Stevens, the letters now provide Temple access to a former sense of freedom and control. She emphasizes the importance of the letters when she tells the governor about her relationship with Red: "I fell what I called in love with him and what it was or what I called it doesn't matter either because *all that matters is that I wrote the letters—*" (572; emphasis mine). She focuses on her authorship: "So I wrote the letters. I would write one each time . . . afterward, after they—he left, and sometimes I would write two or three when it would be two or three days between, when they—he wouldn't—" (572; ellipsis in original). What the governor hears is that two men were visiting Temple, but she highlights her creativity. When he seeks clarification of events, she continues to discuss the letters. She tells him four times that they were good letters, even alluding to Shakespeare: "you would have wondered how anybody just seventeen and not even through freshman in college, could have learned the—right words. Though all you would have needed probably would be an old dictionary from back in Shakespeare's time when, so they say, people hadn't learned how to blush at words" (574). Writing has been for Temple what Cixous projects it can be:

> An act which will not only "realize" the decensored relationship of woman to her sexuality, to her womanly being, giving her access to her native strength; it will give her back her goods, her pleasures, her organs, her immense bodily territories which have been kept under seal; it will tear her away from the supersized structure in which she has always occupied the place reserved for the guilty. (880)

By focusing on her writing, Temple is able to integrate her past experience with her present and gains access to a subjectivity that, while its effects remain private (the governor and Gavin remain unmoved), is not co-opted in the way that her attempt to reclaim the identity "whore" is.[11]

Just as Cecilia corresponds to Temple, Mohataha, mother to Ikkemotubbe, "the last ruling Chickasaw chief" (618), provides the background for Nancy. Both are illiterate women of color who commit the acts that ostensibly allow their displacement by white society. The description of Mohataha likens her to Nancy; her expression is unreadable, just as Nancy's is at the trial, and while Nancy is repeatedly described as a whore, Mohataha is compared to a madam:

> the inscrutable ageless wrinkled face, the fat shapeless body dressed in the cast-off garments of a French queen, which on her looked like the Sunday costume of the madam of a rich Natchez or New Orleans brothel, sitting in a battered wagon inside a squatting ring of her household troops, her young men dressed in their Sunday clothes for travelling too; then she said, 'Where is this Indian territory?' And they told her: West. 'Turn the mules west,' she said, and someone did so, and she took the pen from the agent and made her X on the paper and handed the pen back and the wagon moved . . . herself immobile beneath the rigid parasol, grotesque and regal, bizarre and moribund, like obsolescence's self riding off the stage. (619)

Mohataha's "capital X on the paper which ratified the dispossession of her people forever" (618) shows that a woman's writing can serve to enforce cultural hegemony. But Mohataha's signature is merely the symbolic act of her people's already inevitable dispossession; it is causal apparently and apparently only, since in reality it was as though, instead of putting an inked cross at the foot of a sheet of paper, she had lighted the train of a mine set beneath a dam, a dyke, a barrier already straining, bulging, bellying, not only towering over the land but leaning, looming, imminent with collapse, so that it only required the single light touch of the pen in that brown illiterate hand, and the wagon did not vanish slowly and terrifically from the scene to the terrific sound of its ungreased wheels, but was swept, hurled, flung not only out of Yoknapatawpha County and Mississippi but the United States too, immobile and intact. (621–22)

Nancy's killing the baby—her one signifying act by which she both becomes a part of the town's written record and history and allows for her own eradication by that town—is also accomplished by a "brown illiterate hand" and similarly completes a seemingly inevitable end. She fulfills for Temple's daughter what may seem to her the inescapable, violent destiny of a woman, in which her and Temple's lives have been cast. Her act reveals the devaluation of life that the violence in her own life has taught her. Throughout the novel, Faulkner emphasizes the cultural forces that impinge upon people's actions, as the portrayal of Mohataha's act shows. Nevertheless, and despite the alignment of Nancy with Mohataha, we must resist the urge to interpret Nancy's action as equally inevitable and determined. Why Nancy kills the child is the irresolvable enigma in the novel.[12] Certainly it serves as a plot device, creating the need for Temple to save Nancy, placing the story within the construct of the judicial system, and inciting the suffering in Temple and Gowan that ruptures the structure of their marriage—the roles they played in it and the suffering they had learned to endure as the result of their circumstances. The fact that the baby is never named, in a novel obsessed with the importance of naming, distances the reader from the reality of her life and supports the murder's greater role as plot function than as moral dilemma.

Yet placing Temple and Nancy's relationship in its cultural context is important for any interpretation of the murder. Despite Temple's identification with Nancy, their relationship remains largely determined by the Southern social structure within which they live, a structure in which the black woman's role as domestic and nanny is to function as mirror and support for the white woman. The black woman's prescribed role is to assist the white woman's fulfilling her role in society as a white woman.[13] Interestingly, Faulkner does not address this historical and cultural role in the prose sections, yet it fits Temple's and Nancy's relationship perfectly, as Temple's description of Nancy for the Governor shows:

> nurse; guide; mentor, catalyst, glue, . . . holding the whole lot of them [Temple, Gowan, and their children] together—not just a magnetic center for the heir apparent and the other little princes or princesses in their orderly succession, to circle around, but for the two bigger hunks too of mass or matter or dirt or whatever it is shaped in the image of God, in a semblance at least of order and respectability and peace; not ole cradle-rocking black mammy at all. (579)

Ironically, in trying to emphasize Nancy's importance, Temple reverts to a definition of the mammy stereotype. Her statement also indicates her limited ability to imagine possibilities for her and Nancy's relationship that extend beyond the limits imposed by that image and narrative, possibilities that break out of the boundaries of disciplined penitentiary space and into a space in which they would no longer have to be what Foucault terms "docile bodies" (*Discipline and Punish,* 138).

In a sense, Nancy fulfills her role by demanding that Temple fulfill her maternal role. When Temple tries to leave with Pete, Nancy repeatedly reminds Temple of her duty to her children. Her exhortations fail, and Nancy sacrifices her own life and that of Temple's infant to ensure that Temple will stay with her family, will continue to enact her role as Mrs. Gowan Stevens. In meeting this requirement, Nancy, as Richard Moreland attests, "betrayed the typical role and trust assigned to her ideologically and economically by her race and gender: to care for people in this predominantly white society in their most vulnerable and dependent stage of life (just as in her previous role as black 'tramp' she was expected to cater to white men in their most socially vulnerable movements of sexuality)" (209). Nancy thus puts her duty to the unity of the family and to the eldest son ahead of her duty to the younger, female child. Nancy is also perhaps asking Temple not to abandon her—is in effect saying, "don't leave me." This possibility depends on whether Temple's need for Nancy is reciprocated. While Nancy may need Temple to ensure her employment, the cultural definition of their relationship as employer/employee works against an equitable reciprocity. Temple's identification with Nancy and the isolation that dominated Nancy's existence prior to her life in the Stevenses' home, however, suggest mutual need as a possibility.

Nancy's motivation aside, the murder forces her and Temple to negotiate separately within the judicial system, which then mediates their relationship. Nancy's attempts to use language as a form of resistance, which are
informed by Mohataha's use of language, differ from Temple's strategies. As
the extreme outsider, being black, poor, female, and a prisoner, Nancy maintains her integrity by refusing to answer to the justice system. When her sentence is passed down, she "quite loud in the silence, to no one, quite calm,
not moving" directs her response to God: "Yes, Lord" (507). Temple, when
she is recounting Nancy's response to the charge of murder, recognizes and
respects Nancy's subversion: "'Guilty, Lord'—like that, disrupting and confounding and dispersing and flinging back two thousand years, the whole
edifice of corpus juris and rules of evidence we have been working to make
stand up by itself ever since Caesar" (607). As Jay Watson observes, Nancy
"short-circuits (and puts in its place) the unfeelingly efficient protocol of the
judicial ceremony" (183). Moreland, noting that Nancy's answer follows the
judge's invocation of God, furthers that interpretation: "she dramatizes again
how such deferrals to higher authorities both insulate those present and also
show their need to insulate themselves from a more compromising understanding of, involvement in, perhaps complicity in, the apparent anomaly of
her crime" (209–10). Nancy is employing the strategy Luce Irigaray terms
"mimicry," which is for a woman

> to resubmit herself . . . to "ideas," in particular to ideas about herself, that are elab-
> orated in/by masculine logic, but so as to make "visible," by an effect of playful
> repetition, what was supposed to remain invisible: the cover-up of a possible oper-
> ation of the feminine in language. It also means "to unveil" the fact that, if
> women are such good mimics, it is because they are not simply reabsorbed in this
> function. *They also remain elsewhere.* (76)

By refusing complicity with the court's judgment, Nancy not only critiques
the judicial system, she also shows that her subjectivity—if not her body—
remains beyond the reach of its power.

In the novel's final scene, Temple and Gavin's visit to the prison, where
Nancy at last gets to speak for herself, she again employs this strategy of
resistance.[14] Refusing to be restricted to a single coherent meaning, Nancy
finally reduces her message to one word: "Believe" (662). Her repetition and
simplicity lend her message incantatory power, just as Cecilia's "passivity"

invests her continual and impenetrable presence with invincibility. Nevertheless, Nancy's "Trust in Him" (657) is problematic in that she seems to have accepted her subjugation to the ultimate male power. Nancy's consideration of her audience, however, affects her message; she makes this and related statements before Gavin drops out of the conversation, before the conversation is carried out solely between her and Temple. Furthermore, since the power over her is male, Nancy assumes she will have to "get low for Jesus" (656). To Nancy, men and women have very different expectations. Her distinction between how men and women listen reveals the impact of her consideration of her audience: "Jesus is a man too. He's got to be. Menfolks listens to somebody because of what he says. Women don't. They don't care what he said. They listens because of what he is" (656). Her statements are therefore addressed to an audience that includes men, and she expects Temple to listen not to the content of her words but to the presence of her being, out of the knowledge of who she is.

Temple and Nancy's relationship is central to the novel; they are identified with each other throughout, particularly by Temple, whose first words echo Nancy's words in the courtroom: "Yes, God, Guilty, God. Thank you, God" (509).[15] Such an echo could be taken merely as mockery if Temple did not persistently align herself with Nancy, as when she refers to the governor as "the first paid servant, a part of whose job is being paid to lose sleep over Nancy Mannigoes and Temple Drakes" (551). A large part of Temple's identification with Nancy is based on the fact that they are both considered "whores."[16] Temple reclaims the word *whore* as her and Nancy's shared identity. By continually referring to them both as "whores," Temple achieves two things. First, she distances herself from her own situation and, paradoxically, from Nancy so that she can maintain control, which her feelings for Nancy threaten. Second, she appropriates society's label for them in order to show her contempt for the misogyny inherent in society's conceptions of women.

Temple's relationship to the word *whore* is complicated, however; despite her anger, she has to some extent internalized the moral judgment inherent in the word. (Indeed, her role as Mrs. Gowan Stevens requires her to make that judgment.) Thus, when Temple first decides that she can no longer stand the burden of maintaining her Mrs. Gowan Stevens persona, she feels that her only choice is to reclaim the identity of Temple Drake by running away with Pete, thereby fulfilling the role of "whore."[17] As she puts it, describing for the governor her reaction to Pete's blackmail, "being Temple Drake, the first way to buy them [the letters] back that Temple Drake thought of, was to produce the material for another set of them" (575). The label "whore," by making an act (whether her rape, and thus not her act at all, or her sexual desire for Red) her identity, casts Temple as the enforcer of her own confinement within that role and makes her the site of her own discipline. Temple accepts, under great pressure from Gavin, the essentialized nature of evil: she states, "Temple Drake liked evil," and "the bad was already there [in her] waiting" (564, 574). This self-blame gives her the illusion of control by making her agent rather than victim, but ultimately keeps her contained within the hegemonic patriarchal constructs and definitions. Temple's own language constructs her narrative. Her vocabulary for women's options is inadequate to provide her with more positive choices.

Temple and Nancy's social identity as "whores" gives them an equality that would not otherwise exist in the relationship of a white woman and a black woman who works for her, a fact that Temple acknowledges even as she tries to assert her superiority, calling Nancy's reasoning "whore morality": "But then, if I can say whore, so can you, cant you?" (597). Temple sets up a parallel between the two of them when she describes the young Temple as "the all-Mississippi debutante" and then says that Nancy "made her debut into the public life of her native city while lying in the gutter with a white man trying to kick her teeth *or at least her voice* back down her throat" (544; emphasis mine). Gavin makes Temple's parallel to Nancy explicit by echoing these words when he describes Temple's plan to run off with Red's brother Pete, "who wouldn't even bother to forgive her if it ever dawned on him that he had the opportunity, but instead would simply black her eyes and knock a few teeth out and fling her into the gutter: so that she could rest secure forever in the knowledge that, until she found herself with a black eye and or spitting teeth in the gutter, he would never even know he had anything to forgive her for" (588). Clearly, the shared experience of misogynistic violence forges the deep bond Temple feels with Nancy.

While Temple relates the violence to the attempt to destroy a woman's voice, she describes her relationship to Nancy in terms of their ability to share language. She tells the governor that she hired Nancy "to have someone to talk to" (554), stating, "it wasn't the Gowan Stevenses but Temple Drake who had chosen the ex-dope-fiend nigger whore for the reason that an ex-dope-fiend nigger whore was the only animal in Jefferson that spoke Temple Drake's language" (579). The sharing of language takes on a spiritual significance for Temple; she describes their communication in religious terms: "acolyte," "sisters," "avocational," "worshipper," "worshipped," and "idol." She is acolyte to Nancy's nun:

> A confidante. You know: the big-time ball player, the idol on the pedestal, the worshipped; and the worshipper, the acolyte . . . You know: the long afternoons, with the last electric button pressed on the last cooking or washing or sweeping gadget and the baby safely asleep for a while, and the two sisters in sin swapping trade or anyway avocational secrets over coca colas in the quiet kitchen. (579–80)

An idealized unity manifests in a shared language and arising out of a shared gender experience is, in many feminist theories, posited as the potential source of resistance, transformation, and change. Cixous, for example, states that "Everything will be changed once woman gives woman to the other woman" (881). Such theories have been criticized for eliding crucial race and class differences among women in an attempt to forge gender unity.[18] While race and class differences ultimately separate Temple and Nancy in Faulkner's text, I hope to show that those differences are what make their unity a form of resistance that has not already been co-opted and contained, precisely because it has remained unimagined.

Temple and Nancy's shared language is never represented in the text. According to Irigaray's concept of patriarchal language, women's language is by definition unrepresentable because the category woman, as other, remains "unimaginable" (85). The interchange between Temple and Nancy that immediately precedes Nancy's suffocating the baby is in the language not of their idealized relating, but of "the phallocentric economy" (Irigaray 78). By agreeing to run off with Pete, Temple denies her subjectivity because she accepts the role of commodity within that economy. As Nancy informs her, her relationship to him is explicitly economic; he will demand money of her. Her acceptance of that commodified role propels the two women back into patriarchal space. Here, in this space, Nancy tries to keep Temple within the nuclear family structure by withholding her money and warning her of the dangers of her precarious position with Pete (596). Here, Nancy accuses Temple: "It was already there in whoever could write the kind of letters that even eight years afterward could still make grief and ruin" (596–97). Here, Temple pulls class rank on Nancy, condescendingly distinguishing them: "Maybe the difference [between us] is, I decline to be one [a whore] in my husband's house" (597). Here, Nancy makes explicit the violence that maintains such hierarchical distinctions, offering, "Hit me. Light you a cigarette too. I told you and him [Pete] both I brought my foot. Here it is" (599). Here, they express the hatred Cixous describes as "the greatest crime against women," that which has "led them [women] to hate women, to be their own enemies, to mobilize their immense strength against themselves" (878).

By contrast, the resistant female space created through the relationship between two women who are multiply othered—as women, as "whores," in Nancy's case as an African American and a drug user, and in Temple's case as a woman with sexual subjectivity—constitutes what Irigaray imagines as "an 'outside' that is exempt, in part, from phallocratic law," an outside from which it is possible "to disconcert the staging of representation according to exclusively 'masculine' parameters, that is, according to a phallocratic order" (68). This is the space that she describes as excluded by patriarchal language, in which "there is no possible place for the 'feminine,' except the traditional place of the repressed, the censured," in which "the question of the woman still cannot be articulated" (68). The power of Temple and Nancy's differences—from other women and from each other—is crucial to the resistant power of this space. The text's suggestion that women's differences are necessary for resistance overcomes the tendency of some feminist theories to universalize gender experience.

Because the possibility of Temple and Nancy's discourse has remained unimagined, it is uncontained. Discourse between two women of Temple's social class would be the scripted language of the patriarchy because these women are invested in the privilege that ensues from their identities, which are defined by their relationships to men. Within such space, Irigaray argues, "women's social inferiority is reinforced and complicated by the fact that woman does not have access to language, except through recourse to 'masculine' systems of representation which disappropriate her from her relation to herself and to other women" (85). In Foucauldian terms, these women are disciplinary sites of their own normalization; thus they maintain their normalized identities and perpetuate hegemony when they are together, even when they are not being observed. While this would not necessarily be true if they rejected their prescribed identities, if they were not invested in the system and the privilege it provides, their rebellion would remain contained within the dominant system of power, which has provided space for resistance. Two poor African American women such as Nancy would also be contained; denied access to the power structures, they are rendered invisible, voiceless, and therefore powerless. The problem, therefore, is how to find a way out of contained space, and not just into another already defined space.

Because genuine connection and communication across racial and class boundaries has been impeded by the forces of hegemony, Temple and Nancy's discourse have remained unimagined and undefined. It therefore has potential power. Temple and Nancy's challenge, as they attempt to resist hegemony and claim subjectivity, is one not just of language, but of narrative, just as the dominant discourse that constrains them operates by reading women as texts not only on the level of language (through labels such as "whore" and "nigger dope-fiend whore") but also on the level of narrative, by controlling their possible stories and how those stories are told. Their problem is the one Carolyn G. Heilbrun poses to all women: "How can we find narratives of female plots, stories that will affect other stories and, eventually, lives?" (42).

Ultimately, Temple and Nancy's language fails them, not because it lacks power, but because they are separated. The failure is anticipated by Temple's limited conception of the possibilities of their interaction. For her, Nancy is the listener that everyone needs:

> Somebody to talk to, as we all seem to need, want, have to have, not to converse with you nor even agree with you, but just keep quiet and listen. Which is all that people really want, really need; I mean, to behave themselves, keep out of one another's hair; the maladjustments which they tell us breed the arsonists and rapists and murderers and thieves and the rest of the antisocial enemies, are not really maladjustments but simply because the embryonic murderers and thieves didn't have anybody to listen to them. (580)

The solution Temple proposes for people's need for listeners—"if the world was just populated with a kind of creature half of which were dumb, couldn't do anything but listen, couldn't even escape from having to listen to the other half" (580)—reveals how one-sided her interaction with Nancy has been. Temple's description of the evolution of a murderer implicates her in Nancy's guilt for the murder of her own child; she failed to fulfill her responsibility to listen to Nancy. (Temple's statement also indicates her tendency to assume too much guilt.) This failure of reciprocity—Temple's failure to transcend her own racist assumptions, which have led her to believe that Nancy will listen but prevented her from realizing that Nancy has subjectivity and thus has her own story to tell—contributes to their failure to tap the potential power of their relationship. The failure is not theirs alone, however, but clearly lies primarily in the conditions surrounding their relationship; the hope promised by their connection across racial difference, their love and ability to communicate, is torn apart by the hegemonic social structure. At the end of the play, Temple has called out longingly to Nancy, has desperately tried to hear what the latter has to say. In another textual move that asserts the similarities of their gendered experience, Nancy is enclosed in the prison, in Cecilia's former place, awaiting her execution. Temple acquiesces to Gowan's command for her presence, "Temple" (664), and leaves, contained between two symbols of patriarchal power, the husband and the lawyer. The final scene, therefore, fails to go beyond the two conventional endings of women's plots: marriage and death.

In the final prose section of the novel, which precedes Temple and Gavin's conversation with Nancy in the jail, Faulkner instructs readers in how to read. In this tutorial, Faulkner presents the idea of a living history by directly addressing and then leading the reader, as a stranger, on a journey of discovery into the prison, through the feminine space of the jailor's wife's kitchen, to the window with Cecilia Farmer's signature. The stranger creates a revisionist history of Cecilia Farmer, starting once again with the civil war women's irreconcilability that had become a part of the mainstream culture: "instead of dying off as they should as time passed, it was as though these old irreconcilables were actually increasing in number" (642). The narrative projects that after a century, in 1965,

> not merely the pane, but the whole window, perhaps the entire wall, may have been removed and embalmed intact into a museum by an historical, or anyway a cultural, club of ladies,—why, by that time, they may not even know, or even need to know: only that the windowpane bearing the girl's name and date is that old, which is enough; has lasted that long: one small rectangle of wavy, crudely-pressed, almost opaque glass, bearing a few faint scratches apparently no more durable than the thin dried slime left by the passage of a snail, yet which has endured a hundred years. (643)

In this way, Faulkner portrays women as the bearers of culture; they maintain its artifacts and pass down its oral history. The host thus answers the stranger's questions "out of the town's composite heritage or remembering that long back, told, repeated, and inherited to him by his father; or rather, his mother: from her mother: or better still, to him when he himself was a child, direct from his great-aunt: the spinsters, maiden and childless out of a time when there were too many women because too many men were maimed or dead" (644–45).

The host and the reader/stranger focus on Cecilia Farmer's signature, and the reader (the character in the text, and by implication and use of the second-person pronoun, the person reading the text) becomes a part of the history by becoming one of the creators of it:

> the faint frail [illegible] meaningless even inference-less scratching on the ancient poor-quality glass you stare at, has moved, under your eyes, even while you stared at it, coalesced, seeming actually to have entered into another sense than vision: a scent, a whisper, filling that hot cramped strange room already fierce with the sound and reek of frying pork-fat: the two of them in conjunction—the old milky obsolete glass, and the scratches on it: that tender ownerless obsolete girl's name and the old dead date in April almost a century ago—speaking, murmuring, back from, out of, across from, a time as old as lavender, older than album or stereopticon, as old as daguerreotype itself. (643–44)

Cecilia's writing has become active, moving, meaning-creating. Indeed, the reader is described as having "heard that voice, that whisper, murmur, frailer than the scent of lavender, yet (for that second anyway) louder than all the seethe and fury of frying fat" (644). Cecilia's voice has become the embodiment of that elusive quality that draws people to live in towns such as Jefferson. The stranger imagines the soldier "drawn . . . by that impregnable, that invincible, that incredible, that terrifying passivity" of Cecilia's look (645). But Cecilia's passivity is an irreconcilable paradox for the stranger, whose created story is insufficient to explain "that passivity, that stasis, that invincible captaincy of soul which didn't even need to wait but simply to be, breathe tranquilly, and take food,—infinite not only in capacity but in scope too" (646–47). Through the stranger's interpretation Cecilia becomes a strong autonomous being with an "invincible captaincy of soul" who contrasts sharply with the frail, static girl bound by the prison window. By re-presenting Cecilia in this way, Faulkner highlights both the impact of point-of-view on historical representation and the importance of recovering female texts, hearing female voices, and re-imagining female plots, thereby inviting a woman-centered reading of the novel.

The extended description of the stranger's interpretation of Cecilia Farmer also reveals how men read women as texts. The stranger's imagination expounds until the image of Cecilia's face becomes "Lilith's lost and insatiable face drawing the substance—the will and hoe and dream and imagination—of all men (you too; yourself and the host too) into that one bright fragile net and snare" (647). Suddenly the weak, anemic, almost ephemeral girl has become a fearsome trap. Men's compulsion to read women evokes a catalogue of interpretations:

> among the roster and chronicle, the deathless murmur of the sublime and death-less names and the deathless faces, the faces omnivorous and insatiable and for-ever incontent, demon-nun and angel-witch; empress, siren Erinys: Mistinguette too, invincibly possessed of a half-century more of years than the mere three score or so she bragged and boasted, for you to choose among, which one she was,—not *might* have been, nor even *could* have been, but *was:* so vast, so limitless in capacity is man's imagination to disperse and burn away the rubble-dross of fact and probability, leaving only truth and dream. (648)

Despite all these negative and ambivalent associations, Cecilia's signature is finally interpreted as a proclamation of identity: *"'Listen, stranger, this was myself: this was I'"* (649). Cecilia established her identity, and her existence in history, by writing her name. [19] The clear implication here is that women need to be read from a sympathetic, woman-centered perspective, and that women need to read themselves and write themselves. This call and the novel's association of violence against women's bodies and their preclusion from language anticipates Cixous: "Woman must write her self: must write about women and bring women to writing, from which they have been driven away as violently as from their bodies—for the same reasons, by the same law, with the same fatal goal. Woman must put herself into the text— as into the world and into history—by her own movement" (875). Cecilia's assertion of identity reverberates in Temple's deeply felt pride in the letters she wrote to Red. The writing, then, frees women's subjectivities from the public disciplinary narratives. As the novel shows, however, such a liberation of the private self, while a necessary precursor to the transformation of those public narratives, is insufficient to effect social change in and of itself. The novel suggests that the connection of women across differences has the potential to counteract those narratives, to bring private liberation to a public space.

NOTES

1. For an analytical overview of feminist narrative theory, see Homans (1994). Faulkner descries the genesis of the novel with the following questions: "I began to think what would be the future of that girl? And then I thought, What could a marriage come to which was founded on the vanity of a weak man?" (Gwynn and Blotner, 96).

2. In Gavin Stevens (Temple's uncle and Nancy's lawyer) and the governor, Faulkner gives these cultural forces voice and name. As Noel Polk suggests, one of *Requiem*'s subjects is "the culture's concerted efforts to bring her [Temple] to judgment for her sexual history. The culture is personified in the ruthless figure of Gavin Stevens, who is . . . a surrogate . . . for the culture itself" (*Children of the Dark House* 158). See also Polk's comprehensive 1981 study of the novel, in which he convincingly argues that Gavin's motives are perverse. Gavin's motivation has been the source of much critical debate. Following Olga Vickery's interpretation, many critics confirm Gavin's stated purpose, saving Temple, and recent critics such as Jay Watson and Karl F. Zender continue to use a therapeutic model for Gavin and Temple's exchanges. Judith Wittenberg, on the other hand, in her Lacanian reading of Temple's speech in both *Sanctuary* and *Requiem for a Nun,* shows that Gavin's ineptitude as an analyst contributes to the decline of Temple's verbal sophistication and psychological awareness, thereby reversing the intended process of therapy.

3. To some extent, the difference in their strategies is analogous to the contrast between French and American feminists Margaret Homans describes (with Nancy's strategy fitting the French model and Temple's the American):

> The French writers who accept the premise that language and experience are coextensive also understand language to be a male construct whose operation depends on women's silence and absence . . . In contrast, most recent feminist criticism in this country has pragmatically assumed that experience is separable from language and thus that women are or can be in control of language rather than controlled by it. ("Her Very Own Howl," 186)

While Homans acknowledges that this characterization is a simplification that does not do justice to the diversity of French and American feminist thought, it provides a useful paradigm. Her point is that the two views are not necessarily mutually exclusive, and combining the two approaches provides more productive possibilities.

4. Janet Wondra uses M. M. Bakhtin's theories to discuss the "linguistic disruptions" with which "Temple's marginalized voice protrudes through a capitalizing language" and points out that "it is specifically these two proper names Temple avoids inhabiting when she chooses to speak of herself in the third person, as if speaking about a character playing a role" (48–49).

5. See also 530–32 for similar exchanges. While Stevens recognizes the bifurcation of Temple's identity, his recognition is problematic: the Temple Drake he sees is different from the Temple Drake that Temple sees (neither of which is particularly accurate). This leads to further fragmentation and multiplication of identities. As Temple says to the governor, "I'm trying to tell you about one Temple Drake, and our Uncle Gavin is showing you another one. So already you've got two different people begging for the same clemency, if everybody concerned keeps splitting up into two people, you wont even know who to pardon, will you?" (578)

6. The importance of naming has been established in the history of the town, which is named Jefferson after the mailman, Pettigrew, who has threatened to turn the townsmen in for charging the replacement of the stolen lock to the U.S. government. After they name the town after him, he tells them they can call the lock axle grease on the ledger and no one will ever find it; hence they can charge what it is—its identity—by renaming it (492).

7. Richard C. Moreland states that

> The emotional achievement of her [Temple's] analysis is much less the salvaging of her marriage with Gowan than her mourning of her daughter and her reunion with Nancy and her surviving child, even though a move in Gowan's direction is made in the last lines and gestures of the play. I am tempted to read this last-minute feint toward a more conventionally romantic, heterosexual ending . . . as a betrayal of the emotional center of the work in the two women characters' developing relationship with each other . . . Temple . . . is in some ways being reintegrated with her alienated selves in Nancy and in 'their' surviving child. (215n. 20)

This provocative suggestion seems to me, like much of the criticism that addresses Temple and Nancy's relationship, to idealize their sameness at the cost of neglecting their differences. I hope to show that their differences are important not only as a cause of their physical and emotional separation, but also as a course of the potential power of that relationship.

8. For Foucault's explication of normalization, see *Discipline and Punish,* 170–84; for his discussion of the containment of difference, see *The History of Sexuality,* 95–96. Gowan's identity is likewise normalized, as he forcefully states: "call it simple over training. You know? Gowan Stevens, trained at Virginia to drink like a gentleman, gets drunk as ten gentlemen, takes a country college girl, a maiden; who knows? Maybe even a virgin, cross country by car to another country college ball game . . ."; and "Marrying her was purest Old Virginia. That was indeed a hundred and sixty gentlemen" (520–21).

9. Lynda E. Boose notes that while

    > we seldom find sons locked inside their father's castles, because retention and separation are not the
    > defining stress lines of the father-son narrative . . . the daughter's struggle with her father is one of sep-
    > aration, not displacement. Its psychological dynamics thus locate the conflict inside inner family
    > space. . . . Within the spatial image, the daughter—the liminal or 'threshold' person in family space—
    > symbolically stands at the boundary/door, blocked from departure by the figure of the father (and/or
    > the son or other male heir to the father's position). For the narrative to progress—for the daughter to
    > leave the father's enclosure—the outside rival male must arrive and create a magnetic pull on the
    > daughter, who otherwise remains within, in psychological bondage to her filial bonds. (32–33)

10. Moreland suggests that Cecilia, as "the writer of *'écriture féminine,'*" exerts an "indirect
    influence" on Nancy and Temple (196). He discusses Nancy and Temple as sorceress and hys-
    teric, respectively. Cecilia's signature (especially considering the stranger's re-reading of it,
    which I discuss later in the paper) could be considered as one of the moments when the fem-
    inine erupts in Faulkner's texts. For an elucidating exploration of such moments, see Minrose
    Gwin's *The Feminine and Faulkner,* in which she employs what she calls "bisexual reading" to
    interpret the bisexuality (the interaction of masculine and feminine) in Faulkner's works.

11. The text seems to anticipate some of the major theories of late twentieth century feminism,
    particularly women's relationship to writing, sexuality, and each other. I will counterpoise
    Cixous's arguments in "Laugh of the Medusa" and Irigaray's in *This Sex Which is Not One* with
    portions of *Requiem* to elucidate my interpretation of Faulkner's text as well as to show how
    those theories work out in practical terms in that text. Cixous's and Irigaray's theories help
    reveal the leaks in the culture's containment of resistance—both the places Temple and Nancy
    attempt to take advantage of and the potential sites for resistance that they fail to realize.

12. Faulkner, explaining his use of the work *nun* to refer to Nancy, characterized the murder as
    follows: "She [Nancy] was capable within her poor dim lights and reasons of an act which
    whether it was right or wrong was of complete almost religious abnegation of the world for
    the sake of the innocent child [presumably Bucky]" (qtd. in Gwynn and Blotner, 196). Polk
    suggests that Nancy may be seeking revenge (*Faulkner's* Requiem, 201). Faulkner's own first
    daughter, nine-day-old Alabama, died in 1931. For a brief account of infant deaths and the
    ensuing grief and suffering in Faulkner's work, as well as a condolence letter he wrote to
    Frances and James Warsaw "Sonny" Bell, Jr., see Fowler and McCool.

13. See Gwin's *Black and White Women in the Old South,* Trudier Harris's *From Mammies to Militants,*
    and Elizabeth Fox-Genovese's *Within the Plantation Household.*

14. This scene is typically read not for underlying motives, but at face value: Temple and Gavin's
    turning to Nancy for answers, which she gives forthrightly. As such, it represents the ten-
    dency, which Toni Morrison discusses in *Playing in the Dark,* for white characters to need black

characters in order to forge identities, as does Temple's dependence on her connection to Nancy throughout.

15. Diane Roberts suggests that Nancy and Temple's relationship reveals Faulkner's awareness "that the South was confronting a social revolution, at the center of which were women and blacks" (219). Although she suggests the potential revolutionary power of their relationship, her interpretation remains fairly conventional; she reads Nancy as supporting the social order and Temple as succumbing to the moral demands of motherhood, according Temple with far less intelligence and awareness of her situation than I do.

16. By making women considered "whores" central, *Requiem* to some extent answers *For Whom the Bell Tolls*, to which Temple refers: "somebody—Hemingway, wasn't it?—wrote a book about how it [rape] had never actually happened to a g—woman, if she just refused to accept it, no matter who remembered, bragged" (576–77). In Hemingway's book, Maria, the victim of a gang rape, is repeatedly referred to as a "whore." Temple's revision as she speaks—when she starts to say "girl," she corrects it to "woman"—is significant: Hemingway writes a character whom rape has paradoxically and perversely made innocent and girl-like; Faulkner writes about a woman facing the social and personal consequences of having been raped.

17. Moreland notes that with this decision "Temple acts out in an exaggerated (symptomatic) form the rejection of the mother in herself and the particular (vs. commodified) woman and lover in herself—as if that rejection is required in order for her to enter into that same system of exchange" (225n. 23).

18. Elizabeth Spelman's excellent study *Inessential Woman* shows how theoretical premises can erase race and class differences and undermine feminists' attempts to create inclusive theories.

19. Moreland posits that

> [t]he lingering promise of such an unassimilated subject's and moment's articulate resistance to the "one boom" of modernity's vast skein, after the modernist experience with the reductive dialectics of enlightenment, civilization, signification, and other systematizations, is fraught with all the anxious ambiguity of the rest of the promises of postmodernity and "woman's writing." Along with the possibility that she would found somewhere a resistant "matriarchy" of farmers . . . is the more paranoid possibility that has occurred to the outlander-reader the possibility that this articulated, legible trace of a maternal, anthropophagic order is an engulfing, devouring, castrating threat. . . . (232)

WORKS CITED

Boose, Lynda E. "The Father's House and the Daughter in It: The Structures of Western Culture's Daughter-Father Relationship." In *Daughters and Fathers,* edited by Lynda E. Boose and Betty S. Flowers, 19–74. Baltimore: Johns Hopkins University Press, 1989.

Cixous, Hèléne. "The Laugh of the Medusa." *Signs* 1 (1976): 875–93.

Faulkner, William. *Requiem for a Nun.* 1952. Reprinted in *William Faulkner: Novels 1942–1954.* New York: Library of America, 1994.

Foucault, Michel. *Discipline and Punish: The Birth of the Prison,* 1975. Reprint translated by Alan Sheridan, 2d ed. New York: Vintage, 1995.

———. *The History of Sexuality.* Vol. 1: An Introduction. 1976. Reprint translated by Robert Hurley. New York: Vintage, 1990.

Fowler, Doreen, and Campbell McCool. "On Suffering: A Letter from William Faulkner." *American Literature* 57 (1985): 650–52.

Fox-Genovese, Elizabeth. *Within the Plantation Household: Black and White Women of the Old South.* Chapel Hill: University of North Carolina Press, 1988.

Gwin, Minrose. *Black and White Women of the Old South: The Peculiar Sisterhood in American Literature.* Knoxville: University of Tennessee Press, 1985.

———. *The Feminine and Faulkner: Reading (Beyond) Sexual Difference.* Knoxville: University of Tennessee Press, 1990.

Gwynn, Frederick L., and Joseph L. Blotner, eds. *Faulkner in the University.* Charlottesville: University Press of Virginia, 1995.

Harris, Trudier. *From Mammies to Militants: Domestics in Black American Literature.* Philadelphia: Temple University Press, 1982.

Heilbrun, Carolyn G. *Writing a Woman's Life.* New York: Ballantine, 1988.

Hemingway, Ernest. *For Whom the Bell Tolls.* New York: Macmillan, 1940.

Homans, Margaret. "'Her Very Own Howl': The Ambiguities of Representation in Recent Women's Fiction." *Signs* 9 (1983): 186–205.

———. "Feminist Fictions and Feminist Theories of Narrative." *Narrative* 2 (1994): 3–16.

Irigaray, Luce. *This Sex Which is Not One.* 1977. Reprint translated by Catherine Porter with Carolyn Burke. Ithaca: Cornell University Press, 1985.

Moreland, Richard C. *Faulkner and Modernism: Rereading and Rewriting.* Madison: University of Wisconsin Press, 1990.

Morrison, Toni. *Playing in the Dark: Whiteness and the Literary Imagination.* New York: Vintage, 1993.

Polk, Noel. *Faulkner's* Requiem for a Nun: *A Critical Study.* Bloomington: Indiana University Press, 1981.

———. *Children of the Dark House: Text and Context in Faulkner.* Jackson: University Press of Mississippi, 1996.

Roberts, Diane. *Faulkner and Southern Womanhood.* Athens: University of Georgia Press, 1994.

Sedgwick, Eve Kosofsky. *Epistemology of the Closet.* Berkeley: University of California Press, 1990.

Spelman, Elizabeth V. *Inessential Woman: Problems of Exclusion in Feminist Thought.* Boston: Beacon Press, 1988.

Vickery, Olga. *The Novels of William Faulkner: A Critical Interpretation*. Revised edition, Baton Rouge: Louisiana State University Press, 1964.

Watson, Jay. *Forensic Fictions: The Lawyer Figure in Faulkner*. Athens: University of Goergia Press, 1993.

Wittenberg, Judith Bryant. "Temple Drake and *La parole pleine*." *Mississippi Quarterly* 48, no. 4 (1995): 421–41.

Wondra, Janet. "'Play' within a Play: Gaming with Language in *Requiem for a Nun*." *The Faulkner Journal* 8, no.1 (1992): 43–59.

Zender, Karl F. "*Requiem for a Nun* and the Uses of the Imagination." *Faulkner and Race,* edited by Doreen Fowler and Ann J. Abadie, 272–96. Jackson: University Press of Mississippi, 1987.

(Re) Reading Faulkner as Father and Daughter of His Own Text

MINROSE C. GWIN

What contemporary readers may find most mysteious and provocative about Faulkner's narrative is the way it produces itself out of what Barbara Johnson might call its own "difference within."[1] *Difference* is by its very nature a slippery and elusive term. I would suggest that it may be an appropriate way of describing the unsettling *fluctuations* of language and meaning that keep such works as *The Sound and the Fury* and *Absalom, Absalom!* always so hauntingly beyond our grasp. Where does this "difference within" come from? In a strangely symbiotic way it seems both to generate and be generated by certain irresolvable contradictions that splinter the identity of the literary text in which they occur. This splintering often makes Faulkner's writing seem to speak against itself, creating a relationship of interior otherness somewhat like that between the conscious and the unconscious mind. Such

---

Reprinted with permission from *Refiguring the Father: New Feminist Readings of Patriarchy*, ed. Patricia Yaeger and Beth Kowaleski-Wallace (Carbondale: University of Southern Illinois Press, 1989), 238–58.

a text suggests, by its own example, that identity is not one thing but rather many; and that those many, and their *own* differences within, may indeed necessitate a rethinking of the whole notion of *character.*

This process of difference may occur at the various levels of language, narrative structure, character, story; in Faulkner's greatest moments it seems to encompass them all and dissolve boundaries between them. As I converse with some of Faulkner's most compelling and problematic fiction, I am listening to the ways in which his stories and his characters speak against themselves, how they come to tell their own subversive stories and so create spaces in Faulkner's texts where things break down and meaning ruptures—spaces where difference finds a voice. For it is in these spaces, if it is anywhere, that the mystery and power of Faulkner move and breathe. It is there that the play of meaning achieves its highest velocity, spinning Faulkner's texts out into infinite patterns of production, and so creating their unending energies.

It is possible, I believe, to read this element of difference within Faulkner's narrative process as being connected to what Luce Irigaray would call a feminine economy. This is an endlessly productive force linked to woman's sexuality and maternity. It is an economy of spending, one that puts into question other economics that rely on a balance of give and take.[2] This feminine difference of Faulkner's has the effect of dissolving boundaries—particularly those between author and character; sometimes, I would suggest, those between text and reader. As feminist reader conversing with male author, I am listening for Faulkner's feminine voices as they rise from within what I will describe as the bisexual spaces of difference that layer his narrative. Within these spaces I am attempting to read female characters in new ways, as they themselves seem to create a tension within Faulkner's art by undercutting and subverting patriarchy—the law of the father, by playing creatively on and within its margins.

Faulkner thus creates a symbolic order of father-author only to allow its disruption—often by a female character's own voice of difference within the patriarchal text. In this sense Faulkner becomes father and daughter of his own text: he authorizes the text's meaning and then relinquishes that authority in favor of difference and play. He thereby frees his art to speak and reproduce its own difference from itself in ceaseless variance—to go, as it were, *somewhere else.* It is impossible to know how this process came about. Yet Faulkner himself seems to have had a sense not only that all of his works "failed" to say what they were meant to, but that those "failures," as we see

in his comments on *The Sound and the Fury,* his "finest failure," were indeed
to be valued *to the extent* that they were failures.[3]

I am appropriating the father-daughter model as a trope for linking sexual difference to narrative process because its dynamics permit us to read
Faulkner in several directions at once and hence to enter those spaces of difference with which we hope to converse. Let me be clear that, in part, I am
thinking metaphorically in a traditional Lacanian sense of the father's associations with power and authority, symbolization and repression. In this
sense the daughter is *of* the father because she is created by him; yet she is
also, because of her femininity, his difference within—that which subverts
the authority of the word by disallowing a univocality that would silence the
process of difference at work within language and narrative.

In a sense, then, I am deposing the paternal metaphor through which
Robert Con Davis, John Irwin, André Bleikasten, and other critics link psychoanalysis to narration because I am reading the daughter as much more
than a linguistic or cultural construct in Faulkner's texts. I am reading her as
female subject, as woman who speaks difference from the position of subject,
as she who can *say* desire, loss, absence, and so who can draw us into the
process of productivity in Faulkner's texts—those processes that evolve only
because the father's authoritative narrative is disrupted by the "daughters" of
his own creation.

These "daughters," certain of Faulkner's female characters, seem intimately and mysteriously related to the productivity of Faulkner's narrative in
a way that his male characters do not; for their feminine difference from
father-author actually creates those bisexual spaces in which difference may
find a voice. These "in-between" spaces affirm difference even as they dissolve our traditional notions of the binary construction of gender.

How do we find these spaces between father and daughter in Faulkner's
texts? We first may need to rethink the notion of *character* and its relationship
to the processes of loss and desire. Recent critical thought about Faulkner has
concerned itself with the pervasiveness of loss in his works and the ways in
which loss initiates narrative desire in both author and character. John T.
Matthews has shown us, moreover, that the tracing of the absent person or
thing in Faulkner's works often has the effect not of reconstructing that which
has been lost, but instead of setting into motion a fluid and creative play of
differences, which, in their very creativity and playfulness, dissolve the possibility of reconstruction or retrieval of the lost one or thing.[4] Loss thereby

triggers the desire to tell stories about what has been lost, a narrative desire that in turn is both absorbed and regenerated in its own playful explorations of the infinite and mysterious spaces left by the absent one or thing. As we know, these processes, as they signify *both* fragmentation and creativity, disorder and expansiveness—as they become themselves by differing from themselves—produce characters who are other to themselves; they are split, fragmented, disordered. They move between what is present and what is absent, and they tell stories of their own inability to cohere, out of their interior differences.

We may think, then, of a Rosa Coldfield as a network of desires and productions rather than the unified, coherent fiction we call "character." Rosa is indeed the example par excellence of the post-structural subject, who, as Houston A. Baker, Jr., points out, is not capable of "speaking" out of wholeness and autonomy, but rather is instead a code that is always in the process of deconstructing and producing self.[5] At the base of such a description is the Derridean notion of the subject's unconscious as a pattern of differences, a "radical alerity" that is unexplainable.[6] This symbiosis of loss and desire that theorists call the subject replays itself in processes that take shape as character, for example, as the Miss Rosa whose narrative desire both plucks out and reweaves the pattern of a culture that has, at once, denied her humanity and propelled her to produce it through imagination. Rosa speaks in those spaces between her own absence and presence as a speaking subject—that is, between what she is not and what she is. She becomes what Julia Kristeva would call a "questionable subject-in-process," one who makes and remakes herself through the utterance of her desire for her own presence.

Rosa's insistent talk may thus be heard, as Kristeva might say, "not [as] the discourse of a repudiated subject, but of one searching for the laws of its desires, operating as a hinge between immersion in the signifier and repudiation (it is neither one nor the other), its status unknown." What I am suggesting, then, is not just the *presence* of absence in Faulkner's narrative but the necessity of that absence of the character's ability to speak the text's difference. The subject must not be whole, for to be whole is to be silent. It is only by negotiating the economy of loss and desire that the subject learns to speak what is not. Rosa Coldfield must have lost her *"world of living marriage"* before she can speak, through her loss of it, its inherent contradictions—its difference within.

Where we may listen to Faulkner, then, may be in those spaces of difference that create and are created out of the tensions of loss and desire, and the inevitable ending that their utterance produces. If we think in the sexual terms of the Oedipal model, we may construe this space of desire and loss as the space between the father and the daughter, in this case, between the male author and the female character. This is the space of sameness *and* otherness. Both the father and the daughter may desire the difference of the other, but their sameness constructs desire as incestuous. To "have" the father, the daughter must lose him, and vice versa.

Here, I would hasten to add, I am not positing worlds of female loss and female lack, as Elaine Showalter describes the androcentric assumptions of Freudian and Lacanian psychoanalysis,[8] but instead am suggesting that we take Luce Irigaray's and Jane Gallop's lead in "reading" psychoanalytic theory in deconstructive ways.[9] What is at stake in our reading of Faulkner is not the father-author's creating of the daughter-character in terms of the authority he possesses. The more interesting and problematic question is: How does man create "character" coded as woman, the "daughter" whose narrative desire and sheer force lead the father-author to relinquish the authority of the word, and thereby create a new kind of narrative process arising from the interplay of difference? In these cases, woman created by man initiates *the difference within* that can make the male text speak against itself; and so becomes, as Alice Jardine says of woman in Western culture and metaphysics, all that "disturbs the Subject, Dialectic, and Truth."[10] By listening to the difference of the feminine, then, we may converse with the spaces between Faulkner and, for example, Caddy Compson, and many of his other female characters as well, as an area of "in-between" in which male creator and female created are present in an ever-heightening tension that generates narrative process. How does the feminine of Faulkner's text rise to speak difference from the position of subject? How does the father's daughter become woman?

This is a process that Hélène Cixous's concept of bisexuality may clarify. In Cixous's schema the term *bisexuality* does not mean neuter.[11] It is, to the contrary, the *exacerbation* of male and female elements in the writer and hence in the writing. Such writing is in a permanent state of tension; it is generated and regenerated by the interaction between the feminine and the masculine, between self and other (in the familial model, between the father and the daughter). It does "not annul differences but stirs them up, pursues them, increases their number." In such writing there is an "in-between" that is "infinitely dynamized by an incessant process of exchange from one subject to another."[12]

Faulkner seems to interact in such a way with some women characters of his own creation, his same-yet-other "daughters" whose disruptive female voices articulate *even as they differ from* his male artistic consciousness. Within what I would describe as bisexual spaces in Faulkner's writing—spaces in which this exchange described by Cixous occurs—that consciousness moves from maleness to bisexuality by allowing, as Cixous says, the mutual and engaged presence of both sexes and through this "self-permission," the "multiplication of the effects of the inscription of desire" in the narrative process itself.[13] How, then, do we approach the connection between the male creator and the creative process and desire of these female voices? How does the feminist reader reread the father? Instead of wresting textual mastery away from the male author as Patricinio P. Schweickart suggests, perhaps we should ponder his divisibility and his interaction with the feminine of his own creation.[14] After all, the poststructural rethinking of subjectivity applies not only to the process we call *character,* which, as Cixous tells us, is inevitably disordered and "unanalysable,"[15] but to the *writing subject* as well, the author who disappears into the spaces of the text and must be read out of those spaces.

Michel Foucault suggests that writing "is primarily concerned with creating an opening where the writing subject endlessly disappears" and enlists us in the examination of "the empty space left by the author's disappearance." We should, he says, "attentively observe, along its gaps and fault lines, its new demarcations, and the reapportionment of this voice; we should await the fluid functions released by this disappearance."[16] In some of the Faulkner's texts this "opening" of the text is, I believe, "the daughter" herself—that is, woman; and the interface between Faulkner, the text's father, and this space of authorial effacement evolves within that bisexual space Cixous calls "the in-between . . . infinitely dynamized by an incessant process of exchange from one subject to another." As Faulkner the writing subject disappears into the rhetoric of the text, the created "daughter" emerges with her own language of desire and loss and subversion and, of course, creativity. Within this bisexual space, the daughter's creative voice is engendered by paternal absence, the father's vanishing—that is, his repudiation of authority, and, just as important, *his willingness to vanish,* to disappear into that opening as his text moves beyond its own boundaries and goes . . . somewhere else.

It has been observed, accurately and perceptively, that Faulkner wrote out of his own experience as a white Southern male in a patriarchal culture. Yet we know also that, paradoxically, Faulkner's texts both explore and explode the boundaries of culture through creative probings of their limits and nuances. It is this disruptive freedom of mind, this willingness to differ from itself in infinitely various ways, that we may find reverberating through Faulkner's narrative and its creative female voices. Within certain bisexual spaces of narrative, then, Faulkner relinquishes the mental of the Lacanian "symbolic father," which, as Robert Con Davis points out, is "the agency of law."[17] He relinquishes the power of the phallus—the authority of the subject presumed to know—to *woman,* the female subject who thus becomes not only the created but also the creator.

I should point out here that, within this bisexual space, my reading of Faulkner offers an opposite conclusion to that of André Bleikasten, who sees fatherhood and sonship in Faulkner as "deeply involved in the *writer's* venture and relate back to his maddest desire: the desire to seize the authority of an original *author*—the authority, that is, of an origin, a founder, a father."[18] To the contrary, I find that Faulkner's texts achieve their greatest power" (and I use that term advisedly) when they *give away* power and control, often to the subversive creativity of female subjects—the daughters who are the difference within and who become, as Jardine would say, "woman-in-effect"— all that signify "those *processes that disrupts symbolic structures in the West.*"[19]

I need to define what I mean by female creativity. Sally Page and Cleanth Brooks view the "creativity" of Faulkner's female characters as inextricable from their reproductive and nurturing functions. Considered in this light, these women characters indeed *must be* either creative or destructive, for their "creativity" must reproduce and nurture the validity of the patriarchal universe in which they live, or it becomes destructive to that milieu. In this paradigm, "woman" becomes the created, the *image* of creation—but not the creator, the doer, the maker, the *agent* of creation.[20] The creativity I will converse with is a different thing altogether: it resides within the female subject who remakes herself and the world through imagination. It is a process engendered by desire that always seeks more than it has, a force from *within* the feminine space rather than one postulated by patriarchal expectation. Born out of sexual difference, it emerges out of the tension between Faulkner's male creative consciousness and its subversive feminine voice that undercuts its own discourse as it expands into new and unknown spaces. It is the bisexual space of Faulkner's texts.

What happens to these female subjects, then, is the same thing that seems to have happened to Faulkner as he created them and their responses to the world. Their creative impulse (and his as irrevocably linked to theirs) transforms the artistic consciousness by temporarily extending its creative boundaries into a new process of interaction that both derives from and intensifies sexual difference at the same time it questions its binary construction. Faulkner does this by allowing the female subject's capacity for creation to remain open and productive. Some of these characters, because of desire engendered by loss, enter what Derrida calls "the play of *différance."* They create new meaning through the disruption of presence, by taking the risk of "meaning nothing."[21] This ability to "play" without seeking center or boundary we find in such diverse characters as Rosa Coldfield, Temple Drake, Charlotte Rittenmeyer, Joanna Burden, Caddy Compson, and Addie Bundren. Tensions between denial and desire, the father and the mother, rigidity and flexibility, repression and sexuality give birth to the disrupted and disrupting female subject's narrative desire and by extension to Faulkner's insistence upon play, upon the plasticity of experience, upon the power of the human mind to break down rigidity and boundary.

If we consider what it means to "play" in the Derridean sense—that is, to disallow the necessity of closure, to defer meaning indefinitely—then we may wish to expand our notion of *character* still further to conceptualize female characters as feminine texts that defer themselves, and differ from themselves, ad infinitum. Their imaginative capacities may have moral negative results; yet their creativity is nonetheless a freeing force for their own psyches, which have been squeezed, compartmentalized, and devalued because of gender.

Emily Grierson "plays" creatively by subverting paternal and societal restraint. She not only breaks the law of the father. Within her own physical space, the bedroom, she subverts the signifiers of marital love—the rose-shaded lights, the tarnished hairbrush, the discarded clothing. She thereby creates new meaning for herself, within the repressive margins of the patriarchal order—inside the father's house.

Addie Bundren insists upon her own subjectivity: "I would be I," she says and she inscribes her different exit in an inescapable way. She knows that one never gets to the end of words, that the search for a center is fruitless, that language is not representative but constitutive. What she speaks and thus what she creates is her own sexuality. As Foucault's *The History of Sexuality* shows us, sexual desire is the stimulus for "a regulated and polymorphous incitement to discourse."[22] In response to the deadening force of the father's law, which decrease her to a living death, Addie redesigns her desire into the images of beautiful "garments which we would remove in order to shape and coerce the terrible blood to the forlorn echo of the dead word high in the air."[23] She becomes woman writing her own body, and as Cixous says, "her flesh speaks true. She *inscribes* what she is saying because she does not deny unconscious drives the unmanageable part they play in speech."[24]

Joanna Burden insists, above all, upon the *process* of her subjectivity, the narrative desire to invent and reinvent herself. It is the very multiplicity of her creativity, her insistence upon "playing it out like a play,"[25] which so frightens and alienates Joe Christmas. She must deny her austere past, "the frustrate and irrevocable years" of the father's law, and re-create herself insistently, compulsively, unilaterally. If we continue to think of the female character as a text, we may see that Joanna Burden *becomes* multiple texts of desire which propels her to reinvent herself variously, yet that same desire deconstructs those texts of herself as part of the ongoing process of invention. In this sense she is not so different from Lena Grove, who is herself the disruptive feminine process *outside* cultural codes, who, like Joanna, is a female subject propelled by loss and desire. Between these two female texts, which are *each* both disruptive and productive, we feel the force of Faulkner's narrative desire in continual process and motion.

But how to read process and motion? Caddy Compson has been thought of as a silent text constructed by her brothers, "a blank screen" imprinted by male fear and desire.[26] I would suggest that we try to "hear" Caddy Compson as the feminine voice of difference within male discourse, as the counter-narrative that speaks the possibility of play. If we can imagine Caddy as the space of woman's multiple and generative libidinal energies, a space that cannot be fixed or mastered, "this sex which is not one," as Irigaray would say, then we may begin to hear her voice from within the folds of Faulkner's text and from within our willingness to be absorbed into the concentric and bisexual spaces *between* the "manifest text" of Faulkner's male creative consciousness and the "unconscious discourse" of its own feminine subjectivity.[27] And so Caddy is never really silent, for her "silence" itself speaks.

Although she speaks as a girl within Benjy's mind, Caddy's voice carries the referential weight of the position of the mother, whose very acts of giving birth, of gestation and nurturance, dissolve the otherness of the other. In Benjy's section Caddy speaks the evaporation of ego boundaries and so creates the difference of maternal space, what Kristeva calls "the *unsettling process* of meaning and subject" rather than "the coherence or identity of either *one* or the *multiplicity* of structures."[28] In many of the scenes created in Benjy's memory, Caddy encloses him within this maternal space that transcends the teleologies of time and distance, and thus becomes their counter-narrative:

> "Why, Benjy," she said. She looked at me and I went and she put her arms around me. "Did you find Caddy again?" she said. "Did you think Caddy had run away."[29]

In such scenes Caddy's voice undercuts some of the very meanings of *The Sound and the Fury,* which, as we have been shown, is indeed about the effects of time and loss.[30] For what Caddy's voice says out of the maternal space created for it in Benjy's mind is precisely *opposite* to what Benjy's narrative as a whole seems to be saying—that originary plenitude can never be regained, that creativity and play have given way to despair, rigidity, meaningless order—to sound and fury signifying nothing.[31]

Let us listen to the Caddy of Quentin's section: "let me go I've got to catch him and ask his let me go Quentin please let me go let me go" (*The Sound,* 202). Here Caddy rises from the repressiveness of Quentin's discourse to speak her desire for Dalton Ames, for entry into a libidinal economy that allows her to give, to spend herself excessively, to play creatively within that half-light between self and other, much as she did within the maternal space she created within Benjy's discourse. At the same time, she speaks *from* Quentin *to* Quentin of the feminine within himself—that which he, entangled in a cultural narrative already written for him, can but desire and grieve for. To embrace the force that is Caddy, "the force and movement which displaces lines,"[32] we may conceive of her character as pervading this section in an organic way—enfolding, burrowing into, and playing within Quentin's mind. Paradoxically she both exceeds and is confined inside his discourse. She is like one of the items Quentin keeps packing in his bag; he tries to squeeze her subjectivity into the objective position required to "pack it away." Of course he fails. The constricted space cannot contain her or her voice. She speaks out of the deepest and darkest spaces of his unconscious, and her voice is a powerful challenge to despair.

With jarring force, her voice erupts from the darkness of Quentin's mind, as in his memory of the dungeon in a childhood book. In this intriguing and paradoxical bisexual space, "the dungeon," as Noel Polk has emphasized, is indeed "Mother herself."[33] Caroline Compson's lack of love has created the dark place from which Quentin cannot free himself. It is a dungeon *built by the mother* and it cannot be escaped, for it is the place of the unconscious where fear lives. It is not only threatening; it is terribly and tragically destructive. Yet the feminine differs from itself: the daughter differs from the mother. Within Quentin's memory rises the voice of Caddy who would become a man, a *king,* in order to *"break that place open and drag them out,"* so as to *"whip them good"* (215).

Within the male mind, then, we see maternal space both as dungeon, the place of castration and anxiety, and as the avenue of escape from it. This is surely the "in-between" of Cixous's theoretical imagination, and one of multiple levels and voices. Within Faulkner's male creative consciousness and its multiple subjectivities we find another male creative consciousness and *its* multiple subjectivities, who are *female* and *both* inhibiting (mother) and freeing (Caddy), and moreover in conflict over the status of the male unconscious and so constituting its difference within.

The Caddy of Jason's section continues to speak the language of difference. Filtered through the alembic of Jason's obsessive ("Once a bitch always a bitch") insistence upon male authority, her voice speaks the tragic results of the cultural objectification of the female subject and the disastrous effects of a system of barter that makes women commodities. Because she is both a sign, a commodity, and a speaker of signs, an exchanger, she cannot negotiate in Jason's phallocentric economy. She cannot get what she wants, nor can she return to being the valuable commodity, a virgin, that she once was. She is therefore doubly trapped in male discourse. Hers is a voice to which feminist readers are particularly attuned, for it is the voice of female subjectivity struggling within a cultural text that seeks its silencing. It speaks out of a tight place and it speaks panic and sorrow and loss. "Oh God, oh God," it cries out (261). To listen is painful and terrible, for what we are hearing is the daughter of patriarchal culture speaking loss, speaking what it means to be denied subjectivity and access to one's own desire.

How do we continue to hear Caddy as she fades from our vision in "the moving wall of grey light," into such a yawning chasm of lostness that she seems actually to "disintegrate into minute and venomous particles, like dust . . . ?" (*the Sound,* 330). Neither Dilsey who endures nor Quentin who escapes can "say" the Caddy whose plurivocity is the difference that female subjectivity and the force of woman create within Faulkner's text. Yet, as

Matthews so persuasively reminds us, *The Sound and the Fury* is about the intimate and mysterious relation between loss and articulation.[34]

Might we ourselves, then, create Caddy through the "grey light" of our own loss of her as the book draws to a close? Might her voice have moved from the space within her brothers' male discourse to another more nebulous (but still bisexual) space between literary text and feminist reader? *For I can still hear Caddy Compson.* She is the voice of alterity to the long list of failed men of Faulkner's Appendix. She speaks in the voice of Melissa Meek who, "trembling and aghast at her own temerity," bursts into Jason's thriving masculine domain and forces him to look upon the face of the woman whose life he negotiated as loss to attain it. If we read the Appendix as this space between text and reader, Caddy still may be heard as the disruptive feminine voice that seeks to give and save and love, and thus speaks the text's difference from itself. Whatever else *The Sound and the Fury* may be and do, surely it leaves us in the space of difference. When we permit ourselves to hear Caddy's voice as it creates this difference, we allow ourselves to enter that opening in the text that Faulkner disappears into, but leaves Caddy's voice to guide us toward.

We may begin conversing similarly with other of Faulkner's female characters—for example, with Rosa Coldfield and Charlotte Rittenmeyer, as feminine texts whose presence creates bisexual spaces in Faulkner's writing. In *Absalom, Absalom!* and *The Wild Palms* these are spaces in which difference mysteriously generates unexpected stories that allow narrative to speak against itself and so to attain a power and tension that it would not have reached otherwise. Rosa Coldfield's telling and retelling of the Sutpen story becomes in the Foucaultian progression of desire, repression, and discourse a cultural necessity—"something akin to a secret whose discovery is imperative, a thing abusively reduced to silence, and at the same time difficult and necessary, dangerous and precious to divulge."[35] This is the sense of things we have from Rosa: that what she thinks she knows, or desires to know, is indeed both dangerous and precious. She is the hysterical woman who reads the inexplicable repressiveness of masculinist ideology articulated in the shared cultural narratives of Thomas Sutpen, Mr. Compson, Quentin, and Shreve. Together these patriarchal narratives, with their culminative authority, devalue woman and silence women who, like Rosa, speak difference from the position of subject.

The men of *Absalom, Absalom!* eventually shut Rosa Coldfield up because they cannot stand the sound of her voice, which so shrilly, insistently tells the story of their own cultural madness. Even silenced, she becomes the uncanny feminine sign of what must be repressed by such a culture in order for it to function. Yet, at the same time, Rosa's creativity, her narrative desire to tell what she has lost, can be linked to the narrative process of *Absalom* itself—its refusal to end, its gaps and ruptures, its own sense of loss.

If we converse with Rosa, we must converse with the ambiguity and anguish of her creativity. She knows the power of the flesh but she must repress her own desire and render it into talk, for her desire to enter the sexual world of *"living marriage"* is always prohibited in a culture that denies white female sexuality, and it is transformed into what Cixous has called the initial act of female creativity: Rosa "unthinks the unifying, regulating history that homogenizes and channels forces."[36] Matthews points out that Rosa must continually defer her desires and thus speaks the loss she feels.[37] I would go on to say that, as a female subject striving to speak her desire in a milieu that denies its existence, Rosa both disrupts and re-creates the racist and sexist culture in which she exists. She creates, for example, the disturbing and terrifying memory of herself and Clytie on the stairs of Sutpen's Hundred; yet she destroys the human recognition she receives in that encounter with her denial of female connection (*"Take your hand off me, nigger!"*).[38] She knows the power of the flesh but she must repress her own desire and render it into discourse. She speaks her loss from a feminine space that disrupts patriarchal culture, yet she cannot help but speak her culture as well, with its complex and pain-filled polyphonies of racial and sexual repressiveness.

Rosa Coldfield thus speaks difference in two senses. She herself is the feminine text of difference within patriarchal culture—that which it must deny in order to maintain its systems—*at the same time* her actions cement patriarchy's fixity and rigidity. Her voice conveys her difference from the father, but it also reveals that she is still his daughter. She is trapped in history. Her feminine voice is that of the hysteric, described by Catherine Clément as one "whose body is transformed into a theater for forgotten scenes, [and who] relives the past, bearing witness to a lost childhood that survives in suffering." For Rosa, as for the hysteric, "this is history that is not over";[39] nor, as Faulkner tells us through the text that is Rosa, will it ever be. "Was" can never be "was," and cultural narratives continue to imprint themselves even upon their own deconstructors. Faulkner creates Rosa Coldfield, and himself, as makers of differences, but also as those who are ever in the process of being bound by their culture even as they are eluding it.

Charlotte Rittenmeyer extends the discourse of love beyond cultural codes, creating it as a living thing that is itself an ongoing process of deconstruction and regeneration. Love does not fail, she tells Harry; it is people who fail. In its very excessiveness, in its tendency to "flood" over cultural boundaries the same way the Mississippi River floods the landscape in "Old Man," Charlotte's desire problematizes the binary structure of *The Wild Palms* by mediating the very motion of difference in this watery bloody book. Her feminine "flooding" leads us into the bisexual spaces, the fluid fluctuations, in Faulkner's writing that allow us a way of reading (and thinking) outside binary opposition, a means of dissolving either/or, male/female, active/passive systems. Her desire speaks the difference within this binary narrative, the possibility of *something else.* Such a possibility implies a connection between woman as a desiring subject and the ways in which Faulkner's art floods beyond its own self-constructed levees.

As Faulkner creates female creativity, then, and compels female subjects to "unthink" the world, we feel his participation in their creative processes. As writing subject, (s)he disappears into the text's bisexual opening between male author and the feminine of his own imagination. When this happens, Faulkner the writing subject is able to become father and daughter of his own text. Faulkner's style and meaning, his narrative desire, become immersed in these female subjects, who(m) he himself has made yet also *is.* Gayatri Spivak's tracing of the position of woman in Derrida's schema seems to articulate the meaning of this immersion: as the image of "originary undecidability," woman can "occupy both positions in the subject/object oscillation."[40] Female characters in Faulkner's texts may be both subject and object in the sense that he creates them, yet in a mysterious way also permits his own subjectivity to become entangled with theirs. They and he are neither daughter nor father, but *both* together, at once.

If we think of the process of the feminine as the space of disruption in these and other of Faulkner's texts, as their difference within, and the female subject, the *woman character,* as the discursiveness of that space, as the rebellious unconscious of patriarchy, then we may begin to reread the father-author within those bisexual spaces of his own creation. And within the synergy between feminist reader and male text, we may find Faulkner in the unexpected "in-between" as he becomes both father and daughter of his own text, as he creates *and participates in the* daughter's own tracings of paternal

absence, her female subjectivity and her narrative desire, *her* creative negoti-
ations of the spaces left by the father.

NOTES

I wish to thank Beth Kowaleski-Wallace and Patricia Yaeger for their many important contributions
to the development of this essay.

1. Barbara Johnson, *The Critical Difference: Essays in the Contemporary Rhetoric of Reading*
   (Baltimore: Johns Hopkins University Press, 1980), 4.

2. Luce Irigaray, *This Sex Which Is Not One*, trans. Gillian C. Gill (Ithaca: Cornell University Press,
   1985), 31. In "The Laugh of the Medusa" Hélène Cixous argues that, "far more extensively
   and repressively than is ever suspected or admitted," writing is generated by a libidinal and
   cultural economy which is marked as masculine and which, because of exaggeration and
   oppositional thinking, often has become "a locus where the repression of women has been
   perpetuated" (249). The idea of excessiveness and expansiveness being marked as feminine
   pervades the thinking of Cixous, Irigaray, and Julia Kristeva, influenced as they are by psychoanalytic theory. Woman nourishes life, Cixous writes; she gives without measuring how
   much; she creates "an 'economy' that can no longer be put in economic terms" ("Laugh of
   the Medusa," 264). Likewise, Irigaray argues that woman's libidinal plurality creates a feminine discourse of desire that replenishes itself, that is "always something more" (*This Sex*, 29).
   And similarly, Kristeva writes that it is probably necessary to be a woman to push theoretical
   reason beyond its limits and thus to create a linguistics of "heterogenous economy," which is
   capable of "accounting for the nonetheless articulated *instinctual drive*, across and through the
   constitutive and insurmountable frontier of *meaning*" (*Desire in Language*, 146). (See subsequent notes for full citations.)

3. See, for example, *Faulkner in the University*, ed. Frederick L. Gwynn and Joseph L. Blotner
   (Charlottesville: University of Virginia Press, 1959), 4–5, 77–78, and *Faulkner at West Point*, ed.
   Joseph L. Fant III and Robert Ashley (New York: Random House, 1964), 48–49.

4. John T. Matthews, *The Play of Faulkner's Language* (Ithaca: Cornell University Press, 1982),
   20–21. In *Faulkner's Rhetoric of Loss* (Austin: University of Texas Press, 1983), Gail Mortimer
   argues that Faulkner's protagonists respond to loss by erecting various kinds of defenses,
   which allow them to feel that they are exerting control upon "the dissolution that is the
   normal state of things" and that Faulkner's rhetorical strategies mirror the tensions between

control and lack of it (4–5). In this schema women represent a lack of control and a projection of male fear. They become "distorted or mythicized beings, the projection of a masculine consciousness at its most vulnerable" (122). To the contrary, I am suggesting that loss and desire are productive generators of the narrative process, which is itself linked to the feminine in Faulkner's texts.

5. Houston A. Baker, Jr., *Blues, Ideology, and Afro-American Literature: A Vernacular Theory* (Chicago: University of Chicago Press, 1984), 1.

6. Jacques Derrida, *Speech and Phenomena and Other Essays on Husserl's Theory of Signs,* trans. and "Introduction," David B. Allison, "Preface," Newton Garver (Evanston: Northwestern University Press, 1973), 152.

7. Julia Kristeva, *Desire in Language: A Semiotic Approach to Literature and Art,* ed. Leon S. Roudiez (New York: Columbia University Press, 1980), 120.

8. Elaine Showalter, "Feminist Criticism in the Wilderness," *Critical Inquiry* 8 (winter 1981): 195. This essay has been reprinted in Showalter, ed., *The New Feminist Criticism: Essays on Women, Literature, and Theory* (New York: Pantheon, 1985), 243–70; and Elizabeth Abel, ed., *Writing and Sexual Difference* (Chicago: University of Chicago Press, 1982), 9–36.

9. See, in particular, Gallop's *Feminism and Psychoanalysis: The Daughter's Seduction* (Ithaca: Cornell University Press, 1982) and *Reading Lacan* (Ithaca: Cornell University Press, 1985); Irigaray's *This Sex Which Is Not One,* previously cited; and *Speculum of the Other Woman,* trans. Gillian C. Gill (Ithaca: Cornell University Press, 1985).

10. Alice Jardine, *Gynesis: Configurations of Woman and Modernity* (Ithaca: Cornell University Press, 1985), 183.

11. I should add that Cixous's "bisexuality" differs from androgyny, defined by Carolyn Heilbrun as that which "suggests a spirit of reconciliation between the sexes." See *Toward a Recognition of Androgyny* (New York: Knopf, 1964), x.

12. Hélène Cixous, "The Laugh of the Medusa," in *New French Feminisms: An Anthology,* ed. Elaine Marks and Isabelle de Courtivron (Amherst: University of Massachusetts Press, 1980), 254.

13. Cixous, "The Laugh of the Medusa," 254.

14. Like Judith Fetterley, who positions herself as a "resisting reader" of some male texts, Schweickart argues that the woman reader must struggle against the text for mastery: "Taking control of the reading experience means reading the text as it was *not* meant to be read, in fact, reading it against itself" (50). See Fetterley, *The Resisting Reader: A Feminist Approach to American Literature* (Bloomington: Indiana University Press, 1977); and Schweickart, "Reading Ourselves: Toward a Feminist Theory of Reading," in *Gender and Reading: Essays on Readers, Texts, and Contexts,* ed. Elizabeth A. Flynn and Schweickart (Baltimore: Johns Hopkins University Press, 1986), 31–62.

15. Cixous, "The Character of 'Character,'" *New Literary History* 5 (1974): 387.

16. Michel Foucault, *Language, Counter-Memory, Practice,* ed. Donald F. Bouchard and Sherry Simon (Ithaca: Cornell University Press, 1977), 116, 121.

17. Robert Con Davis, "Critical Introduction: The Discourse of the Father," in *The Fictional Father: Lacanian Readings of the Text,* ed. Davis (Amherst: University of Massachusetts Press, 1981), 2.

18. André Bleikasten, "Fathers in Faulkner," in *The Fictional Father,* 144–45. In the same volume Thomas A. Hanzo seems to be saying the same thing about narrative in general and Dickens in particular when he argues that, just as the Lacanian term "phallus" produces meaning, so "it is the principle of paternity that may be said to govern narraive, as well as other modes of the generation of meaning" ("Paternity and the Subject in *Bleak House,*" 47).

19. Jardine, *Gynesis,* 42.

20. See, for example, Sally Page, *Faulkner's Women: Characterization and Meaning* (Deland, Fla.: Everett/Edward, 1972), 16, and Cleanth Brooks, "Faulkner's Vision of Good and Evil," *Massachusetts Review* 3 (summer 1962): 697. In an analysis of *Absalom, Absalom!* Thomas Lorch carries this androcentric model to the extreme by arguing that the novel "presents male aspiration and will and the passive, enduring, absorbent Female in more closely balanced conflict than we find in Faulkner's other novels." Thomas Sutpen is Faulkner's most powerful male figure, Lorch finds, but his destruction is wrought by society and women, who "absorb and stifle his creative spark." "Female nature" in Faulkner's fiction is "necessary and good," but only "because it provides the living material for the male to shape and elevate." See "Thomas Sutpen and the Female Principle," *Mississippi Quarterly* 20 (winter 1967): 38–41.

21. Derrida, "Implications: Interview with Henri Ronse," in *Positions,* trans. Alan Bass (Chicago: University of Chicago Press, 1982), 14. Matthews has applied the Derridean model in his previously cited and illuminating study of the structures of Faulkner's language and argues that the language of the narratives "produces meaning from *difference*" and hence "meaning arises from the lack of authoritative, unique, absolute, or central significance" rather than from any sense of conclusiveness or closure (*The Play of Faulkner's Language,* 31).

22. Michel Foucault, *The History of Sexuality,* trans. Robert Hurley (New York: Vintage, 1980), 1:34.

23. Faulkner, *As I Lay Dying* (New York: Vintage, 1964), 167.

24. Cixous, "Sorties," in *The Newly Born Woman,* eds. Catherine Clément and Cixous, trans. Betsy Wing, "Foreword," Sandra M. Gilbert, Theory and History of Literature Series, vol. 24 (Minneapolis: University of Minnesota Press, 1986), 92. Also in "Laugh of the Medusa" Cixous posits the concept *l'écriture féminine,* the writing of the female body, so as to transcend a masculine libidinal economy that lies at the heart of Western thought and literary practice. As Ann Rosalind Jones points out in her essay "Writing the Body: Toward an Understanding of *l'écriture féminine,*" Irigaray and Kristeva share Cixous's opposition of women's bodily experience "to the phallic-symbolic patterns embedded in Western thought." The immediacy of that experience "Promises a clarity of perception and a vitality that can bring down mountains of

phallocentric delusion. Finally, to the extent that the female body is seen as a direct source of female writing, a powerful alternative discourse seems possible: to write from the body is to re-create the world" (366). See Jones's essay in *The New Feminist Criticism*, 361–77. *L'écriture féminine* may indeed be seen as a response to the question posed by Sandra M. Gilbert and Susan Gubar in *The Madwoman in the Attic* (New Haven: Yale University Press, 1979): "If the pen is a metaphorical penis, from what organ can females generate texts?" (7). In *Of Woman Born* (New York: Norton, 1977), however, Adrienne Rich, like the French feminists, envisions woman's writing of the body in more general terms, as touching "the unity and resonance of our physicality, the corporeal ground of our intelligence" (62). See Showalter, "Feminist Criticism in the Wilderness," and Jones for assessments of what they perceive as theoretical problems in the concept of *l'écriture féminine*.

25. William Faulkner, *Light in August* (New York: Modern Library, 1967), 244–45.

26. Bleikasten, *The Most Splendid Failure: Faulkner's* The Sound and the Fury (Bloomington: Indiana University Press, 1976), 65.

27. I am using Robert Con Davis's terms to describe Lacan's model of narrative as a split process that "never reaches a point of stability or wholeness" and therefore "poses a serious threat to the empirically based tradition of interpretation as a transparent and focusable lens, an open subjectivity, through which a detached investigator peers into a stable (possibly pictographic) narrative structure." See 'introduction," in *Lacan and Narration; The Psychoanalytic Difference in Narrative Theory,* ed. Davis (Amherst: University of Massachusetts Press, 1982), 857.

28. Kristeva, *Desire in Language,* 15.

29. Faulkner, *The Sound and the Fury* (New York: Vintage, 1963), 50. Subsequent references will be cited in the text.

30. In his influential essay "Time in Faulkner: *The Sound and the Fury,"* Jean-Paul Sartre says that the true subject of the novel is the human dilemma of being placed in time. See *William Faulkner: Two Decades of Criticism,* ed. Frederick J. Hoffman and Olga W. Vickery (East Lansing: Michigan State University Press, 1954), 180–88. Douglas Messerli focuses upon Caddy as "the *character* of time" (3), and finds that "in her pure dynamism, in pure becoming is life itself without human order" (41). Messerli's essay provides a summary of other thinking on the subject of time in the novel. See "The Problem of Time in *The Sound and the Fury:* A Critical Reassessment and Reinterpretation," *Southern Literary Journal* 6 (spring 1974): 19–41.

31. More optimistically, Matthews finds that loss opens the way to "the fun of writing" and its continual deferment, its "play of failures" (*The Play of Faulkner's Language,* 73).

32. Derrida, *Writing and Difference,* trans. Alan Bass (Chicago: University of Chicago Press, 1978), 28.

33. Noel Polk, in his essay by the same name, points out that the image of Caroline Compson as a jailer is reinforced by her carrying of the keys to the house. Her whining and general repres-

siveness make "of the house itself a prison, the grounds a fenced compound." See "The Dungeon Was Mother Herself," in *New Directions in Faulkner Studies,* ed. Doreen Fowler and Ann J. Abadie (Jackson: University of Mississippi Press), 62.

34. Matthews, *The Play of Faulkner's Language,* 65.

35. Foucault, *The History of Sexuality,* 1:35.

36. Cixous, "The Laugh of the Medusa," 252.

37. Matthews, *The Play of Faulkner's Language,* 124.

38. Faulkner, *Absalom, Absalom!* (New York: Modern Library, 1966), 140.

39. Clément, "Sorceress and Hysteric," in *The Newly Born Woman,* 5–6.

40. Gayatri Spivak, "Love Me, Love My Ombre, Elle," *Diacritics* (winter 1984): 24.

Faulkner and the Politics of Incest

KARL ZENDER

What does incest mean in William Faulkner's fiction? If we ask this question of many of Faulkner's other themes and motifs—of race, gender, region, or history—the answers given today differ from those given twenty or thirty years ago. With some significant exceptions—Eric Sundquist's *Faulkner: The House Divided*, Richard King's *A Southern Renaissance*[1]—this is not true of incest. For most commentators, incest in Faulkner's fiction means today what it has always meant—something religious and something oedipal. In the words of Cleanth Brooks, the most persuasive exponent of the religious interpretation, Quentin Compson's obsession with incest in *The Sound and the Fury* expresses "alarm at the breakdown of sexual morality" by attempting to define a "point beyond which surely no one would venture to transgress." For John T. Irwin, the reigning psychoanalytic interpreter of the motif, incest joins with doubling, repetition, and revenge to enact a doomed

Reprinted with permission from *American Literature* 70, no. 4 (1998): 739–65.

oedipal struggle against the priority of the father over the son and of the past over the present and the future. In its fullest extension, it expresses "the inability of the ego to break out of the circle of the self and of the individual to break out of the ring of the family," and it becomes a symbol "of the state of the South after the Civil War, . . . of a region turned in upon itself."[2]

Few would dispute the explanatory power of these approaches to the incest motif. But each also displays a "tyrannizing unity," to borrow a phrase David Wyatt applied to Irwin's *Doubling and Incest* some years ago.[3] Rather than seeing Faulkner's use of the motif as evolving as his career advances, both interpretations assume the existence of a single, global meaning, repetitively enacted. Whether the characters involved in the act or fantasy of incest are Josh and Patricia Robyn, Horace and Narcissa Benbow, Quentin and Caddy Compson, Charles Bon and Judith Sutpen, or the various members of the McCaslin and Beauchamp families, its meaning remains essentially unchanged. Similarly, the complex equivocality of incest as a literary and historical phenomenon is compressed by these interpretations into a single procrustean shape. Marc Shell begins a provocative recent interpretation of the incest motif in Shakespeare's *Measure for Measure* by speaking of incest as located at either "the perverse periphery or . . . the holy center of human life."[4] But this sense of doubleness, of incest as a site of fascination as well as of taboo, is largely absent in interpretations of the motif in Faulkner's fiction. Very early in his career, Faulkner is reported to have said that incest was not the crime it was thought to be.[5] How he could make this statement, and what he might have meant by it, the current interpretations of his depictions of incest do not purport to explain.

• • •

An alternative to the prevailing approaches is to explore the developmental logic underlying Faulkner's uses of the incest motif, seeking to attach this logic to the larger history of incest as trope, fantasy, and fact. A fruitful place to begin such an attempt, as so often in the study of Faulkner, is with his romantic forebears. Exploring depictions of incest among the romantic poets—particularly those in Shelley's poetry—reveals the importance of a distinction, frequently occluded in discussions of the motif, between parent-child and sibling incest. For Irwin, as for Otto Rank, the leading psychoanalytic explorer of the incest motif, attending to this distinction is unnecessary because, in

Irwin's words, "brother-sister incest is a substitute for child-parent incest—what the brother [that is Quentin] seeks in his sister is his mother" (43); or, as Rank phrases the matter, "one's relationship with siblings is revealed by psychoanalytical research to be a 'second edition,' less intense but unchanged in content, of the etiologically earlier relationship with one's parents." [6]

This line of interpretation is entirely consistent with the essentializing and universalizing logic of classical Freudian theory, in which the Oedipus complex governs all later stages of (male) psychosexual development. But as many recent commentators have argued, it has the unfortunate effect of depoliticizing psychological development by treating the oedipal triangle as an exclusively biological, rather than a cultural, formation.[7] On the subject of his desire to treat the oedipal triangle in this way, Rank is explicit and unapologetic. Observing the frequent concern with issues of "inheritance and succession" in romantic works focusing on parent-child incest, he says that "the revolutionary side of hostility toward the father . . . is revealed by psychoanalysis to be a displacement from the sexual sphere to a less objectionable social or political sphere" (63). Speaking directly of Shelley, he rejects interpretations that "derive Shelley's undeniable opposition to parental authority from a striving for freedom and a need for independence," arguing that etiologically "these traits developed in precisely the opposite sequence. Opposition to the father, which emerged in childhood, was later extended to opposition to all authority" (447).

If we reactivate the distinction occluded by Rank and Irwin, however, a contrary observation immediately suggests itself: among the romantic poets, parent-child and sibling incest are assigned directly opposite moral valences. As Peter Thorslev says in an important study of romantic representations of incest,"[p]arent-child incest is universally condemned in Romantic literature . . . ; sibling incest, on the other hand, is invariably made sympathetic, is sometimes exonerated, and, in Byron's and Shelley's works, is definitely idealized."[8] This contrast between negatively and positively valued images of incest suggests, contra Rank, that whatever reasons for interest in the motif might exist within a romantic poet's psyche, the political meanings assigned to it were consciously and deliberately chosen.

The nature of these meanings has been adumbrated by Thorslev and, more extensively, by Shell. In *The End of Kinship,* his study of incest in *Measure for Measure,* Shell argues that throughout post-classical Western history the Christian cloistered orders embodied an ideal of egalitarian "universal siblinghood," as opposed to the hierarchical and patriarchal structures of episcopal and secular authority; and he argues also that this opposition was expressed metaphorically as a contrast between sibling incest on the one hand and parent-child (specifically father-daughter) incest on the other. In the romantic era, Shell argues further, the ideal of universal siblinghood reconstituted itself in secular terms as the revolutionary ideal of fraternity. As this change occurred, images of father-daughter incest came to be used to express the tyrannical power of the ancient regime, while images of brother-sister incest shadowed forth the new, "fatherless," egalitarian social order that the French and American revolutions were struggling to articulate.

This argument is entirely consistent with the moral and political valuation placed on imagined acts of incest by Shelley and, in a less theoretically explicit way, by Byron. In *The Cenci* and "Laon and Cyntha" (the original, unexpurgated form of "The Revolt of Islam"), Shelley explores both the negative and the positive possibilities. In Count Francesco Cenci's forced incestuous coupling with his daughter Beatrice, Shelley depicts, as Earl Wasserman says, "not only a domestic but a political and religious tyranny as well, the three modes being implicated in each other."[9] Envisioning the God to which Cenci prays a Blakean "Nobodaddy" and the pope whose protection he buys as a corrupt "holy father," Shelley uses father-daughter incest as a comprehensive metaphor for political and religious despotism.

In the earlier, optimistic "Laon and Cythna," Shelley depicts brother-sister incest as a metaphor for human perfectibility. Viewing the incest taboo as an example of "those outworn opinions on which established institutions depend," Shelly envisions its defiance as a way of struggling against "the Anarch Custom's reign." [S]uch is Nature's modesty," he says,

> that those
> Who grow together cannot choose but love,
> If faith or custom do not interpose.
> But because "faith" and "custom" do interpose,
> Children near their parents tremble now
> . . . —one rules another,
> For it is said God rules both high and low.

Combining this belief with an ardently held (if by now somewhat old-fashioned) feminism, Shelley presents brother-sister incest as the ultimate form of egalitarian sexual relations, in which "free and equal man and woman greet / Domestic peace." And projecting the relationship along a historical axis, he presents Laon and Cyntha's union as a trope for the way history will ultimately overcome the setback dealt to the struggle for liberty by the Reign of Terror and the ascendancy of Napoleon Bonaparte. Beginning with a narrator filled with "visions of despair" because "the last hope of trampled France had failed," Shelley arrives finally at a vision of egalitarian incestuous love, reborn in

> a People mighty in its youth,
> A land beyond the Oceans of the West.
>
> . . . .
>
> Nay, start not at the name—America!"[10]

In his early, extensive, and widely documented reading of Shelley, Faulkner would have had access to a more various understanding of the incest metaphor than the ones advanced in most current readings of his fiction.[11] He also could have arrived at such an understanding from within the intellectual and political culture of his own age. It is no exaggeration to say that much left-leaning intellectual and political activity during the 1920s and 1930s was devoted to attempts to literalize romantic metaphors. Certainly this is true of the controversy about incest, and about sexual politics generally, during the modernist era. As Paul Robinson says in *The Freudian Left,* a study of the political implications of the psychoanalytic movement, almost from its outset commentators on psychoanalysis asked whether it implied "a revolutionary or a reactionary attitude toward the human situation. . . . Was Freud truly the apologist of sexual and political repression [they asked] . . . or did his new science contain . . . the promise of gratification, liberty, and peace?" The majority sentiment, as Robinson says, was that "Freud's great enterprise implied instinctual renunciation and political reaction."[12]

But two minority parties, one radical, the other liberal, resisted this conclusion. The radical party consisted of a loose congeries of psychoanalysts and philosophers (for example, Wilhelm Reich and Herbert Marcuse), surrealist litterateurs, and advocates of various forms of sexual liberation. The liberal party consisted of the group of second-generation Freudian theorists and therapists known as the Neo-Freudian Revisionists, whose members included Erich Fromm, Karen Horney, Erik Erikson, and (by the 1930s) Otto Rank.

Both parties extended, although in different ways, the romantic questioning of the incest taboo. For René Guyon, whose *Ethics of Sexual Acts* is a fascinating compendium of the radical sexual thought of the 1920s and 1930s, all forms of the incest taboo are merely conventional. Because "[a] weakening in the moral and social condemnation of incest. . . . usually accompanies the growth of a general tendency to call into question the taboo on sex," he says, "in time the community itself will cease to be interested in this out-of-date taboo."[13] Within the liberal faction, by contrast, no call for a literal abandonment of the taboo exists; but an ameliorative romantic optimism nonetheless reveals itself in the tendency of the Neo-Freudians to view sibling incest fantasy and play as simply a normal and expected stage of adolescent sexual development, fated to be outgrown and therefore not requiring severe cultural or parental disapprobation.

Any writer attuned (as Faulkner was) to the main currents of modernist thought would surely have been aware of these contemporary variations on romantic views about incest. But a further factor, deriving from Faulkner's identity as a Southerner, complicated enormously his relation to both the romantic and the modernist interpretations of the motif. In 1933, speaking of the tendency of Southern writers either to frame "a savage indictment of the contemporary scene" or to "escape . . . into a makebelieve region of swords and magnolias and mockingbirds," Faulkner said that "perhaps the ones who write savagely and bitterly of the incest in clay-floored cabins are the most sentimental."[14] This comment uses an image of rural lower-class incest to express an attitude toward the South familiar to anyone living in America in the twentieth century—an attitude Faulkner later caustically described as "a volitionless, almost helpless capacity and eagerness [on the part of Northerners] to believe anything about the South not even provided it be derogatory but merely bizarre enough and strange enough."[15]

The existence of this attitude among Northerners in the first third of the twentieth century can be verified by even cursory reading in the period's literature of social reform, particularly in works reflecting the assumptions of the then-popular eugenics movement. Untroubled by romantic and progressivist interpretations of incest as a social convention fated to wither away, writers supporting this movement depict incest as the most striking of a variety of threats to the maintenance of a healthy American gene pool posed by lower-class rural immorality. In depictions of "the degenerate hillbilly family, dwelling in filthy shacks and spawning endless generations of paupers, criminals, and imbeciles," as Nicole Hahn Rafter says, these writers create a lurid argument in support of programs for sterilization or long-term incarceration of the genetically "unfit." And while their studies focus on Northern as well as Southern instances of inbreeding and hereditary degeneracy, they are particularly vehement in their depictions of the Southern instances—presumably because in the South the possibility of inbreeding combined with the possibility of miscegenation to compound the geneticists' fears of a lower-class assault on American racial integrity.[16]

Faulkner's regional pride is nowhere more evident than in his rejection of the clay-floored-cabin image of rural Southern incest. Although his depictions of incest become increasingly politically inflected as his career advances (as I will argue), he never avails himself of the "sentimental" view of poorwhite or lower-class black incest as a condition to be pitied or corrected. But the image nonetheless possessed a controlling and complicating power relative to the depictions he did choose to present; it is the tacit counterimage that his (invariably) aristocratic images of Southern incest attempt to deny. Like the hound that fails to bark in Conan Doyle's short story, Faulkner's refusal to depict incest as it was most commonly believed to exist in the South—as it is depicted in Erskine Caldwell's *God's Little Acre,* for example— is an absence that carries profound meaning.

Equally important, Faulkner's regional pride denied him direct access to the progressivist interpretations outlined above; for to accept those views without qualification would imply acceptance of a more general egalitarian (and anti-Southern) political and social agenda as well. This Faulkner was unwilling to do. Instead, by a logic resembling the one that permitted Southern apologists for slavery to speak of the Civil War as the "Second American Revolution," Faulkner began his career by standing the progressivist sexual views on their head; he used sibling incest (and other images of sexual transgression) as a trope in support of, rather than in rejection of, regionalism and political reaction. By a similar logic, he equivocated for a long time over what meaning to assign to images of father-daughter incest. Should such images express the threat posed by Southern patriarchal values to the progressivist dream of social and sexual liberation, as a Shelleyan and modernist logic would require? Or should they instead express the threat posed by Northern progress, liberalism, and egalitarianism to Southern conservatism and belief in the value of tradition?[17]

• • •

Once these various contexts have been brought to mind, the direction of
Faulkner's development relative to the incest motif becomes clear. It consists
of a movement away from Southern chauvinism and conservatism and
toward liberalism—toward, that is, a reactivation of a Shelleyan opposition
between father-daughter and brother-sister incest as political metaphors. But
this movement never reaches its implied goal: incest for Faulkner always
remains tragic, never becoming unambiguously a trope for psychic or social
liberation. What happens instead is a steady increase in the complexity of
Faulkner's treatment of the motif as his career advances—an increase in his
awareness that the causes (and costs) of sexual inhibition are social and historical as well as psychological. This line of development occurs in three
stages, the first consisting of the series of early depictions culminating in the
Quentin Compson section of *The Sound and the Fury*, the second of the linking of incest with race and history in *Absalom, Absalom!* and the third of the
politicized depictions of father-daughter and sibling incest in *Go Down, Moses*.

Faulkner's 1933 comment on the conflict between writing "a savage
indictment of the contemporary scene" and escaping into "a make-believe
region of swords and magnolias and mockingbirds" continues by saying, "I
seem to have tried both of the courses. I have tried to escape and I have tried
to indict. After five years I look back at *The Sound and the Fury* and see that
[that] was the turning point: in this book I did both at one time" ("Introduction," 72). This observation accurately describes the relation between
Faulkner's use of the incest motif in *The Sound and the Fury* and in the two
earlier novels, *Mosquitoes* and *Flags in the Dust*, in which it figures prominently. In *Mosquitoes*, the incestuous byplay between Patricia and Josh
Robyn—twins who call each other by the same nickname—is one of several
vehicles by which Faulkner "indicts" the "contemporary scene" of 1920s
"flaming youth" sexual and social rebelliousness. In *Flags in the Dust*, by contrast, Horace Benbow's quasi-incestuous apostrophes to his sister Narcissa as
a "still unravished bride of quietude [sic]" are the main means by which
Faulkner "escapes" a post–World War I "New South" characterized by mechanization and urbanization, sexually aggressive women, and Northern-
financed economic imperialism.[18]

If we ask how *The Sound and the Fury* does both at one time—how it combines the satire of *Mosquitoes* with the nostalgia of *Flags in the Dust*—a partial

answer is that Quentin Compson is Horace Benbow "placed," in the sense that Horace's nostalgia, endorsed by narrator and author alike in *Flags in the Dust,* is presented as Quentin's alone in the later novel. A fuller answer is that in *The Sound and the Fury* Faulkner begins to bring into visibility (and to subject to critical scrutiny) the reactionary implications of his earlier uses of the incest motif. Like Horace Benbow, Quentin Compson attempts to use fantasies of incest as a way of *not* experiencing life as subject to time and change and therefore inherently political. But Quentin's attempt to use incest in this way is shadowed (as Horace's is not) by an alternative interpretation, in which incestuous yearnings are associated less with resistance to time than with immersion in it.

This alternative interpretation has both a psychological and a cultural dimension. Clearly, Quentin wishes to understand his incest fantasies as asexual in origin and atemporal in effect. They are, he believes, a way of rescinding Caddy's sexual initiation—*"you thought it was them but it was me listen I fooled you all the time it was me"*—and, by extension, of denying the descent of the Compson family and of the South into the modern age.[19] But the second section of *The Sound and the Fury* exposes the futility of this attempt. As many commentators have noted, the section is organized as the slow uncovering of a denied self-understanding, in which meanings for Quentin's experiences contrary to the ones he consciously intends gradually emerge from beneath his evasions and rationalizations. His suicide, which he tries to think of as an act of courage, is revealed to be an act of despair; his apparent affection for his father is shown to mask deep anger and disappointment; his confrontation with Dalton Ames is shown to have ended in intense humiliation; and so forth.

The climactic event of this process is the long, uninterrupted memory sequence in which Quentin encounters Caddy at the branch on the evening of the day on which she loses her virginity. This encounter, centering on a sexually suggestive offer of double suicide—"yes the blades long enough"; "you'll have to push it harder"; "touch your hand to it" (152)—constitutes Quentin's closest approach to success in imposing on incest the meaning that he wishes it to possess, of defiance of time and change. But a second, less frequently noted scene immediately follows, in which Quentin literally attempts to force Caddy to engage in an act of incest. The existence of this second scene—and especially its location, just subsequent to the failed effort to link incest with death—suggests a desire not to arrest Caddy's development but to join her in it. The attempt occurs in the ditch where the bones of the dead horse Nancy molder; and the description of the setting and of the outcome of the attempt—"it was matted with vines and briers dark"; "the ditch narrowed closed she turned toward the trees" (153–54)—intimates a balked desire to encounter time and sexuality positively, to reach that moment of emotional transition in which male entry into the "dark ditch" of sexual maturation merges with acceptance of death and change.[20]

As with this reversal of the meaning Quentin attempts to ascribe to incest, so also with the cultural resonances surrounding the motif. Throughout his career, Faulkner depicts human growth as transgressive, as a process of breaking through psychic or social or ideological barriers. In *The Sound and the Fury* the sexual aspect of this process begins to align with other forms of transgression and therefore to call into question the Southern chauvinism of Faulkner's earlier novels. "[H]es crossed all the oceans all around the world" (150), Caddy says of Dalton Ames, a comment linking her sexual adventuring to a desire to break free of Southern insularity—a link also forged by her willingness to marry (albeit reluctantly) a Northern banker and to remain in the North after the marriage fails.

Similarly, Quentin discerns, even as he abhors, a connection between Caddy's sexual boldness and transgression of racial and class boundaries: "*Why must you do like nigger women do in the pasture the ditches the dark woods hot hidden furious*"; "*It's not for kissing I slapped you. . . . It's for letting it be some darn town squirt*" (92, 133–34). And in his encounter with the little Italian girl (whom he repeatedly calls "sister"), he discovers a parallel linkage inside himself. Interspersing comments about the little girl's status as an immigrant ("eyes like two currants. . . . Land of the kike home of the wop") with memories of *"dancing sitting down"* with a *"dirty girl"* and of jumping in the hog wallow with Caddy, he frames a disquieting but enticing association between sibling incest, racial and class transgression, physical filth, and cultural heterogeneity (125, 134–36).

• • •

In *The Sound and the Fury*, Faulkner begins to question his earlier single-minded association of incest with a backward-looking Southern chauvinism. But the intense subjectivity of the novel's narrative method so severely constricts its range of cultural reference as to cause this questioning to remain tentative and incomplete. As John T. Matthews says in a study of social and cultural "frames" in the novel, the "text behaves as if it has no context. . . . History makes itself felt [in *The Sound and the Fury]* by being forgotten, by making itself into a background blur."21 Faulkner's labor over the next dozen years—his labor in *Absalom, Absalom!* and *Go Down, Moses*—is to turn this background into foreground, to implicate the incest motif (and all other aspects of psychosexual development) in culture and history.

Nowhere is the evidence of this effort greater than in *Absalom, Absalom!* Critics who focus on the relation between *The Sound and the Fury* and *Absalom, Absalom!* tend to emphasize continuities rather than differences— an understandable choice, given their desire to explore, in Irwin's words, "[the] imaginative space that the novels create in between themselves by their interaction."22 But a moment's reflection shows that in *Absalom, Absalom!* Faulkner freely availed himself of his willingness to revise his fictional situations and characters as his understanding of them evolved.23 This willingness manifests itself most noticeably in the omission from the novel of every major character in *The Sound and the Fury* except Quentin, Mr. Compson, and Shreve MacKensie (here renamed "McCannon"), and in the thorough reimagining of the three characters who do reappear.

Mr. Compson as envisioned in *Absalom, Absalom!* is a far more powerful and physically dangerous figure than in the earlier novel. Depicted entirely without reference to either the alcoholism or the economic fecklessness of his former characterization, he advances his misogynistic, cynical, and pessimistic vision of life at a higher level of generality (and apparent plausibility) than in *The Sound and the Fury*. Little more than a failed father in the first novel, a source of his son's despair and of his family's decline, in *Absalom, Absalom!* he is both a parent and an embodiment of a pervasive and insidious cultural attitude. Similarly, Shreve McCannon gains symbolic amplitude in *Absalom, Absalom!* A half-caricatured "fat Canadian youth" (106) in *The Sound and the Fury*, a mirror image of Quentin's arrested development, in *Absalom, Absalom!* he is transformed—through his pipe smoking, his deep-breathing exercises, his blunt speech, and his physical virility—into a mature young man, an image of what Quentin might become, were his developmental impasse to be successfully resolved.

As for Quentin, the key elements of his reconceptualization appear at the outset of *Absalom, Absalom!* in the passage describing him as seeming "to listen to two separate Quentins now—the Quentin Compson preparing for

Harvard in the South, the deep South dead since 1865 and peopled with gar-
rulous outraged baffled ghosts . . . and the Quentin Compson who was still
too young to deserve yet to be a ghost but nevertheless having to be one for
all that.[24] Both halves of this characterization are new–the first because the
pervasiveness of Quentin's suicidal melancholy in *The Sound and the Fury*
allows him to view Harvard (and education in general) only as something to
resist, not as something to prepare for; the second because *Absalom, Absalom!*
radically reconstrues the causes of Quentin's "enghosting," replacing the earlier novel's emphasis on the traumas of family life with an emphasis on
region and history.

Central to this reconceptualization is a repudiation of the construction
Quentin had attempted to place on sibling incest in the earlier novel. The
stories that Quentin hears from Rosa Coldfield and from his father first com-
pel his attention when Rosa speaks of Henry Sutpen's murder of Charles Bon.
At this point, "Quentin was not listening, because there was also something
which he too could not pass" (139). What he cannot pass, he at first believes,
is a version of his own relation to Caddy (and to Dalton Ames and to Sidney
Herbert Head), carried through to the conclusion he had desired but was
unable to achieve, the one for which his incest fantasy was a symbolic substitute:

> *Now you cant marry him.*
> *Why cant I marry him?*
> *Because hes dead.*
> *Dead?*
> *Yes. I killed him.* (139–40)

In the second half of the novel, though, as Quentin and Shreve struggle
to create their own version of the Sutpen story, this *Sound-and-the-Fury*-like
understanding of the meaning of the murder of Charles Bon (and of sibling
incest) disappears. The story that Quentin and Shreve finally come to tell displaces sympathy from Henry, whose life *"sprang in quiet peace and contentment
and ran in steady even though monotonous sunlight"* to Charles Bon, whose life
"sprang in hatred and outrage and unforgiving and ran in shadow" (254), and
whose defining trait is his balked desire for acknowledgment by his father. As
this story emerges, the meaning of sibling incest reverses itself. The issue
ceases to be whether Henry will serve his father's interests by preventing

Charles from committing incest with Judith and becomes instead whether he will find some excuse—in the fact that "kings have done it! Even dukes!" (273)—for defying his father and aligning himself with his brother. Once he succeeds in doing so, in answering affirmatively Charles's "Do I have your permission [to marry Judith]?" (279, italics omitted), the issue alters still further, becoming an exploration of whether Henry can maintain this allegiance in the face of his father's revelation that Bon's mother was part black.[25]

As with Henry, so with Quentin. In the eighth chapter of the novel Faulkner repeatedly signals Quentin and Shreve's empathetic involvement in the story they create by variations on the phrase "not two of them but four" (236). At first the identifications expressed through these variations are aligned as *The Sound and the Fury* would predict, with Shreve paired with the "outlander" Charles and Quentin with the censorious and puritanical Henry: "now it was . . . four of them and then just two—Charles-Shreve and Quentin-Henry" (267). But as the novel advances, the pairings blur, until finally, at the climactic moment, "it was not even four now but compounded still further, since now both of them were Henry Sutpen and both of them were Bon, compounded each of both yet either neither" (280).

This blending together of the four characters occurs immediately after Henry has given Bon permission to marry Judith, suggesting that Quentin sees in Henry's act of permission an alternative to his own repudiation, in *The Sound and the Fury*, of his transgressive sexuality. It suggests that Quentin sees in Henry's allegiance to Bon a model for the integration of the consorting and desiring halves of his own personality, of his "daylight" and "shadow" selves.[26] But for Quentin, as for Henry, this integration can no longer remain confined within strictly psychological limits. Just as Thomas Sutpen's revelation of Bon's black ancestry raises the question of whether "it's the miscegenation, not the incest, which [Henry] can't bear" (285, italics omitted), so Quentin's encounter with the aged and dying Henry at Sutpen's Hundred raises the same question for himself. How far will his defiance of his backward-looking suicidal melancholy extend? Will it consist only of a private effort to free the fantasy of sibling incest from the regressive meaning assigned to it in *The Sound and the Fury?* Or will it expand outward, politically and socially, into an attempt to repudiate as well the taboo against miscegenation?

Versions of these questions have been explored in important and similar ways by Eric Sundquist and Richard King. For both, a central interpretative issue in *Absalom, Absalom!* is how incest relates to miscegenation and how both relate to Faulkner's understanding of Southern history. Sundquist and King both see incest and miscegenation as bearing intrinsically opposed symbolic meanings—meanings that reconfigure in the crucible of Southern history (and in *Absalom, Absalom!*) into a complex interdependence. In King's words: "The taboo against miscegenation . . . [is] the inverse of the incest taboo. This taboo provides the injunction to endogamy, the command to marry within one's group, in this case determined by the pseudo-biological categories of the two races. . . . the incest taboo forbids the identity relationship based upon repetition, while the prohibition of miscegenation forbids the relationship between the 'different.'"[27]

In its Southern context, this intrinsic symbolic opposition undergoes a complex alteration. Prior to the Civil War, Sundquist argues (following Joel Williamson), miscegenation received covert endorsement in the actions, if not in the public statements, of slaveowners. But this tacit approval disappeared at the time of the war, and especially at the time of the Emancipation Proclamation, which seemed to many Southerners to unleash—even to encourage—a specter of universal miscegenation." From the end of the Civil War onward, hysteria over miscegenation dominates Southern racial attitudes. This hysteria intersects with the incest motif in a double way. On the one hand, nostalgic incest fantasies of the sort found in Faulkner's early fiction are its logical outgrowth; they are an understandable if extreme response to its injunction to endogamy," its yearning for an (imaginary) pre-Civil War state of racial purity.

On the other hand, fear of miscegenation leads to a nightmarish further fear of an actual rise in the incidence of combined incest *and* miscegenation. It is worth reminding ourselves that the central fact of the Sutpen action of *Absalom, Absalom!* is the "hiddenness" of Charles Bon's familial and racial status; only because he is unacknowledged both as son and as mulatto can he very nearly enter into an incestuous and miscegenational relationship with Judith Sutpen. And this fictional circumstance reflects a social reality of the post-Civil War South, in which miscegenational family ties were often a known but unacknowledged fact. As Sundquist says, to a Southern imagination the emancipation of the slaves may be said "to have destroyed the mechanisms of control that were a barrier to incest and to have made possible, if not entirely likely, a further mixing, a 'monstrous' violation of blood in which, because both black and white strains could be hidden from view, miscegenation and incest could indeed occur at once."[28]

Viewed in these terms, the arc of Quentin's development, from nostalgic incest fantasies to acceptance of sibling incest to the possibility of acceptance of miscegenation, can be seen to entail a struggle against the entire weight of Southern history. Less evident, because more abstractly presented, is the way Faulkner links this development to the extreme tension between the political right and the political left in the mid-1930s, the time of the novel's creation. In an astute pair of Bakhtinian analyses, Stephen Ross explores the tendency of the various narrative voices of *Absalom, Absalom!* to collapse into a single "monological overvoice," which he identifies with the idea of fatherhood. This "overvoice," he argues, "creates tremendous *authority*, an implied and truth-uttering presence" in which "the word father means a principle of authority far greater than Mr. Compson."[29] Clearly, the most immediate referent for this "principle of authority" is the Southern patriarchal social order, as embodied in Thomas Sutpen's dynastic ambitions and Mr. Compson's efforts at narrative control. But another referent, pervasive at the time of the novel's composition, is European and American fascism, with its ubiquitous rhetoric of "fatherland" and "fatherhood."

Once this alternative referent for the novel's rhetoric of fatherhood has been summoned to mind, it is easy to identify a similar but opposed referent for the novel's fraternal rhetoric; for if right-wing political rhetoric in the 1930s was dominated by tropes of "fatherhood," left-wing political rhetoric was no less dominated by tropes of "brotherhood." In "Ad Astra," a story written around 1930, Faulkner reveals his awareness of these tropes and of their essential meanings. Central to the story is a young German baron's attempt to explain why he has rejected his title and inheritance. His father, the young baron says, "talks of Germany, the fatherland; I say to him, It iss there; so. You say fatherland; I, brotherland, I say, the word *father* iss that barbarism which will be first swept away; it iss the symbol of that hierarchy which hass stained the history of man with injustice of arbitrary instead of moral; force instead of love."[30]

In its furthest implication, Quentin and Shreve's retelling of the Sutpen story seeks to replace a rhetoric of the right with a rhetoric of the left. It seeks to substitute the word "brother," with its connotation of "love," for the word "father," with its connotation of "force." During the sixth and seventh chapters, when Quentin and Shreve retell the story in a fashion consistent with Mr. Compson's earlier narrative, Quentin says that Shreve *"sounds just like Father"* and that *"[m]aybe nothing ever happens once and is finished"* (147, 210). But when they turn in the eighth chapter to creating their own version of the story, one in which Shreve repeatedly says, "your old man was wrong" (275), a voice clearly distinguishable from Mr. Compson's emerges. In its "protective coloring of levity" (225), the voice is identifiably Shreve's. But as Quentin, Henry, and Charles blend and merge with Shreve, the voice becomes theirs as well. Ultimately, the voice aspires to more than this, for it seeks to become "the heart and blood of youth . . . [s]trong enough and willing enough for two, for two thousand, for all" (236). It seeks to express, as Shreve says of Charles Bon, a vision of human possibility in which the "ambiguous . . . dark fatherhead" could be "eluded" and "all boy flesh" could be "brothered perennial and ubiquitous everywhere under the sun" (240).[31]

• • •

The vision of universal brotherhood that Quentin and Shreve strive to create frees the incest motif from the merely private meaning that had dominated its appearances in Faulkner's earlier fiction. Beyond the struggle for sexual competence of *The Sound and the Fury,* yet implicit within it, lies the struggle for political competence of *Absalom, Absalom!* But the choice of Quentin Compson as the agent of this struggle predetermines its failure; however intensely Quentin may empathize with Charles Bon in his sexual and social rebellion, his own suicidal destiny is foreknown. Faulkner's purpose in *Absalom, Absalom!* then is not to state an opinion on the possibility (or impossibility) of maturation but to expand our awareness of the tragic consequences of its absence. In *Go Down, Moses,* in his last significant use of the incest motif, he extends this awareness further by linking the trope ever more explicitly to the Southern history of slavery and to America's political situation on the eve of World War II.

The distance Faulkner had traveled between his early understanding of the motif and *Go Down, Moses* can be measured by his innovations in its use in the later novel. In *Go Down, Moses,* for the first time in his fiction, Faulkner concerns himself with father-daughter as well as sibling incest, and with incest as an overt, not just an imagined, act. Also, he assigns political meanings to father-daughter and sibling incest, echoing the ones Shelley had used in *The Cenci* and "Laon and Cythna." He depicts L. Q. C. McCaslin's incestuous coupling with his daughter Tomasina as an act of sexual tyranny parallel in meaning to the curse of possession by which Southern plantation owners had imposed a structure of domination on an "earth" meant to be held "mutual and intact in the communal anonymity of brotherhood."[32] And in "Delta Autumn" he poises against this *Cenci*-like meaning a liberationist view similar to Shelley's in "Laon and Cythna" by depicting in the affair between Roth Edmonds and his black cousin an attenuated form of sibling incest, in which taboos of race, region, and class are defied (at least temporarily) in the service of egalitarian love.

Similarly innovative is Faulkner's treatment of his white male protagonist. It has long been recognized that Isaac McCaslin is a direct descendant of Quentin Compson—that in the short-story originals out of which *Go Down, Moses* was formed, Isaac's role is occupied by Quentin.[33] But in replacing Quentin with Isaac, Faulkner also re-envisioned him (yet again), this time as free of the psychosexual confusions that had dominated his earlier depictions. Fear of sexual incompetence is clearly not an issue for Ike, as the scene with his wife at the end of Section 4 of "The Bear" shows; and Ike's final celibacy, unlike Quentin's, results from moral choice, not pathology. Also, sibling incest loses its personal urgency in Ike's story. Displaced into a succeeding generation and an attenuated form, the motif loses the direct developmental significance it had possessed in *The Sound and the Fury,* displaying instead only a variation on the political meaning first elaborated in *Absalom, Absalom!*

But *plus ça change.* . . . As many commentators have argued, Isaac McCaslin enacts his own tragedy of failed maturation; for in relinquishing his inheritance from L. Q. C. McCaslin he chooses moral purity over political or social effectiveness.[34] In "Delta Autumn" this choice manifests itself in Ike's inability to accept the libertarian political implications of Roth Edmonds's love affair with a black woman. The phrase quoted above about an Edenic South held "mutual and intact in the communal anonymity of brotherhood" is Isaac's. He returns to the idea it expresses often, always as a fantasized alternative to the world of racial inequality and economic competition in which he actually lives. When he thinks of conversations in the hunting camp as "the best of all talking," for example, he describes them as egalitarian, the talk of men, "not white nor black nor red but men" (18384); and when he looks up at the commissary ledgers as a child, he imagines that they will tell a benign story of "the land which they had all held and used in common . . . without regard to color or titular ownership" (256).

Isaac's encounter with Roth Edmonds's lover at the end of "Delta Autumn" tests this dream of communal brotherhood in the real world. It offers Ike an image of egalitarian social relations not just as a fantasized alternative to life in time but as its goal. When he touches the nameless young woman's hand after learning that she is Tennie's Jim's granddaughter, he senses their kinship, feeling how "the strong old blood ran after its long lost journey back to home" (345). This journey back is more than just a rapprochement between the black and white descendants of L. Q. C. McCaslin, significant as this may be; implicit in it as well is a renewal of the Edenic promise of America, imagined as Shelley had imagined it at the end of "Laon and Cythna," as consisting of egalitarian sexual relations. Further, the touch broaches the possibility of an even more general bonding between the sexes; it is the first instance in Faulkner's contemplation of the incest motif in which the ideal of "brotherhood" broadens into the ideal of "siblinghood." Black, Northern, and well-educated, the young woman offers Ike—"Uncle Isaac," as she calls him—the possibility of kinship across the barriers of sexual and racial taboo and regional chauvinism.

Implicit in the touch as well are the specific political circumstances of America in the early 1940s, with World War II imminent and the Great Depression not yet over. At the outset of "Delta Autumn" these circumstances create in Roth a cynicism about America's future as a nation. What will America be like, he asks, '[a]fter Hitler gets through with it? Or Smith or Jones or Roosevelt or Willkie or whatever he will call himself in this country?" (322). And even if America does survive, he says, "what have you got left? . . . Half the people without jobs and half the factories closed by strikes. Half the people on public dole that wont work and half that couldn't work even if they would. . . . The country full of people to tell a man how he cant raise his own cotton whether he will or wont, and Sally Rand with a sergeant's stripes and not even the fan couldn't fill the army rolls" (322–23).

Ike seeks to counter this cynicism with a superficially attractive but ultimately troubling version of the dream of egalitarian communal anonymity. Elaborating on the metaphor of women and children as "does and fawns," he says that he hasn't "noticed this country being short of defenders yet, when it needed them," and that "[t]he only fighting anywhere that ever had anything of God's blessing on it has been when men fought to protect does and fawns" (322–23). And slightly later, when Roth claims that people are only good when "[a] man in a blue coat with a badge on it [is] watching them," Ike counters his comment with an Edenic image of human sexual union, envisioned as transgressive, saying that "every man and woman, at the instant when it dont even matter whether they marry or not, . . . at that instant the two of them together were God" (329, 332).

The contexts presented in this opening debate place an extreme weight of implication on Ike's reaction to the touch of the young woman's hand. Adding to this weight is the novel's concern with the disappearance of the Southern wilderness—a disappearance Faulkner attributed throughout his career to the South's status as an internal colony of the North. As early as *Flags in the Dust,* Faulkner had depicted the destruction of the forests of the Mississippi Delta by Northern-financed timber merchants, and he had linked an inability to oppose this process to fantasies of sibling incest. Obliged to leave Jefferson after marrying a divorcee, Horace Benbow relocates in Kinston, a logging town in the Delta "financed by eastern capital and operated by as plausible and affable a set of brigands as ever stole a county" (400). "A hardwood lumber concern had bought up the cypress swamps nearby," Faulkner says, with the result that "widows and orpahns [*sic*] in New York . . . were buying Stutz cars" and Mississippians were building "mile after mile of identical frame houses with garage to match" (400). Unable to endure this foreshadowing of his region's future, Horace retreats into nostalgia for his childhood home and into quasi-incestuous longing for his sister Narcissa. [35]

In "Delta Autumn" Ike McCaslin watches the end of the process whose beginning Horace had observed in *Flags in the Dust,* the "retreat year by year" of the wilderness "before the onslaught of axe and saw and log-lines and . . . dynamite and tractor plows" (337), and he reacts similarly, turning aside from the contemporary world into dreams of timelessness. But by the early 1940s the option of timelessness had lost the innocence it had possessed earlier in Faulkner's career. The polarity that had allowed Faulkner to pair sibling incest with Southern nostalgia and to oppose both the North and its values had dissolved under the double pressure of his own intellectual growth and of the urgencies faced by the nation as a whole. But the political choice that this pressure would seem to dictate, of left over right, liberalism over conservatism, nation over region, neither Ike nor Faulkner is ever completely willing to make.

What happens instead, for Ike at least, is a full-scale retreat into racial and sexual hysteria. When Roth identifies America's home-grown Hitler as "Smith or Jones or Roosevelt or Willkie," he levels the distinction between

left and right, depicting the Democratic and Republican presidential candi-
dates of 1940 as equally capable of tyranny. And when he complains about
the "public dole" and governmental controls on cotton farming, he rejects
the social and agricultural policies of the New Deal—a rejection that gains
particular salience when viewed in relation to the New Deal's 1933
Agricultural Adjustment Act, which caused a drastic decline in the amount of
cotton grown and produced fundamental and irreversible changes in the
Southern social and economic order by converting large numbers of black
(and white) tenant farmers into wage laborers. [36]

Ike's failure to respond to Roth in historically and politically specific
terms, his appeal instead to a sentimental populism in which women and
children are envisioned as does and fawns and men raise unbidden to the
defense of the nation, foreshadows his final rejection of Roth's lover. Appalled
by the injustice of the Southern social order, aware of changes wrought in
that order by the New Deal, grief-stricken by the disappearance of the unaxed
wilderness, and incapable of any longer aligning sexuality with nostalgia, he
yet cannot step across the gulf separating himself from the larger "kinship"
expressed in Roth's lover's touch. Declining that touch's implicit utopian
promise, he envisions miscegenational sexual relations nightmarishly, as
*"Chinese and African and Aryan and Jew, all breed[ing] and spawn[ing] together
until no man has time to say which one is which nor cares"* (347). *"Maybe in a
thousand or two thousand years in America,"* he says, in an inadvertent parody
of the liberal dream of progress, *"But not now! Not now!"* (344). [37]

•   •   •

Why the evolution of Faulkner's use of the incest motif stops with his depiction of Ike's hysteria—and, more generally, with the writing of *Go Down,
Moses*—is a question beyond the scope of this essay. But an approach to an
answer can be suggested if we consider for a moment directions taken by
thought about incest in recent years. The sexual radicalism of the 1920s and
1930s clearly still continues (even if often in appallingly debased forms),
with the emergence in the last twenty years of what Benjamin Demott has
called the "pro-incest lobby," whose members range from scholars investi-
gating sexual behavior to letter writers to men's magazines to (most recently)
anonymous fantasists on the Internet. [38] But the last twenty years have also
seen the emergence of a strong countervoice in the form of feminist critiques

of male-centered developmental scenarios. Ranging from objections to Freud's interpretation of childhood incest as female fantasy to confessional accounts of real-life experiences, this countervoice seeks to recenter the story of incest on the female rather than the male participant and to emphasize its costs over its putative benefits.[39].

A number of recent commentators—including John Duvall, Minrose Gwin, Richard Moreland, and Joseph Urgo—have sought to align Faulkner's fiction with this newly emergent voice. Richard Moreland argues, for example, that in extending imaginative sympathy to poor whites in *The Hamlet*, blacks in *Go Down, Moses,* and women in *Requiem for a Nun,* Faulkner anticipates a decentered postmodern politics of class, ethnic, and gender inclusiveness. [40] This is an attractive line of argument, if only because it encourages positive and generous readings of Faulkner's late fiction. But it has largely left unexamined the question of what model for psychic development is to replace the male-centered oedipal model that Faulkner so exhaustively explores. And it verges at times on special pleading as it seeks to discover a postmodern politics in what Minrose Gwin has rightly described, quoting Teresa De Lauretis, as "the chinks and cracks of masculinity, the figures of male identity or the repressed of phallic discourse." [41]

A tragedy at the heart of Faulkner's fiction—at the heart, one is tempted to say, of his anger—is the suspicion that all (male) development is a form of psychic imperialism, a co-optation of some "other" (generational, sexual, radial) in the service of the self. Construed more broadly, this tragedy is a doubt about liberalism as a political ideology—about the structural contradiction between liberalism's advocacy of an ever-expanding political inclusiveness and its tacit commitment to maintaining white male privilege and power. Beyond each level of achieved empathy in Faulkner's fiction stands a further level of exclusion and marginalization. Beyond the aristocratic Charles Bon stands the déclassé Jim Bond, a person also deserving (yet not receiving) Quentin and Shreve's sympathy; beyond Charles Bon as well stands Judith Sutpen, no less than Charles a victim of her father's dynastic ambitions yet never the center of Quentin and Shreve's sympathetic attention; beyond Judith stands Roth's lover, nameless, black, female, and the daughter of a washerwoman, the last of *Go Down, Moses*'s long line of black female victims. Where, Faulkner's fiction seems to ask, does the expansionist economy of liberalism end? How far can its quest for inclusiveness extend if its center in a male-dominated social order—and in the white male psyche—is still to hold?

Yet to suggest that Faulkner's journey into liberalism ends at the point where a decentered postmodern politics begins is only slightly more helpful than to view him as a postmodernist manqué—and not only because the returns are still out on the question of the internal coherence of a postmodern politics of the left. The power of Faulkner's fiction (and of literature in general) lies less in the positions achieved than in the struggle that their achievement entails. "Old man," says the young woman whose touch Isaac McCaslin repudiates, "have you lived so long and forgotten so much that you don't remember anything you ever knew or felt or even heard about love?" (346). Faulkner's career between *The Sound and the Fury* and *Go Down, Moses* consists in large measure of a deepening understanding of what the word "love" means and of the range of inequalities its adherents must struggle to overcome. How the meaning of the word has altered and expanded in the fifty years since *Go Down, Moses,* how it can be expected to alter still further, whether "love" is any longer alone sufficient to heal the divisions that rive our nation—these are issues for writers other than Faulkner to explore.

NOTES

1. Eric Sundquist, *Faulkner: The House Divided* (Baltimore: Johns Hopkins University Press, 1983); Richard H. King, *A Southern Renaissance: The Cultural Awakening of the American South, 1930–1955* (New York: Oxford University Press, 1980).

2. Cleanth Brooks, *William Faulkner, The Yoknapatawpha County* (New Haven: Yale University Press, 1963), 331–32; John T. Irwin, *Doubling and Incest / Repetition and Revenge: A Speculative Reading of Faulkner* (Baltimore: Johns Hopkins University Press, 1975), 59. For an elaboration of Brooks's religious interpretation, see Constance Hill Hall, *Incest in Faulkner: A Metaphor for the Fall* (Ann Arbor: UMI Research Press, 1986). All multiple references in this essay are to the edition first cited and are noted parenthetically in the text.

3. David Wyatt, *Prodigal Sons: A Study in Authorship and Authority* (Baltimore: Johns Hopkins University Press, 1980), 83.

4. Marc Shell, *The End of Kinship: "Measure for Measure," Incest and the Ideal of Universal Siblinghood* (Stanford, Calif.: Stanford University Press, 1988), xi.

5. Ben Wasson, *Count No 'Count: Flashbacks to Faulkner* (Jackson: University Press of Mississippi, 1983), 51–53.

6. Otto Rank, *The Incest Theme in Literature and Legend: Fundamentals of a Psychology of Literary*

Creation, trans. Gregory C. Richter (Baltimore: Johns Hopkins University Press, 1992), 363. Richter's is the first translation of Rank's book into English; Irwin cites the German original.

7. Major assaults on the universality of the oedipal paradigm have come from feminist and French psychoanalytic critics. See, e.g., Gilles Deleuze and Felix Guattari, *Anti-Oedipus: Capitalism and Schizophrenia,* trans. Robert Hurley, Mark Seem, and Helen R. Lane (New York: Viking, 1977). See also Norman O. Brown, *Love's Body* (New York: Random House, 1966); Stephen Frosh, *The Politics of Psychoanalysis: An Introduction to Freudian and Post-Freudian Theory* (London: Macmillan Education Ltd, 1987); and Jeffrey B. Abramson, *Liberation and Its Limits: The Moral and Political Thought of Freud* (London: The Free Press, 1984). For a cogent overview of the debate, focused on *Anti-Oedipus,* see Peter L. Rudnytsky, *Freud and Oedipus* (New York: Columbia University Press, 1987).

8. Peter L. Thorsley, Jr., "Incest as Romantic Symbol," *Comparative Literature Studies* 2 (1965): 47. Thorsley distinguishes three types of incest in romantic literature: parent-child, stepson-step-mother, and sibling. Only the first and third are relevant to Faulkner's fiction.

9. Earl R. Wasserman, *Shelley: A Critical Reading* (Baltimore: Johns Hopkins University Pres, 1971), 86.

10. "Laon and Cythna," in *The Complete Poetical Works of Percy Bysshe Shelley,* ed. Neville Rogers, 4 vols. (Oxford, Eng.: The Clarendon Press, 1975), 2:99–273. The quoted phrases appear in the Preface (paragraph 12); the Dedication (1. 86); Canto 6, Stanza 40 (11. 2686–88); Canto 8, Stanza 13 (11. 3307–3309); Canto 2, Stanza 37 (11. 95–9); Canto 1, Stanza 1 (11. 3, 1); and Canto 11, Stanzas 22 and 24 (11. 4414–15, 4439). A darker version of the same interpretation can be applied to the relationship between Manfred and Astarte in Byron's *Manfred: A Dramatic Poem.* Robert Southey's claim that Shelley, Mary Shelley, Byron, and Claire Claremont were living in "a league of incest" while on the continent is well known. For insightful reading of the incest motif in "Laon and Cythna," see Nathaniel Brown, *Sexuality and Feminism in Shelley* (Cambridge: Harvard University Press, 1979), 212–28; and William A. Ulmer, *Shelleyan Eros: The Rhetoric of Romantic Love* (Princeton: Princeton University Press, 1990), 50–77.

11. For commentary on Faulkner's early reading of Shelley, see Joseph Blotner, *Faulkner: A Biography,* 2 vols. (New York: Random House, 1974), 1:184, 252, 422. Faulkner would have had access to the unexpurgated version of "Laon and Cythna" through the various H. Buxton Forman editions of Shelley's poetry (H. Buxton Forman, *The Poetical Works of Percy Bysshe Shelley,* 4 vols. [London: Reeves and Turner, 1976]; reprinted in 2 volumes in 1882 and 5 volumes in 1892).

12. Paul Robinson, *The Freudian Left: Wilhelm Reich, Geza Roheim, Herbert Marcuse* (New York: Harper & Row, 1969), 3. For similar formulations, see Shell, *The End of Kinship,* 1983–84, and Brown, *Love's Body,* chap. 1.

13. René Guyon, *The Ethics of Sexual Acts,* trans. J. C. and Ingeborg Flugel (1934; reprint, New York: Octagon, 1974), 323–24.

14. William Faulkner, "An Introduction to *The Sound and the Fury* [I]," in *Critical Essays on William Faulkner: The Compson Family,* ed. Arthur F. Kinney (Boston: G. K. Hall, 1982), 71. This introduction exists in three forms. The first two were originally published under the editorship of James B. Meriwether in the *Southern Review* n.s. 8 (October 1972): 708–10, and *Mississippi Quarterly* 26 (summer 1973): 410–15; they are conveniently reprinted in Kinney. The third appears in Philip Cohen and Doreen Fowler, "Faulkner's Introduction to *The Sound and the Fury,*" *American Literature* 62 (June 1990): 262–83. I have quoted from the longer and presumably earlier of the two versions reprinted in Kinney, the *Mississippi Quarterly* version.

15. William Faulkner, *Intruder in the Dust* (New York: Random House, 1948), 153.

16. Nicole Hahn Rafter, ed., *White Trash: The Eugenic Family Studies, 1877–1919* (Boston: Northeastern University Press, 1988), 2. For a particularly striking Southern example of the genre, see Arthur H. Estabrook and Ivan E. McDougle, *Mongrel Virginians: The Win Tribe* (Baltimore: Williams and Wilkens Co., 1926). For general discussions of this school of writing, see Richard Hofstadter, *Social Darwinism in American Thought,* rev. ed. (New York: George Braziller, Inc., 1959), 161–69; Sylvia Jenkins Cook, *From Tobacco Road to Route 66: The Southern Poor White in Fiction* (Chapel Hill: University of North Carolina Press, 1976); Shields McIlwane, *The Southern Poor-White: From Lubberland to Tobacco Road* (Norman: University of Oklahoma Press), 163–240; and George B. Tindall, "The Benighted South: Origins of a Modern Image," *The Virginia Quarterly Review* 40 (spring 1964): 281–94.

17. The clearest expression of Faulkner's uncertainty about which meaning to assign to father-daughter incest occurs in "A Rose for Emily," where two highly sexualized male figures, one patriarchal and Southern, the other filial and Northern, struggle for control of Emily Grierson's affections.

18. William Faulkner, *Flags in the Dust* (New York: Random House/Vintage, 1973), 191.

19. William Faulkner, *The Sound and the Fury* (New York: Random House; Vintage, 1990), 149.

20. Quentin's desires in this episode are not to be taken at face value. As Caddy says, "it wont do any good don't you know it wont let me go" (154). His true developmental failure (in my view) is not his inability to commit incest but his self-concealing response to Caddy's offer to serve as his sexual confidante. "Poor Quentin . . . you've never done that have you," she says; to which he twice replies untruthfully, saying, "yes yes lots of times with lots of girls" (151).

21. John T. Matthews, "The Rhetoric of Containment in Faulkner," in *Faulkner's Discourse: An International Symposium,* ed. Lothar Hönnighausen (Tübingen: Max Niemeyer Verlag, 1989), 55–67. The quoted phrases appear on 55 and 67.

22. Irwin, *Doubling and Incest,* 157, italics omitted. Cf. Estella Schoenberg, *Old Tales and Talking: Quentin Compson in William Faulkner's "Absalom, Absalom!" and Related Works* (Jackson: University Press of Mississippi, 1977).

23. For expressions of this view, see Malcolm Cowley, *The Faulkner-Cowley File: Letters and*

Memories, 1944–1962 (New York: Penguin, 1978), 90; and William Faulkner, Prefatory Note to *The Mansion* (New York: Random House; Vintage, 1973), n.p.

24. William Faulkner, *Absalom, Absalom!* (New York: Random House/Vintage, 1990), 4.

25. Henry's shift from opposing to supporting an incestuous liaison between Charles and Judith bears obvious similarities to the explanation for the origin of the incest taboo proposed by Freud in *Totem and Taboo*. At issue in each case is whether the father or the brothers are to command the sexual favors of the daughter/sister.

26. Cf. Irwin, *Doubling and Incest,* 31, 49–50.

27. King, *A Southern Renaissance,* 126–27.

28. Sundquist, *Faulkner: The House Divided,* 122. In *William Faulkner and Southern History* (New York: Oxford University Press, 1993), 62–71, Joel Williamson makes a convincing case for the existence of a black line of descent from Faulkner's great-grandfather and namesake, William C. Falkner.

29. Stephen M. Ross, "Oratory and the Dialogical in *Absalom, Absalom!*" in *Intertextuality in Faulkner,* ed. Michel Gresset and Noel Polk (Jackson: University Press of Mississippi, 1985), 79; see also Stephen M. Ross, *Fiction's Inexhaustible Voice: Speech and Writing in Faulkner* (Athens: University of Georgia Press, 1989), 212–33.

30. William Faulkner, *Collected Stories of William Faulkner* (New York: Random House, 1950), 417.

31. It is worth bearing in mind that *Absalom, Absalom!* was written in the heyday of the Popular Front and that parallels between sexual liberation and the politics of brotherhood were popular throughout the American Left of the 1920s and 1930s; see John Patrick Diggins, *The Rise and Fall of the American Left,* rev. ed. (New York: Norton, 1992), chaps. 4 and 5. Advocates of sexual liberation expressed alarm throughout the 1930s over the threat posed to their hopes by the rise of fascism. See Wilhelm Reich, *The Mass Psychology of Fascism,* trans. Vincent R. Carfagno (1933; reprint, New York; Farrar, Straus, & Giroux, 1970), and Robinson, *The Freudian Left.* Interestingly, in one of his first overtly liberal political gestures, Faulkner donated the manuscript of *Absalom, Absalom!* to an auction to raise money for a relief fund for Spanish Loyalists. See Blotner, *Faulkner,* 2:1030.

32. William Faulkner, *Go Down, Moses* (New York: Random House/Vintage, 1990), 246.

33. John W. Hunt, "The Disappearance of Quentin Compson," in *Critical Essays on William Faulkner,* ed. Kinney, 366–80.

34. For representative readings of the ethical and moral deficiencies of Ike's act of relinquishment, see Brooks, *William Faulkner,* and Sundquist, *Faulkner.*

35. For a discussion of Northern timber-leasing practices as they apply to *Flags in the Dust,* see Linda Elkins McDaniel, annotator, *Flags in the Dust,* vol. 5 in The Garland Faulkner Annotation Series, ed. James B. Meriwether (New York: Garland, 1991), 135–39.

36. Richard Godden, *Fictions of Labor: William Faulkner and the South's Long Revolution* (Cambridge,

Eng.: Cambridge University Press, 1997), 177–19. I regret that Professor Godden's important study appeared too late for me to make more than passing use of it in this essay.

37. Ike's parody of the language of progress should remind us of Shreve McCannon's description at the end of *Absalom, Absalom!* of how "the Jim Bonds are going to conquer the western hemisphere." "[A]s they spread out toward the poles," he says, "they will bleach out again like the birds and rabbits do. . . . but it will still be Jim Bond; and so in a few thousand years, I who regard you will also have sprung from the loins of African kings" (302).

38. Benjamin Demott, "The Pro-Incest Lobby," *Psychology Today* (March 1980): 11–12, 15–16.

39. My understanding of the feminist critique of liberationist views on incest derives from Judith Lewis Heman (with Lisa Hirschman), *Father-Daughter Incest* (Cambridge: Harvard University Press, 1980), and Karen Meiselman, *Incest* (San Francisco: Jossey-Bass, 1978).

40. Richard C. Moreland, *Faulkner and Modernism: Rereading and Rewriting* (Madison: University of Wisconsin Press, 1990); Minrose C. Gwin, *The Feminine and Faulkner: Reading (Beyond) Sexual Difference* (Knoxville: University of Tennessee Press, 1990); Sundquist, *Faulkner: The House Divided;* and Joseph R. Urgo, *Faulkner's Apocrypha: "A Fable," Snopes, and the Spirit of Human Rebellion* (Jackson: University Press of Mississippi, 1989).

41. Minrose C. Gwin, "Feminism and Faulkner: Second Thoughts or, What's a Radical Feminist Doing with a Canonical Male Text Anyway?" *The Faulkner Journal* 4 (fall 1988/spring 1989): 64.

The "Incredibly Loud. . . . Miss-fire":
A Sexual Reading of *Go Down, Moses*

NEIL WATSON

The South's nightmare history of racial conflict has rightly occupied a central place in critical discussion of Faulkner's novel, *Go Down, Moses*. Eric Sundquist considers Faulkner's exploration of the sexual dimension of that conflict, specifically the tragedy of miscegenation and its conjunction with incest, as "the heart of the South's long, continuing catastrophe" and as the thematic focus of *Go Down, Moses* (131). Yet the assumed primacy of the racial problem in assessing the novel, while probably an accurate reflection of Faulkner's own most pressing and heartfelt interest, is not the only available or useful approach. In fact, sex and sexuality, rather than being treated as an *aspect* or *focal point* of a larger context of racial conflict, may be read as the central "problem" of *Go Down, Moses*. Nor are incest and miscegenation the only taboo subjects that the novel broaches. Human sexuality, both frustrated

Reprinted with permission from *The Faulkner Journal*, Vol. 9, nos. 1 & 2 (Fall 1993/Spring 1994), 113–123.

and consummated, in its acts and implications, is the wellspring from which much of the novel's dramatic and symbolic force flows. Paradoxically, it is also a stream in which Faulkner sometimes seems reluctant to dip more than a toe, lest he, like the violated slave Eunice, drown himself in despair.

Faulkner seems almost totally to marginalize the community of women in *Go Down, Moses*. Correspondingly, the interrelations of the male community assume great complexity and ambiguity, particularly in the sexual arena. Relationships between these two communities, and "normal" (hetero)sexuality, become so problematized as to become unworkable. From the novel's opening section, "Was," it becomes clear that the male/female conflict may be insoluable. Uncle Buck and Uncle Buddy (two hypermasculine signifiers if there ever were such) live in a country "where ladies were so damn seldom *thank God* that a man could ride for days in a straight line without having to dodge a single one" (8; emphasis added). Nevertheless, Uncle Buck is forced to endure a strangely inverted courtship rite, in which he plays the coy and reluctant quarry to Sophonsiba Beauchamp's relentless advances. Foced to pursue his half-brother, Tomey's Turl (who has his own paramour on the Beauchamp plantation), into "bear country," he eventually stumbles into the very den of the bear itself, Sophonsiba's bedroom. Although the comic hunt of "Was" is a satiric progenitor of the deadly earnest hunt of "The Bear," involving a "bear" that the male hunters decidedly do not want to bag, it does involve quite serious considerations, particularly for the dynastic future of the McCaslin household. In fact, the generative potential of both the legitimate and illegitimate McCaslin lines is bound up with the women of the Beauchamp plantation. Sophonsiba Beauchamp will be the mother of the only white male McCaslin heir, Uncle Ike, while the slave Tennie Beauchamp will wed Tomey's Turl and mother the illegitimate McCaslin heirs, who must bear their maternal surname. The assiduousness with which Buck and Buddy act to avoid perpetuating the McCaslin line suggests that they already have some inkling of the curse that seems destined to pursue Carothers McCaslin's offspring, biblically visiting the sins of the father upon the sons and future generations.

The fear and discomfort with which Buck and Buddy regard women, and the lengths to which they will go to avoid admitting a woman into their all-male preserve, foreshadow an undeniable pattern in the novel of failed male/female interactions. That these relationships might prove untenable is unsurprising, given a mindset that seems quite consistent with Claude Lévi-Strauss's definition of culture as being a "total relationship of exchange . . .

not established between a man and a woman, but between two groups of men, [where] the woman figures only as one of the objects in the exchange, not as one of the partners" (qtd. in Sedgwick, 184). The poker game between Buck and Hubert, and later Buddy and Hubert, perfectly exemplifies this female barter system, with Sophonsiba and the slave woman Tennie traded back and forth like so many poker chips. This game is even more demeaning, since each man in this case plays to lose. Victory over Beauchamp at least temporarily forestalls the dreaded female incursion, allowing Buck, Buddy, and Cass to return to their comfortable realm of all-male domesticity, where Uncle Buddy plays both poker-faced master of the household and nurturing mother hen, "sitting on the seat . . . exactly the same way he sat a horse or sat in his rocking chair before the kitchen hearth while he was cooking, holding the whip exactly as he held the spoon or fork he stirred or tasted with" (18).

Of course, Sophonsiba eventually wins the curious courtship battle with Uncle Buck, dynastic urges perhaps providing too strong to overcome. Given her ensuing virtual banishment from the text, however, Sophonsiba's marriage to Buck becomes little more than an exigency of plot. The appearance of Ike McCaslin necessitates the preexistence of some sort of mother, at least to accomplish the delivery, though apparently she has little else to do with the boy's upbringing. What we see of Isaac's childhood is extraordinary in its gender exclusivity; he has at least three fathers in Buck, Cass, and Sam Fathers but has no mother to speak of. Little wonder, then, that he totally fails to understand the woman he eventually marries. She is, as women often seem to be in Faulkner's novels, the consummate materialist, while Ike, like most of Faulkner's troubled male characters, is obsessed with abstractions. Ike's failure to take possession of the farm, which all acknowledge is rightfully his, is inexplicable to her. An unbridgeable gulf exists between their ways of understanding the world. In a bedroom tableau that stands at the heterosexual center of the novel, Isaac's wife (who doesn't get a name) offers her body as the one item of exchange for which she can extract Ike's promise to claim his birthright. Failing that, she turns away from him both literally and symbolically, exercising her only remaining power, withholding what she knows he will not take by force:

> she turned and freed herself and on their wedding night she had cried and he thought she was crying now at first . . . , the voice coming from somewhere between the pillow and the cachinnation: "And that's all. That's all from me. If

> this don't get you that son you talk about, it wont be mine:" lying on her side, her back to the empty rented room, laughing and laughing. (233–34)

One can hardly ignore the bizarre nature of this singular act of conjugal relations between Ike and his nameless wife, the only time during their marriage (including the wedding night) when he even so much as sees her unclothed. Furthermore, this bedroom scene is only the second in the novel in which a man and woman get in bed together, the first occasion having been a comic accident. Such a scene makes explicit a heterosexual futility that pervades the book and highlights the ironic contrast Faulkner draws between Isaac McCaslin and his biblical namesake, who is born to an aged Abraham, disinheriting his older but illegitimate half-brother Ishmael, and goes on to father a nation as numberless as the sands of the shore or the stars in the sky. Ike McCaslin, we know, will go on to be an aged, almost monastic widower, "uncle to half a county and father to no one"(5).

We find Isaac McCaslin in this impotent, almost hermetic state in the penultimate section, "Delta Autumn," making his last appearance in the novel. Uncle Ike seems oblivious to the leering innuendo of Will Legate, with his talk of a doe who "walks on two legs—when she's standing up, that is. . . . But of course a old man like Uncle Ike aint got no interest in nothing like that" (248–49). Indeed, Ike does seem disinterested, childlike in his disregard for the sexual banter in the car. "What?" the old man said. "What's that?" (249). And even as Ike sits miserably on his cot, abject before the realized specter of the doe that walks on two legs, the gulf of failed understanding, his almost total lack of comprehension of the male, remains. "'Old man,' she said, 'have you lived so long and forgotten so much that you don't remember anything you ever knew or felt or even heard about love?'" (268). But Ike has not forgotten; he never really understood to begin with. Not to say that Isaac was or is incapable of love; he loves his comrades and mentors in the hunt, loves the woods and the spirit of the wilderness, and we are told that he cherished his wife (260). Sexually, however, he remains a babe in the woods, almost literally virginal, and women will always be represented for him, sexually, by the turned back of his wife.

Uncle Ike is not the only member of the McCaslin-Edmonds clan whose interactions with women result in failure. Old Carothers's descendants through the "distaff," as Faulkner likes to put it, indeed seem only to come together with women in order to reenact the tragic mistakes of their forbear.

The first we hear of Zack Edmonds's unnamed wife in "The Fire and the Hearth" is that she has died in childbirth, insuring that Roth will grow up in the family tradition, motherless. "It was as though the white woman had not only never quitted the house, she had never existed—the object which they buried in the orchard two days later . . . a thing of no moment, unsanctified, nothing . . ." (36). After the departure of this "object," Zack acquires another, Molly, the black wife of his black cousin, only to relinquish her as well, and nearly be killed for his trouble. It should come as no surprise, then, to see Roth, at age forty in "Delta Autumn," still a bachelor and likely to remain so. His sole foray into romance or, at the least, sexual passion, ends in failure, leaving another kinswoman's unacknowledged child perhaps to begin the whole tragic cycle anew. In Faulkner's novel, women and children are commodities that never seem to be lacking, as Roth the cynic observes. He also says that if the union between man and woman represents (as Ike claims) the incarnation of God, "Then there are some Gods in this world I wouldn't want to touch, and with a damn long stick. . . . And that includes myself" (257).

Though the case seems particularly striking in *Go Down, Moses,* it is not unusual to find white men and women almost completely estranged from one another in Faulkner's fictional world. His black characters, however, more grounded in family, community, and religion than the abstracted and defeated whites, seem more likely to find some stable ground where males and females can successfully interact. Lucas and Molly Beauchamp's marriage has endured, despite the early troubles with Zack Edmonds, and Rider (of "Pantaloon in Black") certainly feels genuine love for Mannie. But wait, as Shreve might say to Quentin. While Lucas and Molly's marriage does survive his obsession with buried gold, Molly's suit for divorce is only barely averted. Lucas also works with single-minded determination to prevent the marriage of his daughter to a man he deems unworthy of his McCaslin heritage, and when that proves impossible, uses the "fact" of their marriage to save his own neck. Finally, even though Lucas and Molly's love is seemingly reaffirmed at the end of "The Fire and the Hearth," where is Lucas by the novel's conclusion? In the closing story, Molly walks seventeen miles alone in the summer heat to plead for Gavin Stevens's assistance. And it is Miss Worsham, Stevens, the editor, and the businessmen of the town square who finally contribute the money to bring her executed grandson back to Jefferson, though we know that Lucas has a fortune of his own in the bank. Nor does Lucas appear for the funeral, though every indication is given that he is still alive. If the relationship between Lucas and Molly really is stable, committed, and affirming, it seems odd that she must rely on complete strangers to help her mourn her loss, a sense of loss that, like most things in their marriage, Lucas apparently does not share.

As for Rider and Mannie, there is no doubt that his grief for her is real and awesome in its power. But because Mannie is already dead by the time "Pantaloon in Black" begins, we can see that love as alive and vital only in a brief flashback or "re-memory." All that the text reveals to us is Mannie as a fading and ghostly image, departing from Rider even as he moves towards it. "But she was going. She was going fast now; he could actually feel between them the insuperable barrier" (106). Love and grief are destructive rather than affirmative forces, as Rider rejects the comfort his aunt can offer, seeking instead a white man on whom to exact with a violent razor's caress some measure of outraged vengeance from a world of apparently irredeemable injustices. The "insuperable barrier" between Mannie and Rider to which Faulkner refers is meant to be the barrier between the living and the dead, but it might just as well be the barrier raised in a text where few terms or conditions can be found to allow for positive relationships between men and women.

Why are male/female, heterosexual terms of attraction so problematized, and eventually unworkable, in *Go Down, Moses?* One answer lies in the novel's devaluing of procreation. What is generally viewed as one of the greatest potential gifts of heterosexual intercourse, its regenerative potential, becomes its chief drawback within the context of *Go Down, Moses,* a means of passing on a flawed patrimony or propagating the tragedy of miscegenation. In renouncing his inheritance to save his son from the cursed McCaslin heritage, Ike assures that he will have no son to save. Even this renunciation proves ultimately futile, as the Edmondses, undeserving heirs to the land that is for Ike the symbol of his cursed, sin-born patrimony, eventually receive that tainted land, with its financial worth and social power. Roth Edmonds completes the circle, reuniting flawed patrimony with kindred offspring of miscegenation (his "doe" is Tomey's Turl's great-granddaughter), creating yet another disinherited son who cannot bear his father's name. In a novel where inheritance can only be impotent futility or unalleviated injustice and disregard, perhaps Faulkner feels justified in not bringing forth too many heirs.

But more than a simple desire to avoid the curse of procreation grounds Faulkner's deliberate marginalization of women in *Go Down, Moses.* The novel at its very core is, as Sundquist recognizes, essentially separatist and divisive. Black and white are, finally, irreconcilable; the consequences of their mixture can only be dire. Male and female are separated as well, and to an even greater degree, since Faulkner does not treat the two with anything like the balance of attention he gives the divisions of black and white. Indeed, the world that Faulkner creates in *Go Down, Moses* confers subjectivity almost exclusively upon its male actors. Such calculated emphasis on the male community brings with it the possibility of some radical, though I hope reasonable, conclusions.

Specifically, with women essentially pushed to the margins of the action, the undertones of homoeroticism so prevalent in the novel are more prominent and interesting. In a book where the bedroom becomes so often the scene of crucial action, it seems at least potentially significant that men are far more likely to be found in bed with each other than with women. Admittedly, there is nothing particularly unusual, especially given time and place, about male family members or pre-adolescent boys sleeping together. However, in an intentionally subversive queer reading, where words like uncle" and "nephew" carry an additional meaning, the continual recurrence of such scenes gives one pause, at the very least. And in a novel where the possibilities and consequences of sexual transgression figure so strongly in the dramatic tension, the presence of males in bed together creates a potential triple threat of forbidden desires, the explicit interracial and incestual taboos juxtaposed with the implicit, still unnamable taboo of homoeroticism.

At the novel's beginning, the reader learns that Cass Edmonds regularly sleeps with his aged bachelor uncle, Buck McCaslin. "Uncle Buddy had waked them in the dark and said, 'Get up out of that bed and damn quick'" (8). However, this discovery is not particularly startling (though it might be if Cass were sleeping with Uncle Buddy, who we are told "could have risked [visiting Sophonsiba Beauchamp] ten times as much as Uncle Buck could have dared" [7]). It is interesting that Buck and his nephew Cass stumble into Sibby's bed as they are searching for a place to bed down themselves in the Beauchamp plantation, and the decidedly female-averse Buck uses this fact in his defense: "say, just for the sake of argument . . . I walked into [her bedroom] and tried to get in bed with her, would I have took a nine-year-old boy with me?" (19). But if the uncle/nephew bed partnership carries little charge in "Was," the ground shifts somewhat by the time we reach "The Old People." Here, we find a twelve-year-old Ike in bed with his twenty-eight-year-old cousin, Cass, in "the strange room and the big deep bed, the still cold sheets until they began to warm to their bodies" (138). Not expecting to be believed, Ike describes to Cass the buck that he has seen, the buck which remains invisible to most eyes. In an argument that functions remarkably well as a paradigm for my reading, McCaslin acknowledges that there are many hidden and misunderstood things (closeted, if you will) that nevertheless exist and can be seen by those who know where to look:

> "there is plenty of room about the earth, plenty of places still unchanged from what they were when the blood used and pleasured in them while it was still blood[.]"
>
> "But we want them," the boy said. "We want them too. There is plenty of room for us and them too."
>
> "That's right," McCaslin said. "Suppose they don't have substance, cant cast a shadow—"
>
> "But I saw it!" the boy cried. "I saw him."
>
> "Steady," McCaslin said. For an instant his hand touched the boy's flank beneath the covers. (139)

I do not wish to be found guilty of the common political ploy of taking certain statements out of context in order to misrepresent their intent. Clearly, Faulkner is talking primarily about the mystical, spiritual representation of nature to which Sam Fathers, and through him Ike and Cass, seem to be provided access. Faulkner may be totally unaware of other implications that might be drawn from the passage; indeed he need not be aware of them. For the purposes of our subversive reading, the subtext is plain enough, illuminated like a lightning flash by that peculiar and oddly charged instant of physical contact, the touching of the flank.

Faulkner's males, especially the ones he seems to admire, derive most of their pleasure from being around other males. This is evident in the annual hunting parties. In "Delta Autumn," Ike muses that the men with whom he hunts are "more his kin than any" (260). In "The Bear," Boon Hogganbeck stubbornly shares his bed with the symbolically masculine Lion, despite orders to the contrary; Lion and the bear embrace, "almost lover like" (177); Boon is seen "astride [the bear's] back, working and probing the buried blade: (177). The hunt as a whole may be taken as metaphor for the book's other pursuits, and the objects of the hunt are, by long-standing tradition, exclusively male. The bear in particular seems to symbolize some wished-for state of idealized freedom from sexual considerations, "so long unwifed and childless as to become its own *ungendered progenitor*" (154; emphasis added). As Sundquist observes, though again in a racial context, "the hunt . . . displace[s] the lust and violence of the subject onto the object of sacrifice" (143). In this case, when the object of the hunt is the potentially desired male body, complicated emotions of shame and fear attend the necessity of its sacrifice, presumably to acceptable societal norms.

Conflicting shame, fear, and desire emerge (and merge) most clearly in "The Fire and the Heart." Roth Edmonds and his black "foster brother" Henry share everything, including their beds, in a kind of prelapsarian innocence: "they were sufficient, complete, wanting, as all children do, not to be understood, leaping in mutual embattlement before any threat to privacy, but only to love, to question and examine unchallenged, and to be let alone" (86). But Roth's discovery of the patriarchal strictures of his white world, and their unalterable and unanswerable demands, brings the idyll to an abrupt end: "then one day the old curse of his fathers, . . . stemmed not from courage and honor but from wrong and shame, descended to him" (86). Denying for the first time Henry's right to share a bed with him, Roth lies awake "in a rigid fury of the grief he could not explain, the shame he would not admit" (87). Though written to dramatize the tragic consequences of racial pride and exclusion, another subtext again inevitably emerges, with particular resonance for any homophiliac reading. Men, in Faulkner's society as well as our own, find it nearly impossible to express love for one another and "be let alone." They find that there is no such thing as benign indifference when they (or we) knowingly and openly sin against rigidly enforced codes of masculine behavior.

Still another bedroom tableau prefigures this scene between Roth and Henry. The battle between Lucas Beauchamp and Zack Edmonds, which takes place on Edmonds's bed, becomes the pivotal paradigm for the whole "problem" of homoerotic tension in *Go Down, Moses,* just as Ike's bedroom battle with his wife is central to the heterosexual dilemma. Lucas and Zack, whose relationship had been the same as Roth and Henry's will be, kneel on either side of a bed, hands gripped, the one representing the male-descended McCaslin line, the other the feminized, woman-born Edmonds:

> they met over the center of the bed where Lucas clasped the other with his left
> arm almost like an embrace and jammed the pistol against the white man's side
> and pulled the trigger and flung the white man from him all in one motion, hear-
> ing as he did so the light, dry, incredibly loud click of the miss-fire. (44)

Faulkner juxtaposes two important symbols, the bedroom and the hunt, in
Lucas and Zack's embrace, complete with phallic representative pistol, which
miss-fires. It is the miss-fire that ultimately resonates, like Faulkner's "incredibly loud" silence about the homoerotic desire, implicit but never explicit in
the text. If, finally, the sacrifice of the object both desired and feared is averted,
the end of the conflict yields not so much a resolution as an armistice, a state
of more or less peaceful coexistence. In this stasis, both arbitrary polarities of
sexual desire seem finally divided, not only from each other, but from the
putative objects of their desire. Within the confines of a traditional (and
artificial) sexual dualism, the expected pairings, whether taboo (male/male) or
"normal" (male/female), fail to take place. Hence, for Faulkner's male community in Go Down, Moses, an aged and singular bachelorhood becomes the
only workable option. These men appear to imagine themselves, as Ike imagines the bear, to be their own "ungendered progenitors," perhaps as one way
to avoid the complications of sexuality that the novel renders so threatening.
These complications—incest, miscegenation, homoerotic desire, children—all
work to undermine ideas or myths of familiar honor and place, castle, and
masculinity, the dubious pillars of Faulkner's Southern world.

Granted that a case may be made for a subtext of homosexual desire in
Go Down, Moses, what becomes significant about this beyond having made
the point? I certainly have no intention of making any claims about Faulkner,
who as far as I know was as straight as they come, nor about his intentions
for the novel. While some of the homoerotic suggestion seems hard to credit
as anything other than deliberate, it ultimately does not matter whether it
shows up on purpose or by accident. I have quite intentionally tried to avoid
any biographical or didactic reading of the text; however, I do feel that the
emergence of a strong subtext of homoeroticism in this modernist work is
important. Eve Kosofsky Sedgwick, whose book Epistemology of the Closet deals
with similar issues in the works of Melville, Wilde, and Henry James, argues
that "the modernist impulse toward abstraction . . . owes an incalculable part
of its energy precisely to" what she calls "turn-of-the-century male homo/
heterosexual definitional panic." In a modernist aesthetic where figuration

becomes the embodiment of sentimentality and thus must be abstracted,"
the figuration . . . abjected . . . was not just the figuration of *any* body . . .
but, rather, that represented in a very particular body, the desired male body"
(167). According to Sedgwick, homo/heterosexual definitional panic, in a culture where, as already noted, all significant exchange takes place between
men, naturally comes about due to the shifting boundaries of prescribed male
homosocial bonding and proscribed homosexuality. The inevitable tension
that arises between these two contradictory goals of patriarchal society results
in the most rigorous enforcement of taboos against homoeroticism in the
institutions where homosocial interaction, "male bonding," is most prevalent
(186). Nor is it surprising to find that in these male-dominated institutions,
whether the armed forces, football teams, or hunting parties, the undercur-
rent of unacceptable desire that accompanies "healthy" homosocial bonding
is sublimated and redirected into channels of (eroticized) violence.

The extent to which homoeroticism appears in *Go Down, Moses* is thus a
reflection of how accurately Faulkner portrays an essentially all-male cultural
subjectivity, what Luce Irigaray calls the "hom(m)osexual" culture, "a sociocultural order which requires homosexuality as its organizing principle"
(Irigaray, 192). Carolyn Porter recognizes this logic at work in *Absalom,*
Absalom!, in "the homosexual desire which surfaces between Bon and Henry
as well as between Shreve and Quentin" (110). The logic works as well, and
on a grander scale, in *Go Down, Moses,* where the domains of power are even
more exclusively male. Read Molly for Judith, Lucas for Bon, and Zack
Edmonds for Henry, and Mr. Compson's analysis of that earlier triangle seems
perfectly suited to our discussion of *Go Down, Moses:*

> it was not Judith who was the object of Bon's love or of Henry's solicitude. She
> was just the blank shape, the empty vessel in which each of them strove to pre-
> serve . . . what each conceived the other to believe him to be . . . seducer and
> seduced. . . . (*AA,* 95)

But for the "incredibly loud" miss-fire of the pistol in "The Fire and the
Hearth," the consummation of Lucas's and Zack's relationship would also
parallel that of Henry and Bon, the seemingly inevitable violent climax of
proscribed desire. The miss-fire symbolizes both a frustrated desire and the
essential impotence of all sexual relationships in a book in which celibacy
seems the only viable alternative.

Go Down, Moses is not, in the final analysis, a "gay-positive" book, nor is it "straight-positive." No sexual expression or desire in the novel comes without its price, a price that to Faulkner never seems worth paying. Procreation brings with it rebirth, not of hope, but of repeated shame and despair. Homoerotic desire remains only a suggested impossibility, inevitably channeled into other, often violent forms of expression. Even celibacy, the abnegation of desire and the abdication of responsibility, becomes nothing more than a futile gesture that destroys the very thing it seeks to save. Yet the very pervasiveness of its despair lends *Go Down, Moses* an instructive and compelling power. In its recognition of the subtext of homoerotic desire that underlies a male-dominated cultural exchange, it is an important document of its time and place. In its bleakness, it eloquently expresses the consequences of some of society's poisonous dualities: black/white, male/female, even gay/straight. Rigorous enforcement of these dualities can only lead, as the novel shows, to an ever more pensive and embattled isolation. This obsessive self-separation leads, finally, to the absurdly "perfect incest," the wish to be one's own "ungendered progenitor." Given the barrenness of this enforced isolation, *Go Down, Moses* ends, appropriately, with a funeral.

WORKS CITED

Faulkner, William. *Absalom, Absalom!* New York: Vintage International, 1990.

———. *Go Down, Moses. Novels 1942–1954,* edited by Joseph Blotner and Noel Polk, 1–281. New York: Library of America, 1994.

Irigaray, Luce. *This Sex Which Is Not One,* translated by Catherine Porter. Ithaca: Cornell University Press, 1986.

Lévi-Strauss, Claude. *The Elementary Structures of Kinship.* Boston: Beacon Press, 1969.

Porter, Carolyn. "A Feminist Approach to Faulkner." *Faulkner and Psychology: Faulkner and Yoknapatawpha, 1991,* edited by Donald M. Kartiganer and Ann J. Abadie, 78–122. Jackson: University Press of Mississippi, 1994.

Sedgwick, Eve Kosofsky. *Epistemology of the Closet.* Berkeley: University of California Press, 1990.

Sundquist, Eric J. *Faulkner: The House Divided.* Baltimore: Johns Hopkins University Press, 1983.

PART III

The Sound and the Fury *and* Absalom, Absalom!, *the Enduring Core*

The Comic Structure of *The Sound and the Fury*

FRED CHAPPELL

Only two things militate powerfully against our reading *The Sound and The Fury* as a comic novel. These are the complexity and density of the background material, and the special intensity of presentation. If we abstract ourselves for a moment from these two strategies, if we somewhat ponder the novel, it begins to take on a much different color from the one it has as we read it page to page. I believe that this personal abstraction away from the work is what Faulkner intends for the reader to experience, since he has arranged the four sections in order of *decreasing* intensity, from the almost unbearable immediacy of Benjy's perceptions to the much cooler (though still not distant) third-person narrative of the final part. . . . And there is too

Originally published in a French translation by Robert Louit, "Structure comique de Le Bruit et la fureur." *Magazine Littéraire*, no. 133 (February 1978): 30–32. The present version in English was made by the author, with corrections of errors. Reprinted with permission from *Mississippi Quarterly* 31, no. 3 (1978): 381–86.

always the fact that not even the shape of the book is clear to us until some-time after we have put it away on the shelf.

Saith the Gospel of Matthew: *Take therefore no thought for the morrow: for the morrow shall take thought for the things of itself. Sufficient unto the day is the evil thereof.* This is a maxim that the American Negro still—alas!—has to take very much to heart, to live his life by. The Biblical injunction may be trans-lated into this American bromide: "Just take it one day at a time, that's all." Of the characters in *The Sound and the Fury,* only Dilsey and a few other black characters are able to live up to this necessary imperative. All the other char-acters are obsessed with the bright ungraspable phantoms they glimpse in the dead past or the stillborn future.

If we take—leaving aside for a moment June 2, 1910—the order of events in present time on April 6–7–8, 1928, we see the following design. April 6 introduces us to Jason; it is entirely his day, a day filled with petty and scur-rilous little triumphs. He cheats Earl his boss out of a half-day's work, brow-beats his mother into more than her normal hysteria, cheats his niece Quentin out of money twice, brutalizes her, insults every person in sight, cha-grins Luster by burning the show tickets, and makes a nervewracking sham-bles of the evening meal. He does all these things because it is his pleasure to do them; he is a monster. But after all, he is a recognizable monster; we find in him much of Scapin, much of Harpagon, and a great deal of Shakespeare's Thersites. Jason is in many respects the monomaniac villain of the stage farce. If *The Sound and the Fury* were presented as a stage farce, we would see this very familiar outline: Act I (April 6), Jason thwarts and bam-boozles all his acquaintances, he seems invincible; Act II (April 7), forces of which he is ignorant, but which he has at least partly set in motion himself (dramatic irony) are moving against him; Act III (April 8), Jason falls; he is robbed (legally, or at least without legal recourse), frustrated, and humiliated; and the lovers (though they are not noble lovers) are united. The biter bit. Neatly done; in fact, it is almost too symmetrical to be a classical farce.

The objection might be brought that Jason is not very much on stage during Act II. And that is true, though we do—through Dilsey and Quentin especially—feel the exacerbating force of his presence. But *The Sound and the Fury* is after all not a play, and April 7 is most concerned with others besides Jason. Here are the springs of motion for the major events of April 7, 1928: (1) Dilsey wants to prepare a suitable birthday celebration for Benjy; (2) Luster must have a quarter so that he can attend the traveling musical show;

(3) Quentin wants to attract a beau in order to escape Jason's tyranny; (4) Benjy is engaged in his unending search to recapture a memory of the presence (and not of the absence) of his sister Caddy.

Each of these desires comes to fruition. Dilsey manages to bake the cake and to set thirty-three candles upon it. The celebration in the kitchen is not entirely successful, however, and Benjy has to be removed to the library. Luster does get his quarter; Quentin gives it to him, and presumably it is a part of the ten dollars given her the day before by Jason to mollify her for being cheated—so that it is Jason who pays Luster's way to the music. Quentin does attract someone, passerthrough-with-the-red-tie, to take her away from Jason's dominance; but actually it is Luster who attracts him by hinting strongly that Quentin is sexually available (the empty prophylactic container). And because he has been removed to the library where a large open fire once burned and because he sees Quentin's escape down the pear tree, Benjy is able to seize two incontrovertible images of his sister's former presence: "Caddy's head was on Father's shoulder. Her hair was like fire, and little points of fire were in her eyes, and I went and Father lifted me up into the chair too, and Caddy held me. She smelled like trees." And finally: "Caddy held me and I could hear us all, and the darkness, and something I could smell. And then I could see the windows, where the trees were buzzing. Then the dark began to go in smooth, bright shapes, like it always does, even when Caddy says that I have been asleep."

This day, April 7, comes to a happy, even blissful, conclusion for its principal questers.

June 2, 1910—the story of Quentin Compson's last day on earth—is set apart from the rest of the novel in any number of ways. Quentin's story is also a comic story, I think, but the comedy is darker and profounder here than in the rest of the book. But if we at once describe Quentin's character as *quixotic,* we shall have come immediately at Faulkner's intention. Quentin's destiny is tragic—as is the destiny of Cervantes' great figure—but his character is comic, like the Don's. The figure of a tragic destiny proceeding from a comic flaw always makes an audience uneasy; we laugh and cry at once, regretting that what must be so is indeed so. The gallant ridiculous man who has for no sensible reason set himself at odds with the universe draws our laughter but our sweetest sympathies also. (Buster Keaton knew this fact, and Chaplin.) Quentin's motives, like Quixote's, spring from literature, from a fairy-tale tradition about an ideal of honor which never really existed in this world. The concept of "honour" that Quentin imagines his forebears to have possessed, they never possessed; we know this well enough from the other stories that Faulkner wrote about them, and from his raffishly ironic treatment of them in the "Appendix." Quentin–against his father's very wise advice— has allowed himself to believe in, to be taken in by, a phony Southern tradition of former glory and high honor. Quentin's forefathers were men who simply did what at the time they felt they had to do; and the things they did were not always honorable, nor even always scrupulously honest.

Because we see the events of June 2, 1910, from inside Quentin's very intense consciousness (like Benjy, he is a lyric poet trapped and maimed by circumstance), and because we already know of his coming suicide, we are likely to lose sight of his comic aspect. Still, Faulkner keeps pushing him at us as a figure of ridicule. On his final day, this knightly protector of Southern womanhood is arrested for kidnapping a little girl (whom he calls "Sister") with intent to molest. This whole scene is laid out as farce, with the uncomprehending outraged brother, the desultorily corrupt hamlet officials, and the properly horrified twittery girls from Boston. If we can manage to see him from outside, the obsessed perfervid Quentin merely looks silly. (*Silly* is what his father calls him.) Afterward, in the clearest analogue to episodes from Cervantes, Quentin attacks Gerald Bland for being a womanizer ("Did you ever have a sister?") and is soundly drubbed for his gallantry. The probable truth of the matter is that Bland is not much a womanizer; all that notion is just loose trashy talk he and his mother indulge in. We sympathize with Quentin for hitting Bland, and sympathize with him all the more because he is whipped, but he is still ridiculous. He is so ridiculous, in fact, that Shreve his roommate can only look at him with bemused amazement.

These two comic episodes are more darkly ironic than most of the other comic epidsodes in the novel, and they point up a strain in Faulkner's work we often overlook. Faulkner likes to employ—I suspect that he enjoys—the cruel physical peasant joke that we find so plentiful in Cervantes, Rabelais, Le Sage, and Smollett. The cruel peasant joke is what Faulkner sees as the world's rough-and-ready rebuff to false idealism.

Faulkner's humor colors everything he writes, of course, and *The Sound and the Fury* is full of characters we recognize as comic at first sight: Luster, Roskus, T. P., Uncle Maury, the horse Queenie (Faulkner's Rosinante), and even the tiresomely predictable mother Caroline are more or less standard comic figures. Some of the episodes are comic in the usual way. Uncle Maury, for instance, has to attend father Jason's funeral with a black eye because he had no better judgment than to send a letter of assignation by an idiot. And some episodes which we fully expect to be sad are presented comically. Caddy's wedding, for example, we expect to be gloomy since it is the last time that Benjy shall ever see his sister. But Faulkner presents it instead as slapstick: T.P., mistaking the wedding champagne for sarsaparilla, gets both himself and Benjy drunk; he then sets up a large box at the window to watch the ceremony, but being drunk he tips the box over backward, trapping Benjy underneath; and Caddy has to rush out in her strange finery to rescue her brother. (Fully to appreciate the joke, a reader must understand what great store Southerners set by such ceremonies as weddings. Champagne hauled into Jefferson, Mississippi, for God's sake.)

Henri Bergson's analysis of the comic character is especially relevant to a reading of *The Sound and the Fury* as comedy. Bergson delineates the comic character as that which acts mechanically, predictably, single-mindedly, no matter what changes occur in the outer circumstances which surround the character. All the Compsons gathered in this novel are almost demonically single-minded. They are in fact so one-purposed that they *never* change. They are the same as adults as they were as children; in fact, Faulkner in presenting them to us first as children invites us to predict their adult characters. We have no trouble in doing so: Jason with his hands in his pockets, and so forth. If comic characters must follow settled routines, never deviating, then this household is straitly comic, for its routine revolves about the well-being of Benjy, and Benjy cannot tolerate any change whatsoever in the strict order of his world. The final public humiliation of Jason is brought about because Luster unknowingly upsets the mechanical order of things, going the wrong way around the statue.

The Compsons are trapped in their comic mechanical orders because present time does not exist for them. Except perhaps for Jason the father they have all given their allegiances to an impossible past, as Quentin and Benjy have done, or to an equally improbable future, as Jason the son has done. Of the principal characters only Dilsey is able to live in present time, to live one day at a time, to see sufficient evil here and now without trying to discover more in past or future. And Dilsey may be the one character in the novel who is not comic, but an appreciably admirable person.

In describing *The Sound and the Fury* as a comic novel, I do not *of course* mean to say that it is a happy novel. It is not. I find its tone, its mood, wistful, regretful, elegiac, tender. But then I don't know that I can think of a great comic novel which is happy. Not *Dead Souls,* not *Oblomov,* not *The Magic Mountain* or *Bouvard and Pecuchet,* not, certainly not, *Don Quixote.*

Faulkner's *Commedia*: Synecdoche and Anagogic Symbolism in *The Sound and the Fury*

JAMES M. MELLARD

I

Since the publication in 1976 of *The Most Splendid Failure,* André Bleikasten's book-length study of William Faulkner's *The Sound and the Fury,* one might surmise that little of consequence could remain undone—certainly not enough for a full "reading" of the novel.[1] Despite the extreme thoroughness of Bleikasten's study, however, some aspects of Faulkner's novel remain that simply have not been dealt with adequately. These aspects include certain image patterns that determine dominant themes and bear directly upon the problems of tropological analysis and anagogic interpretation. Anagogic criticism, though derived from the phases of Scholatic Scriptural interpretation, owes its contemporary visibility to Northrop Frye, who considers it the ultimate level of any literary interpretation. What this contention means for contemporary tropological analysis is simply that the mode of *synecdoche* finally dominates a work. Frye's remarks about the anagogic would also apply

Reprinted with permission from *Journal of English and Germanic Philology* 83 (October 1984): 534–46.

to the trope of synecdoche—where parts are drawn into an organic whole. Specifically, the anagogic strives toward the unification of all lower levels of interpretation by drawing symbols (images) and myths (plots) toward inclusion in a single synecdochic image. The synecdochic becomes anagogic when the unifying image or symbol is given the highest cultural valorization and so stands at the center of the literary universe. Anagogically, says Frye, "the symbol is a monad, all symbols being united in a single infinite and eternal verbal symbol which is, as *dianoia* [theme], the Logos, and as *mythos* [narrative or plot], total creative act."[2] Thus, as Frye says, "Anagogic criticism is usually found in direct connection with religion" (122), but literature (such as much Romantic poetry) that offers an anagogic dimension will be concerned, like religion, with the imaginative limits of human possibilities. "The study of literature," in any case, says Frye of its ideal aim, "takes us toward seeing poetry [that is, any literary work] as the imitation of infinite social action and infinite human thought, the mind of man who is all men, the universal creative word which is all words" (125).

In Western literature, the most prominent synecdochic image and anagogic symbol of such an imaginative limit is Christ. We know that Faulkner associates his novel with the Christian celebration of Easter, thereby inviting readers to make direct connections between characters in the novel and figures in the Christian myth; there is no need to rehearse here the many readings that point out various parallels. Any reading that sees a Christ-figure in, say, Quentin or a Christly "Suffering Servant" in Dilsey clearly is moving toward an anagogic vision of the novel. Though any sweeping interpretation one might make of the work these days is unlikely to be totally innovative, still relatively unnoticed are some important strands of imagery woven through the novel and drawn together—climactically—in the novel's fourth section. These images, rather than focusing upon Christ as the great synecdoche, focus primarily upon *blood, voices,* and the traditional pictorial image of the *Pietà*. The first two images are parts of the major synecdoche, for their full significance only gradually unfolds as Faulkner draws them upward through a series of levels, toward the highest cultural ("spiritual") valorization we find embodied in the novel's dominant, figural, synecdochic image: the *Pietà*-in-Dilsey.

In order to make concrete the novel's anagogic conception—the sense that all lower parts belong to a unified whole—Faulkner resorts to the image of a single human being as a universal container, though were he a Romantic poet he might have chosen another image, such as a plant, as the inclusive symbol. In this novel that image finally is *Dilsey,* rather than Christ, though we understand her synecdochic function because of the analogical matrix created by the pervasive Christian images. References to Christ occur in all sections of *The Sound and the Fury,* particularly in the second, Quentin's section. But in Quentin's section, the allusions to Christ form no synecdoche; their function is not to develop an anagogic theme of revelation and containment, but to pursue Quentin's primary theme of Fall and ultimate alienation. It is Quentin's metaphoric identification with the fallen Adam and the crucified Christ that makes his Christian references appropriate to his character and theme. In such passages as this, for example—". . . Jesus and Saint Francis talking about his sister"[3]—one sees Quentin's obsessive concern with his sister, Caddy, not a concern with religious salvation. The function of the Christian background in the fourth section, by contrast, is to provide an analogical matrix for the full range of humanly imaginable experience comprehended in the "plot" sequence of innocence, fall, death, and rebirth, a range that is both Adamic and Christly, but also a range encompassed by the plot formed by the novel's four sections taken together.

II

There are perhaps any number of specific, potentially synecdochic images that might help convey anagogic significance, but those running throughout *The Sound and the Fury* and, most important, in the fourth section are blood and voices. These two images are always significant in religious rituals and symbol systems, for they connote the spirit of life (blood) and the source of the primal life-breath-word (as in any afflatus). Faulkner works these two images through several levels as the novel's symbolism unfolds. In the earlier sections of the novel, blood has meaning far short of the apocalyptic one the fourth evokes. For Quentin blood has a sexual meaning almost exclusively. In the scene with Natalie, he speaks of hearing rain on the roof "as if it was my blood or her blood" (167); he repeats the phrase with even clearer sexual emphasis: "oh her blood or my blood Oh" (167). Later, both in the novel and in Quentin's experience, in his incestuous confrontation with Caddy over Dalton Ames, he speaks the name *Dalton Ames* and then "felt the first surge of blood" in her throat: "there it surged in strong accelerating beats" (203).

But even for Quentin the image of blood is associated with Christ, for it eventually draws together *eros* and *thanatos*. Getting blood on his tie from a finger cut on a broken watch glass, Quentin thinks of his father: "Maybe a pattern of blood he could call that the one Christ was wearing" (213).

For Jason, Quentin's brother, blood has almost no other connotation than heritage, kinship. He takes that meaning from Mrs. Compson, who constantly complains "about how her own flesh and blood rose up to curse her" (225), meaning both her progeny and the traits they inherited. Jason might have perceived an anagogic significance in the conjunction of flesh and blood, but his view is always pointedly mundane, as when he twists his Mother's phrase quite ironically when replying about his niece, Miss Quentin: "Sure," he says, "that's just what I'm thinking of—flesh. And a little blood too, if I had my way" (225). But the matter of heritage *is* important to Jason, and the question of blood thus comes up in his conversation with the probably Jewish drummer, who says, "I'm an American. My folks have some French blood, why I have a nose like this" (238). For Jason blood is synonymous with lineage, family, name, and pride, however sardonic he is forced to be about these: "I haven't much pride, I can't afford it with a kitchen full of niggers to feed and robbing the state asylum of its star freshman. Blood, I says, governors and generals. It's a damn good thing we never had any kings and presidents; we'd all be down there at Jackson chasing butterflies" (286). Sarcasm aside, Jason still insists at least publicly upon maintaining all that blood usually means socially: "Me, without any hat, in the middle of the afternoon, having to chase up and down back alleys because of my mother's good name" (289–90), he says of himself as he pursues his niece, while admitting at the same time: "Like I say you cant do anything with a woman like that, if she's got it in her. If it's in her blood, you cant do anything with her" (290). Rather than representing an inclusive or sacramental concept, however, blood for Jason is exclusive and restrictive—incarcerating rather than liberating, a burden rather than a blessing. For him, blood never forms a synecdoche capable of unifying and redeeming his miserable existence.

Neither for Quentin nor for Jason has blood any meaning other than merely sacrificial; there is nothing anagogic or sacramental or spiritual in their feelings about blood. While Quentin can associate it with sex and death, sex for him is mere lust and has no connection with the sense of communion that sexual relationships ideally should entail, and death becomes simply a way out of his earthly dilemma—it is escape from life rather than triumph over or redemption into it: blood for him represents loss and finally has no redeeming significance. For Jason, blood is *Compson* blood, and that is little more than an onerous social burden he must bear; it is a sign he somehow has to appear to protect and cherish at the same time he really loathes it; his blood is a stigma, a mark, finally, of disgrace and ignominy, a pattern of blood that yields none of the redemptive meaning of Christ's stigmata.

The potentially synecdochic symbolism of voices is not so obvious as that of blood in *The Sound and the Fury;* the first section is presented from the point of view of a speechless idiot, and in the other sections voices are usually associated with characters other than the narrator. Nevertheless, this imagery is of crucial importance and has essentially the same potential for anagogic, sacramental symbolism as blood. Like blood, images of voices are related to a general religious anagogic symbolism as well as a specific Christian symbolism—the blood might become the incarnate *Flesh* and the voice might become the incarnate *Word*. As the potential synecdochic symbolism of blood is never quite realized in Quentin or Jason (to say nothing of Benjy), so the potential synecdochic, anagogic meanings of voice never become actual for the three brothers. Benjy, of course, has a voice, but the only use to which it can be put is his senseless bellowing. The idiot, standing at the opening of the novel, represents verbal articulation in its very earliest stage—that is one reason his presentation is dramatic. He is human experience at the threshold of meaningful verbalization, so the most symbolic phrase Faulkner attributes to him is "trying to say," and since Benjy is nevertheless an *acting* moral conscience the most telling phrases Faulkner attributes to others in Benjy's presence are "What are you moaning about" and "What is it. . . . What are you trying to tell . . ." (5). Susanne Langer has said, "the first thing we *do* with images is to envisage a story; just as the first thing we do with words is to tell something, to make a statement."[4] At his stage of intellectual and verbal development, Benjy can do nothing but try to say, try to tell, try to make a statement, though he can (or does) envisage a story through the images he views and reviews, and, as has been shown elsewhere, that story is thus dramatically presented and romantically shaped.[5] Were Benjy capable of the word, he might have given us the Word that his romantic vision embodies.

Benjy's wordless bellowing provides Quentin with one of the voices that haunts his imagination. In Quentin's section, the potentially anagogic symbolism of voice and voices begins to show more clearly. Although Quentin obviously represents a stage of verbal development beyond Benjy's, he still remains quite inarticulate in many ways; while Benjy is pre-verbal, Quentin in real sense is pre-discursive, for his interest is generally, like Benjy's, in the image, rather than in the word *per se,* and his interest in words is usually in their lyrical sounds and associations. Quentin has speech, then, but he does not have *the* word yet, so his imagination is plagued by voices that represent the passions of his existence: sex and death, innocence and its loss, all represented in Caddy and Dalton Ames. The voices Quentin hears are presentiments of the tragic archetype into which he fits a story of the fall; that is the significance of the sequence of images that begins "the voice that breathed" (95) and *"the voice that breathed o'er Eden"* (100), and ends with *"the odour of the apple tree"* and *"the voice that breathed o'er Eden clothes upon the bed by the nose seen above the apple"* (130). As we know, that voice, which in the hymn refers to God at the primal wedding, here associates Dalton Ames with Satan's tempting Eve in the Garden. But for Quentin that temptation is merely sexual, the primal marriage becomes a sexual fall, and the Satanic voice becomes the phallic voice of Ames and, perhaps, Herbert Head *"shot . . . through the floor of Caddy's room"* (130).

In symbolism more specifically anagogic, the voice is associated with the calling up of life, the life spirit. For Quentin, its meaning draws very close to this anagogic pattern, for it is connected with the spirit of *Eros* through his vision of human sexuality. Quentin sees all Caddy's lovers bound in the image, but he sees them with a disgust that betrays his fear of life, sex, *Eros.* The way in which this voice draws together Caddy's various lovers is enunciated with an unequivocal statement: *"Quentin has shot all of their voices through the floor of Caddy's room"* (138). Thus inextricably bound to Caddy, her lovers, and her sexual indiscretion, the voices Quentin reports are all one voice and mean to him only one thing; this meaning holds as true for the young men's voices as for the voices of the old people, Colonel Sartoris and Grandfather, whose "voices from beyond the cedars" Quentin could hear murmuring (219), and Mrs. Compson, *"a voice weeping steadily and softly beyond the twilit door the twilight-coloured smell of honeysuckle"* (117). For Quentin that meaning is, finally, death. That is the meaning Mrs. Compson attaches to Caddy's loss of innocence, and that is the meaning Benjy's wordless bellowing would also suggest as, at her wedding, the idiot pulls at her dress, and *"his voice hammered back and forth between the walls in waves and she shrinking against the wall getting smaller and smaller with her white face her eyes like thumbs dug into it until he pushed her out of the room his voice hammering back and forth as though its own momentum would not let it stop as though there were no place for it in silence bellowing"* (154). For Quentin, the idiot's bellowing voice becomes the symbol for all grief and guilt and shame; it is finally, then, a synecdochic voice, but the meaning it contains is negative rather than positive, and so cannot be truly anagogic as well. It represents Quentin's passion, his immolation, perhaps, but it is not ultimately redemptive as the voice shall be to Dilsey.

The image of Benjy's voice perpetuating itself, its momentum somehow resisting a diminution into silence, the bellowing becomes a live, self-generating organism, is directly connected to a developing synecdochic and anagogic significance for voices in Jason's experience. Jason, whether we find him sympathetic or not, stands at the farthest stage of verbal development represented by the Compson brothers. Much as he might represent the super ego to Benjy's id and Quentin's ego, in Carvel Collins' analysis,[6] Jason presents to us the process of verbalization as it reaches the level of discursiveness; his characteristic phrases are "What I says," "I says," and "Like I say," phrases that suggest the goal of Benjy's inchoate "trying to say." Jason's facility with language is one of the delights of his character; Jason is in his element in speech, and his personality type no doubt, in Freudian terms, is as oral as his mode of presentation, which in Frye's terms is *epos,* the Greek for *word.* His attitude suggests that one can articulate everything verbally and rationally, but it suggests further that he has the answer to every question, that, indeed, he has the word—or at least the words. His characterizing response, then, is one he offers to Father, *"I could have told you, all the time"* (63). But Jason's faith in rationality and verbalization is badly shaken when Miss Quentin lights out with the money he had so carefully stolen and hidden away. At the end, therefore, Jason is not far removed from his idiot brother, for as Benjy's voice lives on itself, so does Jason's when he recounts his plight to an unsympathetic sheriff: "Jason told him, his sense of injury and impotence feeding upon its own sound so that after a time he forgot his haste in the violent cumulation of his self justification and his outrage" (378). For Jason no more than for Quentin can the voice bring anything but grief and alienation. While his voice, like Benjy's "sound" that "might have been all time and injustice and sorrow become vocal for an instant" (359), can feed itself and the pain it articulates, it cannot exorcise wrongs or redeem time or injustice or sorrow. That role remains to be articulated in the black preacher's sermon and embodied synecdochically *and* anagogically in Dilsey.

III

These two strands of imagery are brought together in their anagogic significance in the novel's last section. There, the Reverend Shegog's sermon deepens the analogical matrix of images and sets the stage for Dilsey's role as synecdoche and anagoge. The sermon makes manifest the heretofore only potential anagogic symbolism of blood and voices. The Reverend Shegog names the anagogic, sacramental potential the images have had from the very beginning. Launching into the message he must convey as well as experience, the preacher firmly joins the two major images in the synecdoche of Christ-the-Lamb: "Brethren and sisteren, . . . I got the recollection and the blood of the Lamb!" (367), he says, first making references to the redemptive nature of Christ's shedding of His blood; then Faulkner himself suggests the anagogic power of the preacher's voice, which will soon bring *the* Word.

> He was like a worn small rock whelmed by the successive waves of his voice. With his body he seemed to feed the voice that, succubus like, had fleshed its teeth in him. And the congregation seemed to watch with its own eyes while the voice consumed him, until he was nothing and they were nothing and there was not even a voice but instead their hearts were speaking to one another in chanting measures beyond the need for words, so that when he came to rest against the reading desk, his monkey face lifted and his whole attitude that of a serene, tortured crucifix that transcended its shabbiness and insignificance and made it of no moment, a long moaning expulsion of breath rose from them, and a woman's single soprano: "Yes, Jesus!" (367–68)

The message is available now, not merely potential, as heart speaks directly to heart, and, as Faulkner's gloss implies, human experience is shown to have the capability of redeeming itself. But this theme needs reification and reiteration and finds both in yet one more of the many shifts in the preacher's voice, as he says "Breddren en sistuhn . . . I got de ricklickshun in de *blood* of de Lamb," and the congregation "just sat swaying a little in their seats as the *voice* took them into itself" (368; italics mine).

The Reverend Shegog's Easter theme is plain now. But for Faulkner's *novel's* theme, rather than Shegog's, the primary significance of the sermon's imagery, the major items of which *(light, word, golden horns, blood)* all have a similar synecdochic and perhaps anagogic significance, lies in its impact upon central characters. Thus, "In the midst of the voices and the hands," as the sermon ends, "Ben sat, rapt in his sweet blue gaze. Dilsey sat bolt upright beside, crying rigidly and quietly in the annealment and the blood of the remembered Lamb" (370–71). At the conclusion of Shegog's sermon, Benjy Compson, his moaning, bellowing voice stilled, for a moment seems to have found peace and contentment, and the promises of time and justice and sorrow seem finally to be redeemed, if not permanently, at least so long as he and the congregation are rapt/wrapped in the preacher's consummated vision.

But the novel does not end here, nor should it, for Faulkner must find a way to concretize the preacher's anagogic vision. The blood and the voice need to be made even more local than Shegog can make them. The sense of the human tragedy's being contained by a universal comedy, precisely the sense that transforms a simple comedy into a *commedia,* is the essential theme of the preacher's message, but it is also the theme of the fourth section as a whole, which inevitably casts its aura over the entire novel's structure. In the last section this theme is ultimately related more crucially to the roles of Dilsey and Benjy than that of the preacher. His sermon, his *voice,* speaks of the redemptive power of Christ's *blood,* but it is the idiot whose flesh carries inchoate human possibilities for innocence and the old black woman who seems to become those possibilities embodied. This positive, perhaps sentimentalized role Dilsey plays in the novel is well known by most readers. Considering the great mass of fully appreciative criticism, one finds it necessary to point out only that the affirmation we feel after the last section is inevitably connected to the Christian *commedia,* the divine comedy of death and resurrection out of which Dante or Shakespeare or Milton or Michelangelo might have worked. It is this particular conception that stands behind the Easter weekend during which the events in present time take place in the novel and behind the sermon Dilsey hears from the "monkey preacher." But most of all it is necessary to point out that Dilsey contains this *commedia,* an anagogic role suggested in her matter-of-fact pronouncements that "I've seed de first en de last," "I seed de beginning, en now I sees de endin" (371), and in her symbolic role *vis à vis* Benjy as the Madonna, the enduring female and mother.

Benjy and Dilsey participate in an iconographic system of anagogic symbolism within the novel. In the novel's first section, Faulkner makes clear that the idiot represents "innocence" in the world of *The Sound and the Fury*. Although Benjy almost ritually dramatizes this meaning in many ways, there is also an important pictorial dimension to this role in the fourth section. Mr. Compson points toward it in the seemingly irrelevant remark in which he uses the Latin phrase *"Et ego in Arcadia"* (53). Irrelevant not at all, this phrase in fact puts Benjy, along with Jason, Quentin, and Caddy, into an enduring iconic tradition in pictorial art, one in which Benjy continues his role in a conventional pastoral scheme. The most famous pictorial treatment of the pastoral theme Father's tag invokes is that by Nicolas Poussin (dated about 1640–45). A description of the painting, along with an analysis of its meaning, offers a suggestive parallel between the traditional theme and Faulkner's use of it.

> Three handsome shepherds [read: "young people"] are both fascinated and moved by an austerely simple tomb, one of them kneeling on the ground, so as to decipher the half-effaced inscription, *Et in Arcadia ego,* the second explaining its meaning to a lovely girl, who listens to him in a quiet, thoughtful attitude, the third trajected into a sympathetically brooding melancholy. It is as though the youthful people, all silent, were listening to or pondering over this imaginary message of a former fellow being: "I, too, lived in Arcadia, where you now live; I, too, enjoyed the pleasures which you now enjoy; and yet I am dead and buried." We instantly perceive a strange ambiguous feeling which suggests both a mournful anticipation of man's inevitable destiny and an intense consciousness of the sweetness of life.[7]

Such a description, noting the three young men and the beautiful girl, might well evoke Faulkner's Compson children. More surely, Father's intoning of the Latin tag suggests the power of Faulkner's pastoral elegiac theme, the ambivalent relationship between innocence and experience, not just in Benjy's section, but throughout the entire novel. Still, the theme of *Et ego in Arcadia* or *Et in Arcadia ego* is much more elegiac than celebratory. Hence, in order to lift this nostalgic theme beyond the merely sentimental, Faulkner places Benjy in yet one more strongly pictorial, iconic text, one less romantic and idealistic, one more realistic and earthly than Poussin's.

Dilsey's role as the Madonna, therefore, gives life to the blood and the voice of anagogic interpretation by serving as "the Center" from which vitality emanates. She finally completes this last picture and establishes the form

of Faulkner's *commedia*. In this role Dilsey is related to the idiot in the way
that the Virgin Mary is related to Christ. First she is mother to the child: in
the preacher's words—"Ma'y settin in de do' wid Jesus on her lap, de little
Jesus. Like dem chillen dar, de little Jesus" (369); in Faulkner's words—"Dilsey
sat bolt upright, her hand on Ben's knee. Two tears slid down her fallen
cheeks, in and out of the myriad coruscations of immolation and abnegation
and time" (368); and, in Faulkner's words, quoted previously—"Dilsey sat
bolt upright beside [Benjy], crying rigidly and quietly in the annealment and
the blood of the remembered Lamb" (370–71). Surrounded, it seems, in the
"sweet blue," the Virgin's color, of Benjy's rapture, Dilsey and the idiot most
evidently are the Madonna and Child, preparing the way for them to become,
just as appropriately, the Mother and the Crucified Son.

David Williams has remarked upon the conjunction of Madonna, Christ-
the-Son, and yet one more synecdochic image of the Mother-goddess—the
Pietà—in the images of Dilsey and Benjy as they sit in the church listening
to the Reverend Shegog: "At the same time [that Christ is seen as man and
as the infant Jesus], the Negro 'mother' is portrayed in the midst of the congregation, weeping beside her idiot 'son.' . . . The new accent heard in this
double account of the dying god is achieved in the shift of emphasis from
the traditional Protestant image of the Heavenly Son, the Redeemer sent by
the Father, to the conflated pagan figure of the Madonna-*Pietà*."[8] Williams
makes a very telling point about the direction in which these images take
Faulkner's novel, for, noting that Faulkner presents "the essence of sacramental experience—in an authentic native idiom" (11), he insists that despite
the nominal Christianity of Shegog's and Dilsey's religion, Faulkner's emphasis is instead upon the non-Christian, the pagan. Faulkner has traded a "spent
religious icon" (11)—the Christian Madonna and Child—for a more vital new
symbol, Dilsey-as-*Pietà*, "the mother of death mourning her son" (68).

Thus, it finally is in the iconographic image of the Madonna/*Pietà* (in a
passage Williams does not particularly note) that we see Benjy and Dilsey
together,[9] immediately before Luster would drive the idiot to the cemetery:

> Dilsey led Ben to the bed and drew him down beside her and she held him, rock-
> ing back and forth, wiping his drooling mouth upon the hem of her skirt. "Hush,
> now," she said, stroking his head, "Hush. Dilsey got you." But he bellowed slowly,
> abjectly, without tears; the grave hopeless sound of all voiceless misery under the
> sun. (395).

In traditional iconic symbolism, the *Pietà* (as Williams points out) is an ambiguous figure, representing the "terrible" side of the Mother; in Jung, it is pointed out, too, that the *Pietà* is associated with nature's cruel law of death and indifference to suffering. But Dilsey's role is rather to mediate between two less ambiguous "Mothers" in this novel; these are, Williams shows plainly (see 66–73), Mrs. Compson and Caddy, "Terrible Mother" and "Virgin Mother," respectively. Dilsey—in Evelyn Scott's words—is a "holy compromise."[10] She is not indifferent to suffering, as her final scene with Benjy demonstrates touchingly. Speaking comforting words, "You's de Lawd's chile, anyway. En I be His'n too, fo long, praise Jesus" (396), Dilsey wraps Benjy and sends him on the journey—symbolically inevitable—to the graveyard.

Rather than leaving us with a sense of negation, however, the image Dilsey and Benjy project together as the *Pietà* is the one most crucial for understanding the novel's *commedic* structure. In the *Pietà* we see the combination of suffering and serenity, of anguish and hope, that gives concrete meaning to the Christian *commedia* of death and resurrection. In the figure of Benjy we see all the "voiceless misery under the sun," but in Dilsey we see the earthier face of piety and pity, the comforter who can redeem that misery in human terms. So it is Dilsey, having tried all day to restore Benjy's peace, who triumphs when Jason turns Benjy back from the cemetery toward home—perhaps, in a realistic novel, the closest we can come to seeing life triumph over death; it is Dilsey whose values overcome, and it is Dilsey, therefore, who comes to stand for those values often attributed to Christians alone, but which are the property of all benevolent peoples. In Faulkner's *commedia* these values finally come not so much from the religious as from the natural perspective that Dilsey embodies. I agree with David Williams, when he says, "In a structural sense, the icon of the Madonna and the icon of the *Pietà* contain the whole of the [novel's] narrative between them; they give it its 'time' but they also surround that time. In a strictly achetypal sense, they evoke nonhistorical figures embracing creatures who are fully temporal" (94).

IV

What this analysis means, then, despite all the usual Christian readings, is that *The Sound and the Fury* is not finally a Christian novel at all, for the Christian imagery is ultimately to be taken as a backgrounded metaphor, an analogical structure familiar to us by which we can grasp something less familiar.[11] Not a metaphoric Christ, finally, but a fictionally realized Dilsey gives experiential meaning to the novel. Dilsey stands to the novel's characters as Christ stands to humanity, for it is she whose life fleshes out—in all its ambiguity—the redemptive message of the Reverend Shegog. Her total experience incarnates the momentary vision of wholeness the preacher brings. To us, to Dilsey, or to Faulkner, it makes no difference that this vision is only fleeting; it is in Dilsey and in her section, where it has never been more than potentially present until then. Evelyn Scott was absolutely correct, I think, in her early review of *The Sound and the Fury:*

> Dilsey . . . provides the beauty of coherence against the background of struggling choice. . . . Dilsey isn't searching for a soul. She *is* the soul. . . . She is the conscious human accepting the limitations of herself, the iron boundaries of circumstance, and still, to the best of her ability, achieving a holy compromise for aspiration. (28)

Thus, while I can also agree with much that David Williams says of the generally pagan archetypalism of the novel's significant symbolism, I cannot agree with his conclusion about the novel's final "tone of pessimism" (94). Like Eliot's "still point," or Joyce's "epiphany," or Lawrence's ecstatic moment, the momentary glimpse of peace and grace offered to us here gives meaning to the seemingly specious order and serenity Benjy's roaring voice establishes at the novel's conclusion. It is Dilsey, then, who is the synecdochic image embodying the anagogic meaning and form of the novel, for it is she who contains the whole range of human experience—the sweep of innocence and experience, plenitude and vacancy, comedy and tragedy—presented in *The Sound and the Fury.*

NOTES

1. André Bleikasten. *The Most Splendid Failure: Faulkner's "The Sound and the Fury"* (Bloomington: Indiana University Press, 1976).

2. Northrop Frye, *Anatomy of Criticism* (Princeton: Princeton Univ. Press, 1957), 122. For the background of my sense of synecdoche and its place within tropological analysis, see Hayden

V. White, *Tropics of Discourse: Essays in Cultural Criticism* (Baltimore: Johns Hopkins University Press, 1978); White's tropology is rooted in Vico, Burke, and, in some dimensions, Northrop Frye. White suggests that metaphor provides our first step toward understanding something new by the process of similarity; metonymy provides the next step, extending the range of metaphorical identification through establishing difference, cause and effect relations, and spatial extensions; synecdoche is the third step, integrating the discrete pieces of data metonymy provides within a whole greater than the parts; the final phase is the trope of irony, which begins to question the very bases of knowledge or understanding. In White's *schema,* metaphor and synecdoche are integrative, and associated with Romance and Comedic plots, respectively; metonymy and irony are dispersive, and associated, respectively, with Tragedy and Satiric plots.

3. William Faulkner, *The Sound and the Fury* (New York: Vintage, 1963), 403–27. This text is cited throughout this essay.

4. *Philosophy in a New Key* (Cambridge, Mass: Harvard University Press, 1951), 145.

5. See James M. Mellard, "Caliban as Prospero: Benjy and *The Sound and the Fury,*" *Novel: A Forum on Fiction* 3 (1970): 233–48. For another type of approach to plot and structure, see also "Disclosure Plot: *The Sound and the Fury,*" in Austin M. Wright, *The Formal Principle of the Novel* (Ithaca: Cornell University Press, 1981), 218–39.

6. Carvel Collins, "The Interior Monologues of *The Sound and the Fury,*" *English Institute Essays 1952* (New York: Columbia Univ. Press, 1954), 29–55.

7. Irwin Panofsky, *"Et in Arcadia Ego:* On the Conception of Transience in Poussin and Watteau," in *Philosophy and History: Essays Presented to Ernst Cassirer,* ed. Raymond Klibansky and H. J. Paton (New York: Harper Torchbooks, 1963), 224.

8. David Williams, *Faulkner's Women: The Myth and the Muse* (Montreal and London: McGill-Queen's University Press, 1977), 11. I have been aided in my own interpretation—especially in the linking together of images such as *blood, voices, words, light, horns,* and the *Pietà*—by J. E. Cirlot, *A Dictionary of Symbols,* trans. from the Spanish by Jack Sage (New York: Philosophical Library, 1962).

9. The *visual* representation of the *Pietà,* though not necessarily inevitable in this context, is certainly a logical next step for an author so interested in pictorial and sculptural art. Were space available I would also show that the mode of presentation in the entire fourth section is pictorial in James's or Lubbock's terms. Faulkner himself was a talented natural artist (a fact well-known), and he made the protagonist of *Mosquitoes* a sculptor. According to Phyllis Klotman, the image of the *Pietà* is frequently associated with black mothers and their dead sons (dead, usually, as a result of lynchings) in paintings by black artists. Faulkner's consciousness of the image may well have been stirred by a representation of the *Pietà* seen in World War I's most celebrated ad poster glorifying the American Red Cross; in it, a massive, sculpted Madonna/

nurse cradles a wounded, stretcher-bound soldier, an image very close to the one Faulkner offers of Dilsey and Benjy together.

10. Evelyn Scott, "On William Faulkner's *The Sound and the Fury*," ed. Michael H. Cowan (Englewood Cliffs, N.J.: Prentice Hall, 1968), 28.

11. Bleikasten gives an excellent treatment of the Christian interpretation of the novel, but concludes that it "stubbornly resists any attempt to dissolve its opaqueness into the reassuring clarity of an ideological statement" (p. 202). Perhaps the most interesting comment Bleikasten makes in connection with my anagogic reading of the novel is that "Reverent Shegog, the frail vessel of the sovereign Word, may be taken for an analogon of the novelist himself, reaching the point of inspired dispossession where his individuality gives way to the 'voice.' And the mystical vision granted to the preacher may likewise be said to metaphorize the poetic vision sought after by the writer" (p. 205).

Faulkner's Family Dilemma: Quentin's Crucible

GARY STORHOFF

"Home is the thing worth having above everything"

William Faulkner, letter to his mother, 21 October 1918[1]

Perhaps "the family" is the most contested term in contemporary America. Evolved into a mythical construction, the family has been increasingly appropriated by neoconservative politics. Its definition, as championed by the right wing, denotes a "haven in a heartless world," a space defined by its harmony and order, and by the benevolent authority of mutually reinforcing parents—in short, the unproblematic locus of all positive meaning and value. Yet any student of William Faulkner's work understands that this nostalgic, glorified, and cozy conceptualization of the family is too often a sad distortion of domestic reality. In his fiction, Faulkner exposes the conservative myths that cluster about the family as ideological constructions concealing the pain and suffering of the most vulnerable human beings—children, women, the elderly. In Faulkner's "family-centered literature,"[2] we discover the ravages of alcoholism and its effects on the family, miserable

Reprinted with permission from *The Mississippi Quarterly* 51 (summer 1998): 465–82.

marriages that lead to spousal abuse, threats of sibling incest and sibling violence, violence against infants and children, and violence of adult children
against their parents. In short, Faulkner's families are (to use the popular
term) a "dysfunctional" lot indeed!

Because in Faulkner's work the family frequently takes thematic prece-
dence, criticism would do well to explore precisely how his families operate
collectively, and how individual members cling to their dysfunctional patterns of behavior in order to keep an otherwise collapsing family unit intact—
even as they (like Faulkner in his 1918 letter to his mother) desperately
harbor the belief that the family will compensate for the pain and suffering
in the outside world. Faulkner, whose family of origin was chronically alcoholic, knew that sometimes the family makes things worse. For a fruitful
examination of the dynamics of Faulkner's fictional family, we must look
beyond the individualistic psychologies initiated by Freud and his followers.
We must look elsewhere than to the traditional psychoanalytic emphasis on
the individual as an "autonomous psychological entity" and "the family only
as a collection of relatively autonomous people, each motivated by his or her
own particular psychological mechanisms and conflicts."[3] Indeed, a psycho-
analytically oriented interrogation, a perspective that limits the critic's analysis too narrowly to a character's introjected *intra*personal problematic (e.g.,
the Oedipal complex), too often leads the critic away from more complex
triggers of behavior, those that emerge from the family itself. Mainstream
contemporary psychology offers a rich model for interpreting family interaction: family systems theory, founded on the concept of the "undifferentiated
family ego mass" (or enmeshed family identity) that family therapists believe
prevails in families where identity boundaries have disappeared, and where
individuation is almost absent.[4] The therapist's assumption is that to avoid
conflict, such families foster intense loyalty and dependency for the sake of
a false sense of order and harmony. The entire family engages in a "dance,"
a metaphor often used by therapists to characterize the family's ritualized,
rigid, seemingly choreographed collective behavior.

The model of family systems theory—developed by the "Gregory Bateson
Group" in the late 1950s and currently a vast, diverse, international research
and therapeutic project—provides an illuminating explanation of the family's
interactive bonds within the family. Systems theory conceives of the family
as a complex, organic whole, in which an individual member's aberrant
behavior is seen as a consequence of an interplay of emotional forces operating to maintain that family's system. The foundation of family systems

theory lies in general systems theory, communication theory and cybernetics, and with disaffected psychoanalysts. Bateson's ecological systems approach to the family examines the necessary connective elements by which each individual's respective position is fixed and affirmed within the constellation of the family system. In therapist Sal Minuchin's words, the family becomes the individual's "matrix of identity"; he sees in families "[a] mosaic—a puzzle in which each individual self defines the others and the whole defines the self, like an Escher painting in which the end is also the beginning."[5] This critical perspective works from the premise that a troubled person cannot be understood until his/her place within the family as a closed system is acknowledged and addressed directly.

Such a psychological model would be particularly enlightening for Faulkner studies, since the Compson family is a kind of crucible within which the children's characters are created. In Faulkner's works, identity emerges from the family, as Donald M. Kartiganer explains: "Confronting a single member of [Faulkner's fictional families] . . . we soon find ourselves addressing family complexes, synchronic and diachronic systems whose individual units take their meanings from their transactions with each other."[6] Family systems theory introduces to Faulkner criticism the concealed dynamics of the interrelationships of the family, and the covert way patterns designed corporately by the family tend to shape and define each individual member's identity, persisting even into the adulthood of the children. Rather than focusing on a single dyad of the family (especially the mother-son relationship), or on the specific intrapsychic symptoms of an individual family member, a literary aesthetic employing family systems theory attempts to reconstruct and account for the fictional family's consistently chosen behavior patterns.

Systems theory does not dismiss, of course, the cultural and the historical influences that also tend to shape an individual's character; nevertheless, the systems theorist would discover in the individual's *first* social unit, his/her family circle, the primary triggers of a character's behavior patterns. Thus, to explain Quentin's tragedy as the consequence of "the trauma of the Civil War defeat,"[7] as merely a sociocultural derivative of a specific regional and historical context, is misleading in its partial truth. The Compson children's actions, even Quentin's suicide, are the effects of the connective elements of their family, created by them for the collective whole. To see Quentin as "gone insane"[8] also oversimplifies Quentin's dilemma, for Quentin's actions on his last day are plausible if reframed within the context of his family's web of interactions.

In the psychoanalytical critic's excavation of a character's intrapsychic drives and unconscious instincts, too often other more significant, empirical triggers of a character's behavior may be overlooked. A character's behavior may well be an effort to cope with *inter*personal family problems, dilemmas involving the family as a corporate entity, and his/her "solutions" to these problems are the consequences of family patterns and "rules" of which he/she is usually unaware. The discovery of Quentin's unconscious "Oedipal complex," for example, too quickly forecloses investigation of other, usually more readily apparent family dynamics, especially those that reveal Quentin's embeddedness in his family. Perhaps the most sophisticated, eloquent, and influential Freudian reading of Quentin is by John T. Irwin, who writes, "Thus, Quentin's narcissism is necessarily linked with his incestuous desire for his sister, for . . . brother-sister incest is a substitute for child-parent incest—what the brother seeks in his sister is his mother" (43). It is a tribute to Irwin's powerful argument and brilliant insights that a Freudian analysis of Quentin now seems virtually commonsensical.[9] Even if the family's collective behavior as a contributory motivating factor is analyzed, the critic usually employs a familiar Freudian/Lacanian grid. For example, Philip Weinstein, in discussing Mr. Compson as "the most engagingly impotent father in Faulkner's fiction," writes, "We see his failure to shepherd his offspring through the Oedipal crisis, for the role of the father is to *suspend* the possibility of castration over the son's rebellious desires, leading to the latter's successful self-discipline and eventual gender maturation."[10] By focusing almost exclusively on Quentin's "Oedipal crisis," we lose too much of the novel's complex revelation of family interactional patterns.

I

QUENTIN AND HIS ALCOHOLIC FAMILY

"Remember that we deal with alcohol—cunning, baffling, powerful."[11]

Quentin is a test case for family systems theory, since he represents a seemingly obvious case of an unresolved Oedipal crisis. Nevertheless, by placing Quentin within the context of his family habitual patterns of behavior, we can see much more clearly why he makes his choices, even when he is hundreds of miles away from them. As I have argued elsewhere, the Compson family is organized around the alcoholism of Mr. Compson, who stanches the family's emotional bleeding with his ever-constant "hushing," his self-deceptive embrace of stoicism, and his refusal to acknowledge the emotions of his children.[12] The invasion of alcohol in the Compson family has become subtle and deceptive; as the *Alcoholics Anonymous Handbook* states, "Remember that we deal with alcohol—cunning, baffling, powerful" (58). Mr. Compson's alcoholism is central to the creation of the family's basic protocols and operations; in fact, it is a critical family theme that all members of the family support his substance abuse. Using the designation of Peter Steinglass, who links his research on alcoholism with family systems, the Compsons could be described as an "Alcoholic Family": "stress attendant on alcoholism is spread uniformly throughout the family rather than being restricted either to the person who is drinking or to the nonalcoholic spouse."[13] Murray Bowen, a leading theorist of family systems, concurs: chronic alcoholism is a systemic rather than individual symptom, for "alcoholism is one of the common human dysfunctions. As a dysfunction, it exists in the context of an imbalance in functioning in the total family system. . . . [E]very important family member plays a part in the dysfunction of the dysfunctional member" (262).

The core dynamic of the Compson family is the preservation of Mr. Compson's drinking, since it has by the time of the children's adolescence achieved a homeostatic purpose within the closed family circle—that is, his alcoholism is a noxious glue that holds the family together, apart from the world, in a bond of manageable misery. It is important, however, that no family member recognizes this, nor does any member criticize Mr. Compson for his substance abuse, since this might jeopardize family unity. The most important organizing principle stabilizing their family life is denied; the most significant emotional issue affecting them is not expressed. Alcoholism is the figurative elephant in the living room—impossible to ignore but never discussed. Unsurprisingly, this situation sets up terrific emotional incongruities. Psychotherapist and researcher Stephanie Brown remarks that alcoholic families often attempt collectively "to preserve [an] inherent contradiction . . . explanations [and strategies] have been constructed to allow the drinking behavior to be maintained and denied at the same time."[14] As we shall see, contradictions, confused communications, and paradox permeate the Compson family, ultimately leading Quentin to his suicide.

As eldest son, Quentin has his part to play in stabilizing the Compson
family life. Research in alcoholic families reveals how children defend themselves against chaos by adopting roles, which produce a greater degree of pre-
dictability in family routines. Michael Elkin, for example, writes "[Alcohol]
can homogenize and organize very diverse people in predictable patterns."[15]
The discussion of assigned role-playing is pervasive in psychological research
on alcoholism. Most often, children devise "false selves" to accommodate
their roles within the family structure: the "hero," "scapegoat," "lost child,"
or "mascot."[16] The hero, usually the eldest child, assumes the responsibility
within the alcoholic system to recoup the family prestige lost by the parent's
abdication of responsibility and loss of control. As the afflicted parent's com-
plement, the child over-performs as a structural remedy for the parent's
under-functioning because of alcoholism. The child's achievements, usually
won at great psychic cost, deflect attention from the perceived failure of the
parent (with the underlying assumption that the *real* purpose of the hero is
eventually to stop the parent's drinking). Quentin, called by Herbert Head the
"half-baked Galahad,"[17] represents the gendered family hero of the
Compsons—but it is his *entire* family, not simply Quentin's peculiar gentlemanly code or the exigencies of Southern culture, that fosters his heroic role.

In his childhood, Quentin's heroism in his family revolves around his
academic achievements, his efforts supplying a compensatory role in a system distorted by his father's alcoholism. As his father is a notable failure in
the world, his son is a remarkable success. This "fit" of father and son makes
comprehensible their seeming closeness, Quentin's obsession with his father's
last conversation with him, and his need to "confess" to his father his imagined incest with Caddy.

Because Mr. Compson is unwilling to disrupt the regulatory function
Quentin performs and because the family's status quo supports his alcoholism, he unconsciously conceals his own participation in Quentin's role-
formation by displaying a lack of interest in Quentin's academic
achievements, and thereby seems to be a cynical foil to his wife. Her ambi-
tion, he tells Quentin, has been since the eldest child's birth to send him to
Harvard, presumably for the social status she would gain. But textual evidence implies that Mr. Compson is also wrapped up in Quentin's success in
school. He twice "hushes" the family so that Quentin can concentrate on his
studies (62, 72); and he obviously favors his more intellectual son over Jason.
Most important, of course, is his sacrifice of the family legacy when he sells

"Benjy's pasture" to pay for Quentin's tuition. Nevertheless, Mr. Compson mockingly implies that it is only Caroline who is bound up with Quentin's academic career: "for you to go to harvard has been your mothers dream since you were born and no compson has ever disappointed a lady" (178).

Caddy subtly reinforces Quentin's role as family hero. She cooperates in sustaining the family myth of Quentin's heroic "duty" in the university, though she alone seems to understand his pervasive unhappiness as a Harvard student: " . . . *they sold the pasture for you so you could go to Harvard dont you see you've got to finish now if you dont finish he'll have nothing*" (124). Caddy's appeal exacerbates Quentin's sense of guilt over his family's financial sacrifice, since he immediately repeats to himself her words *"Sold the pasture"* (124). She also impresses upon him his own responsibility to Mr. Compson (and by extension, to the family) to succeed, since if he does not enroll, "he'll have nothing." The communication is clear: Mr. Compson's happiness and well being depends upon his children, especially Quentin. Unaware, Caddy joins the family coalition; in complicity with her parents, she too imposes the role of "half-baked Galahad" upon Quentin—a role that is not congruent with his deepest sense of self.

The "real" Quentin shows very little interest in academics.[18] On the contrary, as a child he counts the minutes to the school day's dismissal, he remembers, and his only allusion to his education occurs when he is embarrassed by "Miss Laura" for missing an easy question about the discovery of the Mississippi River (88). Claiming that he prefers that Jason take his place at Harvard, he is lackadaisical at best in his college studies: He has been reprimanded by the dean for cutting lecture courses and compulsory chapel (significantly, he cuts psychology as well [p. 101]), and Shreve asks him, "'Have you got too proud to attend classes too?'" (82).

II

QUENTIN'S DOUBLE BIND

"it will be better for me for all of us"

Why does Quentin not resist his family's demands, but conform to a constructed identity that he appears to disavow? The answer may be found in the family's fundamentally conflictual, even contradictory communicatory system, termed by Gregory Bateson "the double bind—a situation in which no matter what a person does, he 'can't win.'"[19] In a double-bind situation, a family member sends two messages, one explicit message that is contradicted by a second, implied "metacommentary"—often expressed nonverbally, with a gesture or an inappropriate action. The two mutually exclusive messages, according to Bateson, occur on separate logical levels, and are relayed to another family member who is not in a position to recognize their logical inconsistency. Bateson describes the possibility of contradictory messages in one message: "All communication has this characteristic—it can be magically modified by accompanying communication (230). Receiving from his family a mixed, contradictory message produces an impasse in Quentin; thus, the family exerts control over him, though usually all members are unaware of the rules they have constructed corporately. From Bateson's ecological, systems perspective, such communication impedes growth and may lead to mental instability—presumably Quentin's condition.

Among the Compsons, Quentin's schooling is a battlefield of double-bind messages: He is expected to overachieve while simultaneously his achievement is devalued within the family. The family's explicit message to Quentin—"Be a great student"—is overruled by a secondary, occluded metacommunication—"Your studies do not matter." Given these two levels of contradiction, there is no way Quentin can make a correct choice. Mr. Compson, for example, gives Quentin two coinciding but contradictory messages. He mocks Caroline's ambitions for Quentin's Harvard education (in effect, communicating his indifference to Harvard's "dead sound"), even as he sells his family's legacy for Quentin's tuition (a metacommunication that reverses or qualifies his verbal communication). In a converse relationship with her husband, Mrs. Compson inverts the father's double-bind message to Quentin. She has cherished the possibility of Quentin's going to Harvard since his birth, according to Mr. Compson; yet she tells Herbert Head in Quentin's presence that she really values the practicality and anti-intellectualism of her favorite child, Jason: "Jason will make a splendid banker he is the only one of my children with any practical sense you can thank me for that" (94). Caddy is the one family member who could help Quentin escape from the family's double-bind pattern, but she too is tied to the double bind created for Quentin. By exploiting the guilt he feels over the loss of Benjy's pasture for his tuition and his responsibility for Mr. Compson's happiness, she in effect coerces him to go to Harvard. Given the two levels of contradiction his family insists upon, Quentin finds himself in an "impossible situation" (Bateson, 210) and is in effect stymied.

Quentin's helplessness in responding to his family's irreconcilable messages is magnified in his relationship with Caddy, whom he (as family hero) is enjoined both to protect and to let down. On the one hand, he receives his father's primary message that "Women are never virgins. Purity is a negative state and therefore contrary to nature. It's nature is hurting you not Caddy and I said That's just words and he said So is virginity" (116). But Mr. Compson's dismissal of the importance of Caddy's virginity is contradicted by his nonverbal metacommunication—the suicidal drinking bouts—that reveal his emotional devastation at her apparently indiscriminate and imprudent sexual activity. The two children may intuitively understand this contradiction, but (caught as they both are in the double bind) they are unable to analyze it. Caddy confesses to Quentin that she has "caused" her father's latest bout of drinking: *"Father will be dead in a year they say if he doesn't stop drinking and he wont stop he cant stop since I since last summer"* (124). Quentin callously agrees with her (and presumably with Jason and Caroline) that she is responsible for their father's drunkenness: *"If they* [father and Benjy] *need any looking after it's because of you"* (111). In other words, he tacitly agrees with his father's metacommunication—that Caddy's virginity is a matter of (his *and* his father's) life and death.

In a sense, his reply to Caddy also acknowledges his own culpability. He too feels responsible for his father's suicidal drinking; he too let the family down, since he failed to protect Caddy from "blackguards" such as Dalton Ames. Both Caddy and Quentin shift responsibility for the drinking from the alcoholic parent to themselves. Quentin especially is in an untenable situation: Either he renounces his father's direct statement ("Caddy's virginity is meaningless"), or his indirect metacommentary ("Caddy's loss of virginity is terrible enough to die for"). The father's designation of Caddy's sexual activity as simultaneously natural and as repugnant, inevitable but also to be avoided creates in Quentin an emotional discontinuity, and as Anthony Wilden writes, "[W]hen this confusion occurs in certain power relationships, such as that between parent and child, it may lead to pathological communication which is at least formally equivalent to 'schizophrenic communications.'"[20] Caught in the crosshairs of his family's irreconcilable demands, Quentin must confront his own powerlessness and his failure as "hero" in the family's systemic configuration—a failure that Quentin's family has secretly promoted.

Bateson explains that an individual will inevitably replicate his family's double-bind dynamic in other interactional contexts, since "the complete set of ingredients is no longer necessary when the victim has learned to perceive his universe in double bind patterns. Almost any part of a double bind sequence may then be sufficient to precipitate panic or rage" (207). Given the closed nature of the Compson alcoholic family system, the pattern set up within the context of that system cannot change. Thus, the events of "June Second 1910" provide ample evidence of Quentin's subjugation to the double-bind pattern, even as he prepares for death in Massachusetts. Having learned to live with his father's combined self-indulgence and self-abnegation, having adjusted to his mother's "practicality" and admiration for "dead sounds," having lived by paradoxical injunctions that he cannot recognize, Quentin expects and even yearns for contradictory patterns in other social contexts—far from his family and their immediate influence.

On June 2, Quentin's watch becomes a functional symbol of his family's double bind. Given to him as the treasured legacy of his legendary grandfather—"Grandfather was always right" (176)—the watch alternately communicates and metacommunicates, and oscillates in its meaning from a sign of the family's past grandeur to a concrete representation of human fragmentation and destruction. This object was given to Quentin by his father as a high school graduation present—his graduation obviously a highly symbolic moment for the family, at once a public recognition of his heroic achievement and a meaningless ceremony. Mr. Compson calls the watch "the mausoleum of all hope and desire" (76): paradoxically, the watch represents both hope and the futility of desire. The watch, then, both legitimizes Quentin's effort and signifies the futility of any action, since all life must end in death. Furthermore, the symbol is meant by his father to be both observed and ignored: "I give it to you not that you may remember time, but that you might forget it now and then" (76). So it is that Quentin cannot throw the watch away, or leave it in his room, or in any other way dispose of it: He must at once keep it and repudiate it. In accordance with his father's nihilism (the metacommunication in his father's gift), Quentin is compelled to acknowledge its emptiness by resisting its significance in his life, so he breaks off the hands, as if to assert literally its pointlessness.

On the last day of his life, Quentin obsessively seeks out situations that are substitutions of the double-bind dynamic he adjusted to in his family of origin. Quentin deliberately chooses interactions that are intense recreations of his earlier experiences in his family, but that in reality are systematically escalating and distorted forms of his family's basic pattern. During that afternoon, in Kartiganer's felicitous phrase, Quentin plays "a Hamlet not altogether distinguishable from the fool" ("Quentin," 392); but in doing so, he also serves both ends of his family's claim on him—to be the hero *and* the failure; to create situations where he acts nobly, but at the same time, foolishly and absurdly.

For example, Quentin, appalled by Gerald Bland's sexist bragging about his sexual conquests, strikes out at him in rage (recall Bateson's statement that a perceived double bind might produce rage and panic). Partly an effort to compensate for his humiliation at the hands of Dalton Ames, Quentin's challenge of Bland is a ludicrous effort to be, in Spoade's words, "the champion of dames" (167). This champion, however, devises his own defeat. It is only predictable that he suffers a beating, since Gerald is a trained boxer, a fact Quentin knew before he attacked:

> ". . . Where'd he learn to box?"
>
> "He's been going to Mike's every day, over in town," I said.
>
> "He has?" Spoade said. "Did you know that when you hit him?"
>
> "I don't know," I said. "I guess so. Yes." (166)

Furthermore, Quentin invites his own affront simply by associating with Bland and responding seriously to his talk; Gerald's other companions are not surprised by his boasting, nor by his attitude toward women. They even expect it as Gerald's typical behavior: "'Ah, he was blowing off *as usual,*' Shreve said, 'about his women,'"(166; emphasis added). Playing the fool *and* the tragic hero is Quentin's familiar pattern in his family, and he attempts to reproduce it in Massachusetts.[21] Although his friends are amazed—"Bud, you excite not only admiration, but horror" (167), Quentin's weird behavior, when understood within the context of his family's interaction with him and their expectations for him, could be construed as his solution to the stress and erosion of identity produced by double binding.[22]

His "defense" of the little Italian girl is another unconscious effort to recreate a double-bind situation so that he can reenact his role as "half-baked Galahad." It is surely true that the "little dirty child" reminds him of Caddy, as criticism of this scene has amply noted (e.g., by Matthews, 59–60), but it is also one more opportunity created by Quentin to act heroically and dishonorably at the same time. Quentin arranges a situation that ensures his humiliation and embarrassment, but that also allows him to express his noble intentions: "Poor kid, you're just a girl" (138). The little girl, sent by her family to the bakery to buy bread (with enough money to pay for it), does not need Quentin's rescuing. She never said she was lost, never said she was hungry, never said she needed help. In fact, until the end of the episode, she says nothing at all—a fact that Quentin mistakenly interprets as her inability to speak English. But she does speak English—"'There's Julio,' the little girl said" (139); and presumably, she understands too well Julio's threat: "'Git on home,' Julio shouted at her. 'I beat hell outa you'" (142).

Throughout the episode, she is understandably amused by Quentin's odd behavior and happily enjoys his company and the treats he gives her. In his own mind, however, Quentin writes a script for a drama in which he will "find" her house for her and restore her undamaged to her family: "She sort of took up with me and I cant find where she lives" (129)—though it is Quentin who is a stranger in this neighborhood, not the little girl. His uncertainty about the area is underscored when he has to ask someone the location of the nearest train station (131). When he is arrested, Quentin cannot see that he has unconsciously set himself up for this misunderstanding, though he laughs at the absurdity of his situation. He is oblivious, however, to his having given the impression of being a child-molester. He sees neither himself nor his circumstance objectively, but ludicrously attempts to revive his failed image as gentleman: "Good afternoon," I said [to Mrs. Bland], raising my hat. "I'm under arrest. I'm sorry I didn't get your note. Did Shreve tell you?" (141).

Quentin's remembered confession to his father of incest with Caddy is his final but futile attempt to escape his double-bind situation on June 2. This episode, whether or not it actually took place, exemplifies one of the key differences between classic Freudian and family systems metatheory.[23] Quentin's problems cannot be solved by Quentin alone, by his moving out of the "Oedipal stage" of development; his dilemma is not so much intrapsychic as it is interpersonal. To transcend the Compson's contradictory communicational patterns requires considerable insight into the operations of the *entire* family, how all these members fit together in the "family dance." But for Quentin, the double bind is insuperable.

It may be that Quentin attempts in his confession to provoke his father to take disciplinary action and reinstate his paternal authority, as has often been suggested by critics.[24] Yet this interpretation seems implausible. It is highly improbable that in such an enmeshed family, Quentin would expect that Mr. Compson would mete out any reprisal or punishment, or that he would suddenly assert his authority in any demonstrable fashion. Certainly with his acute sensitivity and his closeness to his father, it is much more likely that Quentin would anticipate no punishment whatsoever. Given this analysis of the covert Compson family system, it is more consistent to see Quentin's confession as his final effort within the family circle to resolve his double bind by imaginatively sustaining both his family roles, as hero and as failure. In his confession, he attempts, as Kartiganer writes, to "alter an unbearable reality through language" (*Thread,* 13) because it is his family's contradictory language that *is* his problem. His task is to cut through the family's ritualized contradiction in communication. If he has seduced and impregnated his own sister, he has both defended her from outside lovers (enacting his role as family hero), but has also simultaneously degraded her (satisfying his claim as family failure). His confession of incest is in reality a problem-solving device, a release from his family's structured communications to him. In effect, Quentin opts to end the family dance.

His father, perhaps intuitively knowing that the entire family system is at stake, parries Quentin's effort to transcend the double bind and instead clings to the family's homeostasis. Instead of expressing anger, sorrow, or compassion for his son, since these responses would validate Quentin's imagined solution, he distances himself from his son's suffering—"i think you are too serious to give me any cause for alarm" (176–77)—then tells him to leave for school immediately: "no you will not do that [commit suicide] until you come to believe that even she was not quite worth despair . . . i think youd better go on up to cambridge right away" (178). Mr. Compson fails his son not because he refuses to assert his paternity, as critics often assert, but because he unconsciously chooses the family's stability, even over the life of his son.

Quentin, in effect, has yet to serve his family's purpose fully. Speaking in the manner of his self-pitying mother, he tells Mr. Compson that his suicide "will be better for me for all of us" (178), perhaps because in Quentin's convoluted thinking, his death will simultaneously enshrine Caddy's loss as of inestimable value, but also signify life's nothingness. But rather than attempt to discuss with his son his tortured family, and perhaps release Quentin from his double bind to save his life, Mr. Compson once again withdraws: "let no man prescribe for another mans wellbeing" (178). So Quentin goes to his death, believing that his last despairing gesture is for the benefit of his family.

By examining Quentin within the context of his family's communications, we discover that his basic problems are less intrapsychic than interpersonal, less a consequence of his unconscious sexual drives than of his family's need for stability and consistency. Of course, this approach, which discloses the whole fictional family and its operations, challenges a contemporary literary shibboleth: the admonition against treating any text, especially Faulkner's, as "realism." Much current criticism commits itself to the qualities of indeterminacy and the infinitely inconclusive confrontation with the Other; to a premise that characters are no more than the "freeplay of the world and of signs without truth and without origin"[25]; to the view that literature is "nothing but a collection of signs and interpretation of signs."[26] However, these assumptions close off analysis of the character's psychology where fruitful questioning should be encouraged.

Faulkner himself thought of his characters as "real," as convincing imitations of human actions. To him, they were "flesh-and-blood people that will stand up and cast a shadow" (Gwynn and Blotner, 47). He described them as "people that I have known all my life in the country I was born in."[27] He humorously imagined a character having a life beyond the text: "when the book is finished, that character is not done, he is still going on at some new devilment that sooner or later I will find out about and write about" (Gwynn and Blotner, 7). Like Charles Dickens, the great nineteenth-century realist, Faulkner apparently experienced severe depressions at the conclusion of writing a novel—a kind of "mourning period," as if for an actual person's loss. Furthermore, he had a Pirandellian sense of his characters creating their own plot, forcing their author "to trot along behind [them] with a paper and pencil trying to keep up long enough to put down what [they say and do]" (Fant and Ashley, 111). And in my experience of teaching Faulkner, I have been most impressed by the comments of those students who, in very moving terms, connect Faulkner's families to their own lives—where in their homes they endure the suffering that Faulkner dramatizes so powerfully.

Seeing the centrality of family systems in Faulkner's work may help us understand—as readers, children, parents, teachers—the challenges that families confront and the interrelational crises his characters negotiate. By stressing "family values" so vehemently in public discourse, we place too great a burden on the conventional, nuclear family as a panacea for America's woes.

Nathan Ackerman, a founding father of family therapy, writes that "the family is called upon to make up to its individual members in affection and closeness for the anxiety and distress that is the result of the failure to find a safe place in the wider world."[28] Unlike so many commentators on the family in the mass media, William Faulkner, in his powerful family novels, knew that even in the home, a "safe place" is no certainty.

NOTES

1. William Faulkner, *Thinking of Home: William Faulkner's Letters to His Mother and Father, 1918–1925,* ed. James G. Watson (New York: Norton, 1992), 118.

2. Arthur F. Kinney, "The Family-Centered Nature of Faulkner's World," *College Literature* 16 (winter 1989): 83.

3. Michael Kerr, "Chronic Anxiety and Defining a Self," *Atlantic Monthly,* September 1988, 35.

4. Murray Bowen, *Family Therapy in Clinical Practice* (New York: Jason Aronson, 1978), 159.

5. Salvador Minuchin and Michael P. Nichols, *Family Healing* (New York: Touchstone, 1993), 286. Perhaps the best general introduction to family systems theory is Augustus Y. Napier and Carl A. Whitaker's *The Family Crucible,* from which I draw my paper's title. Perhaps the most profound, influential work in the field is Bowen's *Family Therapy in Clinical Practice.* Reviews of recent research in psychology may be found in the *Journal of Marriage and the Family* 52 (November 1990).

   For an excellent argument recommending the use of family systems rather than psychoanalytic criticism, see John V. Knapp, *Striking at the Joints: Contemporary Psychology and Literary Criticism* (Lanham, Md.: University Press of America, 1996), esp. 27–112. See also a special issue devoted to family systems theory in *Style* 31, no. 2 (1997).

6. Donald M. Kartiganer, "Quentin Compson and Faulkner's Drama of Generations," in *Critical Essays on William Faulkner: The Compson Family,* ed. Arthur F. Kinney (Boston: G.K. Hall, 1982), 381. Although, to my knowledge, other than in my previous work (see note 17), family systems theory has not yet been applied to Faulkner's works, other critics invariably discuss the family as a crucial Faulkner theme. Cleanth Brooks, for example, sees Faulkner as "a conservative writer who sees the family as the basic unit of the community," in "The Breakup of the Compsons" in *Critical Essays,* p. 23. Judith Wittenberg, however, understands the Faulknerian family as generally deleterious: "The only real 'villains' in the Faulknerian world are a restrictive society that is inadequately responsive to the needs and desires of its individual members and a nuclear family that fails its children by offering poor examples or providing inadequate

affection" (*Faulkner: The Transfiguration of Biography* [Lincoln: University of Nebraska Press, 1979], 335. David Minter discovers what systems theorists would call "multigenerational themes": "[Faulkner] became acutely aware of the forces of human heredity and the flow of human generations" (*William Faulkner: His Life and Work* [Baltimore: Johns Hopkins University Press, 1980], 3.)

7. Daniel J. Singal, *William Faulkner: The Making of a Modernist* (Chapel Hill: University of North Carolina Press, 1997), 117.

8. John T. Irwin, *Doubling and Incest/Repetition and Revenge: A Speculative Reading of Faulkner* (Baltimore: Johns Hopkins University Press, 1975), 35.

9. For a recent Freudian analysis, see Noel Polk, who writes: "Children in Faulkner's work of the period 1927–1932 are prisoners in the dark house of family dysfunction, houses whose darkness is rooted in fear and loathing of the life processes of sex and death, in denial and repression of desire. The dysfunction is Oedipal in its origins and in its more particular manifestations" (*Children of the Dark House: Text and Context in Faulkner* [Jackson: University Press of Mississippi, 1996], 29). See also Deborah E. Barker and Ivo Kamps, "Much Ado About Nothing: Language and Desire in *the Sound and the Fury,"* *Mississippi Quarterly* 36 (summer 1993): 337–93; and André Bleikasten, "Fathers in Faulkner," in *The Fictional Father: Lacanian Readings of the Text,* ed. Robert Con Davis (Amherst: University of Massachusetts Press, 1981), 115–46. For a rigorously Lacanian analysis of the novel, see Doreen Fowler, *Faulkner: The Return of the Repressed* (Charlottesville: University Press of Virginia, 1997), 32–47.

10. Philip Weinstein, *What Else But Love? The Ordeal of Race in Faulkner and Morrison* (New York: Columbia University Press, 1996), 106.

11. *Alcoholics Anonymous Handbook* (New York: Alcoholics Anonymous World Services, 1976), 58.

12. For a discussion of Jason's role in the family system, see Gary Storhoff, "Jason's Role-Slippage: The Dynamics of Alcoholism in *The Sound and the Fury,"* *Mississippi Quarterly* 49 (summer 1996): 519–35; for a discussion of Mr. and Mrs. Compson's marital subsystem and Caddy's role in sustaining it, see Storhoff, "Caddy and the Infinite Loop: The Dynamics of Alcoholism in *The Sound and the Fury,"* *Faulkner Journal* 12 (spring 1997): 3–22.

13. Peter Steinglass et al., *The Alcoholic Family* (New York: Basic Books, 1987), 15. Steinglass, however, emphasizes that the family's enabling of alcoholism is not deliberate or even conscious, since it has become a part of the family's routine: "Because the invasion process occurs slowly, with the family making its accommodation one small increment at a time, it is only after substantial changes have already occurred and are firmly in place that the distance the family has traveled is readily apparent. However, the cumulative effect is nevertheless a powerful one— family regulatory behaviors now actually play a major role in *maintaining* chronic alcoholic behavior" (91).

14. Stephanie Brown, *Treating Adult Children of Alcoholics: A Developmental Perspective* (New York: John Wiley & Sons, 1988), 34.

15. Michael Elkin, *Families under the Influence: Changing Alcoholic Patterns* (New York: Norton, 1984), 71.

16. For a discussion of role-playing in alcoholic families, see J. S. Seixas and G. Youcha, *Children of Alcoholism* (New York: Crown, 1985). For a discussion of sibling subsystems, see Rosalie C. Jesse, "Children of Alcoholics: Their Sibling World," in *Siblings in Therapy: Life Span and Clinical Issues,* ed. Michael D. Kahn and Karen Gail Lewis (New York: Norton, 1988), 228–52.

17. William Faulkner, *The Sound and the Fury* (New York: Vintage International, 1984), 110.

18. Typically, critics extract Quentin from his family identity and describe him either as a brilliant person or as an imposter. Michel Gresset, for example, states flatly that Quentin "does not belong in Harvard" in "The Ordeal of Consciousness: Psychological Aspects of Evil in *The Sound and the Fury,*" in *Critical Essays,* 177; Eric Sundquist complains of Quentin's "vapid philosophizing" in *Faulkner: The House Divided* (Baltimore: Johns Hopkins University Press, 1983), 15; Kinney decries his "myopic intellection" (*Faulkner's Narrative Poetics: Style as Vision* [Amherst: University of Massachusetts Press, 1978], 147). Perhaps the fiercest criticism comes from Philip Weinstein, who writes that "Quentin is a memory box, a porous container of others' throwaway discourse. Unable to consolidate what he has absorbed, unable to shape his own thoughts into the coherence of a temporal project, he is a figure in motley" (*Faulkner's Subject: A Cosmos No One Owns* [Cambridge University Press, 1992], 85).

    Other critics are somewhat more positive. Jackson J. Benson describes Quentin as "an artist within the Romantic tradition" ("Quentin Compson: Self-Portrait of a Young Artist's Emotions," in *Critical Essays,* 223). John T. Matthews comments on Quentin's intelligence in *"The Sound and the Fury": Faulkner and the Lost Case* [Boston: Twayne, 1991], 49), as does Edmund L. Volpe, who writes that "his mind moves rapidly from one thought to another—ideas, allusions, memories flash across his consciousness" (*A Reader's Guide to William Faulkner* [New York: Farrar, Straus, and Giroux, 1964], 91). But seen within the Compson family system, Quentin is *both* the fool and the intellectual, the overachiever and the "memorybox," as he attempts to fulfill his designated family role.

19. Gregory Bateson, *Steps to an Ecology of Mind* (New York: Ballantine Books, 1972), 201.

20. Anthony Wilden, *System and Structure: Essays in Communication and Exchange,* 2d ed. (London: Tavistock Publications, 1980), 117.

21. Quentin's psychic division has been noted by other critics; for example, Donald M. Kartiganer writes, "[Quentin] moves toward a stylization of his life by separating his deeds from his purposes, the conduct of his last day from the impact of its destination" (*The Fragile Thread: The Meaning of Form in Faulkner's Novels* [Amherst: University of Massachusetts Press, 1979], 14).

This split has often been used to "prove" Quentin insane; Irving Howe, for example, writes that Quentin is a "clinical case" (*William Faulkner: A Critical Study* [New York: Random House, 1952], 167). Irwin states flatly that he has "gone insane" (35).

22. For a contrasting view of Quentin's fight with Bland, see Richard Godden, *Fictions of Labor: William Faulkner and the South's Long Revolution* (New York: Cambridge University Press, 1997), 4–44; and Matthews, 55–59.

23. As is often noted, Faulkner once said that Quentin's final conversation with Mr. Compson never took place, but is only imagined by Quentin: "Suppose I say this to my father, would it help me, would it clarify, would I see clearer what it is that I anguish over?" (*Faulkner in the University: Class Conferences at the University of Virginia 1957–58*, ed. Frederick L. Gwynn and Joseph Blotner [Charlottesville: University Press of Virginia, 1995], 262). Yet the event's certainty is ultimately not relevant from a system perspective: This dialogue is how Quentin experiences his father, and as Bateson observes, individuals tend to recreate the double-bind situation again and again.

24. See, for example, Irwin, 113; or André Bleikasten, *The Most Splendid Failure: Faulkner's "The Sound and the Fury"* (Bloomington; Indiana University Press, 1976), 114.

25. Vincent Leitch, *Deconstructive Criticism: An Advanced Introduction* (New York: Columbia University Press, 1983), 104.

26. J. Hillis Miller, "*Wuthering Heights* and the Ellipses of Interpretation," *Notre Dame English Journal* 12 (1980): 100.

27. *Faulkner at West Point*, ed. Joseph L. Fant and Robert Ashley (New York: Random, 1964), 96.

28. Nathan W. Ackerman, *the Psychodynamics of Family Life: Diagnosis and Treatment of Family Relationships* (New York: Basic Books, 1958), 112.

Jason Compson:
The Demands of Honor

LINDA WELSHIMER WAGNER [WAGNER-MARTIN]

"A writer is trying to create believable people in credible, moving situations," William Faulkner said in 1956. Many critical problems exist because Faulkner achieves his aim: his characters are not simply good or evil. The Mink Snopes who appears first as one of the vermin-like cousins becomes a noble if misguided man by the time of *The Mansion*. Joe Christmas as brutal murderer maintains the reader's sympathy because of Faulkner's vivid evocation of his boyhood's shameful rewards. Percy Grim, Drusilla, even Popeye—nearly all of Faulkner's villains are believable people; and this artistry, of making characters credible though sometimes heinous, is in itself enough to place Faulkner among America's great novelists.

In this age of relative moralities, readers welcome Faulkner's view that subtle ambivalences form men. Who can say what determines how good a person becomes? What causes a child to love instead of to hate?—to disregard

Reprinted by permission of the author from *Sewanee Review* 79, no. 4 (1971): 554–75.

codes rather than to build them? Faulkner does not presume to give answers in his fiction. Rather, he charts the life of one central character, and then briefly parallels—or contrasts—lives of other figures. The reader works inductively. Knowing Joe Christmas's heritage in detail makes possible a greater sympathy with Gail Hightower and Joanna Burden, whose histories are similar. And the reader can better understand the complexities of these characters (Faulkner described the elder Hightower as being "two separate and complete people") because they are poised against the uncomplicated Lena Grove, Percy Grimm, and Miss Atkins, for whom life "seemed straight and simple as a corridor."

From the beginning of his writing, Faulkner was able to create such believable characters—sympathetic villains and limited heroes, men for whom decisions were not so "straight and simple." Of these, I think Jason Compson is one of the most interesting—and perhaps the best drawn. As Faulkner himself urged Malcolm Cowley in 1945, when making selections for *The Portable Faulkner,*

> What about taking the whole third section of *The Sound and the Fury?* That Jason
> is the new South too. I mean, he is the one Compson and Sartoris who met Snopes
> on his own ground and in a fashion held his own.

Contrary to the view of critics who damn Jason for his Snopes-like qualities, notice Faulkner's evident admiration—and his identification of Jason as a "Compson and Sartoris," not a Snopes.

The apparent oversimplification in criticism of much of Faulkner's work—Snopes as bad, Compson and Old South as good—seems to stem from George Marion O'Donnell's comment in 1939 that Jason "succumbed entirely to the Snopes' world" while the rest of the Compsons remained Sartoris. Many readers seem to share Lawrence Thompson's view that Jason is another Iago while Quentin is "almost Hamlet-like." Though at times Faulkner speaks of Jason as "vicious," he often has great sympathy for the man as the responsible Compson ("he assumed the entire burden of the rotting family in the rotting house"). Melvin Backman comes closer, perhaps, in seeing Jason as the "comic villain"; yet Jason's situation is essentially more tragic than comic. What choices does Jason have? He must feed and keep his family and its reputation while yet maintaining some sort of pride in himself.

One of the difficulties in understanding Jason's position might be the technical device already mentioned, Faulkner's dynamic characterization through interaction among the characters themselves—and the tensions resulting from such relationships. Scenes of the Compson children playing in the branch or having supper establish both individual personalities and the lines of influence among them. *The Sound and the Fury* as the story of a nearly loveless family sets the pattern Faulkner was to use again and again: the child's experiences as they mold the man. Consequently, Benjy's memories in Book I—of early childhood, especially of Damuddy's death—are necessary to the more oblique characterizations to follow, those of Quentin and Jason. Reading from the relatively objective beginning which Faulkner has given us in Book I, we have little choice but to sympathize with both Quentin and Jason; and subsequently to question the designations of *hero* and *villain* as commonly applied to them.

I

Faulkner first presents Jason as a fat little boy, an outsider. "Jason was playing too. He was by himself further down the branch." Quentin and Caddy are buddies, and even Benjy, the baby, is destined to remain a baby forever (this is the first irony in Jason's life as the "middle" child). From the beginning, Jason has no recourse but power—blackmail through tattling or through physical destruction. From the beginning, however, Faulkner shows that that power is ineffectual.

Jason the loner is also Jason the suspect. "Are you going to tell, Jason?" Caddy asks. Quentin tries to trust Jason, but Caddy's questioning, antagonizing, cancels whatever good Quentin might interpose.

The second irony in Jason's life is the loss of his grandmother, with whom he has slept, just as Benjy sleeps with Caddy. After Damuddy's death, Jason is truly without recourse, without love. As the children discuss their grandmother's illness in the branch scene, Jason walks behind, "with his hands in his pockets." Rather than read this gesture as Versh does, as symbolic of greed, I would suggest it is an accurate indication of Jason's frustration, even fear. Jason is beaten before he starts. The horror in his life is that he knows it.

Jason's patrimony is to head the Compson family. Named for his father, Jason inherits, too, the older man's perspicacity. Jason knows. But he cannot stand liquor, just as he cannot stand the cynicism that defeats his father. Another of the ironies of Jason's life is that he is a fighter. In some ways Mrs. Compson is right when she calls him a Bascomb: Bascombs scrap. But Jason is in other respects a Compson: he maintains the same kind of wishful ideals Quentin tried to establish ("I dont know why it is I cant seem to learn that a woman'll do anything," Jason mutters in his frantic chase after his niece).

Above all other traits, Jason is a dutiful son. What he feels his responsibility to be is central to his characterization in the novel. He needs money; he works and steals to get money. And, too, Jason has always acted as his family expected: as a child, he was the antagonist, largely because people expected him to be. "'I wont.' Jason said, 'I wont mind you.'" The only action Jason takes throughout his childhood is defensive. Caddy demands that she be in charge; no one fights her except Jason, and only outright aggression makes him act, as when Caddy usurps the grandmother's place in the family:

> 'I bet it's company.' Versh said. 'You all better go in the back and slip upstairs.'
>
> 'I dont care.' Caddy said. 'I'll walk right in the parlor where they are.'
>
> 'I bet your pappy whip you if you do.' Versh said.
>
> 'I dont care.' Caddy said. 'I'll walk right in the parlor. I'll walk right in the dining room and eat supper.'
>
> 'Where you sit.' Versh said.
>
> 'I'd sit in Damuddy's chair.' Caddy said. 'She eats in bed.'
>
> 'I'm hungry.' Jason said. He passed us and ran on up the walk. He had his hands in his pockets and he fell down. Versh went and picked him up.

The pathos in Jason's futile silent protest is intensified in the next few lines of this scene. Mr. Compson stands nearby, apparently seeing Jason fall, hearing Versh's admonition. Yet all the elder Jason says is "Where's Quentin." Time stops, caught in the image of Quentin's shirt, blurred, moving slow, in the light from the kitchen. Father stands radiant in the light. Plaintively, Jason tries again: "Caddy and Quentin threw water on each other."

"'They did.' Father said. Quentin came. . . ." And so to supper. Again, the attention is on Quentin, as it usually is. When the meal is over, we see that—with sympathy for nearly all the children—Dilsey has none for Jason ("You, Jason, shut up that crying"). Caddy has already told us what agony his grandmother's absence has been for Jason: "He does it every night since Damuddy was sick and he cant sleep with her." Yet the Caddy who is so tender toward Benjy taunts Jason with "Cry baby." Jason's futile, stock reply comes fast, "I'm going to tell on you"; but again Caddy has the final word, "You've already told. . . . There's not anything else you can tell, now."

Jason cries. He is put to bed with the withdrawn Quentin, who now turns his face to the wall. Jason says nothing in answer to Caddy's last taunt: "'Mother's not coming in tonight,' she said. 'So we still have to mind me.'" Yet when Mr. Compson appears in the doorway—again bringing light—there is hope for a minute. Father, however, only looks at Quentin and Jason. His kiss he gives to Caddy; his benediction, to Benjy.

This bedtime scene closes Part I. Leading to this final scene are several other bedtimes. In each the family is together: Father identified with light, Father protecting Mother—from noise, from tiredness, from her responsibilities. The interchange between Caddy and her mother about Caddy's carrying Benjy gives us not only a telling difference between the two women, but also a poignant summary of Jason's two years since his grandmother's death:

> 'You humour him [Benjy] too much.' Mother said. 'You and your father both. You dont realise that I am the one who has to pay for it. Damuddy spoiled Jason that way and it took him two years to outgrow it, and I am not strong enough to go through the same thing with Benjamin.'

And then, immediately after this reference, Faulkner presents Jason, this time cutting up the paper dolls Caddy has made for Benjy. As Caddy and Jason fight, he loses even more of his identity: "He rolled into the corner, out of the mirror." Jason is punished and only much later, when he cries behind a closed door, is he included in his father's love (the four children on his lap), and then only under threat:

> 'Stop that, now.' Father said. 'Do you want me to whip you again.' Father lifted Jason up into the chair by him. Jason snuffled. We could hear the fire and the roof. Jason snuffled a little louder.
> 'One more time.' Father said.

True to form, Quentin has just defended a girl's "honor" in the matter of a frog (in November). For his fisticuffs, he is loved. In a later scene, the house is quiet because Quentin has to study. Successive scenes give the reader an indelible impression of Jason's position in his home.

'We must be quiet while Quentin's studying.' Father said. 'What are you doing, Jason.'

'Nothing.' Jason said.

'Suppose you come over here to do it, then.' Father said.

Jason came out of the corner.

'What are you chewing.' Father said.

'Nothing.' Jason said.

'He's chewing paper again.' Caddy said.

Hiding in corners, chewing to comfort himself—these are the bleak details Faulkner gives us to introduce the boy Jason. And another key to his character is given in the following bedtime scene, when Dilsey tells Caddy to get Jason ready for bed. As Benjy relates simply, "Caddy unbuttoned Jason. He began to cry."

This opening picture of the Compson family is particularly important, I think, in light of the usual opinion about Faulkner's treatment of families. As Malcolm Cowley says, Faulkner's books "have what is rare in the novels of our time, a warmth of family affection, brother for brother and sister, the father for his children—a love so warm and proud that it tries to shut out the rest of the world." For Jason to be denied that full relationship—as he so evidently is—makes more plausible some of his "non-Compson" attitudes and actions.

II

To define Jason's behavior as "non-Compson" presupposes another standard for judgment. Structurally, Faulkner gives us what appears to be the desired pattern in Quentin's section, Part II—or so we suppose because we read Quentin's thoughts first. We sympathize with him, lulled by the long, sonorous lines of his monologue. We identify with his philosophic concerns—honor, time, woman as symbol—presented so dramatically as they are. Or, perhaps, melodramatically. The smashed watch and the jeweler's window; the grotesque little sister-figure leading Quentin into his ironic arrest; the Bland-Quentin fight–all build compellingly to the greatest melodrama of all: a man's suicide. Reading Quentin's distorted impressions is very different from reading Jason's cryptic insults, but the difference lies to a great extent in the *tones* of the contrasting sections. One of the strengths of the novel is that Faulkner so well manipulates our reactions to these characters (through prose rhythms, diction, and selection of episodes) that we hardly realize that Quentin's concerns are also Jason's; that the problems of honor, time, and human delicacy fall with more weight on Jason's shoulders than they ever did on Quentin's.

Jason says, "Damn little time to do anything in, but then I am used to that"; Quentin thinks, "Father said that. That Christ was not crucified: he was worn away by a minute clicking of little wheels. That had no sister." "It never occurred to me she wouldn't keep her promise . . . ," Jason muses, with no more understanding than Quentin, earlier, "Father and I protect women from one another from themselves our women." "I'm a man, I can stand it," Jason echoes to Quentin's *"I'm stronger than you," "I am not afraid."*

Time, women (as the responsibilities of men, as extensions or "proofs" of men's personal virtue), and that devout concept of honor that Jason, Sr., tried to undermine, but unsuccessfully—these concerns are near-obsessions to both Quentin and Jason. They are Compsons, before any other consideration: "my people owned slaves here when you all were running little shirt tail country stores and farming land no nigger would look at on shares," Jason boasts. And a Compson has certain beliefs: that integrity is more important than success; that men are the heads of their households, respected in their communities and by their children and servants; that men rely on their ancestry for much of their pride; that men are morally and physically stronger than women, and must protect them.

Honor to Quentin is symbolized in Caddy's virginity—the fresh, the pure—undefiled as he himself tries to remain: "'Dont tell me,' I said, 'please sir.'" His position is complicated by his father's refusal to lie. Jason, Sr., must tell Quentin about life as he knows it to be, even though the fact that "no battle is ever won. . . . They are not even fought" damns Quentin from the start. Quentin's ostensible battle is to save Caddy, but he fights Dalton Ames just as he fights Gerald Bland—for the honor of the whole Compson family. His impotence against the "loud world" is illustrated vividly in each fight. With Ames, Quentin faints; Bland methodically boxes him off his feet. For Quentin, with his constant protests to Caddy that *"I'm stronger than you,"* such outcomes prove again the direction his life must take—toward death through water, toward the eternal beginning, and so again, thematically, toward the novel's beginning.

Just as Faulkner has depicted the children playing in the branch, so Quentin turns for help to the past, to feeling again as he did when a child. His father's cynicism, his mother's coldness (*"If I could say Mother. Mother"*), the rest of the world's bastardy, symbolized best by Head ("I've been out in the world now for ten years things dont matter so much then")—these realities did not affect Quentin as a boy, at least not to the extent that they do now. Yet the irony of Quentin's seeking refuge in the past is that his past was no happier than his present. The best-loved of the four children, Quentin still was afraid. The schoolroom held only agony for him; he counted the seconds until he would be free. And night—Benjy's best time of life—was one more agony to Quentin.

> *. . . the long invisible flowing of the stair-railing where a misstep in the darkness filled with sleeping Mother Father Caddy Jason Maury door I am not afraid only Mother Father Caddy Jason Maury getting so far ahead sleeping I will sleep fast when I door Door door*

Fear characterizes Quentin's behavior when Damuddy dies and when he questions both his father and Caddy. We can see it growing in him as he matures. He never escapes from his childhood picture of his parents: ". . . the dungeon was Mother herself she and Father upward into weak light holding hands and us lost somewhere below even them without even a ray of light." It is, in fact, intensified. Quentin's ancestry, his family as a source of strength, he comes to see only as "all the feet in sad generations seeking water." And Quentin's identity itself is shadow-like, evanescent, as so many of Faulkner's images suggest.

Quentin's concern for time is consequently a very natural one. Bad as it has been, his known past is going, and the future lurks ahead, represented by such happenings as Caddy's pregnancy and—perhaps even worse—her hasty marriage to Sydney Herbert Head (to whom Quentin was a "half-baked Galahad"). Harvard provides boat races and the intimacies of Gerald Bland and his mother. Even the Negroes at Harvard are phony! And when Quentin tries to leave Harvard, guilt-ridden because of the pasture's being sold, his father explains that he must stay because it was his "mothers dream since [he was] born and no compson has ever disappointed a lady." The ironies in this speech show Quentin again that his father's values are dead; Mrs. Compson herself has indicated that she is no lady.

This central lack of understanding between father and son is shown more poignantly in the closing dialogue, as Mr. Compson refuses to believe either the tale of incest or Quentin's threat of suicide. The final injustice is his father's description of Quentin's despair as a "temporary state of mind." Quentin answers his father throughout this scene with a single word *temporary*. ". . . No man ever does that under the first fury of despair or remorse or bereavement . . ." Jason, Sr., reassures Quentin—and himself. What his father does not realize is that Quentin's whole life has been a fury of despair. It comes as no surprise when Quentin promises himself, and the roaring world: "A quarter hour yet. And then I'll not be. The peacefullest words."

While Quentin focuses his concern with honor on Caddy and her state in the world (*not* in any particular culture), Jason's attention falls of necessity on being a "good provider." The critics who damn Jason's materialism (because he is concerned with his job, with money, with his car) might consider how Jason's position differs from Quentin's. Quentin is a young student, scarcely twenty, attempting to answer questions that are in themselves almost symbolic because of his personal inexperience. His reliance on this father's views, his virginity, his obsessive interest in abstractions—Quentin is a boy who has never faced life's real problems. As his father prompts when he sends Quentin early to Maine, "watching pennies has healed more scars than jesus."

In strong contrast, Jason has never known any concerns except material ones. "I've got to get on to work." "I'll have to get on. . . ." "I never had time to be [a reproach]. I never had time to go to Harvard like Quentin or drink myself into the ground like Father. I had to work." No wonder Jason thinks it's too late to start training the girl Quentin at seventeen; he was on his own, feeding the family, at not much more than that age. Everything Jason does stems from his desperate need to put up a front, to keep the Compson name—such as it is now—intact. It is Jason, not Quentin, who speaks again and again of responsibilities of one's own flesh and blood, of the ancestry of the family. Jason is proud of being a Compson. But he can be proud only if he protects the family name—from poverty, from slander. Quentin wanted to create sin to justify his own sense of man's innate tragedy, even though he would have had to sacrifice the Compson name. Jason fights irrationally to preserve that family name. It is all he has.

It is from this perspective of breadwinner that Jason must view the girl Quentin. First, Quentin is the reason he has not been given his one chance to get out of Jefferson ("Well, they brought my job home tonight"). The bank position Head had promised him was the only hope Jason had ("What the hell chance has a man got, tied down in a town like this and to a business like this"). The girl Quentin came to represent not only that loss but still another responsibility to a youngster who already had the care of—how many?—his father and mother, Benjy, six Negroes, and Uncle Maury. Jason's initial resentment is intensified now because seventeen years of his work have come into jeopardy: "Once a bitch always a bitch." Now Quentin is dragging the Compson name through the streets of Jefferson, and Jason sees the girl as one final threat to everything he had given his career for—"I've got a position in this town. . . ." ". . . With Mother's health and the position I try to uphold to have her [Quentin] with no more respect for what I try to do for her than to make her name and my name and my Mother's name a byword in the town."

As Jason follows Quentin and the man with the red tie, his thoughts return again and again to Quentin's betrayal of the family name ("she hasn't even got enough consideration for her own family to have any discretion"; "just you let me catch you doing it one time on this place, where my mother lives"; "I'll make him think that damn red tie is the latch string to hell, if he thinks he can run the woods with my niece"), culminating in Jason's finding the flat tire:

> I dont know why it is I cant seem to learn that a woman'll do anything. I kept thinking, Let's forget for awhile how I feel toward you and how you feel toward me: I just wouldn't do you this way. I wouldn't do you this way no matter what you had done to me. Because like I say blood is blood and you cant get around it. It's not playing a joke that any eight year old boy could have thought of, it's letting your own uncle be laughed at by a man that would wear a red tie.

Jason's cruelty to Quentin seems evident throughout the three days of their story—he is rough and vicious; he cheats and lies. Yet Quentin is hardly the direct result of Jason's behavior—she has also been subject to Dilsey's love, to Caddy's efforts to protect her, to Mrs. Compson's ambivalence, to Jefferson. And we must consider that April the sixth, 1928, was the first time Mrs. Compson had turned Quentin's management over to Jason. In the girl's open defiance of her uncle, Quentin asks for the physical treatment she is

about to receive—when Mrs. Compson once again interferes. Jason's
position, however, is clearly defined: if he is to be in charge, he must control
Quentin.

> '. . . dont think you can run it over me. I'm not an old woman, nor an old half
> dead nigger. . . .
>   'I've started this thing, and I'm going through with it.'

April the sixth is no more a typical day for Jason—despite his constant
hurry, his financial manipulations, his purposeless trips to and from the
store—than June second, 1910, is for the boy Quentin. On each day, the
essence of the character's plan for his life is given, dramatized. Quentin seeks
for tranquility and finds some comfort in the young boys' fishing and swim-
ming—the innocent uses of the water which so mystifies him, the past. His
search to find the home for his surrogate little sister, who trusts him implicitly, is bizarre only in its generosity. He does not even pretend to go to class
or to communicate with Shreve. His plans truly take him away from Harvard.
For Jason, being on call in Earl's store is one typical frustration in the midst
of his day-long conflict with his niece. Jason never has enough time. His
stockbroker's telegrams are late, he's too rushed to get blank checks, he can't
read the mail, nor does he have time for lunch. As Jason describes his life:

> I got the car and went home. Once this morning, twice at noon, and now again,
> with her and having to chase all over town and having to beg them to let me eat
> a little of the food I am paying for. Sometimes I think what's the use of anything.
> With the precedent I've been set I must be crazy to keep on. And now I reckon
> I'll get home just in time to take a nice long drive after a basket of tomatoes or
> something. . . .

In contrast, time to Quentin was evil, but it was evil in the abstract. Quentin
lived a leisurely life, never rushing, even when death was near. It is Jason who
has had no time to philosophize about time, no time even to think about it—
or about many of life's more important matters.

    Jason's rushed life is probably the best explanation for his apparent
duplicity. How is it that a man who is so deadly serious about keeping his
family name untarnished can be guilty of forgery and theft? How is it that a

man who reveres family ties can be so harsh to members of his own family? Clearly, Jason has never considered what he is doing with either Caddy's checks or Caddy's child. As Faulkner writes in Part IV of the novel:

> Of his niece he did not think at all, nor of the arbitrary valuation of the money. Neither of them had had entity or individuality for him for ten years; together they merely symbolized the job in the bank of which he had been deprived before he ever got it.

The immensity of the robbery breaks Jason, for this reason and several others. In his code, that money was justifiably his—"that which was to have compensated him for the lost job, which he had acquired through so much effort and risk." Being robbed by his own niece was a double blow: the strong if paradoxical family loyalty was betrayed; and Quentin was "the very symbol of the lost job itself." But perhaps most important to Jason was the fact that Quentin, "a bitch of a girl," had committed the robbery ("If he could just believe it was the man who had robbed him"). Jason's desperate search for the two is prompted not so much by the loss of the money (for the use of which Jason seemed to have no plans) but because "the whole world would know that he, Jason Compson, had been robbed by Quentin, his niece, a bitch." A woman.

III

In Jason's position as "head" of the Compson house, we see Faulkner at his best in characterization. Jason is no different from his father before him—he arranges life so that it bothers Mrs. Compson as little as possible.[1] His mother, we see again in the opening of Part III, still has two approaches to life—"locking up" problems, like Benjy and Quentin; or turning them over to the younger Jason just as she had to her husband. Mrs. Compson, unwilling and consequently unable to cope with anything, is a great believer in forms: the Bible, names (changing Benjy's and forgetting Caddy's), the way it "ought to be." "Not like most people," Mrs. Compson does not understand life. She has no intention of coming close enough to it—or to anyone in it—to understand anything about it. She knows only her own necessities for survival—hers, and beloved brother Maury's, and (she says) Jason's. But we see that she lies in all her comments to Dilsey and the girl Quentin about Jason's being head of the household.

Jason supplies money, but he is subject to Mrs. Compson's will. Faulkner depicts the true relationship poignantly when Jason is frantic to get into Quentin's room before the robbery has been discovered, but only Mother has the keys, "a huge bunch of rusted keys on an iron ring like a mediaeval jailer's." We sympathize when Jason shouts at her, "Give me the keys, you old fool!" Yet we know her reaction before she gives it: "He will never find the right one."

Mrs. Compson, in her seemingly passive rôle as wife and mother, has undermined all her children and her husband as well. Her direct challenge of her husband's authority, "I'm not so weak that I must kill myself with whiskey," lends credence to the importance her son Quentin places on strength. Jason, too, keeps asserting his strength ("stand on my own feet"), as his mother does that of "[us] Bascombs." Quentin remembers that his mother was always a king, never a princess or a fairy; and Jason's memories of his father are of his feet, sheltered, woman-fashion, by his dressing-gown, while he stands at the sideboard.

Faulkner shows vividly the children listening to Mrs. Compson's peremptory commands ("You, Benjamin" or "Jason" or "Caddy"), but turning for love to their father. Their mother lived constantly *for* them, but her protestations usually ended in cold, harmful relationships (as when she claimed she was "protecting" Jason by gossiping in front of him). The structure of the novel gives Mrs. Compson the dominant position in her children's lives that her behavior warranted: Quentin's view of her occupies the center of his meditation. His constant juxtaposing of Mrs. Compson and Mrs. Bland forces the realization that one perversion is as harmful as another. Mrs. Compson's treachery to Caddy—her mistrust, her spying—is one incontrovertible reason for Quentin's despair.

Parts III and IV show another of Mrs. Compson's traits: she sees all life as she wants to see it. Some of the saddest scenes are Jason's championing his father's memory—and Caddy's—only to have Mrs. Compson declare that his words are "bitter." Jason loves his father, and yet he does not argue with his mother. His attitude is strangely similar to that of Dilsey, the great pacifist, who speaks about Miss Cahline as though she were Benjy—"You want to git her started too?"

Dilsey's rôle in relation to Jason is one of disapproval. She "protects" her womenfolk from him; she expects—and usually sees—the worse from him.

But, then, as Mrs. Compson reminds Dilsey, "I know you have never had any tenderness for Jason. You've never tried to conceal it." Wrong as Mrs. Compson is about many things, she seems to describe accurately the childhood scenes Faulkner has already drawn in Part I.[2]

Jason's treatment from Caddy and the girl Quentin parallels that from Dilsey. They also expect him to hurt them, and he does. When Caddy asks Jason to help care for Quentin, she makes no apology for having added to his work. "Listen, Jason . . . , Don't lie to me now." Echoes of "Jason will tell" come into the reader's mind. "Be kind to her. Little things that I cant, they wont let. . . . But you wont. You never had a drop of warm blood in you." And then, after this strange affirmation, the only mention in the novel of the fact that Jason carries his father's name:

> 'Promise, Jason. You have Father's name: do you think I'd have to ask him twice? once, even?'
> 'That's so,' I says, 'He did leave me something.'

The pattern is repeated as the girl Quentin doubts Jason's word about Caddy's money order, and Jason responds irately, "Think I'm lying, do you? . . . Just for that you wont see it."

"Just for that"—a child's phrase. Yet when Jason is treated as an evil child, he has no recourse but to act as he did years before. No one has ever taught him another way. This reaction pattern is the best explanation for that most gratuitously evil of Jason's acts, burning the show tickets which Luster wanted so desperately. As Jason comes into the house for supper, Dilsey scolds him irrationally for being late and for "persecuting" Quentin. The dialogue with Luster follows Dilsey's browbeating. After Luster asks for a ticket, Dilsey interjects her usual negative remark, "Hush yo mouf . . . Dont you know he aint gwine give nothing away?" Jason is stalemated. He tries to sell the ticket for the smallest amount possible, five cents, but Luster has no money at all. And then Dilsey directs him to "Go on. Drop hit in [the fire]."

Contrary to all these scenes of Jason in conflict with the Compson women, we see him as a generous, loving man when he is with Lorraine.[3] Faulkner's inclusion of Lorraine in the novel is the best answer possible to Dilsey's comment that "You's a cold man, Jason, if man you is." Dilsey is truly a Compson woman in this respect, and perhaps in others as Faulkner describes her as "fatalistic," "childlike."

Of these many women characters, it seems strange that none is a mother. Each woman in the novel is characterized chiefly in that respect—whether or not she is motherly. Caddy comes closest, at least early in the novel; but it is her failure to live up to that rôle—symbolized by her father's taking Quentin from her care—that leads to her brother's death. Dilsey's effectiveness as a mother figure is limited through her overwork, her distorted perception, her partiality. One thinks briefly of the loving Damuddy who was not above sleeping with her fat, lonely grandson; but her influence has been too limited. Mrs. Compson makes no pretense at being a mother, or even a woman: she is a lady. Mrs. Bland is a chum.

More important than the fact that there are no mothers in *The Sound and the Fury* is the fact that Mrs. Compson seems bent on refusing a motherly rôle. The comparison with Lady Macbeth in her own violent negation is more than suggested. "Lady Macbeth I always admire," Faulkner commented in 1956. He went on to say that another of his favorite characters was Sarah Gamp—"a cruel, ruthless woman . . . most of her character was bad, but at least it was character." And we can well pay the same tribute to Mrs. Compson.

IV

"When the shadow of the sash appeared on the curtains it was between seven and eight oclock and then I was in time again, hearing the watch." The slow sibilants give a sad tone to all of Quentin's reflections, whether he is thinking of "Shreve's bedsprings and then his slippers on the floor hishing" or "shabby and timeless patience." Quentin's mourning comes to us through imagery—"roof of wind," "lonely and inviolate sand," "murmuring bones"— no less than through the subjects of his thoughts. Everything that happens to Quentin is intensified, refracted, as it were, through the anguish that colors his sight. The cut finger becomes as important as the smashed watch; Spoade's terrapin-like progress, equated with Quentin's own passage toward death, takes place "in a street full of scuttering dead leaves."[4] The sentence pattern which Faulkner chooses for much of Quentin's section—strangely like that in Benjy's part—is grimly appropriate: simple and compound sentences, many beginning with *I* and then continuing with the barest description of the action. The longer sentences, more heavily imagistic, are often those of his father's words, or Quentin's echoes of his father's convictions. Accented with short phrases used like refrains, the long sections of Quentin's monologue have an indelible rhythm—hesitant and tortuous yet building to the more rapid momentum toward the end. Here, all the central images are heightened (Quentin's understated complaint about his mother becomes the "dungeon was Mother" passage); the real and the unreal are as mixed in Quentin's world as the sensory reactions in Benjy's—and increasingly, in Quentin's, Faulkner turns to meaningful synaesthesia: *"eyes unseeing clenched like teeth"* while *"hands can see touching in the mind"*; "my nose could see gasoline. . . ." The confused images leading to Quentin's "smell the beating of hot blood" make him cry against the loud world, roaring away, somehow more defensible.

As Faulkner presents Quentin, he is nearly always alone. He has no need to talk with anyone. Faulkner places him outside the trivia of human interaction (when he needs physical help, Shreve does his talking for him) so that his interior monologue can grow in strength. For emphatic contrast, Faulkner uses the opposite tack for Jason. Jason is never alone; even when he thinks to himself, someone (in the store, the street, his home) is near. Most of Jason's thoughts come to us as fragments of dialogue: by the nature of his life, Jason is usually involved with someone.

"Once a bitch always a bitch" is an appropriate if offensive contrast to Quentin's somber lines. Quentin only thought about his mother; Jason has to do battle with her, in order in some way to control the girl Quentin. Shocking his mother—who thinks and lives in layers of platitudes—is best done quickly and vulgarly. Mrs. Compson's spoken language and Uncle Maury's written circumlocution provide wonderful contrast to Jason's humorous and masculine directness—and make evident the need for Jason to "talk net."

Faulkner emphasizes in Jason's opening speeches the change from Quentin's reflective poetry to Jason's sardonic slang—"gobbing paint on her face," "six niggers," "damn slick-headed jelly-beans," "grub," and, one of Jason's most unsympathetic phrases, "I says." It is noteworthy that on most subjects Jason speaks in a normally colloquial diction, without the heavy sprinkling of slang and crudities. The girl Quentin provokes the latter diction, as do the stock-market manipulators.

So far as imagery is concerned, Faulkner makes very clear that Jason speaks from a man's perspective: Quentin's "face looked like she had polished

it with a gun rag"; her eyes are "hard as a fice dog's"; her nose, red from crying, "looked like a porcelain insulator." And the humor, depending for its
effect on sacrilege and virulence—that certainly is masculine.

Because so much of Jason's section is dramatic in form—the interaction
occurring in April, 1928, or else remembered by Jason as a scene—the rhythm
is crisper, the movement more abrupt. Terseness is economical, too: a great
deal happens in Jason's day, even though at the end of it we know much less
of Jason than we do of Quentin at the end of his day. Quentin refracts every
happening; Jason seemingly reflects them all.

Yet even the most unsympathetic reader can sense that Jason is not
reflecting any of these experiences. Jason is as sensitive to the slights of his
world as Quentin was to his: Jason, however, has to meet those slights and
go on living. In that recognition lies a kind of heroism, I think. Faulkner, too,
wrote of Jason that he sacrificed "what pleasures might have been the right
and just due and even the necessity of a thirty-year-old bachelor." And one
is reminded of Faulkner's praise for Mercutio because he "coped with life,
didn't ask any favors, never whined." Or that for Sut Lovingood, who "had
no illusions about himself, did the best he could. . . . Never blamed his mis-
fortunes on anyone and never blamed God for them."

"The best he could"—not the ultimate answer, perhaps. Given Jason's
very evident handicaps, what recourse does the robbed man have? The closing question of the novel only echoes the earlier ones: what recourse has
Jason—robbed, it seems, of so many things—ever had? There are no simple
answers. Appropriately, Faulkner gives us Jason's only attempt, "a vain
dream"—and that of violence. So it has ever been for Jason. The "puny fury"
of the roadshow roustabout symbolizes Jason's life, in all its incoherent,
bemused struggle.

> Jason glared wildly about, holding the other. Outside it was now bright and sunny,
> swift and bright and empty, and he thought of the people soon to be going qui-
> etly home to Sunday dinner, decorously festive, and of himself trying to hold the
> fatal, furious little old man whom he dared not release long enough to turn his
> back and run.

It looks so simple—"bright and sunny, swift"—and the normalcy of Sunday
dinner (the lure of regular meals for Jason is surely the lure of a normal existence) deludes him for a moment. Then, again, that "fatal, furious little old

man" confronts him. Only Jason's equally "furious desire not to die" saved him from this attack, and from all the others life had set up for him. For it is in Jason's ability to hang on, to exist despite the odds, that he parallels Dilsey and her children.

In that endurance there is more to life than sound, than fury. Or, in Faulkner's words, "man's immortality is that he is faced with a tragedy which he can't beat and he still tries to do something with it." For Jason, life was to be spent existing as well as he could until his obligations to his family were taken care of: "I'm a man, I can stand it." As *The Sound and the Fury* shows so well, standing it took a kind of love, a kind of honor.

NOTES

1. The similarity between Jason and his father in their views of the breadwinning responsibility is evident in their caustic statements: his father's, that Uncle Maury had no need to work since Mr. Compson "could support five or six niggers that did nothing at all but sit with their feet in the oven." Jason's various references to feeding "six niggers" are reminiscent of this, as when he speaks about Dilsey: "She was so old she couldn't do any more than move hardly. But that's all right: we need somebody in the kitchen to eat up the grub the young ones cant tote off."

2. Faulkner gives us reason to feel that Mrs. Compson is again right in her accusations of her husband: "you always have found excuses for your own blood only Jason can do wrong because he is more Bascomb than Compson . . . that's it go on criticise Jason accuse me of setting him to watch her . . . while your own daughter can I know you don't love him . . . you never have yes ridicule him as you always have."

3. Lorraine affirms Jason's potency, his masculinity, and his generosity. We see only kindness from Jason ("Last time I gave her forty dollars. Gave it to her.") even though he closes his discourse on the treatment of women with the brusque "Always keep them guessing. If you cant think of any other way to surprise them, give them a bust in the jaw." This statement is certainly typical of Jason's usual tough diction. I see no reason for Warren's use of this quotation to prove that Jason takes sex as meaningless, loveless.

4. Quentin's antithesis is presented not in Jason but in Spoade—even more than in Bland or Head. Spoade "never increased his pace": he is oblivious to time. It is Spoade who insults Quentin's masculinity, Spoade who looks at him with cold eyes after his arrest.

Opening Pandora's Box: Re-reading Compson's Letter and Faulkner's *Absalom, Absalom!*

DAVID KRAUSE

F aulkner makes Mr. Compson's letter to his son the most compelling object in the Harvard room shared by Quentin and Shreve: "on the table before Quentin, lying on the open text book beneath the lamp, the white oblong of the envelope, the familiar blurred mechanical *Jefferson Jan. 10, 1910 Miss* and then opened, the *My Dear son* in his father's sloped fine hand" (173).[1] This letter brings news of Rosa Coldfield's death and provokes Quentin's and Shreve's late-night re-working of the Sutpen family romance. Faulkner calls our attention ten times to Compson's letter, giving unusual emphasis to its physical description and to Quentin's physical and psychological relation to it, and framing the long second movement of *Absalom* with its words, its readings.[2] Although Faulkner continues periodically to fix the scene in Cambridge, and indeed presents in intense detail the evolving physical and imaginative relations between Quentin and Shreve in Chapters VIII

Reprinted with permission from *Centennial Review* 30, no. 3 (1986): 358–82.

and IX, the letter is not mentioned after Chapter VII, until the novel's second last page. There it re-appears in an extraordinarily powerful scene which might well have ended the book if Shreve had not been allowed his final periodic and, it would seem, insensitive teasing of Quentin.[3] This essay proposes not so much to explicate the contents of Compson's letter as to disclose the circumstances for explication, the necessary conditions for reading. Aware that "paying attention to the reader is . . . a subversive activity which re-opens Pandora's box and undermines our hard-earned 'certainties' concerning literary texts,"[4] this essay risks a close consideration of Faulkner's strategies in presenting Quentin reading his father's letter and manipulating our reading of that reading.

Quentin's reading of Compson's letter takes place within the contexts of a novel unusually full of and reflexive about problematic acts of reading. In Chapter IV of *Absalom,* for example, Faulkner generates at least six different perspectives on reading Charles Bon's letter to Judith Sutpen (129–32), no one of which, nor any combination of which, provides an adequate paradigm of our own reading, or even an adequate reading of the letter.[5] In Chapter VIII, working with Quentin to re-create the story of Bon, Shreve invents several letters which probably never existed and focuses on the ways at least five of these letters might have been received, interpreted, read.[6] And in Chapter VII, we hear of Thomas Sutpen's experiences listening to his teacher read aloud, of his own failure to learn to read for himself, and of his challenge to his teacher: "How do I know that what you read was in the book?" (242). Sutpen's superficially naive question has disturbing, sophisticated repercussions which penetrate far beyond the boundaries of his own relatively innocent illiteracy. In one way or another, responsible critics of *Absalom* must sooner or later confront radical methodological, ontological, and epistemological uncertainties about what is or is not in the book: where, for example, should we locate the chronology and genealogy, *The Sound and the Fury,* the Biblical story of David and Absalom, or even the source of Quentin's presumed knowledge about Bon's parentage?[7]

Confronted with these sorts of problems, then, the more we can disclose about how Faulkner imagines a text-within-his-text might be read, the closer we may hope to come to a disclosure of how *Absalom* imagines its own reading(s).[8] This essay focuses deliberately, as closely as possible, on only one reader within the novel. It does not—should not—promise any reaffirmation of textual certainties, any reassuring solution to the disturbing problems of reading. Such affirmations and assurances would badly mis-represent (mis-read) Quentin's reading, and Faulkner's. Compulsive (re/mis-) readings of Quentin's (re-mis-) readings will disclose that Faulkner conceives of reading as an absolutely central and necessary yet radically disruptive human activity, an activity that implicates the reader in more pervasive, more subversive, and still more radical human problems of knowing, imagining, author(iz)ing, and being. Both Compson's letter and Faulkner's novel remain as intransigent and explosive as Pandora's box. Both remain fundamentally unreadable, *notread,*[9] even as they are and must be read and re-read: "the writing faded, almost indecipherable, yet meaningful . . . shadowy inscrutable and serene" (101). Failures of reading and writing, however, free us to re-read and re-write, helping to keep us human—and sane.

I

We first see Compson's letter lying on its envelope on top of an open textbook beneath a lamp on a table in front of Quentin. Faulkner draws a precise, symbolic picture, one which changes as the evening of old tales and talking wears on. Apparently the letter has distracted Quentin from his studies, Jefferson has distracted him from Cambridge, the South from the North, the past from the present, the emotional from the rational, the subjective from the objective, the unconscious from the conscious. Whatever Quentin's textbook (perhaps it is a history book, since later Shreve compares Ellen's manipulation of Bon and Judith to "the campaigns of dead generals in the textbooks" [321]7), in displacing it his father's letter demands a different strategy of reading, one more sensitive to the unexpressed and repressed play of subconscious, private, intimate associations, to "all the voices of his heredity and training" (342). In writing to Quentin, in the very act of addressing him as *"My dear son,"* Mr. Compson has made demands on him, demands Quentin can neither accept nor reject easily. Compson's salutation (which we read twice on page 173) invokes the rich patriarchal concerns signaled by the book's title, and resonates nicely with the key war-time scenario between Sutpen and Henry: *"—Henry, Sutpen says My son"* (353).

A letter always "requires and presupposes an I *and* a Thou, an I-for-a-Thou, and a Thou-for-an-I;"[10] yet this kind of inter-subjectivity may be at once peculiarly intimate and intimidating in the linear, ancestral relationship

between father and son. It may be unusually problematic for either the I or
the Thou, the father or the son, to establish the kind of healthy identity, the
self-possessed subjectivity, which any genuine reciprocity or inter-subjectivity
necessarily presupposes. Obviously it is problematic for Quentin, who not
only hears his own father talk about "the father who is the natural enemy of
any" (104), but who seems at times—like Henry—to feel that he may be just
an illusion which his father begot (347–48): *"apparently not only a man never
outlives his father but not even his friends and acquaintances do"* (277; see also,
for example, 261–62). And Compson finds it problematic to remain properly
paternal without slipping into oppressive paternalism; his letter reveals something of the strain, sounding a bit detached, impersonal, perhaps unfatherly.
Only once after its salutation does Compson's letter gesture openly (if parenthetically) toward Quentin as Other: *"It will do no harm to hope—You see I have
written hope, not think. So let it be hope.—that the one cannot escape the censure
which no doubt he deserves, that the other no longer lack the commiseration which
let us hope (while we are hoping) that they have longed for"* (377; emphasis added).
And even this gesture toward Quentin as the Other seems reductive—direc-
tive, manipulative, appropriative; characteristically, Compson mediates on
fate and death, rather than communicating love to his son.[11] Or so it seems.

Seems: because in watching Quentin trying to read (or not read) his
father's letter and in trying to read that letter for ourselves, we should not forget what Compson tends to forget about Bon's letter: Bon does not write to
Compson, but to Judith: Compson does not write to us, but to his son. We
cannot read as if we were Quentin and the letter were addressed to us. And
this "necessary *difference* in meaning of the letter when read later by someone
other than the one addressed" is crucial and inescapable. Our act of reading
Compson's letter—or Bon's letter—becomes, like Compson's act of reading
Bon's letter, an attempt at (re-)appropriation, at re-direction, at theft: "to
become Novel (or to play a role in the novel), letters must be read by someone other than the one to whom they are addressed." They must become *literally* a communication between someone who is not the writer and someone
who is not the reader."[12] They must become literally, in Compson's words,
"letters without salutation or signature" (100). And it is then not simply a
matter of adjusting our strategy of reading to allow for the fact that the letters do not belong to or even address us, though we must begin with such an
adjustment. A purloined letter, a fictionalized letter, must always to some
degree, in some fundamental way, remain irrecoverable, indecipherable,

unreadable—as Bon's letter remains to Compson, and Compson's to us. Our problem, then, reading Compson's letter and reading Faulkner's *Absalom,* is this: how can we recover and yet release the irrecoverable; how can we read the unreadable, and yet not confuse it with or reduce it to the readable?

Returning to the room at Harvard, the opening tableau of the novel's second movement, we should further observe that while we read the first part of Mr. Compson's letter, Quentin does not; he has apparently read it earlier and now he feels, smells, hears whatever the letter has "attenuated up from Mississippi and into this strange room . . . bringing with that very September evening itself" (173–74). The letter, moreover, breaks off with the phrase *"I do not know that either"* [173–74]), which seems to give Quentin an opening, a chance to move beyond his father's reading of Rosa's life and death, of the Sutpen story, of human nature, beyond reading his father's letter, into an imaginative or psychological space where he can do his own reading. And this seems to be what Quentin attempts to do in those 204 pages which disrupt his father's letter, interrupting, opening his reading.[13] But Quentin's reading is almost always tightly circumscribed by his father's.

Probably the easiest way to begin to recognize and measure the extent of Compson's circumscription (and inscription) to his son is to count the number of times Quentin says "Father said" when trying to re-tell the Sutpen story. In only the last ten pages or so of Chapter VII, for example, Quentin says "Father said" twenty-three times—occasionally four or five times in a single page (282, 283, 287). The density of these deferrals to authority at this point in the narrative is especially ironic and revealing, since Quentin has just vigorously asserted himself, trying to wrest control of the story from Shreve; "Wait, I tell you! . . . I am telling" (277). Within five lines of Quentin's tense, defensive, assertion, the unidentified narrative voice takes over briefly, acknowledging Mr. Compson's authority four times, and very soon going way to Mr. Compson's voice (378). Then Shreve's "No . . . you wait. Let me play a while now" (280) not only (re)emphasizes his narrative struggle with Quentin, but exposes the voices of the narrator and Compson as "not-language" (9)—"still born and complete in a second" (22) in Quentin's unconscious. And Quentin does not let Shreve play yet; the unidentified narrator manages to transfer the talking back to Quentin (280). But Quentin's voice is his father's (and Shreve's): "'Don't say it's just me that sounds like your old man,' Shreve said" (261); and it is here, after (or in) one of his most self-assertive moments with Shreve, that Quentin almost completely submits or

defers to his father (281–91). Moreover, in this section we shift to Wash
Jones's perspective (286–90), and even seem to be inside Jones' head (287) as
he transforms here, however, that Mr. Compson more-or-less controls the
view-point and voice, and Mr. Compson more-or-less mythologizes Sutpen.

These abrupt transformations and dislocations of narrative voices in the
last several pages of Chapter VII represent only an unusually noticeable and
important (because so compressed and self-conscious) version of the novel's
characteristic strategy of narrative ventriloquism. Though on the surface it
remains surprisingly readable, Chapter VII emerges as probably the most contrived and sophisticated movement of *Absalom* in its vocal modulations and
textual sedimentations. After all, earlier in the chapter Sutpen himself,
"Quentin's Mississippi shade," somehow manages to emerge—"a thousand
times more potent and alive" than in life (280)—to recount a brief part of his
own story. Through subtle manipulation of narrative voices and the reader's
engagements with the textualizations of those voices, Faulkner manages to
subvert or transcend the distances between story and source, between reader
and Thomas Sutpen, creating for a few pages (especially 240–43) a compelling
illusion of immediacy, not unlike that "by outraged recapitulation evoked"
between Miss Rosa and Quentin in the novel's opening pages (8): "the
invoked ghost of the man . . . began to assume a quality almost of solidity,
permanence" (13). Faulkner's technique generates some deliberate indeterminacy about who is speaking and who is not, about what is in the book and
what is not, about presence and absence, seducing even the most disciplined
of readers into an intimate, if illusive, engagement with a remote, elusive narrative voice. And, significantly, this narrative voice talks about the importance of learning to read.

Sutpen's talk about reading and Faulkner's sedimentation of the filtered
narrative voices, like Quentin's repeated deferrals to the authority of his
father's voice, affect the dynamics, the quality and consequences, of Quentin's
engagement with his father's letter—and, in turn, are affected by that engagement. Because Sutpen cannot read he must submit to the authority of a
teacher who reads aloud to him. Moreover, just as he cannot read or interpret
books for himself, Sutpen cannot read or interpret himself or others; he cannot recognize or realize his own identity, even his "own name" (242); his
awareness or understanding of human experience remains severely circumscribed by the voices of others' readings. Similarly, Quentin, though of course
not literally illiterate like Sutpen, finds himself confronting an unreadable

text, or at least a text *he* cannot (re-)read; finds his "curious repressed calm voice" (218) haunted, almost literally, by the oppressive ghostly voices of others: including his father's, his grandfather's, Sutpen's—and as Shreve rather cruelly insists in the end, Jim Bond's (378). And similarly, Quentin's problems with reading threaten his identity. Additionally, the elliptical movement of the narrative itself in Chapter VII—between Shreve's "so he just wanted a grandson" (217) and Sutpen's "all I wanted was just a son" (292)—works to emphasize that identity involves (inescapably) inheritance, genealogy, paternity—"one ambiguous eluded dark fatherhead" (299). As Quentin and Shreve re-examine Sutpen's identity, or, more accurately, his attempt to cerate, to design an identity for himself as father and grandfather, Quentin broods over the way his own identity has been determined through the inheritance of his father and grandfather. He broods over the letter. He resists the appropriation it represents to him. Significantly, during Chapter VIII, while Quentin and Shreve re-examine Bon's identity, or, more accurately, his attempt to design an identity for himself as son and grandson through discovering, disclosing a father—a disclosure which would depend on receiving from that father an acknowledgement, a *letter* which never comes (326–27)—Quentin seems able to ignore or displace or repress the letter from his father.

The second paragraph of Chapter VII (repeated and refracted later) establishes in exquisite circumstantial detail the brooding relationship Quentin cultivates with his father's letter:

> He sat quite still, facing the table, his hands lying on either side of the open text book on which the letter rested: the rectangle of paper folded across the middle and now open, three quarters open, whose bulk and raised half itself by the leverage of the old crease in weightless and paradoxical levitation, lying at such an angle that he could not possibly have read it, deciphered it, even without this added distortion. Yet he seemed to be looking at it, or as near as Shreve could tell, he was, his face lowered a little, brooding almost sullen. (217–18)

While Quentin is obviously not shown here reading the letter in any ordinary sense of that word (in fact, "he could not possibly have read it"), his brooding reflects an intense concentration upon the letter, a mystical rapport evidenced not only by the position of his hands on the table, but by the "paradoxical levitation" of the letter—*"now* open" (emphasis added). Since there is no textual evidence that Quentin has handled the letter, Faulkner apparently wants to cultivate the ambiguity or the illusion that Quentin has some sort of extraordinary, almost mystical, relationship with his father's letter. This relationship, moreover, remains qualified or defined by the current unreadability of the letter, an unreadability emphasized by the letter's position, the distortion, the resistance to attempts at deciphering.[14]

II

Quentin's brooding over the letter, his talking to it—"talking apparently (if to anything) to the letter" (255)—would seem to press beyond mere moodiness or sulkiness toward an effort to bring something within the text (or within himself?) to life, toward a kind of nurturing: that is, toward the radically literal sense of brooding as sitting on eggs in an effort to hatch them. Indeed, though the metaphors perversely elide, blurring and expanding, another passage presents the letter as egg-like ("fragile"), and describes what Quentin's imaginative brooding has hatched, released. We see Quentin and Shreve "facing one another across the lamp lit table on which lay the fragile Pandora's box of scrawled paper which had filled with violent and unratiocinative djinns and demons this snug monastic coign, this dreamy and heatless alcove of what we call the best of thought" (258). What may seem at first a casual reference to Pandora's story, merely an accident of colloquial speech, actually participates fully in *Absalom's* exploration of the "female principle" (116), of the myths of *"all the unsistered Eves since the Snake"* (144), and of "the dread and fear of females" (265) which inhibits most, if not all, of the novel's males. And even more importantly and disturbingly, Faulkner's appropriation of the myth here also insinuates Pandora's box deeply in the problems of reading—for Quentin, for Faulkner, and for us—exemplified and amplified throughout *Absalom*.

Faulkner had originally referred to the *envelope* as a "fragile trivial pandora's box—and significantly, dropping the adjective "trivial" (see Langford, 266). So he wants us to see the letter itself as having depth (the dimensionality of a box), and to associate whatever energies are released from that paper/container with the scrawling, the language, the words on the paper; and he does not want us to dismiss this image as trivial. In short, Faulkner forces the question implicit in his metaphor: how is Compson's letter (the "scrawled paper") like Pandora's box?

This question is made all the more difficult to answer responsibly since no single authoritative version of Pandora's story has survived transmission. Since the myth itself has been mis-represented and *mis-read* in transmission, this apparently innocuous allusion opens up the kind of archaeological abyss which threatens virtually any act of reading: how does a reader disclose/ enclose what Faulkner's reference means? How does a reader cope with textual sedimentation, worth layers of textuality or inter-textuality? How does he engage the relevant prior texts? How, in short, does a reader know what's in the book and what's not?[15] To pose these kinds of questions within a text, even implicitly, is to open a Pandora's box, to release violent and ratiocinative textual energies, to flirt with unreadability—to subvert the readable.

But how, more specifically, perhaps even more literally, is Compson's letter like Pandora's box? And how, in turn, might Faulkner's novel be seen to be like Compson's letter? Is the letter in some way a synecdoche for the novel?

Perhaps surprisingly, a scholarly article (published in 1900) about the nature and meaning of the box almost always associated with Pandora helps disclose a fuller explanation of Faulkner's metaphor. Jane E. Harrison explains convincingly that the so-called box is really a large jar or urn—more precisely, a burial urn or pithos—and that "the Pithoigian of Pandora was a release of maleficent ghosts from the grave" on a kind of Athenian Halloween: "The Pithoigia, the opening of graves, existed no doubt before the earth became anthropomorphized into a goddess. It was merely a ghost and ancestor cult: when the form of the earth goddess emerged in human shape, she was its natural patron: her spirits, the ghosts, were the source of all good and evil: she was Pandora . . ."[16] Like Harrison, Faulkner associates Pandora with a "ghost and ancestor cult" and her box with a grave full of "violent and unratiocinative djinns and demons." Compson's letter, in fact, not only describes how *"they had to use picks to break the earth for the grave"* for Miss Rosa (377), but itself *becomes* a kind of grave which encloses or entombs (or en-graves) her at least until Quentin's act of reading exhumes her, releases her—"name and presence of volatile and sentient forces"(100)—into his "snug monastic coign" (this coign is itself tomb-like, as is Rosa's room, and Henry's room, and even Quentin himself: "he was a barracks filled with stubborn back-looking ghosts still recovering" [12]).

If in constituting what it describes—Rosa's burial—Compson's letter becomes (not merely resembles) Pandora's pithos, its self-conscious attention to *hope* seems not merely important but uncanny. The most curious, ambiguous, unreadable feature of the Pandora myth—even more problematic than the nature of the box or the sex of whoever opened it—is the fate of Hope: did Hope escape from Pandora's box into the world or not? And what might be the consequences of its escape or containment? Rossetti's sonnet on Pandora, for example, which Faulkner almost certainly knew, ends ambivalently remarking of the escaped spirits: "Whither they go / Thou may'st not dare to think: nor canst thou know / If Hope still pent there be alive or dead."[17] Compson writes: *"It will do no harm to hope—You see I have written hope, not think. So let it be hope. . . . let us hope (while we are hoping) . . ."* (377). Compson remembers Bon's letter—*"Stop what? You will say. Why, thinking, remembering—remark that I do not say, hoping—"* (131); and I think that his self-conscious ambivalence about hope (also evident in his description of the redworm) implicates his letter still more deeply in the myth of Pandora. Of course the problem of hope is inherent in Compson's philosophical determinism, his fatalism; the capacity to hope would moderate Compson's cynicism. Does Compson's letter, then, contain or exclude or release hope? Like Pandora's box, yes and no.

Graves and letters, interment and inscription, are associated by Judith as she hands on Bon's letter to Quentin's grandmother; according to Compson, Judith conceives of both gravestones and scrawled papers as ways "to make that scratch, that undying mark on the blank face of the oblivion to which we are all doomed" (129). A less-discussed scene, Quentin's quail hunt with his father, resonates closely with Judith's speech and presents a graphic image of graves and undying marks—and reading:

> the two flat heavy vaulted slabs, the other three headstones leaning a little awry, with here and there a carved letter or even an entire word momentary and *legible* in the faint light . . . (188). Quentin looked at the three identical headstones with their faint identical lettering, slanted a little in the soft loamy decay of accumulated cedar needles, these *decipherable* too when he looked close. . . . Quentin had to stoop and brush away some of the cedar needles *to read* the next one (190) . . . . he brushed the cedar needles away, smoothing with his hand into *legibility* the faint lettering, the *graved* words (191). . . . he knew who had ordered and bought that headstone before *he read the inscription* on it,. . . . He had to brush the clinging cedar needles from this one also *to read it,* watching these letters also emerge beneath his hand . . . . (210, my emphasis)

If the text of Compson's letter is a kind of grave, these graves are a kind of text—both constituted by *"graved words."* And the emphasis in this graveyard scene falls insistently on the problematic *legibility* of these *graved words,* on the nature and consequences of Quentin's reading—a decipherment which is also a disinterment, an opening of Pandora's box: "It seemed to Quentin that he could actually see them" (189). This act of disinterment, then, like the act of opening Compson's letter, or Pandora's box, releases "violent and unratiocinative djinns and demons." It makes present an absence, an absence rather macabrely stressed by the narrator: "(. . . there could have been nothing to eat in the grave for a long time) though the lettering was quite legible" (188). But this "presence" is ghostly, shadowy, something like what Derrida calls the *trace* produced by *graved words,* by language: "The trace is not a presence but is rather the simulacrum of a presence that dislocates, displaces, and refers beyond itself. The race has, properly speaking, no place, for effacement belongs to the very structure of the trace. Effacement must always be able to overtake the trace; otherwise it would not be a trace but an indestructible and monumental substance. . . . [The text] proposes both the monument and the mirage of the trace, the trace as simultaneously traced and effaced, simultaneously alive and dead, alive as always to simulate even life in its preserved inscription. . . ."[18]

Quentin discovers in reading his father's letter, as well as in reading the Sutpen gravestones, the difficulty of transcending or subverting or arresting the interplay of tracings and effacings, of presence and absence, of now and then, of conscious and unconscious, of life and death—the difficulty of reading. Similarly, in attempting to read Quentin's readings we necessarily re-enact his discovery. This pursuit of Faulkner's allusion to Pandora's box has simultaneously traced and effaced Quentin's reading—and our own—while entangling us ever more inextricably in the textuality of the text. Once opened through an act of reading, the ghost-ridden text, like any genuine Pandora's box, does not re-close itself, cannot be re-closed, through it threatens to enclose or entomb others: "Nevermore of peace. Nevermore of peace. Nevermore Nevermore Nevermore" (373).

III

Several pages after the nearly buried allusion to Pandora (which the above paragraphs only begin to exhume), her box, the letter, recedes from our consciousness, if not from Quentin's and Shreve's. The intimacy between the two roommates grows, as they respond to "Quentin's Mississippi shade," presumably Sutpen, but just possibly Rosa as well, "who dying had escaped it completely" (280). We no longer see Quentin talking to the letter, but we cannot always be sure that he talks *to* Shreve, or Shreve to him. Some kind of dialogue Quentin was having or conjuring or repressing or exorcising between himself and the letter.[19] Throughout Chapter VIII, collaboration and apparent imaginative communion grows between Quentin and Shreve. There no longer seems to be any pressure to finish (re-)reading Mr. Compson's letter. The physical environment presents itself in detail—for example, "Shreve stood beside the table, facing Quentin again though not seated now" (293)—without any mention of the letter. Their playing even transforms their environment—"Not two of them in a New England college sitting-room but one in a Mississippi library sixty years ago" (294), and Quentin and Shreve themselves become "as free now of flesh as the father who decreed and forbade, the son who denied and repudiated" (295). But if on the level of narrative Sutpen decrees and Henry denies, there emerges on the psychological level the trace of Compson decreeing and Quentin denying, the trace of the letter to be (re-)read.

Quentin avoids the letter, turning to Shreve, as Henry turned to Bon: "Quentin and Shreve stared at one another—glared rather . . . There was something curious in the way they looked at one another . . . a sort of hushed and naked searching" (200). This intense mutual searching replaces (or seems to displace) Quentin's solipsistic scrutiny of the letter; reading each other rather than the letter, they become as transparencies—or mirrors—to each other. Again, on page 303, we are told, "They stared—glared—at one another. . . . the two of them creating between them, out of the rag-tag and bob-ends of old tales and talking, people who perhaps had never existed at all anywhere," and again the narrator does not mention the letter. Nor does he allude to the letter in perhaps the most remarkable of all those passages representing creation as collaborative discovery, as "some happy marriage of speaking and hearing wherein each before the demand, the requirement, forgave condoned and forgot the faulting of the other—faultings both in the creating of this shade whom they discussed (rather, existed in) and in the hearing and sifting and discarding the false and conserving what seemed true, or fit the preconceived—in order to overpass to love, where there might be paradox and inconsistency but nothing fault nor false" (316). In this passage, perhaps more explicitly and eloquently than anywhere else in the novel, conversation proposes itself as an alternative to reading.[20] One of the faultings which the narrator claims Quentin and Shreve "forgave condoned and forgot" is the tendency to conserve only what "fit the preconceived." A marriage of true minds—or voices—apparently requires not that preconceptions be sifted and discarded, but only that their conservation be acknowledged and overpassed. But Compson's letter waits on the desk to be (re-)read, a sign that Quentin, at least, remains bound by his preconceptions to an extent that may inhibit his free entry into "some happy marriage of speaking and hearing." And the dynamics of Chapter VIII, pretty much controlled by Shreve, do not necessarily or exactly validate the narrator's poetic vision of conversation as marriage, or imagination as love. Even as the narrator claims the greatest freedom for the roommates, Quentin (and probably Shreve as well) continues to be circumscribed by his father's letter, by his past, his assumptions, his inhibitions.

To the extent that internal psychological and imaginative restraints inhibit the free play of love and creativity, pressuring or permitting Quentin and Shreve to fit their version of "what seemed true" only to the pre-conceived, the two students find themselves reading even when not reading, submitting to the authority of pre-texts, pre-readings. And they can see or read only that which confirms their individual, private conceptions, assumptions, expectations about what might be true. Ultimately, they sustain no genuine inter-subjectivity; what seem to be moments of self-transcendence prove illusory, even mutually debilitating. The narrator's recognition or suspicion of constraints within the happy marriage of speaking and hearing" was anticipated by Shreve's obtuseness about the infant born to Sutpen and Milly Jones (292), and in turn, anticipates the imaginative divorce which separates Quentin and Shreve irreconcilably in Chapter IX: "You can't understand it" (361).

Any illusion of sustained intimacy or communion between the two young men disintegrates in the book's final movement; any marriage of minds had been temporary, if not wholly illusionary. The roommates go to

bed, and Quentin retreats not only into the darkness but deeper into solipsistic and (apparently) mystical reveries, refusing to respond to Shreve. All of
Quentin's senses are re-activated as he re-lives his journey with Miss Rosa to
the Sutpen mansion, and he "lay still and rigid on his back with the cold New
England night on his face and the blood running warm in his rigid body and
limbs, breathing hard but slow, his eyes wide open upon the window, thinking 'Nevermore of peace. Nevermore of peace. Nevermore Nevermore
Nevermore'" (373). The more insistently Shreve pressures Quentin to respond
to his questions and remarks, the more Quentin withdraws into himself, into
his unconscious, and the greater the chasm between them, until at last Shreve
concludes his remarks about Rosa, saying "and so she died" (376). This abrupt
remark signals an extraordinary return of the repressed, the re-emergence of
the letter from Compson announcing that death and burial:

> Quentin did not answer, staring at the window; then he could not tell if it was
> the actual window or the window's pale rectangle upon his eyelids, though after
> a moment it began to emerge. It began to take shape in its same curious, light,
> gravity-defying attitude—the once-folded sheet out of the wisteria Mississippi
> summer, the cigar smell, the random blowing of the fireflies. "The South," Shreve
> said, "The South. Jesus. No wonder you folks all outlive yourselves y years and
> years and years." IT was becoming quite distinct; he would be able to decipher the
> words soon, in a moment; even almost now, now, now.
>   "I am older at twenty than a lot of people who have died," Quentin said.
>   "And more people have died than have been twenty-one," Shreve said. Now
> he (Quentin) could read it, could finish it—the sloped whimsical ironic hand out
> of Mississippi attenuated, into the iron snow: . . . (376–77)

The structure of this scene—subtle, fragments, yet precise, the result of
painstaking revision—give symbolic import to Quentin's act of reading, a
reading which is not a reading, of a text which is not a text.[21]
    Quentin has been staring at the window of his Cambridge room through-
out Chapter IX, just as in Chapter VIII he had stared at Shreve, and in
Chapters VI and VII he had stared at the letter. His staring has blurred distinctions between inside and outside his own mind, his own vision: *"You cannot know yet whether what you see is what you are looking at or what you are
believing'; "your illusions are a part of you like your bones and flesh and memory"*
(314, 348). The window (like Compson's letter) reflects rather than reveals,

inhibits rather than exhibits. In Quentin's mind, and even the reader's, the Harvard window seems to merge with a window at Sutpen's mansion—"Miss Coldfield screaming harshly, 'The window! The window!'" (375); or, "and then for a moment maybe Clytie appeared in that window from which she must have been watching"(375–76); or even, "Henry would recall later how he had seen through the window beyond his father's head the sister and the lover in the garden" (294). Still more immediately, and still more interestingly, "the window's pale rectangle upon his eyelids" merges with "the rectangle of paper folded across the middle" (217), the letter from Mr. Compson, a merger marked and submerged by the ambiguous pronoun *it*—"*it* began to emerge. *It* began to take shape. . . ." Not until the *it* further emerges as "the once-folded sheet" can we recognize the letter, a letter no longer physically within our field of vision, or Quentin's, bringing with it the sensations of the South, accompanied by Shreve's sardonic commentary. Though he speaks, apparently in response to Shreve, Quentin seems detached from, all but oblivious to, his roommate, intent upon the emergence of the letter, a letter which now seems to have nothing to do with Shreve or Shreve's material world. If Shreve has somehow helped Quentin deal with his memories, that help has now placed Quentin beyond Shreve's understanding or touch, alone with his father's letter—a letter he needs compulsively to read and re-read: "It was becoming quite distinct; he would be able to decipher the words soon, in a moment; even almost now, now, now." These *nows* perhaps blur in Quentin's consciousness and the reader's with those of the previous September at Sutpen's: "'Now,' she said, 'We are on the Domain.' . . . But Quentin was already aware of that. Before she spoke he had said to himself, 'Now Now.'" (363). And perhaps they blur even further with those of Bon as he arrives at Sutpen's Hundred for Christmas, "saying *Now. Now. It will come now*" (333). An almost erotic anticipation builds as Quentin finally approaches the potential release of (re-)reading his father's letter, a release which is also a surrender (as was the approach to the old mansion for Rosa—and Bon); Quentin (like Rosa—and Bon) would seem to seek ultimate release and surrender in death—or, at least within the limits of *Absalom, a kind* of death that is withheld: "sleeping, the little death, the renewal"(275).

In this final scene Quentin can be seen to read the letter only as an act of total recall, an act of memory which transcends or consumes the materiality of the text at once locating the letter within Quentin and Quentin within the letter. Through this act of interpenetration or appropriation all distance between Quentin and his father's letter seems to collapse, dissolve; the text seems to become part of Quentin, Quentin part of the text. However reluctantly, Quentin opens himself to the letter and the letter opens itself to him, in a process involving an apparent suspension of self—of subjectivity— which results from Quentin's absolute attention to the text, the object, a process which seems to alter the very text(ure) of his consciousness. At last accepted, fully engaged through concentration and memorization, Compson's letter appears to mesh with the fabric of Quentin's self, becoming an integral part of the text(ure) of Quentin's identity: "He was a barracks filled with stubborn and back-looking ghosts" (12).[22]

At the end of *Absalom*, then, Faulkner re-presents his most radical act of (re-)reading. He discloses Quentin's inscription within the texts of his past, his lineage, his memories, and subverts any comfortable notions about how such problematic, patriarchal texts can be read. Faulkner refuses to handle Compson's letter as if it were what Roland Barthes has called a "text of pleasure: the text that contents, fills, grants euphoria; the text that comes from culture and does not break with it, is linked to a *comfortable* practice of reading." Instead, he allows Compson's letter to disrupt both Quentin's consciousness and the textuality of *Absalom* itself. Through the letter and its reading the novel exposes itself as a "text of bliss: the text that imposes a state of loss, the text that discomforts . . . unsettles the reader's historical, cultural, psychological assumptions, the consistency of his tastes, values, memories, brings to a crisis his relation with language."[23] Quentin's crisis mimics but does not duplicate that of *Absalom's* readers. In some ways the pressures on readers of the novel are not only less fictional but more extreme than those on any reader in the novel, even Quentin/ Faulkner demands that his readers somehow accommodate, for example, both Quentin's visionary, ontological poetics of reading and Compson's more pragmatic epistemological maneuvers, "tedious and intent, poring" (101). This crisis of accommodation makes Faulkner's assertion "that when the reader has read all these thirteen different ways of looking at the blackbird, the reader has his own fourteenth image of that blackbird which I would like to think is the truth" sound trivial and untrue—or, at best, nostalgic.[24] Faulkner's Pandora's box is not so easily controlled, closed.

Unlike some readers of *Absalom*, Faulkner does not sentimentalize or idealize or privilege any mode of reading within his novel's repertoire, does not offer any simple paradigm for getting at "the truth" of a fourteenth image through reading, and does not endorse even Quentin's reading as "success-ful."[25] Rather, Faulkner insistently demonstrates that "if reading must not be content with doubling the text"—as Compson tries to do—"it cannot legiti-mately transgress the text"—as Quentin does—"toward something other than it, toward a referent (a reality that is metaphysical, historical, psychobio-graphical, etc.) or toward a signifier outside the text whose content could have taken place outside of language, that is to say . . . outside of writing in general."[26] Through his reading/writing of reading in *Absalom,* Faulkner rup-tures his own text, displacing reductive, nostalgic notions of centered textual truth and releasing a true play of decentered readings. He opens Pandora's box. He shows that "reading does not consist in stopping the chain of sys-tems, in establishing a truth, a legality of the text, and consequently in lead-ing its reader into 'errors'; it consists in coupling these systems, not according to their finite quantity, but according to their plurality (which is a being, not a discounting): I pass, I intersect, I articulate, I release, I do not count."[27] Only in this open, liberating, unstable way—passing, intersecting, articulating, releasing—can Faulkner's "fragile pandora's box of scrawled paper" be read in all its blissful and truthful unreadability.

IV

Recognizing *Absalom's* surprising self-consciousness about its own traces of epistolarity, that is, recognizing that most of the major scenes of reading are letter-readings, can only deepen our recognition of the book's self-consum-ing poetics of reading. While it would be an obvious and unconvincing dis-tortion to force *Absalom* into the epistolary genre (just as it is a distortion to force it into the "historical novel" genre), it needs to be stressed that the novel does originate in two or three acts of reading letters, acts of trying to say what the letters themselves do not, will not, or cannot say. Two or three, because in addition to Bon's letter which originates much of Chapters I–IV and Compson's letter which originates most of Chapters VI–IX, Rosa's letter to Quentin— "—the quaint, stiffly formal request which was actually a sum-mons, out of another world almost—the queer archaic sheet of ancient good notepaper written over with the neat faded cramped script" (10)—deserves notice. In a way although its specific content is withheld from us, it origi-nates the entire novel, and not just on the level of narrative, but on that of hermeneutics. Rosa's letter provokes Quentin's first act of misreading within (or just before) the novel: "he did not recognize [it] as revealing a character cold, implacable, and even ruthless' (10). This mis-reading not only antici- pates but necessitates all those problematic acts of (re-)reading—Quentin's, Compson's, Sutpen's, etc., as well as Faulkner's and ours—which generate the novel. Rosa's letter, though thoroughly displaced, radically absent from *Absalom,* functions in a sense as (not just another, but) *the* "pandora's box of scrawled paper" from which all the other ghostly presences emerge—includ- ing those of Bon's and Compson's letters.

These *aporiae* of epistolarity in *Absalom* enclose and disclose Faulkner's reflexivity, his extreme self-consciousness about the problems of writing and reading novels.[28] Faulkner's appropriation of epistolary situations and strate- gies can be better understood in contrast to more conventional uses of the genre, such as Samuel Richardson's.[29] Faulkner has more problematic, pre- dictably more modern conceptions of letters and novels, of identity and love, than Richardson; yet in this novel about uncertain identities, doomed loves, and empty choices, he repeatedly plays with the possibilities of a successfully written and read letter—Bon's to Judith, Compson's to his son, even those invented by Shreve, and Rosa's note to Quentin—in ways which suggest that in the process of discovering fiction's inadequacy as history he tests its via- bility as personal correspondence: *"unsolicited communication"* (315). Faulkner uses his letters and their readers to disclose an emptiness, an absence that cannot quite be made a presence. His scenes of letter reading become medi- tations on the difficult problems of communication, of intersubjectivity, of selfhood, of authority, of choice, of love—problems which necessarily inhibit, literally dis-compose or de-construct, his writing of a novel and our reading of that novel. Such discomposing and deconstructing, however, humanizes as it frees author and reader to re-write and re-read.

With admirable economy and poise, Quentin's Grandfather Compson gets close to the heart of this paradoxical freedom; "language (that meager and fragile thread, Grandfather said, by which the letter surface corners and edges of men's secret and solitary lives may be joined for an instant now and then before sinking back into the darkness where the spirit cried for the first time and was not heard and will cry for the last time and will not be heard then either)" (251). With this meager and fragile thread of language man simultaneously constructs and de-constructs—closes and opens—his fragile pandora's boxes, concealing and revealing (effacing and tracing) his ghostly, ancestral selves in (unwritten and unread) acts of writing and reading.

NOTES

1. William Faulkner, *Absalom, Absalom!* (1936; reprint, New York: Random House: Vintage Books Edition, 1972). All page numbers refer to this accessible edition and will be given parenthetically in the text.

2. See *Absalom*, 31, 173–74, 207, 217–18, 238, 255, 258, 265, 275, and 377. A comparison of the original manuscript and the published text of *Absalom* reveals that Faulkner consistently paid scrupulous attention to the placing and phrasing of each reference to Compson's letter. Each passage shows evidence of tinkering; some are pasted in (173, 275); one added (207); one—cancelled from Chapter VIII (350–51). See Gerald Langford, *Faulkner's Revision of Absalom, Absalom!: A Collation of the Manuscript and the Published Book* (Austin: University of Texas Press 1971). Despite methodological and mechanical weakness, Langford's work provides a convenient and adequate collation.

3. Shreve's last words parody remarks Compson attributes to Bon (*Absalom*, 116).

4. Rudolf E. Kuenzli, "The Intersubjective Structure of the Reading Process: A Communication Oriented Theory of Literature," *Diacritics* 10 (1980): 47.

5. See my article, "Reading Bon's Letter and Faulkner's *Absalom, Absalom!*," *PMLA*, 99 (March 1984): 225–41.

6. See my article, "Reading Shreve's Letters and Faulkner's *Absalom, Absalom!*," *Studies in American Fiction* 11 (fall 1983): 153–69.

7. Two of Faulkner's best readers, Joseph Blotner and Cleanth Brooks, cannot even agree on what they read in Compson's letter to Quentin. Blotner says that, "The letter conveyed news not only of Miss Rosa's death but of the destruction by fire of the Sutpen mansion. Henry and Clytie within it" (*Faulkner: A Biography* [New York: Random House, 1974], 2:926). Brooks, noting that the letter is dated January 10, says that "Quentin (at home for the Christmas holidays) must have got all the gory details when the ambulance came back to Jefferson" ("The Narrative Structure of *Absalom, Absalom!*," *Georgia Review* 29 [1975]: 385). Blotner errs: Compson's letter as we read it makes no mention of the fire, or Henry or Clytie; moreover, even if we could infer that we read only edited portions of the letter, the rhetoric of the text demonstrably presupposes a prior knowledge of the fire and its immediate consequences: "She remained in the coma for almost two weeks . . ." (173). Brooks infers: recognizing that the

letter *begins in medias res,* and noting its date, he says that Quentin must have been in Jefferson, on Christmas break from Harvard when Rosa's return to Sutpen's Hundred precipitated the fire, the deaths of Clytie and Henry, Jim Bond's escape, and Rosa's coma. Nothing in the text of the letter or of the novel as a whole supports Brooks' inferences. Yet unless (for example) there was an earlier letter from Jefferson bringing news of the fire—and there's no textual evidence for this—Brooks is almost as certainly as right as Blotner is wrong. And *The Sound and the Fury,* of course, supports Brooks. But why cannot Blotner and Brooks agree on what is in Compson's letter and Faulkner's *Absalom?* Why do they have so much trouble reading?

8. Paul de Man offers a caveat: "This procedure in fact begs the question, for we cannot *a priori* be certain to gain access to whatever [the author] may have to say about reading by way of such a reading of a scene of reading . . . if reading is truly problematic. . . . then the scenes in the novel that literally represent reading are not to be privileged." Nevertheless, de Man, who himself offers a compelling reading of reading in Proust, would not "prevent us from questioning the passage on actual reading, if only to find out whether or not it does make paradigmatic claims for itself." *Allegories of Reading* (New Haven: Yale University Press, 1979), 57–58.

9. Here I consciously imitate Faulkner's use of such words (not words?) *as not language, not people, and not husband;* and I also echo Judith; "Read it if you like or don't read it if you like" (127); and Compson: "even to read or not to read as the stranger saw fit" (129).

10. Homer Obed Brown, "The Errant Letter and the Whispering Gallery," *Genre* 10 (1977): 581.

11. For a helpful discussion of Compson's philosophical poses and narrative strategies, see Donald M. Kartiganer, *The Fragile Thread: The Meaning of Form in Faulkner's Novels* (Amherst: University of Massachusetts Press, 1979), 76–87.

12. Brown, "The Errant Letter. . . ." 583.

13. See John T. Irwin. *Doubling and Incest/Repetition and Revenge: A Speculative Reading of Faulkner* (Baltimore: Johns Hopkins University Press, 1975), esp. 113–14.

14. In revising the original draft of page 217 Faulkner deleted two phrases which would have made clear: first, that Quentin has in fact already read the letter; and second, that Quentin is not trying to (re-)read the letter in the present scene. The manuscript draft simultaneously lacks the precision and the suggestive ambiguity of the published version. Juxtaposition of the two passages provides an excellent example of Faulkner's meticulous attention to detail and nuance in re-writing: ". . . open book on which the letter lay, the oblong of paper folded across the center and open, or half open, _ open, whose bulk had raised half of itself from the old crease in weightless and levitation paradox, and lying at such an angle that, regardless of this added distortion, *he could not have deciphered the writing even if there were need, even if he had not already done it learned that contents, But he was not trying to read it.* He just faced it, immobile, his face lowered and looking almost sullen a little, brooding" (Langford, 229, my emphasis).

15. The seminal study by Dora and Erwin Panofsky, *Pandora's Box: The Changing Aspects of a Mythical Symbol* (New York: Pantheon, 1956), includes versions of the myth in poetry, drama, and painting: for example, Hesiod, Spenser, Milton, Hawthorne, Swinburne, Calderon, Voltaire, Goethe, Rosso, Fiorentino, Paul Klee. Did Faulkner derive his notions of Pandora's box from any of these sources, or only from Bullfinch? In what ways might it matter?

16. "Pandora's Box," *Journal of Hellenic Studies* 20 (1900): 104 and 108.

17. Cited by Panofsky (110), from Dante Gabriel Rossetti, *Poems* (Boston, 1870) 272; on Pandora and Hope, see Panofsky, 27–33.

18. Jacques Derrida, *Speech and Phenomenon*, trans. David B. Allison (Evanston: Northwestern University Press, 1973), 156–57.

19. Faulkner manages to sustain this replacement or displacement by strategically erasing two brief passages near the end of Chapter VIII: the first, a description of Shreve originally occurring after the italicized Civil War scenes and before Shreve's voice resumes (350); the second, a description of Quentin and the letter after Shreve "ceased again" (351): "Quentin had not moved, still brooding apparently over the open letter which lay on the book on the table before him" (see Langford, 344–45). This cancelled reference to Compson's letter, it should be noted, would have followed quite naturally and aptly the account of Bon writing his decisive letter to Judith at the end of the War: " . . . and Henry read it and sent it off" (349). That Faulkner here chooses to suppress his impulse to juxtapose so effectively the novel's two central, originating texts—Bon's letter and Compson's—suggests that he wants to sustain the illusion of Quentin's intimacy with Shreve, *and* to defer the letter's reappearance until the novel's brilliantly orchestrated finale.

20. For a very different, very suggestive discussion of this key passage, see John T. Matthews, *The Play of Faulkner's Language* (Ithaca: Cornell University Press, 1982), 15–17, 159–60.

21. In re-working this scene Faulkner adds this crucial phrase: "he could not tell if it was the actual window or the window's pale rectangle upon his eyelids;" and "in a moment; even almost now, now, now" (see Langford, 361). Gary Williams, virtually alone among critics of *Absalom*, pays some close attention to this scene, in "Quentin Finally Sees Miss Rosa," *Criticism* 21 (1978): 331–46.

22. See George Steiner, "'Critic'/Reader,'" *NLH* 10 (1979): 423–52. Compson has most of the qualities which Steiner attributes to his fiction of the "critic;" Quentin, most of those attributed to the "reader." See also Georges Poulet, "Criticism and the Experience of Interiority," *The Structuralist Controversy*, ed. Richard Macksey and Eugenio Donato (1970; reprint, Baltimore: Johns Hopkins University Press, 1972), 56–72. And consider Roland Barthes: "Reading involves risks of objectivity or subjectivity (both are imaginary) only insofar as we define the text as an expressive object (presented for our own expression), sublimated under a morality of truth, in one instance laxist; in the other, ascetic," *S/Z*, trans. Richard Miller (New York: Hill and Wang, 1974), 10.

23. Roland Barthes, *The Pleasure of the Text,* trans. Richard Miller, (New York: Hill and Wang, 1975), 14.

24. *Faulkner in the University,* ed. Frederick L. Gwynn and Joseph Blotner (New York: Vintage, 1965), 274. For a suggestive reading of this statement, see Gary Lee Stonum, *Faulkner's Career: An Internal Literary History* (Ithaca: Cornell University Press, 1979), 131–32.

25. See Karl F. Zender, "Reading in 'The Bear'": "Crippled by custom or by fear, many of [Faulkner's] characters cannot sustain the labor of interpretation. But these failures remain their own. Because they are presented in a context of negative authorial judgments and are balanced against *successful acts of reading such as Quentin's and Shreve's,* these failures do not imply a general breakdown in the relation of the mind to the world" (*Faulkner Studies* 1 [1980]: 94, my emphasis). Compare the recent article by Allan Chavkin who asserts that "Faulkner's celebration of the imagination and its heightened moments of perception is at the heart of this affirmative work;" and more specifically, that Quentin's "imaginative exploration of the past and his ability to interpret it suggest that only the human mind can defeat time and that his sophisticated approach to complex reality is the alternative to Sateen's simplistic one." "The Imagination as the Alternative to Sutpen's Design," *Arizona Quarterly* 37 (1981): 117 and 116. Though seldom as explicit or sentimental, most critics of the novel have tended to agree (more-or-less) with Zender and Chavkin that Quentin shows us how to read well. A notable exception is James Guetti who discusses "Quentin's failure to understand the story he articulates," in *"Absalom, Absalom!* The Extended Simile," *Twentieth-Century Interpretations of Absalom, Absalom!,* ed. Arnold Godman (Englewood Cliffs: Prentice-Hall, 1971), 92; reprinted from *The Limits of Metaphor* (Ithaca: Cornell University Press, 1967), 69–108.

26. Jacques Derrida, *Of Grammatology,* trans. Gayatri C. Spivak (Baltimore: Johns Hopkins University Press, 1976), 158.

27. Barthes, *S/Z,* 11.

28. Janet Gurkin Altman notes that novelists tend to turn to the letter-form when they want—as Faulkner so obviously wants in *Absalom*—to "most openly reflect upon the relation between story telling and inter-subjective communication and begin to question the way in which writing reflects, betrays, or constitutes the relations between self, other and experience." She also observes that the "epistolary situation evokes simultaneously the acts of writing and reading," that "the letter is by definition . . . the result of a union of writer and reader;" and that, "In no other genre do readers figure so prominently within the world of the narrative and in the generation of the text," *Epistlarity: Approaches to a Form* (Columbus: Ohio State University Press, 1982), 186 and 188.

29. On Richardson's epistolary aesthetics, see Roy Roussel, "Reflections on the Letter: The Reconciliation of Distance and Presence in *Pamela," ELH* 41 (1974): 375–99.

Absalom, Absalom!: The Movie

JOSEPH URGO

The view that *Absalom, Absalom!* is William Faulkner's greatest novel, his most complex and rewarding literary work, makes it easy to forget that the novel was written for the most part in Hollywood while Faulkner was a paid scriptwriter. He would work on the novel early in the morning before going to the studio to write screenplays, participate in story conferences, and work on location at various film projects. The novel contains a number of indelible images, including a central one in which Quentin and Shreve sit across "a strange lamplit table" to collaborate on the Sutpen story. The two students, together in a foreign environment, sit in the "strange room" and contemplate one another's perspectives and insights "across this strange" juxtaposition of intellectual energies.[1] The collaboration, the "strange" meeting of talents, produces a compelling historical narrative. Whether their story is "true enough" is a matter of some debate, but what is unquestionable is the

Reprinted with permission from *American Literature* 62, no. 1 (March 1990): 56–73.

amazing productivity of their joint effort. In one night they outline an American epic. Quentin and Shreve, as collaborators, must have originated not in Faulkner's experience as "sole owner and proprietor" of the apocryphal county but in his successful record as an employee in the Hollywood studio system. Only there did he sit regularly at strange lamplit tables across from interlocutors in order to get a story told. *Absalom, Absalom!* is about history and mythmaking and narrative and storytelling and all the rest, so aptly and thoroughly explicated over the past decades, but it is about one more thing as well. *Absalom, Absalom!* is about movie-making, and the production of images and moving pictures under the strange, forced, and often brutal conditions of an environment foreign to everyone, Hollywood.

Students of Faulkner have been misled by early-day Faulkner scholars and by Faulkner himself into believing that his Hollywood experience was a drain on his creative powers in the 1930s.The ten years between 1929 and 1939 are considered his major period, when he produced a string of literary masterpieces, including *The Sound and the Fury, As I Lay Dying, Sanctuary, Light in August, Pylon, Absalom, Absalom!, The Unvanquished, The Wild Palms, The Hamlet,* and dozens of short stories. Recent scholarship only adds to this list, and we must now include numerous screenplays, story treatments, and actual scripts in this phenomenal bibliography.[2] Faulkner spent four months in 1932 working at MGM studios, three weeks in July 1934 at Universal Studios, five weeks in December-January 1934–1935 at Twentieth Century Fox, and two separate periods in 1936, one for three months and another, into 1937, for a full year. Conventional thinking on his career confuses these profitable and largely successful stints as film scenarist in the 1930s with his less successful experiences in Hollywood in the next decade, the years Joseph Blotner refers to as Faulkner's "bondage." Faulkner, of course, is legendary in his complaints about the movie industry, and his letters home are sprinkled with expressions of impatience with the working conditions. But he was also involved in a passionate love affair with young Meta Carpenter during much of his Hollywood time in the 1930s, and so letters home to his wife Estelle, at least, are of dubious credibility. In any case, as Bruce Kawin points out, students of Faulkner's career must keep separate the work he did in Hollywood in the 1930s and the work he did there in the 1940s. In the 1930s, Kawin argues, "Faulkner was definitely using his film writing to advance his own thinking, to try out versions of his stories, and to gain a large audience for his own work."[3] His six months' experience with filmmaking prior to and simultaneous with the writing and revision of *Absalom, Absalom!* (begun early in 1934 and completed in January 1936) made that novel possible in many ways. Primarily, *Absalom, Absalom!* is a celebration of *collaboration* as a fruitful human exercise toward creating new works of art and reaching new levels of comprehension. Faulkner learned this in Hollywood.[4]

Absalom, Absalom! marks a break in Faulkner's narrative strategies as dramatic as the breakthrough represented by *The Sound and the Fury*. In that novel, as in *As I Lay Dying*, his use of multiple narration is characterized by the individual narrators' lack of dialogic interaction with one another. Benjy, Quentin, and Jason may each have a say in representing the Compson story, but they do not say it to each other, only to the reader. Narrator interaction in *As I Lay Dying* is similarly low, with the Bundren family members talking into a kind of narrative "space" and competing for the reader's vote of confidence. Critical attention to the novel has even featured a debate among readers over which narrator is most credible, creative, or insightful into the family (or the human) condition, with one reader going so far as to privilege the six-year old Vardaman.[5] In *Sanctuary* and *Light in August*, perspectives on events clash and collide with greater violence but still without significant or productive interaction. Horace listens to Temple Drake but puts none of her story to use in his feeble defense of her. *Light in August* in particular plays out this early Faulknerian technique of competing storylines, as the twin tales of Joe Christmas and Lena Grove parallel and intersect one another but do not face each other, except in the mind of the reader.

In *Absalom, Absalom!*, however, the various narrators are not talking into space but directly *at* each other and, at times, doing so by force or summons. The reader is seldom appealed to for verification or even sympathy and is invited only to witness the collaborative, creative processes which unfold over the course of the novel. This is not to say that readers cannot make or have not made judgments concerning the relative reliability of the various narrators. All the participants have personal stakes, of varying degrees, which influence their points of view. The difference between *Absalom, Absalom!* and the novels which precede it is not the fact of multiple perspective, or of perspectivism as fundamental to a modernist worldview. The difference between *Absalom, Absalom!* and its predecessors is that perspectives are folded over one another to provide a single, recognizable text, or series of pictures, *by two of the narrators themselves*—and not solely by the reader. In the same way that a director, in collaboration with writers and producers and technical assistants, makes a film from the various scenes, shots, and file footage at his disposal, Quentin and Shreve make a Sutpen story from materials which Quentin produces and Shreve ultimately shapes, or directs, into a coherent pattern. And when they're working, Shreve, echoing Faulkner's own immediate sense of *Absalom, Absalom!* as "the best novel yet written by an American,"[6] proclaims, "It's better than Ben Hur, isn't it. No wonder you have to come away now and then, isn't it" (271).[7]

Rosa Coldfield summons Quentin to her house in 1909 because she wants the Sutpen story produced. She is thinking that Quentin will write it down, "remember this and write about it . . . and submit it to the magazines," but Quentin does not seem to be thinking about writing. *"It's because she wants it told,"* he thinks, but never does he think or voice an intention to write anything. Instead, Quentin repeatedly *sees*, or envisions, Rosa's story of Thomas Sutpen as a potential visual production. "Out of quiet thunderclap he would abrupt (man-horse-demon) upon a scene peaceful and decorous as a school-prize water color," in Quentin's hearing—although the only medium in which "quiet thunderclap" is conceivable is on film. "Quentin seemed to see them," the Sutpen family, "the four of them arranged into the conventional family group of the period," as Rosa speaks in the opening chapter. Soon, however, this "fading and ancient photograph itself would have been seen enlarged and hung on the wall behind and above the voice" of the old woman, like a movie screen, "and of whose presence there the voice's owner was not even aware" (12). As Rosa sketches the character, Thomas Sutpen, Quentin is enthralled and begins to fill that movie screen he has shrewdly placed behind her with dramatic or cinematic possibilities. "Quentin seemed to watch resolving the figure of a little girl. . . . She seemed to stand, to lurk, behind the neat picket fence of a small, grimly middleclass yard or lawn. . . ." As he "watches," Quentin is already altering the story, mingling Rosa's words with his own imagination. "It (the talking, the telling) seemed (to him, to Quentin) to partake of that logic-and reason-flouting quality of a dream," in which long-elapsed periods of time are conveyed in an instant, filmic images communicating instantaneously what "a printed tale" would take much longer to evoke (21–23).

From Rosa Coldfield Quentin gets what was known in Hollywood in the 1930s as a "property," or a story idea. When Faulkner worked at MGM the head of the Story Department was Sam Marx. According to Kawin, Marx kept track of four hundred stories per week, "from optioned novels to intriguing paragraphs in the newspapers."[8] Quentin's "intriguing paragraph" is famous:

> *It seems that this demon—his name was Sutpen—(Colonel Sutpen)—Colonel Sutpen.*
> *Who came out of nowhere and without warning upon the land with a band of strange*
> *niggers and built a plantation—(Tore violently a plantation, Miss Rosa Coldfield says)—*
> *tore violently. And married her sister Ellen and begot a son and a daughter which—*
> *(Without gentleness begot, Miss Rosa Coldfield says)—without gentleness. Which should*
> *have been the jewels of his pride and the shield and comfort of his old age, only—(Only*
> *they destroyed him or something or he destroyed them or something. And died)—and*
> *died. Without regret, Miss Rosa Coldfield says—(Save by her) Yes, save by her. (And by*
> *Quentin Compson) Yes. And by Quentin Compson. (5–6)*

This paragraph condenses the novel as a whole, including the major elements of the Sutpen story and the principle of collaborative check and revision (and the authoritative "Yes," explained below). It also demonstrates the continuing hold this story has on the present generation.[9] At the end of the first chapter, Rosa demonstrates to Quentin the dramatic possibilities of this property by creating for him the scene where Ellen finds Judith and Henry watching their father fight with his slaves in the barn. Even though Rosa admits, "I was not there," she portrays vividly the scene which captures more of this property, or this story idea's key elements: sibling relations, racial and sexual divisions and attractions, violence, power, and, of course, the motif of witnessing events which convey images of siblings, race, sex, violence, and power.

Quentin gets a number of additional scenes from his father. Actually, the second step in the MGM production process, as Faulkner would have known, would be for a writer (or writers) to compose a story "treatment." This is a short narrative or outline based upon the story idea, broken into major scenes and containing major plot developments and, possibly, some dialogue. It was not uncommon for competing story treatments to exist, or for one treatment to be rejected in whole or part and sent to another writer for revision. Much of Faulkner's work at MGM involved revising and improving existing story treatments. In Mississippi (or in Yoknapatawpha, anyway), Quentin receives story treatments from his father and from Rosa. His father's contains such scenes as Sutpen's "courtship" of Ellen, the wedding of tears, Henry's dramatic ride into Jefferson, Mr. Coldfield's exile in the attic, and Ellen's bedridden request to Rosa to protect her children. While Mr. Compson speaks, Faulkner repeatedly presents images of darkness illuminated, as if the story itself possessed the potential to illuminate a darkened room, as if the story were taking form in a movie theater. We learn, for example, that Quentin is waiting for it to be "dark enough" to visit Miss Coldfield; that "the only alteration toward darkness" off the Compson porch "was in the soft and fuller random of the fireflies"; that the Compson porch light, "the single globe stained and bug-fouled," is the only light that keeps the father and son from sitting in total darkness (and which will illuminate Bon's letter later on); and that Mr. Compson's cigar, "the coal glowing," comes in and out of Quentin's vision (108–9).[10] These illuminations are carried through to the Harvard sitting room, as mentioned earlier, when Quentin and Shreve sit at the table, "glaring" eye to eye "beneath the lamp." The projections of light in Mr. Compson's narrative reinforce his sense that his narrative is itself a projection of images from the past, some of which he can imagine and some of which, try as he does, he cannot.

Mr. Compson thinks in pictures, not moving pictures (as, we shall see, his son conceives) but static pictures, like photographs. In fact, his metaphor to explain how Charles Bon initiated Henry Sutpen into his New Orleans life is drawn from photography. According to Mr. Compson, Bon watches Henry study his image and ape his manners, "watching the picture resolve and become fixed." Bon continues to show Henry one "plate" after another, with Henry "waiting for the next picture which the mentor" (or the director, Quentin, would see) intended for him. Bon, in Mr. Compson's imagination, carefully arranges it so that "the exposures" come to Henry in a way "so brief as to be cryptic, almost staccato, the plate unaware of what the complete picture would show, scarce-seen yet ineradicable" (137–38). Bon is manipulating Henry's subliminal responses, arranging his "exposures" in Eisenstein montage sequences, creating emotions and reactions in Henry by the rapid direction of images ("plates") into Henry's subconscious. Mr. Compson's description of the effect of Bon's skillful manipulation of images, "seen by Henry quickly and then removed," is as well a description of the effect of viewing a powerfully evocative film: "Without his knowing what he saw it was as though to Henry the blank and scaling barrier in dissolving produced and revealed not comprehension to the mind, the intellect which weighs and discards, but striking instead straight and true to some primary blind and mindless foundation of all young male living dream and hope . . ." (138). With Henry's emotions tilting, *"I will believe! I will! I will!,"* he is ready to accept anything Bon tells him "before [he] had time to know what he had seen." Bon's skill has on Henry the same effect that a film has on one's senses, where images appear too fast for the intellect to judge and analyze before the emotions either accept them as true or reject them as false.

What must have shocked and initially repulsed Faulkner about movies was the *captive* demands of the medium. Unlike reading or listening, one cannot interrupt a movie, or interfere with it, while it is running.[11] One of the first stories about Faulkner at MGM, apparently occurring on his first day in Culver City, California, concerns his experience in the projection room. "The film was hardly underway when Faulkner said to the projectionist," in Blotner's version of the story, "'How do you stop this thing?' There was no use looking at it, he said, because he knew how it would turn out. Then he asked for the exit and left." He did not return for over a week, claiming to have wandered in Death Valley. Later he would admit to being "flustered" and "scared" by the entire experience of coming to Hollywood to work for $500 a week, and by the fuss made over him.[12] This anecdote is particularly telling. Faulkner's refusal to sit through a movie once he saw how it was working and where it would end displays a resistance to being manipulated by an inferior production (it was *The Champ* [1931], a prizefighter picture starring Wallace Beery)[13] and illuminates further Quentin's well-known and similar frustration, in *Absalom, Absalom!,* at having "to listen to it" again and again when he knew perfectly well how it turned out (and when he was himself waiting to tell the story). Faulkner would not be comfortable in Hollywood until he met Howard Hawks and began to learn and practice the art of making movies himself.

In *Absalom, Absalom!* Quentin listens to his father long enough to stop paying attention and envision or create his own scene. Once a story treatment was approved at MGM in the 1930s, a writer was then assigned to provide a temporary screenplay (also called a dialogue continuity). There were often second, third, and other subsequent versions, and each contained wholly realized scenes and complete dialogue sequences. The temporary screenplay was passed around to various writers, the director, and others, and continually edited and altered or completely revised. At the end of chapter 4, Quentin creates the equivalent of a "dialogue continuity" for the scene where Henry stops Bon at the gates to Sutpen's Hundred. This key scene in the story is completely realized, including background setting, characterization, costume, and dialogue.

(It seemed to Quentin that he could actually see them, facing one another at the gate. Inside the gate what was once a park now spread, unkempt, in shaggy desolation . . . up to a huge house where a young girl waited in a wedding dress made from stolen scraps. . . . They faced one another on the two gaunt horses, two men, young . . . with unkempt hair and faces gaunt and weathered . . . in worn and patched gray . . . the one with the tarnished braid of an officer, the other plain of cuff, the pistol lying yet across the saddle bow unaimed, the two faces calm, the voices not even raised: *Dont you pass the shadow of this post, this branch, Charles;* and *I am going to pass it, Henry).* . . .

The same pattern is repeated in chapter 5, where Quentin is "not listening" to Rosa's story treatment but is envisioning another scene, another temporary screenplay. This time the scene is set in Judith's bedroom, with "old intricate satin and lace" on the bed, with Henry described as "hatless," and with "shaggy bayonet-trimmed hair," "gaunt worn unshaven face," and "the pistol still hanging against his flank." The two of them, Judith and Henry, are "speaking to one another in short brief staccato sentences like slaps," followed by their actual dialogue. The "staccato" sentences, of course, were popular in the movies of the 1930s, and Faulkner had written some of his own in the film version of "Turn About" (called *Today We Live [1932]*) on which he worked for Hawks. By this point in the novel, Quentin has fully accepted the story treatments he has heard and is prepared to take the property with him and "produce" it.

Faulkner met Hawks in 1932. Kawin describes a striking commonality between the very powerful men. "Both were reserved and private, gentlemanly and soft-spoken. Each was a perfectionist in his chosen field." They were one year apart in age. Both flew planes and had read Conrad and Hemingway with appreciation. "They even wore similar tweeds, and each lost a younger brother to a freak plane crash." Also, both liked to drink with commitment and abandon. They would go on "dove hunts," or drinking weekends, with regularity. They would both tell tall tales about their pasts. They enjoyed a twenty-year association, "an effective working relationship based on mutual respect" and what Kawin accurately calls a "special intimacy."[14] For Faulkner, the friendship was certainly unique in his life. He drank with Hawks, something he did alone or with hunting friends; he worked productively with Hawks, something he seldom did successfully or consistently with someone else; and he respected Hawks's abilities as a professional filmmaker.

What did Faulkner get from Hawks? First, the notion, demonstrated over the course of various Hollywood projects, that collaboration has its value and could produce results. George Garrett, who knew Faulkner in Hollywood in the 1930s, writes of what he terms a "truth about Faulkner—an ability to work well and closely and honestly with another writer when he had to."[15] Second, Faulkner saw demonstrated in Hawks that filmmaking was a natural manifestation of twentieth-century civilization which attracted people as serious about storytelling as he was. And third, Faulkner saw that there was something in the Hollywood production process itself which reflected the human capacity to create. Hawks did not necessarily *tell* him these things, but by virtue of their friendship and their working relationship, Faulkner came to see them and use them in his fiction.

Hawks bought Faulkner's short story "Turn About" before the two men had met, and he hired Faulkner in 1932 to write the temporary screenplay. He did so in five days, producing a work of rare (for Hollywood) quality of which producer Irving Thalberg reportedly said, "Shoot it as it is." Later, however, Thalberg told Hawks that the screenplay had to be rewritten to include a starring role for Joan Crawford. Faulkner's original story, a World War I tale set in England, has no females in it. Apparently without missing a beat, Faulkner rewrote the temporary screenplay with the Crawford role, adding love and sibling rivalry to a story about war experience and courage. The result is a much more complex and engaging work than "Turn About" was or was meant to be. The story was also renamed and the film released in 1932 as *Today We Live.*

When a story is adapted to the screen, Faulkner learned working with Hawks in 1932, it need not be a faithful adaptation—it need not even resemble the original property—in order to be a "successful" film adaptation. It simply has to work as a screen story. This is precisely what Quentin and Shreve demonstrate, in principle, in the cold Harvard sitting room as they work toward the creation of fully realized scenes in their "temporary screenplay" of the Sutpen story. Of course, no mention of filmmaking is made in the novel (aside from one reference by Mr. Compson to "a broken cinema film" [258]), but moviemaking, I think, provides a good model for what happens in the novel, particularly in the second half, or the Quentin-Shreve portion. The two young men sit across "a strange lamplit table" that is similar, perhaps, to the work space Faulkner shared during his Hollywood collaborations. The environment, in Cambridge, Massachusetts, is as "strange" to

Quentin as California surely was to Faulkner. Faulkner uses the word "strange" three times in the first paragraph of chapter 6, where the Harvard setting is introduced. As with moviemaking, Quentin and Shreve are involved in a collaborative exercise based upon something written.[16] Mr. Compson's own "intriguing paragraph," or his letter, lies on the table over the course of their collaboration. Faulkner continues to "illuminate" the settings of the second half of the novel with actual lights and memories of light. Shreve is portrayed "leaning forward into the lamp" on the table, and Quentin is "seeing the fireflies" from the previous September in Mississippi (227).

Chapter 6 begins with Shreve's rapid and irreverent, but insightful, summary of the Sutpen story—a full synopsis, actually—to which Quentin, who "owns" the property, says "Yes" at key pauses or when Shreve solicits approval. Shreve's flippancy might resemble the jaded attitude of a man like Sam Marx who, keeping track of four hundred stories a week, might assume a similar callousness, even if occasionally moved by something in his files. Throughout Shreve's narrative Quentin is envisioning scenes, perhaps on the authority of Rosa's assurance, from chapter 1, that one need not have been present to "see," or to project. For example, Quentin sees the delivery of the tombstones (237–38) and the confrontation between Charles Bon (the younger) and Judith. (Judith, significantly, receives Bon "sitting there beneath the lamp.") Although Mr. Compson had told Quentin that there was "nobody to know what transpired that evening between him and Judith," Quentin casts the scene effectively. This time it is Faulkner's narrator who says, "Yes, who to know if he said anything or nothing" (259–61).

Following the narrator's "Yes" to Quentin's dialogue continuity, an italicized segment narrates Quentin's childhood forays to the Sutpen house, to which Quentin says "Yes." The collaborations at work at this point are numerous and the lines of narrative origin are often confusing. Quentin, Shreve, Mr. Compson, Rosa, and Faulkner's narrator all collide and collaborate to advance the story, to produce, as Shreve says at the beginning of chapter 7, something "better than theatre," something "better than Ben Hur." Faulkner interrupts the story at one point and attempts to explain the principle of collaborative effort in naturalistic terms. Quentin thinks *"Yes. Maybe we are both Father. Maybe nothing ever happens once and is finished"*—least of all a story treatment or an understanding or working through of a story or "property." *"Maybe happen is never once but like ripples spreading"* in a pool, the "pool" being Faulkner's metaphor for the human mind, *"the pool attached like a narrow umbilical water-cord to the next pool which the first pool feeds, has fed, did feed, let this second pool contain a different temperature of water."* As Quentin's mind is "warm" with Mississippi air and Shreve's is "cool" with Canadian air, the ripple will take a different course in either pool, will *"reflect in a different tone the infinite unchanging sky"* (326). According to the analogy, creation, reflection, and collaboration are interchangeable and inextricable. One thing *Absalom, Absalom!* certainly does, then, is to challenge conventional notions about authors, intentions, and accountability.

The image of the Hollywood studio must have staggered anyone who worked there or visited there and who, like Faulkner, knew the power and place of storytelling in human history.[17] Thousands of people and millions of dollars centered in one place for the production of tall tales in the machine age: this is what surely "flustered" and "scared" Faulkner at first but which kept him returning in order to participate in the process. The progress of a story from property to synopsis to treatment to temporary screenplay (revised, edited, and rewritten by many hands) and then to final screenplay, and again altered and revised on the set, only to be edited in a cutting room into a motion picture—this was hundreds of years in the life of a "story" or tale condensed into about a year of intense, collaborative effort. The "production" of a motion picture provides the twentieth century with a renewed understanding of the collaborative nature of human intelligence and human creation, and certainly raises questions about individualism or intellectual independence as essences or as more than ideological constructs.[18] Quentin, Faulkner claims early in *Absalom, Absalom!,* "was not a being, an entity, he was a commonwealth" (9)—a *product* of many *"pools"* feeding his mind and feeding off of his mind, linked organically (and hence inescapably) by *"umbilical"* connection. In filmmaking, the collaborative nature of the medium makes it difficult, and often impossible, to attribute credit for specific contributions beyond influence; as difficult, perhaps, as it is to attribute sources to an author's final work. The question of who did what, who wrote this or that line or who is responsible for this or that scene, is often impossible to pinpoint in film study. In the same way that a machine, or a factory, objectifies human thought in its operations, filmmaking can be said to objectify the human creative process in *its* operations. Although *Absalom, Absalom!* (like many other Faulkner novels) contains filmic elements—montage, collision, suspended time—what is most filmic in *Absalom, Absalom!* is not specific, cinematic techniques but the presentation of the creative process in a reified manner.[19] Garrett describes the collaborative screenwriting process in a sentence which could easily be applied to what happens in Faulkner's novel. "In any collaboration," Garrett explains, "it is, finally, impossible to distinguish who contributed what since ideas, notions, whims must be blended and fused together into a unity which is largely inextricable, into the sources of the bits and pieces which make up its parts."[20] In *Absalom, Absalom!,* creation is a *production,* a series of collaborations, exchanges, dialogues, revisions, individual breakthroughs or brainstorms checked by individual corrections, for which the only sign of authority or truthfulness is the audience's (or the listener's or the reader's, or sometimes Faulkner's) assent: the "Yes" spoken so frequently in the novel.

Chapter 8 continually stresses collaboration and features collaborative images which unite not only Quentin and Shreve but also Quentin, Shreve, and their objects, Henry and Bon. This joint effort takes place "in the lamplight, the rosy glow" as "not two of them but four" (367) inhabit the illumination. Quentin and Shreve are "both thinking as one . . . the two of them creating between them . . . shadows not of flesh and blood but shadows" produced by a pair of voices "quiet as the visible murmur of their vaporising breath" (378–79). When Faulkner describes "not two but four of them riding the two horses" (417) to New Orleans, "four of them and then just two— Charles-Shreve and Quentin-Henry," he describes a setting in which the two creators, Shreve and Quentin, inhabit the same space with their visible creations ("Jesus, you can almost see him," Shreve says of Bon [371]), as if on film, before them. Having made these "shades," the creators (or producers, rather) envision and embody them simultaneously, "First, two of them, then four; now two again" (431), like an enthusiastic matinee audience. When the "four of them" sit "in that drawing room of baroque and fusty magnificence which Shreve had invented and which was probably true enough," we might imagine Quentin and Shreve sitting in the projection room, alternating, in their joint consciousness, between identifying with their projections and assuming their roles as producers. "Four of them there, in that room in New Orleans in 1860, just as in a sense there were four of them here in this tomb-like room in Massachusetts in 1910" (419).

Chapter 8 culminates in the production of two major scenes, a "temporary screenplay" concerning Bon and Henry, presented in the text in italics. Faulkner prefaces the scenes with a recapitulation of the continental symbolism involved in "Shreve, the Canadian" and "Quentin, the Southerner."

The first scene is brief, establishing Bon's predicament in 1864–65, leading to his confrontation *"in which there was no flicker, nothing"* in the way of recognition from Sutpen, followed by his decision to go ahead with the marriage to Judith, culminating in Sutpen's summons of Henry to his tent. The italics then break off, as the "scene" is interrupted by Shreve's talk of details concerning the source of Quentin's knowledge about Bon's secret. The next italicized portion is more detailed in its screenplay format. The setting is made clear: *"bivouac fires burning in a pine grove"* with Rebel and Yankee pickets *"so close that each could hear the challenge of the other's officers."* Henry is again presented as *"gaunt and ragged and unshaven."* Then, in screenplay language, Henry receives the summons from the orderly:

> *The orderly does not return with him. . . . The sentry gestures him into the tent. He stoops through the entrance, the canvas falls behind him as someone, the only occupant of the tent, rises from a camp chair behind the table on which the candle sits, his shadow swooping high and huge up the canvas wall. . . . They sit, one on either side of the table, in the chairs reserved for officers, the table (an open map lies on it) and the candle between them.*

This is the language of a screenplay, defining movements simply and directly, setting scenes, identifying key props. The italicized "temporary screenplay" includes dialogue as well, some of it in the staccato style of the 1930s, as when Bon reacts to Henry's objection to the marriage:

> —*Yes. . . . I gave him the choice. I have been giving him the choice for four years.*
> —*Think of her. Not of me: of her.*
> —*I have. For four years. Of you and her. Now I am thinking of myself.*
> —*No, Henry says.—No. No.*
> —*I cannot?*
> —*You shall not.*
> —*Who will stop me, Henry?*
> —*No, Henry says.—No. No. No.*

The chapter, and the novel, culminates in this demonstrated ability by Quentin and Shreve to project and produce a Sutpen screenplay—to transfer their collaboration into a single, coherent series of images and dialogue. In the final chapter which follows, they discuss what their production means (and prove singularly inept at understanding what they've created). Significantly, now that the production process is completed, "the single light bulb" in their room is turned off and they lie in their beds in "the iron and impregnable dark." In this darkness Quentin recalls his trip to the Sutpen house with Rosa, a trip that took place in unilluminated darkness as well. His conversation with Henry Sutpen is particularly flat, perhaps because it is recalled rather than projected, with private and not public (or collaborative) origins. Quentin then envisions Rosa's return to the house three months later, and he "could see that too, though he had not been there," thus closing the novel with the same references to vision and sight with which the novel had opened. In fact, the words "Quentin could see" or "he could see" are repeated five times in three pages at the end of the book.

Quentin has succeeded in "producing" Rosa's property (although a case could be made for some of it, at least, belonging to his father). In its final form and emphasis, however, it resembles its original version only slightly. The mark of Quentin as producer (with a specific reason to want this story told) and of Shreve as *auteur* (with a specific, identifiable style) transforms Rosa's story tremendously. Rosa is far from the center of the story, for example, and Sutpen's ogre-like qualities are humanized to tragic proportions. The last lines of the "intriguing paragraph" from the opening chapter state that Sutpen died *"Without regret,"* save by Miss Rosa, *"And,"* in the final line, *"by Quentin Compson."* The story is "by Quentin Compson" now, and the "regrets" are, finally, his alone for its quality and its content. The story is also "by Shrevlin McCannon," who deserves "screen credit" for his collaboration and direction. By the last pages of the novel, Quentin does not even bother to correct Shreve's reference to "Aunt Rosa" instead of *Miss Rosa*—it's not her story anymore. Quentin's "director," however, continues to prod him for additional material. Shreve's "Why do you hate the South?" and Quentin's *"I don't hate it!"* are rhetorical in both question and answer, a reopening of the collaboration, not an ending to it. In this way, Faulkner's ending to *Absalom, Absalom!* indicates that the Sutpen story is not even Quentin's or Shreve's anymore. Once produced, it is out of their hands and into the public realm, another story property for subsequent collaboration and correction. Rosa got her story told all right, but not in a way she would find satisfying.

Faulkner had hoped that *Absalom, Absalom!* would become *someone's* movie, however. After completing the revisions and corrections on the galleys of the manuscript, he planned to try to sell *Absalom, Absalom!* to

Hollywood. "I am going to ask one hundred thousand dollars for it or nothing," he told his agent Morton Goldman in September 1936. He stated similar intentions to publisher Harrison Smith. "I am going to sell the manuscript to the movies myself, and see what luck I have."[21] He had no luck at all, and one can only imagine the way in which producers in Hollywood might have reacted to the prospect of making *"Absalom, Absalom!:* The Movie." *Gone With the Wind,* also published in 1936, would become Hollywood's Civil War epic, released by MGM at the end of the decade.

Nonetheless, a movie *could* be made based upon *Absalom, Absalom!,* although it would resemble Truffaut's *Day for Night* (1973) more than it would Selznick's *Gone With the Wind* (1939). In Truffaut's self-reflexive work, it is not always clear whether a scene is taking place in the film or in the movie ("Meet Pamela") which is being made by the characters in the film. It *is* clear, moreover, that the progress and character of "Meet Pamela," a movie based on "a real life story," are continually affected by incidents which happen on the set and by the actual lives—love affairs, jealousies, pregnancies—of the people making the film. Filmmaking, in *Day for Night,* represents the mind's capacity to blur reality and illusion, by virtue of its creativity, so that the line between the real thing and the projected "shade" (to use Faulkner's term) is not easily discernible, nor is it really very important. "People like you and me," the director says to the star of "Meet Pamela," "are only happy in our work—making films." Films keep going on while life may stop and start, and personal fortunes rise and fall. "Personal problems will have to wait," the director commands. "The film is king." This is what director Truffaut (who also portrays the director of "Meet Pamela" in the movie) was interested in portraying on film in *Day for Night,* and also what Faulkner succeeds in portraying in print in *Absalom, Absalom!.* David Cook asserts that *Day for Night* asks the question, "Are films more important than life?"[22]—to which the film as a whole answers, Yes. Similarly, *Absalom, Absalom!* implicitly asks, "Are created projections more important than documented history?"—to which the answer "Yes" is made repeatedly by Quentin Compson (and by William Faulkner).

NOTES

1. The quotations are from William Faulkner, *Absalom, Absalom!* (1936; reprint, New York: Vintage, 1987). All further references to this text will be parenthetical.

2. For his Hollywood career in the 1930s, see Bruce Kawin, *Faulkner's MGM Screenplays* (Knoxville: University of Tennessee Press, 1982), and Kawin, *Faulkner and Film* (New York: Ungar, 1977). Elisabeth Muhlenfeld most recently perpetuates the idea that *Hollywood* intruded upon Faulkner's literary career. In her excellent study of the composition of *Absalom, Absalom!*, she states that he "was forced to spend a considerable part of this period in Hollywood," and implies that this "forced" activity impeded his work on the novel. See *William Faulkner's* Absalom, Absalom!: *A Critical Casebook* (New York: Garland, 1984), xii. Kawin is one scholar working to correct this misconception, pointing out, for example, that screen writing and fiction writing were Faulkner's "two careers" and that "his two careers were integrated throughout most of his creative life," to the advantage of each. See *Faulkner and Film*, 125.

3. "Faulkner's Film Career: The Years with Hawks," *Faulkner, Modernism, and Film*, ed. Evans Harrington and Ann J. Abadie (Jackson: University Press of Mississippi, 1979), 174.

4. One clue to the importance of Hollywood to *Absalom, Absalom!* can be taken from the original manuscript itself. Page 1 gives the title and date and has this notation: "Begun, Oxford, 1935/Continued, California, 1936/Finished, Oxford, 1936." The final page of the manuscript records the title and this notation: "Mississippi, 1935/California, 1936/ Mississippi, 1936/Rowanoak, 31 January 1936." See Gerald Langford, comp., *Faulkner's Revision* of Absalom, Absalom!: *A Collation of the Manuscript and the Published Book* (Austin: University of Texas Press, 1975), 22–23.

5. Joseph R. Urgo, "William Faulkner and the Drama of Meaning: The Discovery of the Figurative in *As I Lay Dying*," *South Atlantic Review* 53, no. 2 (1988): 11–23.

6. Faulkner made the comment to Hollywood colleague David Hempstead upon handing him the original manuscript, just completed, and asking him to read it. See Joseph Blotner, *Faulkner: A Biography*, one vol. ed. (New York: Random House, 1984), 364, 358. Significantly, Faulkner had collaborated with Hempstead, during the composition of *Absalom, Absalom!*, on a film for Hawks.

7. *Ben Hur* was produced by MGM in 1925, a lavish spectacular directed by Fed Nibles, costing over $4.5 million to make. It was reissued with sound in 1931. Shreve, of course, could not know the film version in 1910, but Faulkner surely knew of it as one of his employing company's largest efforts.

8. *Faulkner's MGM Screenplays*, xvi. Information in this essay concerning the production process at MGM is largely indebted to Kawin's invaluable work.

9. David Paul Ragan, *William Faulkner's* Absalom, Absalom!: *A Critical Study* (Ann Arbor: UMI

Research Press, 1987), 21, claims that this paragraph "outlines all the facts which can be known with certainty about the man" and "underlines the means through which information about the Sutpen family is to be conveyed throughout the novel."

10. J. R. Raper, "Meaning Called to Life: Structure in *Absalom, Absalom!*," *Southern Humanities Review* 5 (1971): 9–23, points out the "methods acquired during his flirtation with the movies in the 1930s" which Faulkner applied to *Absalom, Absalom!* including the contrast between brightness and dimness. Raper also explicates Faulkner's use of montage, close-up and distance, conflicts between events and their duration, and other filmic techniques. A good study of Faulkner's cinematic stylistics is also Claude-Edmonde Magny, *The Age of the American Novel: The Film Aesthetic of Fiction Between the Two Wars* (New York: Ungar, 1972), esp. 178–224.

11. The VCR era, of course, changes this to some extent.

12. Blotner, 305.

13. Then again, Faulkner may have found the film's story line too familiar. It concerns an alcoholic boxer and his young, agonizing son, done in the melodramatic, overly sentimental style of the era—a mawkishness Faulkner would certainly object to and not want to sit through.

14. *Faulkner's MGM Screenplays,* xviii.

15. Garrett, "Afterword," Joel Sayre and William Faulkner, *The Road to Glory: A Screenplay,* ed. Matthew J. Bruccoli (Carbondale: Southern Illinois University Press, 1981), 163. Faulkner collaborated with Sayre on *The Road to Glory* (1936) while at the same time working early mornings on *Absalom, Absalom!* Tom Dardis points out, in his brief study of Faulkner's film career, that he preferred to work with a collaborator than to work alone in Hollywood and that he worked well with others—*Some Time in the Sun: The Hollywood Years of F. Scott Fitzgerald, William Faulkner, Nathanael West, Aldous Huxley, and James Agee* (New York: Penguin, 1981), 79–150.

16. For an excellent study of Shreve and Quentin as narrative voices see Francois Pitavy, "The Narrative Voice and Function of Shreve: Remarks on the Production of Meaning in *Absalom, Absalom!*," in Muhlenfeld, 189–206. Carolyn Porter, "William Faulkner: Innocence Historicized," in Harold Bloom, ed., *William Faulkner's* Absalom, Absalom! (New York: Chelsea, 1987), 57–73, makes a convincing case for Shreve's narrative presence in the novel as early as chap. x and refers to the novel as representing "the process of communal storytelling" (86).

17. MGM was a good place for Faulkner to learn this first hand. MGM produced one feature film *every week* in the 1930s, the largest output of any studio in the history of filmmaking. "There was no film so big that MGM couldn't produce it, no talent so large that MGM couldn't buy it"—David Cook, *A History of Narrative Film* (New York: Norton, 1981), 269–70.

18. For a thorough presentation of production theory in historical studies, see Richard Slotkin, "Myth and the Production of History;" *Ideology and Classic American Literature,* ed. Sacvan Bercovitch and Myra Jehlen (Cambridge: Cambridge University Press, 1986). For a demon-

stration of the relationship between film making and the production of history, see Slotkin's novel, *The Return of Henry Starr* (New York: Atheneum, 1988).

19. As Francois Pitavy points out, in *Absalom, Absalom!* "the act of producing the narrative is itself fictionalized." See "The Gothicism of *Absalom, Absalom!'s* Rosa Coldfield," *"A Cosmos of My Own": Faulkner and Yoknapatatvpha 1980,* ed. Doreen Fowler and Ann J. Abadie (Jackson: University Press of Mississippi, 1980), 203. Estella Schoenberg makes a similar point, claiming that "the novel is about the creation of a story"—*Old Tales and Talking: Quentin Compson in William Faulkner's* Absalom, Absalom! *and Related Works* (Jackson: University Press of Mississippi, 1977), 135.

20. Garrett, 162.

21. *The Selected Letters of William Faulkner,* ed. Joseph Blotner (New York: Random House, 1977), 96.

22. Cook, 467.

PART IV

Style, Humor, Genre, and Influence

Faulkner's Narrative Styles

J. E. BUNSELMEYER

The vision at the heart of Faulkner's works is of life as a process of accretion, of overwhelming connectedness. This vision is embodied in the syntactic style that characterizes Faulkner's narration and marks phrase rhythms as "Faulknerian." Works as different as *The Hamlet* and *Light in August* share a syntactic style that equates events and ideas, past and present, by piling up clauses; the style transforms an individual experience by linking it to everything around it. Stylistic analysis identifies the dominant features of Faulkner's characteristic style as well as the variations in style that create differences in tone, ranging from comedy to thoughtful contemplation. Specifically, speech act theory and transformational analysis of grammatical patterns yield insights into the ways by which narrative syntax creates tone and point of view.

The communication of point of view is, perhaps, the basic "transaction" of literary language.[1] In literary and ordinary narratives, events are related

Reprinted with permission from *American Literature* 53, no. 3 (1981): 424–42.

from an evaluative viewpoint (for example, in the tellable tales imposed upon dinner guests). In *Toward a Speech Act Theory of Literary Discourse,* Pratt considers this evaluative attitude as inherent in "the literary speech situation" because the author or speaker is "not only reporting but also verbally *displaying* a state of affairs, inviting his addressee(s) to join him in contemplating it, evaluating it, and responding to it. His point is to produce in his hearers not only belief but also an imaginative and affective involvement in the state of affairs he is presenting and an evaluative stance toward it."[2] In Faulkner's tales, the evaluative stance varies from comic detachment to empathy with a character's contemplation; these differences in tone and point of view are created by different syntactic styles.

The stylistic features that mark the contemplative tone all inherently involve evaluation because they present syntactic relationships. Narration differs from the mere recounting of events—in intent and in style—as Labov has pointed out. He found that when events were merely reported, they were phrased in the simple past tense; when evaluation was built into the narration, it was through "departures from basic narrative syntax," through syntactic transformations that "suspend the action," introduce evaluation, and transform experience by framing it in a point of view.[3] Thus, the syntactic style in which a tale is told alters the way events and characters are evaluated. Faulkner's contemplative style, which draws readers into the process of thought and evaluation, is marked by many of the syntactic features noted by Labov in the evaluative sections of natural narratives, literature's closest kin. The foregrounded features that cluster in Faulkner's contemplative passages are:

- *negatives,* which define what is by what is not and invite judgment of both through comparison, providing in Labov's words, "a way of evaluating events by placing them against the background of other events which might have happened, but which did not" (380–81);
- *appositives,* which are so lengthy and so numerous that the original noun is lost sight of as it is amplified and absorbed by all the things it stands for and can be equated with;
- *double modifiers,* which "bring in a wider range of simultaneous events" (Labov, 388), inviting an evaluation of the relationship between attributes;

- *comparisons* that explicitly evaluate what is by what it is like;
- *or-clauses* that embed the consideration of alternative forms of action or perception and invite evaluation through juxtaposition.

These syntactic tendencies have in common a "mode of ordering" experience; an act is amplified, often doubled or tripled, through comparisons, negative comparisons, or-clauses, doubled modifiers, and appositives.[4] In Faulkner's narration of contemplation these stylistic features cluster together, forming foregrounded patterns that absorb the reader in the process of thought and engage him in an evaluative point of view.

Faulkner's comedy is free of these stylistic features. The comic passages are marked by a very different syntactic style that does not suspend the action, but rather pushes it onward by piling up individual events. Stacking separate actions into coordinate syntactic structures eliminates the evaluation inherent in subordination. In Faulkner's comic passages, actions are accumulated, one at a time, as the sentence grows to the right; the right-branching kernels move from one action to the next so rapidly that there is no pause for evaluation or contemplation. This syntactic style creates a more distanced comic perspective on the narrated events. The viewpoints of comedy and contemplation differ; Freud even thought that contemplation interfered with the comic affect.[5] In Faulkner's prose, this interference is quite literal at the level of syntax, for his contemplative style breaks up the flow of action by embedding evaluation. His right-branching comic style speeds the flow of action; by heaping up deeds, the style minimizes each event and creates a distanced attitude toward the action. These contrasting patterns of syntactic expansion create the differing tones of comedy and contemplation; the quality the two styles share is the "Faulknerian" sense of crowded accumulation.

Differences in the tone and styles of comedy and contemplation are nicely illustrated by the opening passages of the two sections of "Was."[6] These passages also illustrate that central to both styles is a kind of syntactic accretion that suits a thematic view of life as composed of interconnected layers of relationships between times and people. The first section presents the contemplative introduction to Isaac and to thematic perspectives on the past and possession.

1

appositive	Isaac McCaslin, 'Uncle Ike,' past seventy and
doubling	nearer eighty than he ever corroborated any more,
appositives	a *widower* now *and uncle* to half a county *and father*
negative	to *no* one.
negative	this was *not* something participated in *or*
or-clause/neg.	even seen by himself, *but* by his elder cousin,
appositives	McCaslin Edmonds, grandson of Isaac's father's
	sister and so descended by the distaff, yet *not-*
negative	*withstanding* the inheritor, and in his time the
appositive	bequestor, of that which some had thought then and
triple adj.	some still thought should have been Isaac's since
clauses	his was the name in *which* the title to the land
	had first been granted from the Indian patent
	and *which* some of the descendants of his father's
negative	slaves still bore in the land. But Isaac was *not*
appositives	one of these:—a widower these twenty years, who
negative	in all his life had owned *but* one object more
doubling	than he could wear and carry in his pockets and
	his hands at one time, and this was the narrow
	iron cot and the stained lean mattress *which* he
	used camping in the woods for deer and bear *or*
or-clauses	for fishing *or* simply because he loved the woods;
negatives	*who* owned *no* property and *never* desired to since
neg./comparison	the earth was *no* man's but all men's, *as* light and
double adj.cl.	air and weather were; *who* lived still in the
triple adj.	cheap frame bungalow in Jefferson *which* his wife's
clauses	father gave them on their marriage and *which* his
	wife had willed to him at her death and *which*
appositive	he had pretended to accept, acquiesce to, to humor
negatives	her, ease her going but which was *not* his, will *or*
or-phrases	*not,* chancery dying wishes mortmain possession *or*
appositives	whatever, himself merely *holding* it for his wife's
	sister and her children who had lived in it with
doubling	him since his wife's death, *holding* himself

comparison	welcome to live in one room of it *as* he had during
or-clauses	his wife's time *or* she during her time *or* the
	sister-in-law and her children during the rest of
	his and after.
neg./or-phrase	*not* something he had participated in *or* even
appositive	remembered except from the hearing, the listening
	come to him through and from his cousin McCaslin
doubling	born in 1850 and sixteen years his senior and hence,
	his own father being near seventy when Isaac, an
appositive	only child, was born, *rather* his brother than
comparisons	cousin, and *rather* his father than either, out of
appositive	the old time, the old days.

The entire last paragraph is an appositive to the preceding one; within each paragraph the numerous appositives continually qualify and equate, separating subject and verb until often the connection between the subject and the action of the verb is lost sight of. In the first paragraph, there is no verb, for there is no meaningful action for Isaac to make (except to refuse to act). Appositives have the syntactic effect of deleting agents present in the deep structure and thus diminishing actors and events in the surface style. In the deep structure: (Isaac was) "past seventy"; (Isaac was) "a widower"; (Isaac was) "uncle to half a county"; (Isaac was) "father to no one." (McCaslin was) "grandson of Isaac's father's sister"; (McCaslin was) "descended by the distaff"; (McCaslin was) "the inheritor"; (McCaslin was) "the bequestor." In the surface matrix, only eight lines into the passage, both Isaac and McCaslin are transformed into all the other nouns their names can be equated with (widower, uncle, grandson, descendant), which all imply their relationship to others. The act of apposition decreases individuation and emphasizes relationships; the appositives move the surface style even further into the realm of the passive and away from direct, active statements such as "McCaslin bequeathed." In Faulkner's surface syntax, McCaslin's action of bequeathing is transformed into McCaslin's identity as inheritor and bequestor; the syntactic apposition absorbs McCaslin's potential for individual action into a network of equated relationships. The over-all structure of the passage has the same effect: the individual sections have no individual existence, for each depends for meaning upon its relationship to what comes before and after. The last paragraph is an appositive to the preceding one, and the second paragraph begins with a pronoun that has no antecedent: "this was not something." Such pronouns usually refer back to something, but here the only referent is Isaac's appositional identity. Such syntactic structures allow for inconclusive paragraph structure and punctuation, which reinforce the thematic point of view that there are no clear beginnings or endings to events. Thus, the vast number of appositives establishes through style, two themes: that there are few isolated actions or actors in life's legends, and that legends grow, a bit at a time, until they inundate consciousness.

The overwhelming maze of relationships is reinforced by other elements of style—by numerous or-phrases and adjective clauses and by the redefinition of things by their opposites, through negation. Like the appositives, the adjective clauses are a kind of doubling, for they keep giving further information about the preceding clause: "that which some had thought then and some still thought should have been Isaac's since his was the name in which the title to the land had first been granted from the Indian patent and which some of the descendants of his father's slaves still bore in the land." Isaac and his home are qualified by many such clauses: "who in all his life," "who owned no property," "who lived still," "which his wife's father had given," "which his wife had willed," "and which he had pretended to accept." The clauses continually redefine what has gone before in light of the past. The or-constructions also expand description in an evaluative direction: "which he used camping in the woods for deer and bear or for fishing or simply because he loved the woods"; "holding himself welcome to live in one room of it as he had during his wife's time or she during her time or the sister-in-law and her children during the rest of his and after." Like the appositives, this syntactic construction leads further away from the initial starting point to all the things that might be substituted for it, and thus presents the point of view that actions and people can and do replace each other. The process of defining things by other, surrounding things is extended by Faulkner's use of negatives to identify. Isaac "owned no property and never desired to since the earth was no man's." Isaac's repeated relationship to his house is that he will not own it; the important thing about his relationship to the story he tells is that he does not own it either since he did not participate in it. Definition of reality or relationships by what they are not pulls into the reader's consciousness twice as many things at once: not just Isaac who owns no land, but those who think he should, and those who do not; not just McCaslin owned the land and participated in the annual race, but also Isaac who refuses ownership and who provides a narrative frame for a story about men who would possess and own each other. This redefinition by negation, like the strings of adjective clauses, stretches the reader's consciousness by the syntax, which embeds all the added details into the middle of the sentence, between subject and verb—if the process of apposition has not eliminated the subject and verb altogether. The heavy embedding reaches the limits of what the mind can contain and makes the reader feel, through syntax, the numbing sense of a world in which numerous connections and interrelationships are at least as real as action.

In contrast to the contemplative tone that opens the first section of "Was," the second section begins with the comic creation of action. The style of the narration shifts dramatically:

2

When he and Uncle Buck ran back to the house from discovering that Tommy's Turl had run again, they heard Uncle Buddy cursing and bellowing in the kitchen, *then* the fox *and* dogs came out of the kitchen *and* crossed the hall into the dogs' room *and* they heard them run through the dogs' room into his *and* Uncle Buck's room, *then* they saw them cross the hall again into Uncle Buddy's room *and* heard them run through Uncle Buddy's room into the kitchen again *and this time* it sounded like the whole kitchen chimney had come down *and* Uncle Buddy bellowing like a steamboat blowing *and this time* the fox *and* the dogs *and* five or six sticks *of* firewood all came out of the kitchen together with Uncle Buddy in the middle of them hitting at everything in sight with another stick. It was a good race.

The syntax creates the rhythms which move the reader through the bizarre race around the house; it also creates the point of view that the race and the characters involved in it are bizarre. The lengthy sentence is clear because the kind of transformation employed to join elements is right-branching. As the reader moves through the sentence each clause follows, in time and logic, whatever preceded it: "When he and Uncle Buck ran back . . . they heard Uncle Buddy cursing . . . then the fox and the dogs came out . . . and they heard them run . . . then they saw them cross the hall." The perception of this series of separate, fast actions is due to the syntax, which grows toward the right, rather than embedding appositives and adjective clauses between subjects and verbs. The few participial phrases pass unnoticed in the general foregrounding of the right-branching syntactic style. The separate actions are equated by the separate independent clauses of nearly equal length. The right-branching achieves a rhythmic power suitable to a race and is appropriately broken by the ironic, staccato generalization: "It was a good race." Such variation in phrase rhythm focuses attention on the short sentence, which is repeated at the very end of the story, as a kind of refrain, applying satirically not only to the bumbling hunt of the fox and dogs but also to the equally bumbling semi-annual hunts of Buck and Buddy for Turl and of Sophonsiba for a husband. The piling up of separate actions, through right-branching independent clauses, creates a galloping rhythm that reduces each individual deed to blurred insignificance.

The difference in tone between the first and second sections of "Was"—between the contemplative introduction and the comic tale—is due to the difference between the evaluative embedding of appositives, negatives, and adjective clauses and the accretion of quick, right-branching actions. Yet both syntax patterns share the "Faulknerian" quality of accumulating things of equal weight: neither syntax pattern grants grammatical priority to certain individual actions over others. In action or contemplation the characters' and readers' minds must sort through an accumulation of related, rather equated events for significance.

The sense of connectedness of all actions, past and present, which is conveyed by the syntactic styles, is also expressed by the circular, repetitive structure of "Was." The hunt is a recurrent ritual enacted to confirm a social code that is outdated; the story is ended as it was begun. Just as the syntax parallels and equates events, so does the patterning of the parallel hunts: Buck's for Turl and Sophonsiba's for a husband—both Buck and Turl head for the woods. The hunter and hunted are further equated by the similarity of the animal metaphors that express the dehumanization and entrapment of both—for example, when Uncle Buck's "gnarled neck thrust forward like a cooter's" as he began to "flush," "circle," and "bay" Turl (8). Their entrapment by codes from the past is further suggested by the settings: Buck and Buddy have given over the unfinished big house to the numerous slaves they pretend to possess and have no real use for; Sophonsiba pretends to have dignity by insisting that others call the ramshackle plantation Warwick: "when they wouldn't call it Warwick, she wouldn't even seem to know what they were talking about and it would sound as if she and Mr. Hubert owned two separate plantations covering the same area of ground, one on top of the other" (9). A similar discrepancy exists between the names of the characters and their reality. Buck and Buddy eschew their anachronistic birth names, Theophilus and Amodeus; Sophonsiba tries to live up to hers and fails. Tommy's Turl is named, like a race horse, as his mother's issue; his absence of a surname is the semantic symbol of his enslavement. He proves twice a year that his own enslavement also enslaves those who pretend to own and name him. In the frame story Isaac rejects pretensions at ownership, which others presume his last name entitles him to. Even the archaic stage props to the ritual hunt (for example, Sophonsiba's sending Buck the red ribbon from around her throat) underline the absurdity of living by social codes of the past, which sanction possession and which categorize "Tomey's Turl's arms that were supposed to be black but were not quite white" (29) differently from Buck's and Buddy's. Obviously, "Was" examines the semantics of racism, the ways in which words from a world which "was" continue to determine perceptions, influence actions, and enslave people. The encoding of present reality by anachronistic verbal "maps"[7] from the past is reflected in the setting, the names, the title, and the structure of the action of "Was," as well as in its syntactic styles. Whether the narrative syntax of "Was" is comic or contemplative, it conveys the entrapment of man in an accretion of relationships.

The comic and contemplative styles are present throughout Faulkner's works, as the following analysis of passages from *Light in August,* "The Bear," *The Sound and the Fury, As I Lay Dying, The Hamlet,* and *The Reivers* illustrates. As in "Was" the narrative styles may be mixed in a given work: there are contemplative passages in comic novels such as *The Reivers* and comic passages in novels about subjects such as dying and burying that are not ordinarily considered comic. The difference between narrative styles and tones is due to a difference in the degree of concentration of stylistic features; as Doležel points out in *Statistics and Style:* "The overall character of style is called forth by the *degree* of presence (or absence) of a certain mode of expression, rather than by its exclusive use (or complete suppression)."[8] The degree of embedded evaluation or the degree of foregrounding of right-branching actions creates differences in narrative tone. Of course, there are mixed tones between comedy and contemplation. This somewhat binary distinction of the ends of Faulkner's narrative continuum is intended to clarify how variation in syntactic style contributes to varieties of tone and differences in point of view.

In *Light in August,* "The Bear," and *The Sound and the Fury,* the process of evaluation is presented in the same syntactic style that begins the first section of "Was" and from the same empathetic point of view. The many embeddings not only reflect the contemplative style of mind or act as a "mirror of the mind," to use Chomsky's phrase;[9] they also involve the reader in sorting through relationships between the elements embedded through apposition, negation, or-clauses, double adjectives, and explicit comparison. The effect of these transformations in the narrative syntax is to engage the reader in the act of evaluation, for example, in the thoughts of Joe Christmas as he weighs the strangeness of his experience:

	That night a strange thing came into his mind.
neg./doubling	He lay ready for sleep, *without* sleeping, *without*
comparison	seeming to need the sleep, *as* he would place his
negative	stomach acquiescent for food which it did *not*
or-clause	seem to desire *or* need. It was strange in the
negatives	sense that he could discover *neither* derivation *nor*
doubling/neg.	motivation *nor* explanation for it. He found that
	he was trying to calculate the day of the week.
comparison	It was *as though* now and at last he had an actual
double adj.	and urgent need to strike off the accomplished
appositive/neg.	days toward some purpose *or* act, *without* either
or-phrases	falling short *or* overshooting.[10]

The words describe the process as well as the content of thought. The syntactic style defines states of thinking and feeling by what they lack through the foregrounding of negatives, which imply an evaluation of the thoughts "by placing them against the background" (Labov, 380) of absent qualities: derivation, motivation, explanation. Through the negatives, the passage presents the point of view that such explicit connections are absent (regardless of the motivations and explanations that might be given afterward). By bringing into consciousness both what is and is not present in the process of thought, the syntactic style invites a point of view toward contemplation. The or-clauses, comparisons, and doubling of adjectives and nouns also "bring in a wider range of simultaneous events" (Labov, 388) and invite comparative evaluations of sleep and hunger, desire and need, days and acts, and of the sense of timelessness and its inherent opposite—the need to order time. The viewpoint that thought is a process of relating and connecting is built into the syntactic style.

The same narrative style marks other passages that present contemplation and creates the same effect of engaging the reader in an evaluative stance, a point of view. For example, the contemplation of the meaning of the wilderness and of the bear involves an attitude toward both the process and the object of contemplation.

negative	He had already inherited, then, without ever having
double adj.	seen it, the big old bear with one trap-ruined foot
	that in an area almost a hundred miles square had
appositive	earned for himself a name, a definite designation
comparison	like a living man:—the long legend of corn-cribs
appositives	broken down and rifled of shoats and grown pigs
doubling	and even calves carried bodily into the woods and
appositive	devoured . . .—a corridor of wreckage and destruc-
doubling	tion beginning back before he was born . . . [11]

Syntactically, the bear is transformed into a legend through apposition; by further apposition, the legend of his actions is transformed into a corridor of wreckage and destruction. The bear is continually defined by all the things he stands for and can be equated with: he is "an anachronism, indomitable and invincible out of an old dead time, a phantom, epitome and apotheosis of the old wild life . . . the old bear, solitary, indomitable, and alone; widowered childless and absolved of mortality—old Priam reft of his old wife and outlived all his sons." The appositives extend the relationship between the bear and the past back to Priam. The bear and its legend are also expanded as they are defined by negation: it has not been seen; it speeds "not fast but rather with the ruthless and irresistible deliberation of a locomotive"; it is "not malevolent but just too big, too big for the dogs which tried to bay it . . . too big for the very country which was its constricting scope"; it is "not even a mortal beast." The negation extends the awareness of what the bear might have been, but is not (not fast, not malevolent, not mortal) and thus implies an evaluation of what it is. Like the appositives, the negatives bring additional layers of meaning into consciousness; both syntax patterns separate subjects and verbs, and obscure direct connections between agents and events. Often the order of subject and verb is reversed, further obscuring conventional syntactic connections and involving the reader in the process of sorting through the parts of the sentence for significance: "a corridor of wreckage and destruction beginning back before the boy was born, through which sped, not fast but rather with the ruthless and irresistible deliberation of a locomotive, the shaggy tremendous shape." The bear's action is introduced as a clause describing further the appositive (corridor); the actor comes last. Other sentences are patterned with the same inverted syntax: "the doomed wilderness . . . through which ran . . . the old bear." Like the characters, the reader senses but does not know the cause for events (the subject of the sentence) until last. A syntactic style which minimizes subjects or absorbs them by apposition is the perfect style for establishing the narrative perspective that the process of life is less a process of individual action than of the contemplation of intricate relationships and interconnections.

Quentin's contemplation of time and its relationship to action concludes with an explicit statement of a point of view that is also latent in the syntax patterns that transform experience into evaluation.

	When the shadow of the sash appeared on the curtains
	it was between seven and eight o'clock and then I was
	in time again, hearing the watch. It was Grand-
	father's and when Father gave it to me he said,
comparison	Quentin, I give you the mausoleum of all hope *and*
doubling	desire; it's rather excruciating-ly apt that you
	will use it to gain the reducto absurdum of all
	human experience which can fit your individual
neg.comparison	needs *no* better than it fitted his *or* his father's.
or-phrase/neg.	I give it to you *not* that you may remember time,
negative	*but* that you might forget it now and then for a
negative	moment and *not* spend all your breath trying to
negative	conquer it. Because *no* battle is ever won he said.
negative	They are *not* even fought. The field only reveals to
doubling	man his own folly *and* despair, and victory is an
doubling	illusion of philosophers *and* fools.[12]

The explicit comparisons, negatives, or-phrase, and doubling of nouns and modifiers all have the same effect: of transforming the event, the gift of the watch, into an evaluation of life. The syntax emphasizes what cannot be won, conquered, fought, remembered, possessed, and establishes the point of view that is stated explicitly in the concluding *coda*: life's actions reveal "to man" only "his own folly and despair." The closeness of this vision of life to the passage in *Macbeth* that contains the novel's title is reinforced by the closeness of Faulkner's syntactic style and the style of Macbeth's speech in despair:

negative/appositive	Life's but a walking shadow, a poor player
doubling	That struts and frets his hour upon the stage
appositive	And then is heard no more. It is a tale
doubling	Told by an idiot, full of sound and fury,
negative	Signifying nothing.

(V, v, 24–8)

This is not to say that Faulkner found his style as well as his title in *Macbeth*, but merely that the contemplative tone in both is established through a nearly identical syntactic style that suits the vision of life as a succession of shadows signifying nothing.

This vision is reinforced not only by the syntactic structures of Faulkner's narrative style, but also by the over-all, architectural structure of these works. The four-part structure of *The Sound and the Fury* is an extended apposition that equates each character's evaluation of the significance of events. The relationship between the four points of view is parallel; they pile on top of each other, creating layers of consciousness. The recurrent hunts in "The Bear" and "Was" are also parallel; the action progresses in a cyclical fashion. Just as the over-all structure of "Was" moves in a circle, so does the structure of *Light in August*, which ends as it begins with Lena's meandering. Faulkner's larger narrative structures are of a piece with the syntactic structures of his narrative style. Both structures embody a repetitive vision of life's events which is consistent with Quentin's contemplative evaluation, inherited from his father and his father's father—"that no battle is ever won" and that "victory is an illusion of philosophers and fools."

This vision is shared by Faulkner's comic novels, which also present life as movement in a circle. The difference is in the focus: the comic passages focus on the foolishness of the moments when men believe their actions can result in victory. In these moments, characters direct their actions in a linear fashion toward a goal that is never reached; the linear, right-branching syntactic style captures both the direction of the actions and the insignificance of each individual motion. The piling up of parallel actions equates the deeds and creates a sense of accretion and speed. In short, the narrative syntax creates a comic perspective.

The horse auction in *The Hamlet* contains the ancient comic contest between greed and gullibility. From the point of view of victims and losers, such events are not funny; from the more distanced perspective of the spectator, they are. As in the second section of "Was," Faulkner engages his audience in the distanced comic stance through the syntactic style of the narration. In *The Hamlet* the cavorting of the uncaught, but bought-and-paid-for, horses is presented in a right-branching style that contrasts with the highly embedded, evaluative style of contemplation. Because the comic style has little embedding, the right-branching of clauses and phrases of equal weight allows one action to supplant another rapidly.

> "Get to hell out of here, Wall!" Eck roared. He dropped to the floor, covering his head with his arms. The boy did not move, *and* for the third time the horse soared above the unwinking eyes *and* the unbowed *and* untouched head *and* onto the front veranda again just as Ratliff, still carrying the sock, ran around the corner of the house *and* up the steps. The horse whirled without breaking or pausing. It galloped to the end of the veranda *and* took the railing *and* soared outward, hobgoblin *and* floating, in the moon. It landed in the lot still running *and* crossed the lot *and* galloped through the wrecked gate *and* among the overturned wagons *and* the still intact one in which Henry's wife still sat, *and* on down the lane *and* into the road.[13]

The dominant stylistic feature is the repetition of "and," an equating conjunction that does not invite evaluation in the same way as subordinating conjunctions, which express relationships in causality or time. "And . . . and . . . and . . ."—the horse runs on as the men ran on in "Was." The foregrounding of the right-branching is so heavy that the few embedded elements do not deter the flow of the action: the two participial phrases are placed toward the right; the one adjective clause is insignificant. The style is distinguished by the high "degree" of right-branching; a statistical count is not necessary to understanding that the comic tone is conveyed by a cohesion of syntactic features of a distinctly different kind than those associated with contemplation. The same comic tone and style dominate Ratliff's retelling of the episode at the general store: "It was in my room *and* it was on the front porch *and* I could hear Mrs. Littlejohn hitting it over the head with that washboard in the backyard all at the same time. *And* it was still missing everybody everytime. I reckon that's what that Texas man meant by calling them bargains: that a man would need to be powerful unlucky to ever get close enough to one of them to get hurt" (314). Ratliff's concluding *coda* provides the point of view he wishes his auditors to adopt, but the comic stance is implicit in the preceding sentences describing the repetitive movements of the horse. The principle of repetition is the comic principle underlying slapstick humor such as the Marx brothers'; in Bergson's terms, such repetition is comic because its mechanical nature reminds man of the limitations placed on his vitality by mechanical and bodily forces. The repetitive style may be funny merely because "repetition overdone or not going anywhere belongs to comedy, for laughter is partly a reflex and like other reflexes it can be conditioned by a simple repeated pattern," as Frye points out.[14] The repeated patterns of this syntactic style parallel the patterning of the action; the rapid, mechanical repetition reminds Ratliff and the reader of the absence of thought that gets men gulled.

The comic occasion in Faulkner's novels is often an occasion when action is taken without contemplation. In the contemplative passages, characters realize that no goal is ever achieved; in the comic passages characters act without thinking of ultimate futilities. In *The Reivers* the illusive goal is winning a race; the comic perspective toward this hope is present the moment the horse is—when Millie announces:

> "Man standing in the back yard hollering Mr. Boon Hogganbeck at the back wall of the house. He got something big with him."
>
> We ran, following Boon, through the kitchen and out into the back gallery. It was quite dark now; the moon was not high enough yet to do any good. Two dim things, a little one and a big one, were standing in the middle of the back yard, the little one bawling "Boon Hogganbeck! Mister Boon Hogganbeck! Hellaw. Hellaw" toward the upstairs windows until Boon overrode him by simple volume:
>
> "Shut up! Shut up! Shut up!"
>
> It was Ned. What he had with him was a horse.[15]

The amusing point of view is due to some extent to the verbal excess: the repetition of "Boon Hogganbeck! Mister Boon Hogganbeck! Hellaw. Hellaw" and

"Shut up! Shut up! Shut up!" conveys the excitement of the characters, the emotional excess that overrides contemplation. The repetition of similar phrasing at the beginning and ending of the passage reinforces this perspective: "He got something big with him"—"What he had with him was a horse." This syntactic style is the perfect style for races—of men and horses—because the syntax captures the sense of motion; for example, in the two races in *The Reivers:*

> I *cut him* as hard as I could. He broke, faltered, sprang again; *we* had already made McWillie a present of two lenghts so *I cut him* again; *we* went into the second lap two lengths back *and* traveling now on the peeled switch until the gap between him *and* Acheron replaced Ned in what Lightning called his mind, *and* he closed it again until his head was once more at McWillie's knee . . . (272–73).
>
>   . . . McWillie whipping furiously now *and* Lightning responding like a charm, exactly *one neck back; if Acheron* had known any way to run sixty miles an hour, *we would too—one neck back; if Acheron* had decided to stop ten feet before the wire, *so would we—one neck back* (297).

The right-branching syntactic style captures the actual movement of the action as in "Was" and *The Hamlet;* the repetitiveness of the passages suggests that nearly all races are repetitive and doomed to be lost by a head. The comic limitations are no different from those recognized in contemplation, but such races are comic because the actors keep moving toward a mere illusion of victory.

This illusion is also at the heart of the absurdist comedy of the bizarre funeral procession in *As I Lay Dying.* Death and burying can only become subjects for comedy when they provide the occasion for the living to assert what Langer calls "the vital feeling"—the human tendency to "seize on opportunities," to grab a little more of life.[16] However, the "opportunism" becomes absurd when its goals become unworthy of the expenditure of energy—merely to go to town or to get new teeth. The opportunism of Faulkner's absurdist comedy is less "brainy" than the "opportunism" Langer thinks underlies comic greed. In fact, the lack of thought is what makes the opportunism absurd as the characters, the mules, and the mother's coffin all swirl off in the flood:

> Cash tried but she fell off *and* Darl jumped going under he went under *and* Cash hollering to catch her *and* I hollering *and* Dewey Dell hollering at me Vardaman

you Vardaman you vardaman *and* Vernon passed me because he was seeing her
come up *and* she jumped into the water again *and* Darl hadn't caught her yet. . . .

The mules dived up again diving their legs stiff their stiff legs rolling slow *and*
then Darl again *and* I hollering catch her darl catch her head her into the bank
darl *and* Vernon wouldn't help *and* then Darl dodged past the mules. . . .

"Where is ma, Darl?" I said. "You never got her. You knew she is a fish but
you let her get away."[17]

The syntactic style makes the actions swirl around each other, inundating
opportunity for thought. The piling up of the repetitive actions is highlighted
by the repetition of "and" and of specific words. Vardaman, who narrates this
bizarre parody of crossing to the other world, is, of course, limited in contemplative abilities by his age. His perception of this accretion of separate
actions is not so different from Benjy's in *The Sound and the Fury*: "*They* took
the flag out, *and they* were hitting. Then *they* put the flag back *and they* went
to the table, *and* he hit *and* the other hit. *Then they* went on, *and* I went along
the fence" (23). The repetitiveness of the actions described is emphasized by
the style in which they are described. Of course, Benjy's syntax represents the
epitome in lack of contemplation; he literally cannot connect, relate, and
evaluate events, and while this is not comic in an acknowledged idiot, it is
in men who pretend to reason but share Benjy's style of mind. Benjy and
Vardaman are pathetic because they are caught by age and inheritance in the
accretion of actions they did not cause and cannot understand. The pathetic
quality about them is directly connected to their lack of ability to think. As
Freud reminds us, human nature laughs at the pathetic—at children and
idiots and "hump backs"—perhaps because "we see an unnecessary expenditure of movement which we should spare ourselves if we were carrying out
the same activity" and "our laughter expresses a pleasurable sense of the
superiority which we feel in relation" to another (254–55). In this sense,
Vardaman and Benjy are expansions of the comic quality of other Faulknerian
characters who are involved in activities they do not fully comprehend, the
futility of which they have not contemplated.

Many of the actions that occupy the comic scenes in Faulkner's novels
might become tragic if the characters involved engaged in contemplation of
their insignificance, if the style in which they were presented involved evaluation. As Richard Sewall points out, one critical aspect of tragedy is contemplation, graduation "from the condition of pain and fear to the condition

of suffering—which is the condition of pain and fear contemplated."[18] Faulkner's comic style embodies the lack of contemplation in its rapid, right-branching accumulation of actions. The more contemplative passages are marked by a syntactic style that imposes continual evaluation of what is by all that is related to it—by all that precedes it, stands in opposition to it, or can be equated with it. The contemplative or comic point of view grows from the style of the narration, regardless of whether the author or a character is doing the narrating. This consistency between style and tone accounts for the consistency between passages with different formal narrative structures and for the persistence of the "Faulknerian" voice in the voices of different characters. A further sense of consistency in Faulkner's narrative style derives from qualities shared by the contemplative and comic styles, which both present an inundation of consciousness—by thought or by action. The syntactic accretion that marks Faulkner's narrative styles transforms individual experiences through syntactic connections that create a world in which everything is related. Both the contemplative and comic styles convey relationships between layers of experience, reinforcing through style the persistent Faulknerian themes of the interconnectedness of all times, peoples, and actions.

NOTES

1. John Searle, *Speech Acts: An Essay in the Philosophy of Language* (Cambridge, Eng.: Cambridge University Press, 1969), 17, discusses speech as an active transaction.

2. Mary Louise Pratt, *Toward a Speech Act Theory of Literary Discourse* (Bloomington: Indiana University Press, 1977), 136.

3. William Labov, "The Transformation of Experience in Narrative Syntax," *Language and the Inner City* (Philadelphia: University of Pennsylvania Press, 1972), 371–73 and 388.

4. Richard Ohmann in *Shaw: The Style and the Man* (Middletown, Conn.: Wesleyan University Press, 1962) argues that "We order experience as we order language. . . ."

5. Sigmund Freud, "Jokes and the Comic," trans. James Strachey, in *Comedy: Meaning and Form*, ed. Robert W. Corrigan (San Francisco: Chandler, 1965), 261.

6. William Faulkner, "Was," in *Go Down, Moses* (New York: Modern Library, 1940), 3–4.

7. S. I. Hayakawa coined the terms "maps" and "territories" in *Language and Thought in Action* (New York: Harcourt, Brace, 1939), esp. chap. 2 on "Symbols."

8. Lubomir Doležel, "A Framework for the Statistical Analysis of Style," in *Statistics and Style*, ed. Lubomir Doležel and Richard Bailey (New York: American Elsevier, 1969), 10–11.

9. Noam Chomsky, *Reflections on Language* (New York: Pantheon, 1975), 4.

10. *Light in August* (New York: Modern Library, 1932), 317.

11. "The Bear," in Go *Down, Moses*, 192–93.

12. *The Sound and the Fury* (1929; reprint, New York: Random, Vintage, 1946), 93.

13. *The Hamlet* (1931; reprint, New York: Random, Vintage, 1958), 308.

14. Northrop Frye, "The Mythos of Spring: Comedy" from *Anatomy of Criticism* (1957; reprint, New York: Atheneum, 1970), 168.

15. *The Reivers* (New York: Random, Vintage, 1962), 115.

16. Suzanne Langer, "The Great Dramatic Forms: Comic Rhythm," from *Feeling and Form* (1953), as reprinted in *Comedy,* ed. Marvin Felheim (New York: Harcourt, Brace, Jovanovich, 1962), 248 and 243.

17. *As 1 Lay Dying* (1930; reprint, New York: Random, Vintage, 1957), 143–44.

18. Richard B. Sewall, *The Vision of Tragedy* (New Haven, Conn.: Yale University Press, 1959), 6.

Why Did the Snopeses Name their Son "Wallstreet Panic"? Depression Humor in Faulkner's *The Hamlet*

ANDREA DIMINO

When applied to Faulkner's *The Hamlet,* the term "depression humor" may at first seem as troublesome as the "jerky" span of mules that the legendary horse trader Pat Stamper palms off on Ab Snopes: "e'en after we was in the road and the wagon rolling good one of them taken a spell of some sort and snatched his-self crossways in the traces like he aimed to turn around and go back . . . they was a matched team in the sense that neither one of them seemed to have any idea as to just when the other one aimed to start moving"(38).[1] Thoughts of economic depression pull us in one direction: the hints of mortgage foreclosures scattered throughout the novel; the degraded life of the tenant farmer Mink Snopes, who kills his more prosperous neighbor with a shotgun oiled with bacon grease because he can't afford oil; pathetic, gray Mrs. Armstid, who weaves by candlelight to buy her sons some shoes. The novel's humor, however, pulls us into a world peopled by a

Reprinted with permission from *Studies in American Humor* 3 (summer-fall 1984): 155–72.

host of intriguing con men, from formidable Stamper with his "eyes the color of a new axe blade" to froglike Flem Snopes to V. K. Ratliff, the shrewd sewing-machine salesman and raconteur (29–30). Yet ultimately Faulkner manages to duplicate the horse-trading legerdemain of the masterful Stamper by convincing us to accept both our mules, economic depression and humor, as a "matched team."

The novel's theme of economic depression includes not only depictions of financial struggle, class conflict, mortgage foreclosures, and a lowered standard of living, but also a broader inquiry into Southern and, more generally, American economic values. The Snopes' invasion of Frenchman's Bend, for example, is sympathetic of the social upheaval brought on by economic forces, an upheaval poorly understood and experienced as absurd. And in countless other instances, economic decline generates what I call dialogue of value in the novel. In both realistic and antirealistic modes, in comedy and in serious narrative, Faulkner dramatizes such issues as the nature of meaningful work, the validity of the Protestant ethic, the relation of Southerners to the land, the nature of cash money as opposed to tangible goods, the incursion of the machine into the human psyche, and the relation of economics and sex. The novel's comic theme of the difference between Northerners and Southerners, introduced in Ratliff's goat-trading scheme, is especially important in this regard, since it evokes the South's crisis of identity and crisis of values after the Civil War, including the problems of industrialization in the "New South" and the Northern domination of the Southern economy.

Both the setting and the composition of *The Hamlet* are closely connected with economic dislocation and depression. The novel takes place from 1902 to 1908, a period that includes the panics of 1903 and 1907, the latter brought on, according to Theodore Roosevelt, by "the speculative folly and the flagrant dishonesty of a few men of great wealth."[2] In Yoknapatawpha County, the country around Frenchman's Bend has been hurt by the catastrophic decline in cotton prices in the nineties, and we can see a nightmarish image of these hard times in the farm that Ab Snopes rents from Jody Varner; the gate is "choked with grass and weeds like the ribs of a forgotten skeleton" (18).

The novel was composed during hard times as well. Faulkner began writing *The Hamlet* (as "Father Abraham") in 1926–27, when the South was already suffering from the decline that was to become the Great Depression; and during the Depression he published several stories that were later incorporated into the novel. In the novel itself, published in 1940, Faulkner addresses some of the crucial economic questions of his time, portraying the evils of the tenant farming and sharecropping system and associating Flem Snopes with usury, manipulative secrecy, and even mechanization.[3] We see similar concerns in such contemporary works as H. C. Nixon's essay "Whither Southern Economy" in *I'll Take My Stand,* which discusses the inadequacy of the tenant system and the "crop lien" system in Southern agriculture and warns Southerners of the accelerating tempo of life in an industrial society, a tendency foreshadowed by Flem Snopes's buggy with its "speeding aura of constant and invincible excursion" (89).[4] *The Hamlet* thus reflects the economic problems of the first decade of the twentieth century and presages the greater depression to come.[5]

Economic decline provides the impetus for the novel's reenactment of American history on two fronts: as Faulkner charts the evolution of the American economy in *The Hamlet,* from Ab Snopes's barter to Flem's capitalist shenanigans, he also charts a literary history of American humor, from its folk origins, reflected in Ratliff's mock-oral stories, to literary black humor. Under the pressure of economic decline, however, the more traditional comic stories of the first half of the novel are all invaded in some way by portents of black humor. The critical point in this comic history, which signals the shift from nineteenth- to twentieth-century humor, comes almost midway through the novel, when a pregnant Eula Varner is married off to Flem Snopes. The story of this rustic Venus, a symbol of "abundance and munificence," has evoked the expansive atmosphere of a tall tale, but Eula's marriage to squat, bland, passionless Flem precipitates a crisis both in Ratliff's economic consciousness and in the novel's humor (159). In portraying Ratliff's effort to transcend his outrage at the waste of Eula's marriage and to create humor once again, Faulkner captures the basic tension of depression humor, the need to reconcile the Edenic abundance of America with the realities of waste and hardship. [6]

SOME FOOLS AND THEIR MONEY

The novel's economic dialogue begins with a portrayal of the change in the region's highest social class. Faulkner opens *The Hamlet* with an unforgettable image of the antebellum Old Frenchman's place in ruins; by the turn of the century, when the story takes place, the once-fertile plantation has reverted to jungle and the local people have taken to tearing down the magnificent house for firewood, so that the original economic and aesthetic value of the plantation is no longer accessible. Sold to banks during the Reconstruction, the nameless Frenchman's plantation has been taken over by the chief man in the area, Will Varner. Folksy, Rabelaisian Will performs a complex economic function for the local people, acting as farmer, usurer, and veterinarian at the same time. Skeptical of the Cavalier tradition, Uncle Will affably criticizes the greed at the basis of plantation life: "'I'm trying to find out what it must have felt like to be the fool that would need all this . . . just to eat and sleep in'"(6). Since Will is good-natured, and the local people seem to accept this ascendency, the reader glides quickly over the facts that Will and his son Jody deal heavily in foreclosed mortgages, and that the threat of foreclosure hangs over many of the farmers. Jody's plan to cheat his new tenant farmer, Ab Snopes, maps out a scenario similar to foreclosure: at some point after Ab has planted his crop but before he can reap some profit, Jody will drive Ab out of the country by revealing that he knows of the barn-burning in Ab's past. If we can identify mean and devious Ab as a "subversive" comic character in the nineteenth-century tradition of humorous rascals and rogues who flaunt the morality of "reputable" society, including Faulkner's favorite rogue, G. W. Harris's Sut Lovingood, we can also note that "reputable" Jody is subversive in his own way.[7] In the metaphor derived from fencing that describes Jody's habitual levity, the "poste and reposte of humor's light whimsy," we see reflected Jody's willingness, at least formerly, to allow some give and take in his economic dealings (10).

In Ratliff the relation between economic activity, social ease, and a humorous psychological poise seems more solidly balanced. Ratliff first appears as a reincarnation of the nineteenth-century oral taleteller; he hides his sharp insight into human nature behind an affable mask. The son of a tenant farmer, Ratliff combines his shrewd trading in sewing machines, land, and other commodities with a certain egalitarian social activity; functioning as a mail service and one-man news bureau, he knows everyone on his 50-mile route. Though Ratliff must be more prosperous than most of the people around Frenchman's Bend, his personality seems to transcend class categories, and thus it is appropriate that the first comic story he tells in the novel represents a defusing of a class conflict—clearly one major option of depression humor. Cold and bitter Ab Snopes, who moves from one tenant farm that "'aint fitten for hawgs'" to another, has—deliberately?—tracked some horse-manure on the hundred-dollar French rug in the house of his landlord, Major de Spain (20). When de Spain insists that Ab's womenfolk clean the rug, they ruin it, whereupon he demands twenty bushels of corn in payment. Ab then sues him and has the fine reduced to ten bushels. But this partial vindication doesn't satisfy Ab; the same night de Spain's barn burns to the ground.[8]

This comic story contrasts two kinds of value: the judge's concept of value sets up an equivalence between an expensive French rug and bushels of corn, whereas Ab's psychological scales of value balance his economic exploitation at the hands of landlords like de Spain with his destructive revenge. Ab's ten bushels of corn are worth as much to a poor man like Ab as a barn is worth to de Spain. By tracking manure on the rug, Ab is probably suggesting that de Spain values the rug more than his tenants—or that landlords treat their tenants like horse manure. The barn-burning thus marks the subversive comic triumph of Ab's sense of value over the values of law and society. When Ab announces that he is leaving the farm, de Spain reminds him of his farming contract. "'I done cancelled it,'" Ab says (17). He may be down, but he isn't out. Ratliff's good-humored telling of the story and his refusal to assert Ab's proven guilt suggest that he may still feel some sympathy for the class of tenant farmers he was born into; but we may also assume that Ab does not really pose a serious threat to the prosperity of people like de Spain, the Varners, and Ratliff.

Ab's attempts at self-aggrandizement also form the core of Ratliff's second comic anecdote, "Fool About a Horse," which he tells the farmers lounging at Varner's store. Like the barn-burning story, this anecdote works toward a comic denial of loss and failure in Ab's life as a tenant farmer. "Fool About a Horse" takes place some twenty years before the narrative present. As a tenant after the Civil War, Ab prizes his eye for horseflesh because it lifts him above his identity as a shiftless and sorry farmer. Ratliff himself, as a neighbor's child of eight, accompanies Ab to town on the day that Ab is carrying $24.68—his wife's savings of four years—to buy her a milk separator. Ab learns that this new horse, which he has acquired by barter, was originally owned by Pat Stamper, who set in motion a series of trades in which eight "'actual Yoknapatawpha cash dollars'" had got "'to rattling around loose'" (34). Ab then determines to vindicate "'the entire honor and pride of the science and pastime of horse-trading in Yoknapatawpha County'" by beating

Stamper at a trade (34). Ratliff insists that honor, not profit, is Ab's motive. But the existence of a cash nexus sets up a different system of values in Ab's mind, initiating what proves to be a dangerous process of abstraction. Somehow cash diminishes the physical reality of the horses: "'So here we come,'" Ratliff says, "'easing them eight dollars . . . up them long hills . . .'" (35). A less vivid and personal commodity, cash represents a snake in the garden, a value alien to Yoknapatawpha County.

Comparing Ab and Stamper to two "'first-class burglars,'" Ratliff describes the confrontation between them as a contest of social equals who trade for pleasure as well as gain, even though Stamper is fabulously successful and Ab is not. Ab makes a basic decision about value when he decides to trade his sorry horse and good mule for Stamper's slightly inferior span of mules. But Stamper's black hostler, an artist in horseflesh, has groomed the mules to have only a temporary semblance of value. First they won't pull together; then they go on a rampage and collapse in a heap. Doomed, desperate, and drunk, Ab sacrifices his wife's new milk separator in a second trade in which he acquires his original mule and a new hog-fat horse. When it starts to rain and the new dark brown horse turns into a bay, he realizes that Stamper has merely disguised Ab's original horse by dyeing it and blowing it up with a bicycle pump valve. In order to retrieve the milk separator, Mrs. Snopes must trade not only Ab's original mule and horse but her only cow as well. Still undaunted, Mrs. Snopes runs the milk separator again and again with the same gallon of borrowed milk, enacting a comic version of Camus's myth of Sisyphus. Though Ab is comically unregenerate, in the manner of nineteenth-century comic rogues, his wife at least has confronted the absurd. [9]

Our fascination with Stamper's legerdemain blocks our sympathy for Ab's vulnerability, even though he is now a farmer without a mule or cow; since he tried to beat Stamper, he only receives comic justice when he is whipped. But Stamper has precipitated what Ratliff calls a natural process of "souring" in Ab. At some point after Stamper eliminated Ab from horse-trading, he "'just went plumb curdled'" and became the mean old man we see at the start of the novel (29). In order for the story to remain comic, Ratliff must end it here, before the unknown moment when the curdling actually happens.[10] Ratliff must not cross the line between a "depression" story and one that depicts the irrevocable death of Ab's spirit.

Ab's "souring" at the hands of a shrewder trader brings about a definitive change in his family's economic activity, since, in a repudiation of traditional values, Flem decides that there's no profit in farming.[11] Accepting the bribe of a clerkship in the Varner store, which Jody hopes will prevent Ab from burning his barn, Flem becomes the agent of further change. Up to now the raw power relation between Varner and the other farmers has been tempered by a set of social forms; Will and Jody often leave the store untended, trusting people to pay for the goods themselves; when Jody makes a mistake in his own favor in adding up the bills, he also makes a joke: The Varner's extend credit with an air of generosity, even though they charge interest. Flem, however, is allied with the legalistic and the mechanical. He makes Will pay for the wad of chewing tobacco from his own store, tries to deny everyone credit, and never makes a mistake—or at least never gets caught at it. Most important, through Flem we gain a heightened sense of the mechanical aspect of economic gain in general and the charging of interest in particular, a perception that will fuel the novel's black humor.

Though Faulkner exploits for comic purposes the incongruity of the blandly repulsive Flem as a big shot in Frenchman's Bend, he also uses Flem to demystify, through parody, the economic activity of more traditional social leaders like the Varners, and even Ratliff. The process of economic gain can, from a certain distance, seem almost magical; the herd of scrub cattle that Flem owns is "transmogrified" overnight into a herd of superior Herefords (61). But at the bottom of this magical transformation, akin to the magical feats of Pat Stamper in horsetrading, lies a foreclosed lien at a Jefferson bank. Similarly, when Ratliff goes to Tennessee because his sewing machine business forces him to raise cash, we find comedy in his discovery of a territory ripe for exploitation, like "the first white hunter blundering into the idyllic solitude of a virgin African vale teeming with ivory, his for the mere shooting and fetching out" (55). Yet we begin to wonder about the "naturalness" of the economic system of Frenchman's Bend when we see Will Varner and Flem sitting together at the yearly settling of accounts with Will's tenants and debtors, resembling "the white trader and his native parrot-taught headman in an African outpost" (61).[12] Part of the mystery behind Flem's acquisition of capital is illuminated by the comic anecdote that Bookwright, a successful yeoman, tells to Ratliff. Bookwright has overheard a black sawmill worker explaining how easy it is to borrow money from Flem Snopes: "'He lent me five dollars over two years ago and all I does, every Saturday night I goes to the store and pays him a dime. He aint even mentioned that five dollars'" (70). The earlier image of the ceaseless milk separator has thus foreshadowed Flem's discovery of a true perpetual motion machine: the charging of interest.

Flem's new citified clothes evoke another theme of depression humor, the emergence of sharper class distinctions. We find comedy in the puniness of Flem's tiny, machine-made black bow tie. But Flem's tie and Will's are the only ones in Frenchman's Bend, setting them apart from the farmers. It is significant that when we learn of the tie, we also learn of Flem's ultimate social station: when he becomes president of the Sartoris bank in Jefferson, he will have the little ties made for him by the gross.

The basic social conflict inherent in Flem's financial machinations— which turns out to be a regional conflict as well—affects the form of the final comic incident in Book One of the novel. The story begins as a traditional high-spirited comedy, as Ratliff appears to us as a confidence man, the Southern version of a clever Yankee peddler. He allows Flem to overhear his telling the farmers that he has a contract to buy goats for a Northerner who wants to start a goat farm. Ratliff wants Flem to rush out to buy the only existing local herd of goats before him, and then to try to sell the goats to Ratliff so that he can confront Flem with a couple of financial notes connected in a complex way with Flem's cousins Mink and Isaac Snopes. In the story that Ratliff dangles before Flem as bait, however, we find an opposition that deepens the economic dialogue of the novel. According to Ratliff, Southerners are like philosophic materialists: they start goat ranches because they already have too many flesh-and-blood goats; Northerners are idealists who start with abstractions, with rules and syndicates, diplomas and measurements.

Implicit in this Northerner-Southerner dichotomy is the contrast between the traditional concrete barter economy of Frenchman's Bend, represented earlier by Ab's pre-Stamper horse-trading, and the new, more abstract economy of the Stamper-inspired cash dollars, Flem's notes, and Varner's and Flem's charging of interest. The "Northern" complexity of Flem's manipulation of notes in the cash economy dizzies even an experienced man like Ratliff, schooled in the "science and pastime of skullduggery" (82). Flem has given his cousins Mink and Ike two notes in exchange for their two ten-dollar inheritances from their grandmother, and somehow Flem has collected on the notes several times, activating another perpetual motion machine. Moreover, Ratliff finds that he cannot use traditional social pressures to shame Flem for neglecting his cousins. Ratliff is forced instead to undergo the disorientation characteristic of black humor, which stands in contrast to his earlier folk humor: Isaac Snopes, whose inheritance Flem seems to have used as his original fund of capital, turns out to be an idiot.

Flem's brand of economics thus short-circuits what started out to be a traditional comic story.[13] Though Faulkner presents the blasted face of Ike Snopes as a vision of a generalized absurd injustice toward humankind, the "Gorgon face of that primal injustice which man was not intended to look at face to face," the uncovering of Ike as the original source of the note and of Flem's capital suggests a more specific, though oblique, questioning of the change in the economy of Frenchman's Bend (85). Again, the elusive value of cash money, now further abstracted into notes, seems to be the villain. If the Old Frenchman in the plantation economy is a greedy fool, and if Ab Snopes the tenant farmer is a fool about a horse—and the fool of the Cavaliers—Ike Snopes in a capitalist economy is an absurd fool.

From Goddess to "Gal-Meat": Eula Varner and the Dialogue of Value

Flem's rise to power in Book One represents a story of social upheaval characteristic of depression humor. Flem Snopes has now replaced Jody Varner as the heir to Will's power—it is Flem, not Will, who sits in meditation at the Old Frenchman's place at the end of this Book. Ratliff's comic poise is not upset by his failure to beat Flem in the goat-trading incident, however. Thinking that he has merely "quit too soon" in his calculations, Ratliff does not abandon his basic conception of economic and social value (88). But Faulkner complicates the situation in Book Two, "Eula," by juxtaposing a radically different system of value to the stable local values that Flem has upset. This "system" is centered and symbolized in Will's daughter Eula.

Faulkner defines Eula's Dionysic, paradoxical world of value in part by focusing on the role she plays in disrupting the life of the schoolmaster, Labove, a young man from a poor farming family who teaches school in order to put himself through the state university. A walking parody of the Protestant ethic, ascetic and humorless Labove fills every moment of the day with ceaseless work. His first crisis of value echoes the Southern crisis in traditional agrarian values. He learns that his football skill is more important than his intellect, and that preparing a field for a football game claims more human energy than farming. There is no provision in Labove's system of value for entering into a relation with Eula; at best he can try to deflower her, to hurt her, or to "kill" her symbolically (121). Comparing Eula to an infinitely fertile field Labove perceives that Eula's future husband "would not possess her but merely own her . . . by the dead power of money," an analogy that suggests a shallow and futile aspect of American economic life (119).

It falls to Ratliff to forge an explicit interpretation of Eula's meaning in relation to the dominant system of values. The narrator has spoken earlier of the displacement of a younger group of Eula's suitors by an older one in terms of the novel's theme of economic depression: they are "last summer's foreclosed bankrupts" (132). When Will Varner married off a pregnant Eula to Flem Snopes—her lover, Hoake McCarron, has fled—Ratliff regrets the death of everyone's dream of possessing Eula. But he denies the tragedy of Eula's ruin and marriage, reducing Venus to "gal-meat" wasted on all of Frenchman's Bend as well as Flem (149). Slovenly, unclean, with her tawdry negligees and cheap shoes, Eula is reduced not only to an offense to the puritanical virtue of cleanliness and propriety, but also to a "moral natural enemy of the masculine race" whose power over men destroys their own system of value (149). Apparently, once the failure of depression calls into question the efficacy of other traditional puritanical virtues like hard work and thrift, the threat of a riotous reaction to these virtues—a threat embodied in Eula—evokes an even stronger repression.

The counterpart in comedy of Ratliff's declaration of "male" value is the story of Flem in hell that Ratliff spins himself just after he remembers Eula in the train, leaving on her honeymoon. The anecdote relates the confrontation of two supreme con men: Flem Snopes arrives in hell to redeem the soul he sold to the Devil, and by insisting on legal technicalities and resisting mere human temptations, he manages to drive the Prince of hell from his throne, just as the real Flem has driven Jody from his rightful place as Will's heir. Ratliff's anecdote marks a subtle but definite shift in the novel's humor, since, unlike the earlier comic stories that he relates to Jody and the farmers, it takes place only in his head. Though it resembles traditional American comic stories, the isolation of this anecdote, its turning inward, foreshadows the increased psychological and social disorientation that results from Flem's marriage and concomitant gain in power.

Ratliff's ultimate view of Eula's value resolves comedy into a matter of economics. Unable to forget her attraction in spite of his rationalizing, he is left with anger: "what he felt was outrage at the waste, the useless squandering: at a situation intrinsically and inherently wrong by any economy . . . as though the gods themselves had funneled all the concentrated bright wet-slanted unparadised June onto a dung-heap, breeding pismires" (159–60). The death of the dream of Eula, like the death of the American dream of abundance for all, propels Ratliff into satire, the form of humor that can best tap his anger. Substituting a physical outrage for a social one, Ratliff relates a crude and bitter anecdote of a poor woman who copulates with Flem in return for a nickel's worth of lard, and then says, "'Mr. Snopes, what you ax fer dem sardines?'" (164). Since the American tall tale is expansive, and dependent on the myth of abundance, the anticlimactic deflecting of the erotic tall tale of Eula into a satire involving Flem and cut-rate sex reflects a basic deflating and satirizing tendency of depression humor.[14]

"The Prime Maniacal Risibility": Black Humor, the Snopeses, and the Dialogue of Value

Together with the story of Eula, the sheer proliferation of Snopeses in *The Hamlet* works profound change in the novel's modes of depression humor. The comic antics of the Snopeses in the first half of the novel, evoking nineteenth-century "subversive" humor, pave the way for the twentieth-century humor of the second half. As Walter Blair and Hamlin Hill note, "some subversive humor has a significantly modern flavor. Some of it aims, in one of its channels, directly toward contemporary black humor and comic savagery."[15] In the Snopeses' skewed relation to the world of meaningful work and coherent social roles and in their destruction of the secure norms of Frenchman's Bend, we see mirrored an absurd depression America that has broken down.

Different aspects of the depression work crisis are embodied in different Snopeses. Ab's "immobile" bovine daughters signal a loss of energy, like "a carved piece symbolizing some terrific physical effort which had died with its inception . . ."(19). Eck Snopes, moving in slow motion, gives us a dreamlike vision of a chasm between the worker's intention and the finished product: "there was a definite limitation of physical coordination beyond which design and plan and pattern all vanished, disintegrated into dead components of pieces of wood and iron scraps and vain tools" (66). Economic unpredictability takes the shape of frenetic, weasel-like I. O. Snopes, who explodes in a "furious already dissipating concentration of energy vanishing the instant after the intention took shape"(64). He adds a sardonic wrinkle to the novel's debate between concrete Southerners and abstract Northerners; inept at any kind of manual work, he eventually installs himself as the new school professor in Frenchman's Bend, complete with lenseless spectacles. Rodent-faced I. O., who talks in a steady stream of mangled proverbs, is not only a strange new version of the American comic stereotype of the learned fool, but also a parody of Benjamin Franklin's proverb-spouting Father Abraham, who tells colonists how to succeed in spite of the drain on their wealth caused by British tariffs—another example of a colonial economy.[16]

Snopes humor takes yet another form in Issac Snopes the idiot. At first the uncoordinated Ike seems to be another version of the comic work crisis: he does his chores at the boarding house in a mechanical series of steps, so that if he misses one of the steps he must start over again. Nevertheless, his outrageous mock-heroic love for Jack Houston's cow helps him to transcend his mental and physical limitations, and in recounting Ike's story Faulkner joins the bizarre Snopes humor to an exalted lyrical strain. Ike's idyll with the cow, a travesty of romance, has important ramifications for the novel's dialogue of value. His love for this bovine Juno links his story to that of Eula, the bucolic Venus, and like Eula he threatens some of the norms of Frenchman's Bend. In an almost Chaplinesque ballet, Ike innocently handles the fifty-cent piece that Houston has given him as a bribe to leave the cow alone. This scene strips away our notion of the conventional value of the coin, allowing us to see it as something strange and questionable. We never know whether Ike's dropping the coin involves clumsiness or a repudiation of mercenary values: the action remains absurd.

Ike's idyll deepens our sense of an absurd universe, since of all the novel's characters, only an idiot achieves a fusion of work and love: his work in caring for his beloved cow. Faulkner also links Ike unequivocally with the triumphant union of the Northern abstract and the Southern concrete; the diadem of flowers with which he crowns the cow is both concrete fodder and symbolic coronet, imaging forth the glory of their love. In contrast, both the "normal" and the abnormal characters who plague Ike are allied with an array of questionable values. The raging "puritanical" farmer, whose grain Ike steals to feed the cow, has grimly eked out a living in an endless round of labor (191). His hate-filled "marriage" to his embattled land parallels Flem's marriage to Eula, the human counterpart of an infinitely fertile field. Launcelot "Lump" Snopes, Ike's cousin, exploits Ike's love by inviting the farmers to a peep show in which Ike copulates with the cow. Most important, Ratliff himself faces a radical test of his values when he decides to stop the peep show, allying himself with society's "reputables" rather than the "subversives." He knows that he is robbing Ike of his only happiness, yet he rejects moral relativism in favor of repression and suppression. In one of the funniest scenes in the book, Ratliff forces the Snopeses to convene a family conference to separate Ike from his cow, a conference that creates humor out of a contrast between concrete and abstract measures of value. The local minister employs a traditional Protestant method of interpreting the beefing of Ike's cow, finding the exalted symbolic value of purification in the actual butchering. When Ratliff insists that the Snopeses buy the cow from Ike, the family wrangles about dividing the price of the cow. Eck asks his cousin I. O., who is trying to bamboozle him, "'How do I need fifteen dollars worth of moral value when all you need is a dollar and eighty cents?'"(204).

Holding a wooden effigy of his dead cow, Ike seems to share the fate of the murdered farmer Jack Houston, becoming the "victim" of a "useless and elaborate practical joke at the hands of the prime maniacal Risibility . . ."(188). This practical joke turns even grimmer in the story of Ike's cousin Mink, which signals a turn to grotesque black humor. [17] The beginning of Mink's story mingles the pathetic, the tragic, and the absurd. Mink, a tenant farmer, murders his yeoman neighbor Jack Houston because he is insulted when Houston demands a repayment for the cost of pasturing a bull that Mink has allowed to wander; this tragic vengefulness repeats Ab Snopes's vengeful comic barn-burning in a darker key. Moreover, Mink's marriage picks up on a major theme in Eula's story, the relation of the economic despoiling of the land to the ruin of women's virginity. In logging the virgin timber, Mink's father-in-law has founded a cruel and chimerical economic structure, a "furious edifice of ravished acres . . . which had been erected overnight and founded on nothing, to collapse overnight into nothing, back into refuse . . ."(238). These multiple repetitions of earlier episodes point to the "cyclical" nature of black humor, in which "characters enact constant, recurrent situations rather than live unique histories."[18]

In describing Mink's later life Faulkner makes the most explicit statements in the novel about the degradation of tenant farming and sharecropping; the meager crops, the endless succession of dilapidated cabins for which

Mink pays "almost as much rent in one year as the house had cost to build" (219). This somber story modulates into grotesque black humor after Mink kills Jack Houston. Not only does Mink torture his own body with near-starvation and a reversed pattern of sleeping and waking, but he is unable to distance himself from Houston's corpse after his amoral cousin Lump reveals that Houston had at least fifty dollars in his pockets when Mink shot him. Lump sticks to his cousin like a leech in order to force him to show where he hid the corpse; the sheriff is also skulking around for the same purpose. The comic battle between Mink's furious grasping at his last chance for freedom and Lump's loud monomania culminates in a grotesque vision of Mink recovering the stinking mutilated corpse out of a rotting tree while Houston's dog attacks him. At the end of the episode Faulkner reveals the basic contrast implicit in the black humor of Mink's story, the contrast between his grotesque degradation and the middle-class society he cannot enter. As the sheriff brings Mink in a surrey to Jefferson, we catch a momentary glimpse of the prosperous town-dwellers, the "clipped lawns," the children in "bright garments," the "neat painted gates," the comforting dinners at twilight (257).

THE INCORPORATION OF YOKNAPATAWPHA

If a grotesque character like Mink or a subversive character like Ab Snopes can gain revenge against society only by killing their neighbors or burning their barns, Flem can beat the society that would condemn him to tenant farming by turning into what Ratliff has called a Northerner, that is, someone who manipulates abstract values. Throughout the novel the comic resurfacing of the North-South dichotomy has been symptomatic of the dislocation in the Southern economy and culture triggered by the Civil War and its aftermath. Not only does Flem represent the changes that have occurred in the New South, but he also foreshadows even more sweeping changes in the future.

The fourth and final book of *The Hamlet*, "The Peasants," reflects the comic "Northernness" of two con games that help propel Flem into the world beyond Frenchman's Bend, the spotted horse auction and the "salting" of the Old Frenchman's place with fake buried treasure. In essence Flem becomes a comic version of another Faulkner character born into the lower classes, Thomas Sutpen in *Absalom, Absalom!,* the man who tries to beat society by joining it. But Flem's Northernness is also a threat to comedy, since the humor of the spotted horse episode reveals a radically double form, part humorous, part pathetic or tragic; and the basic comic framework of the salted treasure episode is blurred by a curious dreamlike atmosphere and strained by a strong measure of grotesque black humor that threatens to break the form entirely.

The spotted horse story starts out as a traditional comedy. Returning from his Texas honeymoon in the company of an affable cowboy and a kaleidoscopic herd of spotted ponies, Flem bursts into the village with the aura of a circus parade like a Yoknapatawpha P. T. Barnum who will entertain the yokels while he bilks them. In bringing the horses to Frenchman's Bend, Flem seems to have achieved a comic revenge for his father's "souring" at the hands of Pat Stamper. Flem is even more of a master of illusion than Stamper was, since the number of horses appears to double in the moonlight and double again when they stampede. We can never ascertain the actual value of the horses because they are intangible, existing as "'Transmogrified hallucination'" in "mazy camouflage" or "mirage-like clumps" (276). The novel's debate between the Southern concrete and the Northern abstract thus finds a fitting embodiment in these elusive creatures, who partake of both qualities. They burst out of the lot when the auction is over, and none of the new owners ever succeeds in catching them.

Ultimately, however, the actual relation between Flem and the horses remains ambiguous; as the trial at the end of the episode reveals, no one can prove that Flem owned them. The question of the ownership of the horses brings to a head a theme that has already appeared in connection with the Snopeses. The farmers have long been aware that Flem has used his numerous cousins as pawns or shills in his economic shenanigans, creating an absurd confederation that challenges the farmers' belief in honest, rugged individualism. But the traditional value of family bonds—even in a family as bizarre as the Snopeses—obscures the radical newness and impersonality of Flem's strategy. In the horse auction Flem succeeds in evading his individual responsibility by forming a hidden business relationship with the Texan which represents an embryonic stage of the process that Alan Trachtenberg has called "the incorporation of America": "the emergence of a changed, more tightly structured society with new hierarchies of control, and also changed conceptions of that society, of America itself."[19]

Throughout the novel Flem and other Snopeses have been associated with many of the changes in cultural and social values that Trachtenberg discusses. Ab Snopes, hoodwinked by the horse trader Pat Stamper, finds himself a victim of one change: the increasing professionalism of American life. In A. B. Longstreet's story "The Horse-Swap" *(Georgia Scenes,* 1835), which has been suggested as a source of Ab's "fool about horse" story, the seemingly naive old farmer manages to beat the boastful horse trader. But Ab, the amateur, doesn't stand a chance in the late 1870s against the wily expert Stamper. As I have mentioned, the Snopeses also represent an absurd questioning of traditional American conceptions about the value of labor, and Flem's organization of his tribe to further his capitalistic ends can be seen as a comic image of a corporate body—all Snopeses except Mink usually manage to avoid personal liability. Flem's usury and other economic activity, linked with calculation and rationalization, embody a new centralized power in the area, for he affects people in all classes of local society.

The novel's images of mechanization, one of Trachtenberg's main themes, center on Flem as well. As an early sign of his encroaching on Jody Varner's power, he takes charge of the Frenchman's Bend cotton gin, and his constant mechanical chewing of tobacco foreshadows his major feats of mechanization: his transformation of Henry Armstid into a machine in the salted treasure episode and his appropriation of Eula. After Henry Armstid has lost his farm in Flem's salted treasure scam, he digs himself "back into the earth which produced him to be its born and fated thrall forever until he died" (359). It is fitting that Flem's marriage to Eula crystallizes in Ratliff's vision of Eula's "calm beautiful mask" being whisked away by a train, since the railroad is the "age's symbol of mechanization and of economic and political change" (147).[20] Courted by her lover, McCarron, in a buggy, the new Mrs. Flem Snopes vanishes behind a "moving pane of glass" at the railroad station (149). Moreover, because of the marriage Ratliff succumbs to the commercial spirit of the age in reducing Eula the earth goddess into "gal-meat," a commodity like the spotted horses. The horse auction thus signals a crisis of value that extends far beyond Yoknapatawpha County. In the new, impersonal society comically mirrored by the horse auction—the Yoknapatawpha equivalent of the Wall Street stock exchange?—a shadowy Flem pulls the strings, backed up by the pistol-toting Texan.[21]

The trial following the horse auction, in which Mrs. Armstid and the Tulls sue Flem and Eck Snopes, combines pathos, satire, and black humor; the old Justice realizes that legal niceties can't relieve the pain and uproar caused by the rampage. Like the Prince in Ratliff's earlier vision of Flem in hell, he cries "'I can't stand no more!'" (332). Ultimately Mrs. Armstid fails to get her five dollars back from Flem, receiving a nickel's worth of candy instead, and the Tulls are awarded possession of Eck's worthless horse, which has disappeared—a vision of a system in which people get out much less than they put in.[22]

The novel's depression humor culminates in Flem's ultimate con game in Frenchman's Bend, as Flem swindles Ratliff, the impoverished farmer Armstid, and the prosperous yeoman Bookwright by salting the Old Frenchman's place—his wedding gift from Will Varner—with bogus buried treasure. In this episode, Ratliff, usually a solitary traveler, allows himself to be "incorporated" into a group venture that includes an unstable impoverished man like Armstid; the three men dig in frenzy at night and purchase the Old Frenchman's place from Flem. No longer a recounter of comic stories, Ratliff becomes part of a far blacker joke than the ones he tells. This leveling of Ratliff, now the partner of half-crazed Armstid, reflects another aspect of black humor, "the tendency toward total democratization in which all characters become interchangeable machine parts."[23] Ratliff's motivation in this episode combines the rational and the irrational. Ratliff has always believed that the Old Frenchman's place was valuable simply because Will Varner owned it, and throughout the novel has regarded himself as an "heir" of sorts to Will's affably shrewd dealing. The treasure has not been found, he reasons, simply because people digging surreptitiously at night have not been able to dig deep enough. But Ratliff, caught up in the madness characteristic of grotesque black humor, also falls prey to a money-hunting sickness akin to the "'Pat Stamper sickness'" that dooms Ab Snopes (31). Ratliff knows that the money he is hunting was supposed to have been coined before the Civil War, but he never looks at the dates on the coins he unearths. With the deception of Ratliff, we have descended to a level where Americans, "democratized" by black humor, are seen as economic fools, baffled by a puzzle that a child could figure out.

The wholesale process of leveling at the end of the novel insists upon the existence of an economic subtext in *The Hamlet*. From the beginning of the novel we have seen a close connection develop between Flem and the Varners, which seems to be an "outrageous paradox" at first, but is later cemented by marriage; now we see shrewd and affable Ratliff finally lock horns with Flem—unsuccessfully—for gain rather than honor (89). Perhaps if we scratch a humorous but ambitious man like Will Varner or Ratliff, we will find a Flem Snopes, with his "tiny predatory nose like the beak of a small hawk"—the Yoknapatawpha version of what Teddy Roosevelt, during the panic of 1907, called the "predatory wealth" of the Northern fat cats (89, 51).[24]

The novel's treatment of depression crystallizes in the final episode in the financial ruin of Henry Armstid, who in return for his share of the Old Frenchman's place has given Flem a mortgage on his farm. For Faulkner and for other southerners, Armstid's failure is an important representative case for the South, since one of the greatest evils of economic depression lies in its destruction of the Southern yeomanry. The prime villain in this threat is the outrageously exploitative credit system with which the Southern farmer was saddled. In order to get money to grow his crops and pay his mortgage, Armstid would have to borrow. In this context, Flem's identity as a usurer and holder of mortgages becomes central.

In 1938, two years before *The Hamlet* was published, the National Emergency Council's "Report on Economic Conditions of the South" informed President Roosevelt that one of the South's most serious problems was the lack of credit facilities that could deal leniently with low-income farm people. In general, Southerners paid much higher interest rates than did other Americans: C. Van Woodward, writing about the period from 1877 to 1913, reports estimates that under the crop-lien system farmers paid from thirty percent to seventy percent interest.[25] Ultimately this credit system funneled money to the North. To use the terminology of Ratliff's parable of Northern and Southern approaches to goat-ranching, Flem's extortion of enormous amounts of interest from poor blacks and white farmers brands him as a "Northerner," that is, someone more concerned with the abstract uses of money than with fundamental questions of value and social responsibility. Flem has modeled himself on rapacious Northern contemporaries like J. P. Morgan, Hill, Harriman, Frick, and Rockefeller, men whose frenzied speculation and ruthless pursuit of self-interest helped to bring about the ruin of smaller fish in such events as the panic of 1907. Eck Snopes's naming his son "Wallstreet Panic," so that the boy could get rich like the folks who ran the panics of 1907, presents us with a naive comic view of the South spawning its own enemies—people who would not scruple to plunge it into depressions because of their itch for power and personal gain.

NOTES

1. *The Hamlet* (New York: Random House, 1964). Further page references in the text will be to this edition.

2. Caused largely by "an inflexible money structure and the spectacular overcapitalization of trusts," the panic of 1903 seemed "curious" in that 1902 had been a prosperous year; the causes of the panic of 1907 were also the subject of a "heated debate" (George E. Mowry, *The Era of Theodore Roosevelt and the Birth of Modern America, 1900–1912* [New York: Harper Torchbooks, 1962], 173, 219). The enigma of the business cycle thus encouraged a feeling of normality that contributed to black humor. In *The Hamet,* the vagaries of the business cycle are even displaced onto the natural cycle of the seasons, producing an exceptionally cold winter and a "long summer" (the title of Book Three).

3. Though mechanization was introduced in Southern agriculture in the 1880s it did not cause social problems in the cotton growing area until the 1930s. See Pete Daniel, "The Crossroads of Change: Tobacco, Cotton, and Rice Cultures in the Twentieth Century," *Journal of Southern History,* in press.

4. Twelve Southerners, *I'll Take My Stand: The South and the Agrarian Tradition* (New York: Harper and Brothers, 1930). The tenant system and the crop lien system evolved in the South during the thirty years after the Civil War.

5. For studies of the problems of cotton farmers during the entire period, see Pete Daniel, "The Crossroads of Change" and *Breaking the Land* (Champaign: University of Illinois Press, forthcoming). In addition to such trials as the disruption of the First World War, the collapse of the cotton market in 1920, and problematic government intervention, Southern cotton farmers had to endure the invasion of the boll weevil, repeated Mississippi floods, and the 1930 drought.

6. A fundamental aspect of depression humor thus corresponds closely to what Louis D. Rubin, Jr. . calls "the great American joke": "the clash between the ideal and the real, between value and fact," between the "theory of equality and the fact of social and economic inequality" ("Introduction," in *The Comic Imagination in American Literature,* ed. Louis D. Rubin, Jr. [New Brunswick, N.J.: Rutgers Univ. Press, 1973], 13, 9).

7. Other subversives include Longstreet's Ransy Sniffle, James Russell Lowell's Birdofredum Sawin, Hooper's Simon Suggs, and Locke's Petroleum Vesuvius Nasby. See Walter Blair and Hamlin Hill, *America's Humor* (New York: Oxford University Press, 1978), 187–99.

8. "*In Cornbote:* A Feudal Custom and Faulkner's 'Barn Burning,'" Brenda Eve Sartoris notes the implicit contrast between English and European feudal society and the tenant farming society in "Barn Burning" (1939), a story Faulkner rewrote for *The Hamlet* (*Studies in American Fiction* 11, no. 1 [1983]: 91–94). Ab's payment in grain, or "cornbote," for de Spain's rug

reflects his low social standing, since feudal "villeins" had to pay in grain and only freehold-ers had the right to pay in money. In "Barn Burning" Faulkner depicts the anguish of Ab's son, Colonel Sartoris Snopes, over class differences, but in *The Hamlet* Faulkner exploits the comparison between feudal and Yoknapatawpha society for comic purposes. We perceive not only the comic incongruity between feudal ideals of social reciprocity and Yoknapatawpha reality, but also the irony that Southern society has not progressed beyond feudalism.

9. Though he does not mention this episode, Richard Boyd Hauck invokes Camus's myth of Sisyphus in discussing American absurd humor, including Faulkner's (*A Cheerful Nihilism: Confidence and "The Absurd" in American Humorous Fiction* [Bloomington: Indiana University Press, 1971], xi-14, 167–200). The "American Sisyphus," like Mrs. Snopes, chooses creative activity in a meaningless world. Hauck suggests that the characters in *The Hamlet* "sense that the Snopeses are only part of some universal joke created by some unknown jokester" (185).

10. The comic distortion of a normal economic process—the substitution of a mechanical milk separator for Mrs. Snopes's naturally productive cow—has a noncomic parallel in Ab's subse-quent alienation. In comparing Ab to milk, Ratliff uses a natural metaphor, but elsewhere the dead and lifeless post-Stamper Ab is compared to rust or iron and seems like a machine, fore-shadowing later black humor (97–98).

11. As a break with Southern tradition, Flem's repudiation of farming and Ab's total post-Stamper alienation go hand in hand. In the "fool about a horse" story, Ab's horse-trading mirrors his identification and solidarity with classes higher than his own: the horse-symbol occurs, of course, in the term "Cavalier" and in the ruling class's designation of itself as "the chivalry." W. J. Cash attributes the solidarity of common Southern whites and the planter class to their shared—and relatively recent—frontier origins; see *The Mind of the South* (New York: Knopf, 1941).

12. These two references to imperialist colonies evoke C. Vann Woodward's analysis of the "colo-nial economy" of the New South, an economy under the domination of Northern interests. Instead of creating Southern magnates, industrialization put into place an economy con-trolled by people like Rockefeller, the Morgans, the Mellons, and the DuPonts, who invested in corporations (*Origins of the New South, 1877–1913* [Baton Rouge: Louisiana State University Press, 1951], 291–320). Faulkner's comic references to a colonial economy not only fore-shadow this domination but throw into doubt Southerners' adherence to their traditional val-ues: Varner and Ratliff are acting like Northerners.

13. We find a nineteenth-century analogue to Flem's repeated collection on the same note in the "subversive" story of the roguish Davy Crockett reselling the same skin at a trading post over and over; see Blair and Hill, *America's Humor*, 196–97.

14. An economic analogue is implicit in Constance Rourke's description of American tall tales, which were marked by verbal and imaginative "inflation" (*American Humor: A Study* of the

National Character [Garden City, N.Y.: Doubleday Anchor Books, 1953], 60). Rourke finds in tall tales and talk "an exhilarated and possessive consciousness of a new earth and even of the wide universe." Once people like Labove and Ratliff despair of such a "possession" of Eula, the tall tale is doomed.

15. *America's Humor,* 199.

16. Father Abraham's exhortation on the way to wealth appears in Franklin's preface to *Poor Richard Improved* of 1758. The germ of *The Hamlet,* Faulkner's 1926–27 narrative, was also called "Father Abraham."

17. In Mathew Winston's formulation, "grotesque black humor has the characteristics common to all black humor," but is marked by an "omnipresent threat of death" that manifests itself in an obsession with madness and with "the human body, with the ways in which it can be distorted, separated into its component parts, mutilated, and abused" *("Humor noir* and Black Humor," in *Veins of Humor,* ed. Harry Levin [Cambridge, Mass.: Harvard University Press, 1972], 282–83.

18. Ibid., 280.

19. *The Incorporation of America: Culture and Society in the Gilded Age* (New York: Hill and Wang, 1982), 3–4.

20. Ibid., 57.

21. In contrast to Flem, the farmers are so committed to the traditional value of individuals that they never "incorporate" except in cases of emergency: in order to hem in and capture the spotted horses they form a long line, but the horses break through. Real-life Southern farmers, though they formed associations like the Farmers Alliance and the Farmers Union, never succeeded in duplicating the "incorporating" success of financiers and industrialists.

22. In analyzing the doubleness of the spotted horses episodes, in which victims like Mrs. Armstid reverse the comic caricatures of "unfeeling clowns," Myra Jehlen concludes that ‑Faulkner has almost succeeded in using [comedy] to comment on its own assumptions, and thus uncover its ideological basis—but not quite, for he does not . . . make the victims . . . completely human" *(Class and Character in Faulkner's South* [Secaucus, N.J.: The Citadel Press, 1978], 146).

23. Winston, p. 279.

24. Quoted in Mowry, p. 221.

25. Woodward, p. 180.

Knight's Gambit: Poe, Faulkner, and the Tradition of the Detective Story

JOHN T. IRWIN

Like the machine gun, the detective story is an American invention. We can assign its origin to a specific author and story. The author is Edgar Allan Poe, and the story the 1841 tale "The Murders in the Rue Morgue." The detective genre has, of course, enjoyed worldwide popularity since Poe's day, but perhaps because of its native roots it has always had a special place in American literature, in both popular and serious fiction. Needless to say, Faulkner is a major inheritor of Poe in this genre, and I would even go so far as to maintain that *Absalom Absalom!,* with its two young narrators puzzling over the facts of a very old murder trying to understand the motive, represents in some sense the culmination of the gothic detective form.

What I would like to discuss is Faulkner's relationship to the genre's origin (Poe's Dupin stories) in his own practice of detective fiction, that is to say, the way in which Faulkner interprets or inflects various conventions and

Reprinted with permission from *Arizona Quarterly* 46, no. 4 (1990): 95–115.

images associated with the genre, devices that were for the most part invented by Poe. And I would like to center my discussion on Faulkner's 1949 collection *Knight's Gambit*.

Let me begin with a fairly clear cut example of Faulkner's work in the genre, the story called "An Error in Chemistry," first published in *Ellery Queen's Mystery Magazine* in 1946 and awarded a second prize in the magazine's annual contest for the best stories to appear in its pages during the year.[1] (The first prize that year, by the way, went to a writer named Manly Wade Wellman for a story with an American Indian setting called "A Star for a Warrior.") What I would like to discuss is the story's relationship to the first and third of Poe's Dupin tales—"The Murders in the Rue Morgue" and "The Purloined Letter." As you recall, "The Murders in the Rue Morgue" is a "locked-room" mystery. A mother and daughter have been brutally murdered in their apartment, and when the police arrive at the scene they find that all the apartment's windows and doors are locked from the inside and that the killer has escaped without leaving any trace of his "means of egress,"[2] a puzzle that Dupin must solve on his way to unraveling the still deeper puzzle of the killer's bizarre identity. In "The Purloined Letter," on the other hand, we are confronted with a "hidden-object" mystery. A compromising letter has been stolen from the Queen by the Minister D——, and the police have rigorously searched the Minister's home and person without turning up the missing object. Dupin is certain that if the letter is to be of any use to the Minister in blackmailing the queen, it must be ready to hand, which is to say that it must be hidden somewhere in the Minister's residence. And the mystery then turns upon the fact that the missing object is undoubtedly present within a finite physical enclosure (the Minister's house) without, as it were, making a physical appearance during the minute searches conducted by the police. Dupin solves the mystery by realizing that the Minister has hidden the letter under the very noses of the authorities by not seeming to hide it at all, by simply turning the letter inside out, readdressing it to himself in a feminine hand, and then leaving it in plain sight in a card rack hanging from the mantelpiece.

As you might conclude from this brief description of the two stories, "locked-room" and "hidden-object" mysteries are structurally related. In the former, a physical body (that of the murderer) is absent from an internally sealed space without there being any apparent means of egress; while in the latter a physical object is present within what we might call an externally sealed space (externally sealed because all the possible hiding places for the object outside the space have been logically eliminated) without the object's making a physical appearance. In the former instance (the locked room) we are certain that what we seek *is not inside a given space,* in the latter (the hidden object) that what we seek *cannot possibly be outside it.* Indeed, part of the peculiar force of the hidden-object and locked-room types of detective stories is that they seem to present us with a physical embodiment, a concrete spatialization, of the very mechanism of logical inclusion/exclusion on which rational analysis is based—present us with this as an apparent confounding of rational analysis.

Now it seems clear that Faulkner had registered the structural resemblance of these two types of mysteries, for in "An Error in Chemistry" he creates his own combination of a locked-room and a hidden-object problem. The tale begins with Joel Flint telephoning the sheriff to say that he has killed his wife at the home of his father-in-law Wesley Pritchel. When the sheriff arrives, he finds the killer Flint and the body of the victim. But Wesley Pritchel has locked himself in his room and won't come out. The sheriff sees Pritchel looking out the window, and the assumption is that Pritchel had witnessed the crime. In the sheriff's account to Gavin Stevens, Faulkner goes out of his way to emphasize the locked-room aspect of the scene by having Stevens ask whether Pritchel's room was locked from the inside or the outside. "On the inside," the sheriff replies.[3] And to compound matters, it seems to the sheriff that Joel Flint, who phones the authorities, waits for them to arrive, and then freely confesses to his wife's murder, is in search of his own locked room. As the sheriff says, "It's like he *wanted* to be locked up in jail. Not like he was submitting to arrest because he had killed his wife, but like he had killed her so he would be locked up" (112). So the sheriff locks Flint up, and the next morning Flint's cell is empty. As the narrator, Chick Mallison, describes it, "He had not broken out. He had walked out, out of the cell, out of the jail, out of town and apparently out of the country—no trace, no sign, no man who had seen him or seen anyone who might have been him" (116). And as he says later, "It was as if Flint had never been here at all—no mark, no scar to show that he had ever been in the jail cell" (120). Concerned about the witness's safety with Joel Flint on the loose, the sheriff sends his deputy out to Wesley Pritchel's place with instructions "not to let that locked door—or old Pritchel himself, if he comes out of it—out of his sight" (117). The deputy reports that Pritchel is still in his locked room and that he doesn't leave it even for his daughter's funeral.

Joel Flint's plan is remarkably simple: The motive is greed. Three northern businessmen have offered Wesley Pritchel a sizable amount of money for
his farm, but Pritchel won't sell. And even if he did, he would never give any
of the money to his son-in-law, whom he despises. So Flint decides to kill
Pritchel and then use his talents as a make-up artist (Flint had performed for
years in vaudeville billed as "Signor Canova, Master of Illusion, He Disappears
While You Watch Him" [129]) to impersonate Pritchel, sell the farm, and
pocket the money. The only problem with the plan is that while Flint might
be able to fool someone like Gavin Stevens, who has only seen Pritchel twice
in his whole life, or Chick Mallison, who has never seen him, Flint would
never be able to fool his own wife, who is Pritchel's daughter. Consequently,
Flint has to kill his wife, who would be a witness not necessarily to Pritchel's
murder but to the fact of Flint's impersonation (and thus implicitly to the
fact that something had happened to remove from the scene the man he was
impersonating). And the brilliance of Flint's plan is that he decides to reverse
the usual sequence in the murders of an intended victim and a witness,
which is to say, he decides to kill the witness (his wife) first and then kill the
real victim (Pritchel) later. And he is able to accomplish this plan precisely
because he has duped the authorities into misinterpreting the roles of Pritchel
and of Flint's wife in the affair. He has created the illusion that his wife was
the intended victim (when the sheriff asks Flint why he killed her, Flint says,
"Why do men ever kill their wives? Call it for the insurance") and that his
father-in-law was the witness.

All of which casts a somewhat different light on the locked-room aspect
of the case. The standard locked-room problem requires that the murderer
and victim be together at the moment of the crime in the same internally
sealed space. But in Faulkner's version of the problem, the locked room has,
so to speak, been split and doubled. There are two locked rooms, the jail cell
containing the killer Joel Flint, locked from the outside, and Wesley Pritchel's
bedroom containing the victim, locked from the inside. At some point during the night after he has been jailed for the murder of his wife, Joel Flint
escapes from his cell. Faulkner doesn't say how this was accomplished, but
in telling us that Flint had worked in vaudeville as an illusionist and escape
artist, he has in effect finessed the question. For unlike Poe, Faulkner is not
really interested in the mechanics of how the killer got out of the locked
room without leaving any physical evidence of his means of escape.

Once Flint is on the loose, he goes to his father-in-law's farm, makes his way into the locked bedroom, and kills Pritchel. Flint then disguises himself to look like Pritchel and in turn tries to make the victim's corpse look like Flint. He obliterates Pritchel's face with a blow from a shovel and then buries him in a shallow grave with a scrapbook full of Flint's press clippings from vaudeville. Flint then locks himself in the bedroom, and by the next morning when the sheriff discovers Flint's escape and sends the deputy out to Pritchel's farm with instructions "not to let that locked door . . . out of his sight," it is Flint disguised as Pritchel behind that door. And it is Flint who stays there during the funeral of Pritchel's daughter, since he doesn't want to risk having his impersonation discovered by people who might have known Pritchel well. The way Flint has it figured, if he simply stays in the locked room, acting as if he were afraid that the escaped killer might still come back to eliminate the witness to the crime, then the only people that he may ever have to confront in his disguise are the three northern businessmen who want to buy Pritchel's farm, and they have only seen Pritchel once before.

Flint's illusionary feat is ingenious, and so is Faulkner's. For in the very act of creating Flint's plan, Faulkner has, right before our eyes, reversed the standard structure of a locked-room mystery. When the law arrives at Pritchel's farm the first time, there hasn't in fact been a locked-room murder. Pritchel's daughter has been killed outside the house, and the person inside the locked room is the witness to the crime, who fears for his life. But when the law arrives at Pritchel's farm the second time in the person of the deputy who, after Flint's escape has been sent to check on the old man's safety, Pritchel's bedroom has now almost certainly become the scene of a "locked-room" murder. But with this difference: it is now the killer who is present in, and the victim's corpse that is absent from, the internally sealed space. And this reversal in regard to the occupant of the locked room grows out of that earlier reversal in the order of the murders, the killing of the witness prior to the killing of the real victim, a trick that Faulkner, like any master of illusion, can't help calling our attention to when he has the puzzled sheriff remark, "It don't make sense. If he was afraid of a possible witness, he not only destroyed the witness before there was anything to be witnessed but also before there was any witness to be destroyed. He set up a sign saying 'Watch me and mark me'" (115). And that is, of course, just what Flint did, because as an illusionist he knows that the way to pull off a trick is to draw the audience's attention in one direction while doing something in another, that is, to make the audience misinterpret what it is they are seeing.

Flint in effect tricks the sheriff into misreading the roles of the three people at the scene of the crime. When Hub Hampton arrives at Pritchel's farm the first time, he finds a triad of murderer, victim, and witness. He sees, correctly enough, that Flint is the murderer; but he reverses the other two roles in the triad, even though he senses that there is something amiss in his reading of the roles. He says to Gavin Stevens, "The wrong one is dead" (114)— by which he means that if the motive for the murder was greed, as Flint's remark about his wife's insurance suggests, then the amount of money to be gained from the insurance is trifling compared to the amount to be gained from the sale of Pritchel's farm to the three northern businessmen. But for Flint to get his hands on that money, the victim would have to be Pritchel.

Faulkner's manipulation of the triad of murderer, victim, and witness in the tale has a familiar ring to it. As I argued in *Doubling and Incest*, Faulkner has a predilection for triangular or triadic structures, most obviously for the Oedipal triangle—a structure that he tends to inflect in a variety of ways by substituting different figures in the three roles. Thus, for example, in *Absalom, Absalom!* he substitutes for the standard triad of father, mother, and son the figures of brother avenger (Henry Sutpen), sister (Judith), and brother seducer (Charles Bon), while keeping intact the same structural relationships, the same sexual tensions, associated with the standard triad of the family romance. And as I further argued, the structural principle that governs the dynamics of this triangular relationship is the narcissistic principle of doubling, whereby one figure in the triangle tries to play more than one role within it, as when the son desires to usurp the father's role and thus enjoys a dual relationship to the mother—that of both son and husband.

The ultimate goal of the structural principle of doubling, as it operates within the Oedipal triangle, is the collapsing of all three roles into one. And something very like this is what happens in the triangular structure of murderer, victim, and witness in "An Error in Chemistry." In the sheriff's interpretation of the initial crime scene, Flint's real intended victim Pritchel appears to play the role of the witness, an appearance that deceives the sheriff and that ultimately makes it possible for the murderer also to play the role of the witness when Flint kills Pritchel and assumes his identity. As the narrator says at one point in commenting on the resemblance in physical build of Flint and Pritchel, "he and his father-in-law could easily have cast that same shadow which later for a short time they did" (110), and we know that for Faulkner the image of the shadow almost always evokes the notion of doubling.

Victim as witness, murderer as witness—it is as if the roles of the two people actively involved in the crime (murderer and victim) had been collapsed into that of the passive observer (and indeed, the dynamic principle at work here is a kind of death drive that seeks a state of quiescence, of absolute passivity, for the self). Moreover, it is not without significance that the persons who fill these three roles are already linked together in a triangular family relationship as father-in-law, son-in-law, and daughter, the male-male-female structure of the Oedipal triangle. (We might note that in Faulkner's fiction a locked room or a closed door often signifies the site not of a murder but of a primal scene, a fantasized scene of parental intercourse in which the child interprets the sounds of lovemaking as the sounds of violence perpetrated by the father against the mother.) At one point in the tale, Gavin Stevens gives his own reading of the triangular structure of the crime as a kind of shadow-play, "That triumvirate of murderer, victim, and bereaved—not three flesh-and-blood people but just an illusion, a shadow-play on a sheet—not only neither men nor women nor young nor old but just three labels which cast two shadows for the simple and only reason that it requires a minimum of two in order to postulate the verities of injustice and grief" (121).

But at this point we should pause and ask ourselves if Faulkner hasn't in fact performed another illusion before our very eyes in regard to the "locked-room" character of the story, another disappearing act as startling as the murderer's switching places with the victim in the role of the witness. We suggested a moment ago that when the deputy arrives at Pritchel's home the morning after Flint's escape and stations himself outside the locked bedroom door, he confronts in effect a locked room mystery, finds an internally sealed space that is the scene of a murder, though in this instance the sealed space contains the living body of the killer rather than the dead body of the victim. Yet isn't it precisely upon that difference in the degree of animation of the room's occupant that the "mystery" in a locked-room problem hinges? Corpses can't lock doors, so to find a corpse alone in a room whose doors and windows have been locked from the inside is mysterious. But where's the mystery in finding the internally sealed space occupied by a living murderer, even if that murderer is disguised as the victim he has done away with in that locked room? The only thing that might resemble a mystery here is how Flint got out of the locked jail cell and then into Pritchel's locked bedroom to kill him, but as we said, Faulkner finesses that problem by making Flint an escape artist. What Faulkner has done in effect is to switch, under the reader's nose, the type of problem that lies on the other side of the locked door. He has set up a situation that bears the obvious marks of a locked-room puzzle, but when we open that locked door we find that it has changed into a hidden-object problem.

Instead of a purloined letter, the object that everyone is seeking in Faulkner's tale is the missing killer. However, like the purloined letter, whose appearance was altered by turning it inside out, readdressing it to the Minister D—— in a feminine hand, and then leaving it in plain view in the Minister's drawing room, the killer has also altered his appearance and hidden himself in plain sight. And just as part of altering the purloined letter's appearance was the turning of the letter inside out, so part of altering the murderer's "appearance" in Faulkner's tale is the turning of the locked-room mystery's spatial coding of killer and victim inside out. Which is to say that the person who should be outside the internally sealed space (the killer) is inside it, and the person who should be inside that space (the victim) is outside it (buried under the feed room in the stable).

From what we have said so far it should be clear that Faulkner was a profound student of the origin and conventions of detective fiction and that he wrote his own detective stories with an eye to situating them within the tradition of that genre that had been originated by a fellow southerner almost a hundred years before. However, what we must add is that while it may be interesting to discuss a tale like "An Error in Chemistry" in terms of its manipulation of traditional detective story devices and thus Faulkner's inflection of the genre's origin in Poe, that is, interesting to give a reading of it in terms of literary history, it is much less satisfying to read "An Error in Chemistry" simply in terms of the pleasures of a standard detective story. For the tale is marred in two important ways.

First, Faulkner's decision to make the killer a former vaudeville illusionist and escape artist inevitably strikes the reader as being itself a kind of vaudeville trick, an illusion that lets Faulkner escape from the traditional challenge of coming up with a solution to the locked-room problem different from the one which Poe originated. As any student of the genre knows, this is a challenge to which detective story writers have consistently addressed themselves over the years. (Indeed, one might note in passing that if the author of a detective story is going to allow himself the liberty of making the killer an illusionist and escape artist, then he might as well go all the way and make his killer the invisible man or superman. A large part of our interest in murder mysteries depends upon the killer's being someone with ordinary human powers like you and me—not a ghost or a creature from outer space.) Second, the way in which Flint's imposture is revealed and his capture effected is not the result of Gavin Stevens's analytic investigations but of an accident: Flint disguised as Pritchel makes the mistake of mixing a cold toddy in Stevens's and the sheriff's presence by trying to dissolve the sugar in raw whiskey, the kind of mistake that a southerner like Pritchel would never make, but that the northerner Flint would. Seeing this, Stevens and the sheriff leap upon Flint, wrestling him to the floor and wrestling him out of some of his make-up—a climax that leaves the reader with the feeling that he has witnessed, if not a *deus ex machina*, at least an instance of *justitia ex ampulla*, justice poured out of a bottle.

All of which leads me to suggest that as a writer of detective fiction Faulkner is most successful when he takes the conventions of the genre and shapes them to his own materials, his own obsessive concerns, rather than when he competes with the genre's originator on terms that are almost wholly Poe's. The reason for this is fairly straightforward. Faulkner's strengths as a fiction writer tend to be in the direction of character and setting and in the poetry of the language, while the detective story is a form that essentially favors plot and has a low tolerance for highly developed characterization or highly evocative language. Indeed, in the history of the genre one finds not great characters but rather great caricatures. From Dupin to Holmes to Poirot, we are confronted not with fully-rendered personalities but with monsters of idiosyncrasy, figures conveyed through one or two odd traits as trademarks. Yet to say that the detective story is a form which essentially favors plot is not to imply that Faulkner has a weakness when it comes to plotting; it is simply to say that the specialized kind of plot which forms the core of the genre demands a type of ingenuity that was the great strength of the genre's inventor, but not of Faulkner, as "An Error in Chemistry" and several of the other tales in *Knight's Gambit* make clear. It is only when Faulkner pushes the detective story to the limits of the short story form that he is able to bend it to his own artistic will, as he did with the tale that gives the collection its title. And it is on the story called "Knight's Gambit" that I would like to focus the rest of my discussion.

Faulkner originally wrote "Knight's Gambit" as a short story, completing it by January 1942. He described it as "a love story, in which Stevens prevents a crime (murder) not for justice but to gain (he is now fifty plus) the child-hood sweetheart he lost 20 years ago" (Blotner, 2:1097). Some four years later in early 1946, Faulkner began revising and expanding the tale, stretching it from short story to almost novella length before it was completed in November 1948. What I would like to concentrate on is the way that Faulkner took two devices that originated with Poe—the imagery of a chess game used to evoke the battle of wits between detective and criminal, and the notion of the detective's having a personal motive for becoming involved in the solu-tion or prevention of the crime—and, by annexing these devices to standard Faulknerian material, made them his own.

The action of "Knight's Gambit" begins on the evening of December 4, 1941, three days before the Japanese attack on Pearl Harbor. Gavin Stevens and his nephew Chick Mallison are playing chess at home when a young man named Max Harriss and his sister burst into the room. The brother and sister are the spoiled children of Melisandre Backus Harriss, a childhood friend of Chick's mother. Max Harriss has come to demand that Stevens, as the county attorney, take action to get Captain Sebastian Gualdres out of their house, to have him deported if need be. Young Harriss says that Gualdres, an Argentine fortune hunter whom the Harriss family had met dur-ing their foreign travels, was at first engaged to his sister but has since jilted her and intends to marry his mother. Harriss wants Gavin Stevens to inter-vene, challenging the older man by asking, "You're the Law here, aren't you?"[4] And Harriss implies that if Stevens doesn't act, then he (Harriss) will take matters into his own hands and kill Gualdres.

The situation is a familiar one in Faulkner's fiction. A young man con-fronts his father or a father-surrogate (an older man who represents author-ity, who embodies a patriarchal Law) and demands to know what the older man is going to do about the womenfolk, whether he intends to protect the young man's sister or mother from an interloper, which is to say, to protect the womenfolk from themselves. One thinks of Quentin Compson and his father in *The Sound and the Fury* and of Henry and Thomas Sutpen in the story that Quentin helps narrate, *Absalom, Absalom!*. And indeed the father-son analogy certainly applies to the confrontation between Gavin Stevens and Max Harriss. For as we learn in the course of the story, Stevens had been briefly and secretly engaged to Harriss's mother when she was a girl of sixteen, and the implication is that, had they married, Stevens would have been the father of her son, much as he is to become her present son's step-father by the story's end. Moreover, young Harriss's real father, a New Orleans bootlegger, was murdered, and just as the role of Max's father has been vio-lently vacated once before, so now Max is threatening to make it violently vacant once again by killing the man who plans to marry his mother—a state of affairs that, given Stevens's feelings about Max's mother, is not lost on the county attorney. Which is simply to say that when young Harriss presents himself to Stevens in a situation that we recognize from other Faulkner fiction as being that of a son confronting a father to demand that the father exer-cise paternal authority, he is, from Stevens's point of view, in effect chal-lenging Gavin to exhibit his *own* qualifications to fill the role of stepfather, challenging him to exhibit an authority that is not only able to protect the womenfolk by repulsing the intruder but also able to make the son obey the paternal will by not breaking the Law, by not killing the prospective step-father—a matter of no small importance if Stevens himself ultimately intends to fill that role.

Part of the tale's artistry is that, by having Harriss and his sister interrupt Gavin's and Chick's chess game in order to tell their story, Faulkner is able to assimilate the details of their story to the imagery of chess and thus able to evoke young Harriss's challenge to Stevens in chivalric terms, to present it as a contest, a joust, between a younger and an older knight. As I mentioned earlier, chess is associated with the detective genre from the very beginning. In the first Dupin story, "The Murders in the Rue Morgue," the narrator cites the game as an example, along with draughts and whist, to illustrate the workings of that analytic power which he considers the essence of detection, and in the third Dupin story, "The Purloined Letter," Poe presents us with a scenario that is strongly reminiscent of a chess game—there is a king and queen, and there is a battle of wits between two knights (Dupin is a *Chevalier*, and we must assume that his double, the Minister D——, is at least of equal rank), a battle for possession of a letter that concerns the queen's honor and that could, in the Minister's hands, reduce the queen to being a pawn. Given the game's presence at the genre's origin, it is not surprising that the image of a chess game is one of the most frequently used figures for the battle of wits between detective and criminal in the form's history, a figure of the detective's attempt to double the thought processes of his opponent so as to end up one move ahead of him. This doubling of an opponent's thoughts, in which one mentally plays out possible moves, countermoves, and responses against an antithetical mirror-image of one's own mind, at once reflects the kind of thinking that goes on in a chess game and is reflected in turn by the physical structure of the game itself in which the opposing pieces at the start face each other in a mirror-image relationship.

Faulkner would have been exposed to an especially interesting example of the association of chess with both the detective genre and the image of chivalry in the project that he worked on in late 1944—the screenplay of Raymond Chandler's *The Big Sleep*, on which he collaborated with Leigh Brackett and Jules Furthman. Chandler's detective Philip Marlowe always keeps a chessboard in his apartment with a problem laid out on it. At one point in the novel, Marlowe returns home to find that there is another kind of problem laid out in his apartment—his client's daughter, the nymphoma- niacal Carmen Sternwood, naked in his Murphy bed with monkey business in mind. Predictably enough, Marlowe's chivalrous spirit immediately turns to thoughts of chess: "I went . . . across the room . . . to the chessboard on a card table under the lamp. There was a problem laid out on the board, a six-mover. I couldn't solve it, like a lot of my problems. I reached down and moved a knight."[5] Several moments later, he adds, "The move with the knight was wrong. I put it back where I had moved it from. Knights had no mean- ing in this game. It wasn't a game for knights" (146). Yet for all his tough talk Marlowe doesn't take advantage of his client's mentally unstable daughter.

Indeed, Chandler had always thought of Marlowe as a kind of modern knight-errant: the detective in search of the solution like a knight in quest of the Grail. Chandler had named an earlier version of his detective Mallory, alluding to the author of the *Morte D'Arthur;* and references to Arthurian romance fill the novels. In *The High Window,* for example, Marlowe is described as a "shop-soiled Galahad";[6] while in *Farewell, My Lovely* Velma Valento, the woman that Marlowe has been in quest of throughout the novel, hides her identity behind the name Helen Grayle. And of course one of the Marlowe novels is even named *The Lady in the Lake.* The tone of Marlowe's slightly ironic, somewhat battered chivalry is set at the very beginning of *The Big Sleep,* when he comes to the home of his client General Sternwood and notices above the front door a "stained-glass panel showing a knight in dark armor rescuing a lady who was tied to a tree and didn't have any clothes on . . . he was fiddling with the knots on the ropes that tied the lady to the tree and not getting anywhere. I stood there and thought that if I lived in the house, I would sooner or later have to climb up there and help him" (1).

It is a short step from Chandler's Marlowe (read Malory), a chess-playing detective and modern knight-errant who uses his wits to uphold his personal code of chivalry, to Faulkner's Gavin Stevens, another chessplaying detective whose own chivalrous nature (as evidenced in his encounters with Eula Varner Snopes and her daughter Linda) is evoked by his Christian name's suggestion of King Arthur's nephew and most famous knight, Gawain. (Recall in this regard that the failed knight in Faulkner's 1926 gift-book for Helen Baird, *Mayday,* is named Galwyn.) But the difference is that where Chandler and Faulkner both use the game of chess, with its kings and queens and knights, to evoke the chivalrous character of their detectives, Faulkner, with an eye to the game's presence at the origin of the genre in Poe's Dupin stories, also uses the game to evoke that basic structure of the analytic act which both chess and detection share—that alogical attempt to project an image of the opponent's mind as an antithetical mirror-image of one's own mind so that one can anticipate the opponent's next move and end up one jump ahead of him, a form of mirror doubling that, as we said, is reflected in the physical structure of the game itself. Indeed, at one point Faulkner alludes to this mirror-image aspect of chess when he has Gavin reply to Chick's apparent dismissal of chess as "a game" by remarking, "Nothing by which all human passion and hope and folly can be mirrored and then proved, ever was just a game" (192).

Faulkner evokes the structure of mirror doubling shared by chess and analytic detection at the very start of "Knight's Gambit." When Max Harriss and his sister burst into Gavin's study, interrupting the chess game, Chick remarks almost in passing that the brother and sister look so much alike that "at first glance they might have been twins" (135). Now there is an obvious appropriateness in having a brother and sister who look like twins interrupt a game whose physical structure involves a mirror-image symmetry in the opening alignment of the pieces, an alignment that evokes the opposing black and white chessmen as antithetical twin images of each other. And this appropriateness was to become even greater some eight years after the appearance of "Knight's Gambit" when, with the publication of *The Town* in 1957, we learn that one of the chessplayers in this scene, Gavin Stevens, is himself a twin.[7] Gavin's twin sister Margaret is Chick Mallison's mother, and as Chick implies on several occasions in *The Town* the twinship of his mother and uncle seems almost to involve their knowing each other's thoughts—apropos the kind of mental doubling associated with analysis in chess. Thus, when the Harrisses burst in on the chess game between Gavin and Chick, a brother and sister who look like twins confront a man who is playing a game of mirror-image symmetries against the son of his twin sister. And what all this twinning and mirroring is ultimately meant to make the reader notice is that the relationship between Captain Gualdres and Max Harriss is the mirror image, the antithetical double, of the relationship between Gavin Stevens and Chick Mallison.

In each case there is an older man and a younger: in one instance the older man is a father-figure for the younger (Gavin and Chick), while in the other the older man aspires to a role that would involve his becoming a father-figure for the younger (Gualdres and Max). And in both cases the father-figure's task is to bring the young man from adolescence to maturity, to conduct a kind of rite of passage by establishing, through a veiled, and sometimes not so veiled, competition with the young man, the older man's authority to instruct him, a paternal authority able to command the young man's respect and thus allow him to learn from the older man. But while this instructive competition or competitive instruction has been eminently successful in the case of Gavin and Chick (Chick not only respects his uncle, he idolizes him), it has been a disaster in the case of Gualdres and Max.

The competition in the latter case turns upon skills that are quite literally knightly—riding, fencing, and romantic dalliance. As Max Harriss's sister describes it to Stevens, her brother is "the rich young earl" and Gualdres "the dark romantic foreign knight that beat the young earl riding the young earl's own horses and then took the young earl's sword away from him with a hearth-broom. Until at last all he had to do was ride at night up to the young earl's girl friend's window, and whistle" (183). One senses a sexual overtone to the first two of these knightly skills (riding a horse and using a sword) that is made explicit in the third, and one further senses that this competition between the older and younger man for the affection of the same woman (the young Cayley girl) is a displacement of the Oedipal struggle initiated by Gualdres's aspiring to marry Max's mother. But where the instructive competition between Gualdres and Max involves skills that are literally knightly, the competitive instruction between Gavin and Chick involves a sublimation of knightly combat into the mental combat of chess and into the verbal fencing that accompanies Gavin's and Chick's games. Indeed, to emphasize the parallel between these two types of combat, Faulkner has Chick momentarily best his uncle in a discussion of the relative sensitivity of younger men and older men and has Gavin reply, "All right. . . . *Touché* then. Will that do?" (174). But then Gavin beats Chick again at chess and becomes sarcastic, and Chick says that Gavin would probably have a better game by playing against himself, "at least you'd have the novelty of being surprised at your opponent's blunders" (176). To which Gavin replies, "All right, all right. . . . Didn't I say *touché?*" (176).

The fact that Chick every so often scores a hit in his verbal fencing with Gavin suggests why this competitive instruction of the nephew by the uncle works so well, for though Chick may come to the end of these encounters feeling chagrined, he never feels hopeless or humiliated, never feels that he hasn't had some degree of success in making his uncle treat him like a man. But it is precisely a sense of humiliation that Max Harriss continually feels in his encounters with Gualdres, for in just those areas in which Max most prides himself (riding and fencing), Gualdres beats him as if he were a child. Or as Max's sister says, "it wasn't even because of Mother. It was because Sebastian always beat him. At everything" (181). It is worth noting here, as regards the kinship of Gavin and Chick, that in those cultures with communal rites of passage for young men, the relative usually given the responsibility for the young man's initiation to adulthood is the maternal uncle rather than the father, the communal wisdom apparently being that the Oedipal tensions between father and son are such that a male relative from the mother's side of the family is a more effective initiator of the son, particularly if the initiation ceremony involves, as is usually the case, the son's symbolic death and rebirth.

The artistry involved in Faulkner's assimilation of the knightly combat of Max and Gualdres to the mental jousting of Gavin's and Chick's chess games depends in large part, of course, upon the fact that the game of chess, according to virtually every psychoanalytic reading of its structure and symbolism, is a ritual sublimation of father murder played out as the checkmating of the king. The word "checkmate" is from the Persian "shah mat," the king is dead. As the psychoanalyst and chess master Reuben Fine points out, since "genetically, chess is more often than not taught to the boy by his father, or by a father substitute," it naturally "becomes a means of working out the father-son rivalry."[8] And as another chess critic has noted, "chess is a matter of both father murder and the attempt to prevent it. This mirror function of chess is of extreme importance; obviously the player appears in both a monstrous and a virtuous capacity—planning parricide, at the same time warding it off; recreating Oedipal fantasy, yet trying to disrupt it. Yet the stronger urge is the monstrous one; the player wants to win, to kill the father rather than defend him."9

It is because Gavin has done his work so well in sublimating Oedipal tension, in conducting his nephew from adolescence to maturity through a prolonged rite of passage symbolically evoked by their combative encounters across the chessboard, that Gavin is able to outwit Max Harriss, prevent the son from breaking the patriarchal law by killing the prospective stepfather, and establish his own right to fill the role of stepfather by virtue of his having commanded the son's respect and obedience. And the agency by which Gavin establishes his authority over Max Harriss is in some sense his relationship with Chick, establishes this authority not merely in the sense that he has demonstrated his ability to be an enabling father-figure in his shepherding of Chick from boyhood to manhood, but in the sense that he has literally created through his relationship with Chick a bright young adult who is his devoted helper, an assistant bright enough to know when patriarchal commands must be obeyed and when they must be set aside. And this latter knowledge is crucial, for it is Chick, of course, who brings Gavin the piece of information that allows him to foil Max's plan—the information that Rafe McCallum had sold his wild stallion to Max that afternoon—brings it to his uncle even though Gavin is shut up in his study working on his translation of the Old Testament, that labor of twenty years which no one is allowed to interrupt once he has closed his study door, as Chick says, "nor man woman nor child, client well-wisher or friend, to touch even the knob until his uncle turned it from inside" (207). But Chick has come to maturity as a young man so confident of his own judgment, or rather, so confident of his uncle's respect for his judgment, that he bursts into the study and disturbs his uncle in order to deliver the piece of information that he senses is somehow critical (though he himself doesn't quite know how), disturbs this imposing, white-haired father-figure in the task of translating the patriarchal law.

Together with McCallum, Gavin and Chick hurry to the Harriss mansion aiming to thwart Max's plan, and it is part of the wittiness of Faulkner's plot that the method which Harriss has chosen to eliminate his intended victim constitutes a kind of double entendre, evoking that sexual overtone to the chivalric skill of horseback riding that we mentioned earlier. Gualdres owns a blind mare that he keeps in a separate stable at the Harriss place and that he rides every night, but the people of Jefferson have come to feel that the mare is itself a blind to cover Gualdres's nightly romantic adventures, that Gualdres has trained the mare to gallop around the empty paddock at night at varying gaits as if it were being ridden so as to conceal the fact of its rider's absence in search of young women. The humor of Max's plan turns upon his having removed the mare from its stable and substituted McCallum's wild stallion, so that when Gualdres comes for his (k)nightly ride, he'll find an animal that will jump up and down on top of him rather than the reverse— a switch in the gender of the animal to be ridden that smacks faintly of French farce, as if the seducer had gotten by mistake into the husband's bedroom rather than the wife's. No doubt, Max considers this an appropriate demise for the expert rider and swordsman who had galloped his horse up to the Cayley girl's veranda and tried to beat Max's time. (We might note in passing that horseback riding as a sexual metaphor was used more than once by Faulkner during this period. In the film version of *The Big Sleep*, which Faulkner worked on between writing "Knight's Gambit" as a short story and rewriting it as a novella, Philip Marlowe and Vivian Rutledge, played by Humphrey Bogart and Lauren Bacall, engage at one point in a verbal fencing match in which they appraise each other's romantic possibilities as if they were sizing up the physical abilities of racehorses. Having given her estimate of Marlowe, Vivian Rutledge invites Marlowe to reciprocate, and he says, "Well, I can't tell till I've seen you over a distance of ground. You've got a touch of class, but uh . . . I don't know how . . . how far you can go." To which she replies, "A lot depends on who's in the saddle." One recalls that when Faulkner first met Lauren Bacall during the filming of *To Have and Have Not* he told an acquaintance that "Bogie's . . . new girl friend" was "like a young colt" [Blotner, 1156].)

Gavin, of course, saves Gualdres from entering the dark stable and having his brains bucked out, and Faulkner evokes their confrontation as a kind of chivalric combat between the two prospective suitors of the widow Harriss, a duel in which Gualdres's knightly skills are no match for Gavin's prowess in intellectual jousting honed over the chessboard. With a certain *noblesse oblige,* Gavin begins the conversation in the native tongue of his rival, and Faulkner underlines the at once humorous and knightly character of their encounter by having Chick remark that he could understand some of the Spanish because he had read *Don Quixote* and *The Cid.* Gavin structures this verbal exchange as if it were a wager: he bets Gualdres that he doesn't want to enter the darkened stable. And for this life-saving piece of information, Gualdres agrees to marry the young Harriss girl and take her away with him, thus leaving the widow Harriss free for someone else.

And it is with this final ploy of Gavin's that we can see most clearly that other device which Faulkner took from Poe's Dupin stories to use in "Knight's Gambit"—the detective's personal motive for becoming involved in the solution or prevention of the crime. The trajectory of the development of the detective genre within the Dupin stories runs from the pole of physical violence in the first story (the brutal murder of a mother and daughter by a killer ape) to the pole of intellectual violence in the third story (the mental victimization involved in the blackmail of the queen by the Minister D——). And just as the movement from the first to the third Dupin story seems to involve a muting of the form, a sublimation or attenuation of the crime's violence, so this movement also involves a progressive simplification or reduction of what constitutes the mysterious element in the tale. In the first Dupin story, "The Murders in the Rue Morgue," we are not only confronted with the problem of "who done it," or more precisely "what done it," but also with the problems of "how he done it" (the locked room mystery) and "why he done it" (the senseless savagery of the crime). But by the time of the third Dupin story, "The Purloined Letter," we know at the outset who took the letter, how he took it, why he took it, and what use he intends to make of it. The only mystery is how the Minister D—— has concealed the letter in his home so that the police can't find it.

It is as if the inventor of the genre in producing a series of detective stories had to find an ongoing challenge to his ingenuity in order to spur his imagination to new heights, and that that challenge was to see how much he could pare away or reduce the mysterious element in the tale, the element that needed solution, and still have a detective story. But what happens in "The Purloined Letter" is that with the attenuation of the mysterious element in the crime, its reduction to a single, circumscribed problem, a mysterious element from another quarter enters the story toward the end to fill the vacuum—the mystery of the detective's motive for taking the case. For though at first it seems that Dupin becomes involved in the affair of the letter because he is being well-paid or because he is a supporter of the queen's cause (both of which are true), we learn at the end that the real reason for his taking the case is that he has an old score to settle with the Minister D——. The Minister had done Dupin "an evil turn" once in Vienna which Dupin told the Minister

"quite good-humoredly" he would remember (3:993). Consequently, Dupin
goes to the trouble of retrieving the letter himself from the Minister's residence, so that he can substitute for it a duplicate letter informing the Minister
who it was that made the switch and brought about his downfall.

Something very like this scenario of creating a new source of mystery
from the detective's motives, as the mysterious element in the crime is being
reduced to a bare minimum, occurs in "Knight's Gambit." We know at the
start by his own admission who the prospective killer is, we know the
intended victim and the reason for the crime, and we know that it will be
committed within a few days. The only thing we don't know is how it will
be done. But as those standard mysterious aspects of the crime are being
pared away in the course of the story to a single problem, another mystery is
emerging, the problem of the identity of the man who was secretly engaged
to Max's mother when she was a girl of sixteen. The realization that it was
Gavin Stevens comes about simultaneously with our realizing that Gavin's
involvement in preventing the murder has not been simply in an official
capacity, but rather has been a personal involvement in order to win the
hand of the woman he was once engaged to. For if he allows Max's plan to
succeed, then as county attorney he will have to handle the case, and I think
that it is still conventional wisdom in the South, as elsewhere, that the best
way to advance one's suit with a wealthy widow is not to prosecute her only
son for first-degree murder.

But Gavin's problem is more difficult than that, for there are two other
obstacles—the lovestruck daughter and the foreign suitor. And the solution
that Gavin works out makes us realize how early in the affair he had begun
planning to turn matters to his own ends if the situation permitted, how
early he had begun to think of the matter not as a chess game but a chess
problem, as Faulkner suggests when he has Gavin, at the end of the evening
when first Max Harriss and his sister and then Miss Harriss and the Cayley
girl interrupt his chess games, sweep the board clean and set up a chess problem "with the horses and rooks and two pawns" (192). Of course, in Gavin's
personal chess problem, the object is not to checkmate the king (indeed, it is
precisely that Oedipal content he tries to repress), but rather to capture the
queen. And the alignment of pieces in his problem is somewhat different
from the one he sets up on the board for Chick: there are two dark knights,
one older, one younger (Gualdres and Max), one white knight (the white-
haired Gavin, read Gawain), a young dark queen (Max's sister), an older white

queen (the widow Harriss), and one white rook (the widow's property). The solution goes like this: in exchange for Gavin's saving his life, the older dark knight settles for the young dark queen and half the white rook, or as Gavin puts it, "a princess and half a castle, against some of his bones and maybe his brains too" (218). And in exchange for Gavin's saving Max's life as well, which is to say, for Gavin's preventing him from committing murder and perhaps being executed, the young dark knight acknowledges Gavin's authority and accepts that penalty which small town prosecutors have for years offered to local boys as an alternative to being charged with a first offense—he joins the army. (Indeed, part of Faulkner's wit in setting the story on the eve of America's entrance into the Second World War is the way that this allows him to bundle up all the Oedipal conflict, adolescent mischief-making, and chivalrous yearning for desperate glory and ship it off to the front in the persons of Max, Gualdres, and Chick.) With all the obstacles removed from his path, the white-haired knight rides up to the empty castle and captures the white queen.

But we should have expected this conclusion in a story named "Knight's Gambit," for while there is no chess opening called "the knight's gambit," Chick does tell us that his uncle's favorite opening move was pawn to queen four, that is, the first move of the queen's gambit. And Gavin had said to his nephew during one of their chess games, when Chick had forked Gavin's queen and rook, that in that situation you should always take the queen and let the castle go because "a knight can move two squares at once and even in two directions at once," but "he cant move twice" (176). Chick later applies this remark about the knight's being able to move in two directions at once to Gualdres's attentions to both the widow Harriss and her daughter, but surely Faulkner means for the reader to apply the remark to another knight who in one move was able to carry out his public duty by preventing a murder and at the same time accomplish the most personal of goals, the winning of a wife.

In his reworking of this device of the detective's personal motive for involving himself in the investigation, as in his annexing of the imagery of chess to the detective story, Faulkner shows his debt to Poe, but he also shows how far he could expand and develop such devices when he joined them to the kind of material that was closest to his imagination, thus revealing himself not only as a worthy successor but a formidable competitor of the genre's originator.[10]

NOTES

1. Joseph Blotner, *Faulkner, A Biography,* 2 vols. (New York: Random House, 1974), 1201. All subsequent quotations from Blotner are taken from this edition.

2. Edgar Allan Poe, *Collected Works of Edgar Allan Poe,* ed. Thomas Ollive Mabbott, 3 vols. (Cambridge, Mass.: Harvard University Press, 1969–78), 2:551.

3. William Faulkner, "An Error in Chemistry" in *Knight's Gambit* (New York: Random House, 1978), 113. All subsequent quotations from "An Error in Chemistry" are taken from this edition.

4. William Faulkner, "Knight's Gambit" in *Knight's Gambit* (New York, Random House, 1978), 137. All subsequent quotations from "Knight's Gambit" are taken from this edition.

5. Raymond Chandler, *The Big Sleep* (New York: Random House, 1976), 144. All subsequent quotations from *The Big Sleep* are taken from this edition.

6. Raymond Chandler, *The High Window* (New York: Random House, 1976), 161.

7. William Faulkner, *The Town* (New York: Random House, 1961), 45, 181, 302, 305.

8. Reuben Fine quoted in Alexander Cockburn, *Idle Passion: Chess and the Dance of Death* (New York: Simon and Schuster, 1974), 42.

9. Cockburn, 101.

10. This essay was originally delivered as a paper at the seventeenth annual Faulkner and Yoknapatawpha Conference at the University of Mississippi. The author wishes to thank Professors Evans Harrington, Ann J. Abadie, and Doreen Fowler for inviting him to participate in the conference. A longer version of this essay will appear in the volume of papers from the conference to be published by the University of Mississippi Press.

Madame Bovary and *Flags in the Dust*: Flaubert's Influence on Faulkner

PHILIP COHEN

Along with works by Conrad, Dickens, Shakespeare, Keats, and Melville, Flaubert's *Madame Bovary* (1856) is a book which William Faulkner repeatedly claimed he read once a year.[1] While doubting the complete veracity of Faulkner's formulaic answers to the routine question concerning his favorite writers, critics have, nevertheless, acknowledged Faulkner's enormous respect and admiration for Flaubert. Generally, comments on the nineteenth-century novelist's influence on Faulkner have been extremely brief and limited to the example Flaubert set as a dedicated craftsman trying to achieve the perfect style.[2] Cleanth Brooks has speculated that Faulkner may have drawn on *The Temptation of Saint Anthony* for "the visionary scene experienced by Elmer in Venice [in Faulkner's unfinished and posthumously-published *Elmer*], a piece of prose Faulkner liked so well that he incorporated some of it in *Mosquitoes*" and may have made use of Emma Bovary for his

Reprinted with permission from *Comparative Literature Studies* 22 (fall 1985): 344–61.

creation of Charlotte Rittenmeyer in *The Wild Palms;* Caroline Gordon's 1948 essay "Notes on Faulkner and Flaubert," however, has given more than a cursory glance at the relationship between the two novelists, examining Faulkner's lyrical modification in "Spotted Horses" of Flaubert's use of detail.[3] More recently, Albert J. Guerard in *The Triumph* of *the Novel* has offered a series of brief but extremely illuminating comments on the affinities between *Madame Bovary* and *Sanctuary.* [4]

Flaubert's *Madame Bovary* provided Faulkner with more than an example of artistic integrity, however; it probably also served as a model for the Horace Benbow-Belle and Harry Mitchell triangle in Faulkner's *Flags in the Dust,* his third novel and his first in the Yoknapatawpha County cycle (called Yocona County in the novel), which appeared in a badly cut and edited form in 1929 as *Sartoris.*[5] The illicit relationship between Horace and Harry's wife, Belle, seems to be indebted to Léon's adulterous relationship with Charles Bovary's wife, Emma, for essential elements of character and plot. The absence in *Sartoris* of much material dealing with Horace and Belle's adultery obscures both the relationship between *Flags in the Dust* and *Madame Bovary* and Faulkner's growing mastery which enabled him to transform the *Bovary* material, using it to broaden his treatment of post-World War I despair and alienation in *Flags in the Dust:* Horace is as cut off from the community of Jefferson as the returned aviator Bayard Sartoris and Byron Snopes are. This expansion in the scope of *Flags in the Dust* may be seen especially in Faulkner's portrait of Horace Benbow, which draws upon and transforms elements of *Madame Bovary* and which was also heavily cut in *Sartoris.*[6] Faulkner's imagination may have fused specifically southern details with some of the essential characteristics of Belle and Harry Mitchell which he probably derived from *Madame Bovary,* but his treatment of Horace in *Flags in the Dust* demonstrates that he was not merely rewriting Flaubert's novel, southern style, in part of his own.[7] Flaubert's novel probably exerted some influence on *Flags in the Dust's* realism and anti-bourgeoisie sentiments; it may even have been a contributing factor in Faulkner's decision, after exploring postwar Georgia in *Soldiers' Pay* and literary New Orleans in *Mosquitoes,* to return to the land he knew best, his own northern Mississippi, in his third novel.

Faulkner's use of *Madame Bovary* in *Sanctuary,* in which he returned to Horace and his relationships with Narcissa, Belle, and especially little Belle, suggests that he may have drawn upon Flaubert's novel when he initially dealt with this material in *Flags in the Dust.* In the original text of *Sanctuary,* three direct allusions to *Madame Bovary* occur. Early in the novel, Horace meditates on why Belle divorced her husband, Harry, in order to marry him. Perhaps, he speculates, it was "because Harry insisted on calling her Little Mother in public."[8] Emma Bovary is similarly irate with her husband, Charles, for calling her "little mamma" during her pregnancy.[9] In *Flags in the Dust*, Faulkner had used the same allusion: there Harry "called Belle 'little mother' until she broke him of it" (TS, 296; FD, 174; S, 187). On their way to Goodwin's house, Popeye suddenly crouches against Horace, "clawing at his pocket and hissing through his teeth like a cat" as an owl wings by. "He smells black," Horace thinks to himself, "he smells like that black stuff that ran out of Bovary's mouth and down upon her bridal veil when they raised her head" (OS, 25). Horace here refers to the moment in Flaubert's novel when Madame Bovary senior and Madame Lefrancois lift Emma's head while dressing her in her wedding gown in preparation for her laying out (MB, 259).

The image of that poisonous black liquid sullying the bridal veil, an emblem of innocence—which it does not do in *Madame Bovary*—excited Faulkner's imagination as a potent symbol for the power of corruption, and he made use of it a second time in Chapter 5 when Horace's quasi-dream about his long-dead mother turns into a nightmare:

> She had been an invalid, but now she was well; she seemed to emanate that abounding serenity as of earth which his sister had done since her marriage and the birth of her child, and she sat on the side of the bed, talking to him. With her hands, her touch, because he realized that she had not opened her mouth. Then he saw that she wore a shapeless garment of faded calico and that Belle's rich, full mouth burned sullenly out of the halflight, and he knew that she was about to open her mouth and he tried to scream at her, to clap his hand to her mouth. But it was too late. He saw her mouth open; a thick black liquid welled in a bursting bubble that splayed out upon her fading chin and the sun was shining on his face and he was thinking He smells black. He smells like that black stuff that ran out of Bovary's mouth when they raised her head. (OS, 60)

In this surreal vision of evil's corruption of innocence and purity, Faulkner combines Ruby's calico dress, Belle's sullen mouth—the connection between Emma Bovary and Belle is made explicit here—Popeye's black suit, and Emma's black vomit to create a microcosmic scene symbolic of the entire novel's thematic import: the discovery of the power and pervasiveness of evil.

Although the second reference to *Madame Bovary* survived into the 1931 *Sanctuary,* the first reference and Horace's nightmare vision did not, nor did a more oblique reference to *Madame Bovary* in which Horace thinks of Belle "as she moved there in a series of pictures rich with sullen promise; thinking of that aura of voluptuous promise with which sheer discontent can invest another's wife" (OS, 65).[10]

More difficult than demonstrating *Madame Bovary's* influence on work besides *Flags in the Dust* is trying to determine exactly when Faulkner first read the novel. Faulkner claimed he was influenced by Flaubert, and the evidence suggests he initially read *Madame Bovary* in the early 1920s.[11] Perhaps Faulkner's friend and mentor Phil Stone included a translation of *Madame Bovary* along with the numerous other works of poetry and fiction that he loaned Faulkner in the early years of their friendship, or perhaps Faulkner read the novel while working at the Doubleday bookstore in Lord & Taylor's New York store in 1920. The possibility also exists that Faulkner first read the novel in French: he told a Japanese audience in 1955 that he had taught himself French by "reading Flaubert, Balzac, Laforgue, and Verlaine,"[12] and indeed he took courses in French during the University of Mississippi's 1919–1920 academic year and published adaptations of four Verlaine poems in *The Mississippian* in early 1920. His 1922 *Mississippian* essay on Eugene O'Neill mentions *Madame Bovary,* but no one, to my knowledge, has observed that Faulkner mistakenly locates the action of the novel in the Rhone valley, southeastern France, instead of in Normandy, northwestern France:

> Some one has said—a Frenchman, probably; they have said everything—that art is preeminently provincial; i.e., it comes directly from a certain age and a certain locality. This is a very profound statement; for Lear and Hamlet and All's Well could never have been written anywhere save in England during Elizabeth's reign . . . nor could Madame Bovary have been written in any place other than the Rhone valley in the nineteenth century. [13]

Either Faulkner had not yet read the novel, or his first reading of it, whether in French or in English, had not been a thorough one. Faulkner may even have read *Madame Bovary* during his 1925 travels in Europe, possibly while he was in France, where he visited Rouen and doubtless learned it had been the birthplace of Flaubert and had provided the locale for *Madame Bovary.*[14] All we say now with any certainty, as I will show here, is that

Faulkner was thoroughly conversant with *Madame Bovary* by the time he wrote *Flags in the Dust.*[15]

Flaubert's portrait of Emma Bovary, of a narrowly provincial bourgeoisie obsessed with "the lusts of the flesh, the longing for money, and the melancholy of passion" (MB, 83), reappears in the essential features of Harry Mitchell's unfaithful wife, Belle. Belle resembles Emma in her unrestrained sexual passions, pervasive materialism, and thwarted romantic aspirations for a refined lover and a genteel life of refinement. Sensual to the point of corruption, Belle is as "cannily stupid" as Emma Bovary (TS, 277; FD, 159; S, 178). Like Emma, Belle is a voluptuous woman deficient in intellect and driven by her physical desires, even though Horace and she apparently refrain from sexual intercourse until after her divorce. Described as "a hot-house bloom, brilliant and petulant and perverse" (TS, 284; FD, 167; not in S), Belle with her "scented flesh," her eyes like "hothouse grapes," and her mouth "redly mobile, rich with discontent" (TS, 287; FD, 168; S, 183) is as sensuous in nature as Emma. Her perfume and "rich voluption" (TS, 415; FD, 243; S, 257) exude an odor so powerful that Horace believes himself saturated with it. Desirous of those "marvels where all would be passion, ecstasy, delirium" (MB, 126), both Emma and Belle embark on an increasingly frantic course of deceit and corruption in their devotion to an ideal of passionate, sexual love.

Both women share a pervasive materialism. Like Emma, whose extravagant purchases from Monsieur Lheureux ultimately lead to her undoing, Belle is essentially a provincial bourgeoise who desires money and the style of life it engenders. A southern nouveau riche possessed of Emma's social aspirations, Belle lives in a horrifyingly ugly house and lacks any genuine sense of taste. Before obtaining her divorce, Belle asks of her lover, "Have you plenty of money, Horace?" (TS, 416; FD, 243; slightly different in S, 257); when she realizes his "Of course I have" (TS, 416; FD, 243; S, 257) was a lie, her love for Horace becomes sullen rage, revealing the grasping avarice beneath her genteel pretensions. In fact, the new town in southern Mississippi (called Kinston in *Sanctuary*) where Horace and Belle live after her divorce in a rented house next to a rented garage is notable for only one attribute:

> Yes, there was money there, how much, no two estimates ever agreed; whose, at any given time, God Himself could not have said. But it was there, like that afflatus of rank fecundity above a foul and stagnant pool on which bugs dart spawning die, are replaced in mid-darting; in the air, in men's voices and gestures,

seemingly to be had for the taking. That was why Belle had chosen it. (TS, 542; FD, 342; not in S)

Belle's bourgeois nature also reveals itself in her dissatisfaction with her own class and in her pretensions to a refined world. Here, too, she resembles Emma who yearns for a more genteel, less common existence than her life in Tostes and later Yonville as the wife of a rural doctor affords her. We first meet Belle entertaining some of Jefferson's ladies with a card party at which she serves "edible edifices copied from pictures in ladies' magazines and possessing neither volume nor nourishment" (TS, 35; FD, 24; S, 27). After educating "the group in which she moved to tea as a function in itself and not as something to give invalids or as an adjunct to a party of some sort" (TS, 284; FD, 168; not in S), Belle also holds afternoon teas near Harry's tennis court at which even Harry is obliged to take his cup.

Like Emma, Belle is portrayed as a sullen and fiercely discontented woman who turns to deception and adultery in a futile attempt to find the romance with which her good-natured but oafish husband fails to provide her. During little Belle's piano and dance recital, little of which appears in *Sartoris,* Belle constantly glowers "with cold and blazing irritation, enveloping, savage, disdainful of who might see" as "the heavy thump-thump-thump of Harry's heels" sounds above everyone while he takes the men upstairs to the bathroom for a drink (TS, 319; FD, 186; not in S). Presumably, Belle married Harry for his money, but now her romantic illusions are affronted by his lack of gentility. Belle's discontent with Harry, a leit-motif in the novel, appears whenever Horace thinks of her. Just as Emma forsakes Charles for Léon, whom she perceives as a far more refined figure, so Belle leaves her husband for someone she believes is a real poet, not merely the "son of a carpenter, of whom Belle had made a poet" earlier (TS, 285; FD, 168; not in S). Ironically, the genteel Horace possesses neither money nor a romantic passion for Belle, the two things she desires in a lover; similarly, Emma finds not love but disillusionment in her affairs.

A vain poser like Emma, Belle too is often engaged "in the unflagging theatrics of her own part in the picture" (TS, 283; FD, 167; not in S). While her sister Joan harbors no sentimental notions whatsoever, Belle indulges in shallow romantic posturings, playing "saccharine melodies" on a piano with "a sense for their oversweet nuances" (TS, 309; FD, 180; S, 194) and "building with her hands and for herself an edifice, a world in which she moved romantically, finely, and a little tragical" (TS, 309; FD, 180; slightly different in S, 194). Faulkner underscores this point when Belle informs Horace, "I want to have your child" and then rushes madly away from him in fear when her own child comes quietly into the room (TS, 311; FD, 181; S, 195).[16] While Harry fawns on little Belle clumsily, Belle treats her daughter just as cruelly as Emma does Berthe. Always telling little Belle to go somewhere else and play, Belle seems only too glad to give Harry custody in order to obtain her divorce earlier. Deceiving others, self-deceived, and deceived by others—she cheats on Harry, entertains seriously the notion that Horace is her ideal lover, and is enraged when Horace tells her of his affair with Joan—Belle resembles Emma who sees in her first lover, Rodolphe, an elegant man of refinement when he is merely the crassest of Don Juans.[17]

Although Belle Mitchell is, in many respects, modeled after Emma Bovary, Faulkner's southern Emma is a cruder, less subtly complex portrait of a rural bourgeoisie than Flaubert's. Because Emma descends gradually into a pit of depravity during the course of *Madame Bovary* while Belle appears completely corrupt from the beginning of *Flags in the Dust,* the latter is more transparently a vulgar prostitute. Certainly Belle struggles not at all over whether to have an affair, whereas Emma does. Belle's comparative lack of complexity may derive from her role in the novel as a minor character; Faulkner does not provide the interior portrait of her mind which Flaubert gives us of Emma. As revealed by his creation of Belle, however, Faulkner's reading of *Madame Bovary,* while not doing justice to the intensity of Emma's desires, is essentially correct: Belle is every bit as "irritable, greedy, voluptuous" (MB, 215) as Emma Bovary.

In *Madame Bovary,* Emma's husband is characterized as a slow-witted, kind-hearted provincial physician whose lack of elegance and refinement irritates her. So wanting in perceptiveness is Charles that he never realizes that his wife loathes him and never suspects that she has been unfaithful to him until the end of the novel when he discovers the love-letters which both Léon and Rodolphe had written her. In his ignorance, Charles even plays the eager cuckold: he "persuades" Emma to stay in Rouen without him to see the rest of *Lucia de Lammermoor,* at Léon's urgings. Nevertheless, Charles is one of the few characters in *Madame Bovary* who is basically good-intentioned. Lacking the meanness of soul which his neighbors and his wife possess, he forgives Emma's slights and insults because he loves her so intensely. Flaubert's emphasis on Charles's love for Emma and Berthe provides a foil to

Emma's lack of love for Berthe and himself, a constant reminder of Emma's pride and stony heart. Ultimately, Charles provides the only touches of pathos in the novel, most notably when his grief over Emma's death reduces him to a bankrupt, broken man.

Harry Mitchell, Faulkner's relatively prosperous cotton speculator who has the misfortune of being married to Belle, may owe his origins as much to Flaubert's novel as to Faulkner's imagination and observation. Like Charles, Harry is hen-pecked and slow-witted and clumsy. With "his squat legs and his bald bullet head and his under-shot jaw of rotting teeth" (TS, 296; FD, 174; S, 187), Harry is the antithesis of the romantic lover Belle so ardently desires. At little Belle's recital, Harry's "stridently, tactlessly overloud" voice (TS, 315; FD, 183; not is S) brays above the guests as he carelessly scatters cigarette ash and clumsily embraces little Belle. As Harry becomes progressively drunker, his trips to his upstairs liquor supply grow more and more audible and embarrassing to Belle. Like Charles, Harry is completely ignorant of his wife's true feelings toward him and is on very friendly terms with his wife's lover, who is his favorite tennis partner.

In Faulkner's novel, as in Flaubert's, the cuckolded husband remains basically good-natured despite his coarseness: "He would give you the shirt off his back. . . . he was ugly as sin and kindhearted and dogmatic and talkative" (TS, 296; FD, 174; slightly different in S, 187). Devoted to his wife—"I'd kill the man that tried to wreck my home like I would a dam snake" he tells Horace (TS, 303; FD, 178; slightly different in S, 191)—Harry also worships little Belle, treating her with awkward but sincere affection. Faulkner manipulates Harry's unreturned love for pathos, highlighting Belle's proud disdain for little Belle and him. Just as Charles is broken by Emma's death and the revelation of her love affairs, Harry's life crumbles when he discovers Belle is leaving him for another man: he becomes a picture of dumb suffering with his "dogged inarticulateness and his hurt groping which was partly damaged vanity and shock, yet mostly a boy's sincere bewilderment, that freed itself terrifically in the form of movie subtitles" (TS, 415–16; FD, 243; S, 257; also see TS, 547; FD, 346; not in S). When young Bayard Sartoris sees Harry drunk and preyed upon by an unscrupulous woman and a waiter in a Chicago speakeasy, the man's situation is as pathetic as Charles's rapid and complete deterioration in *Madame Bovary*.

The one substantial difference between Charles and Harry lies in Faulkner's presentation of the latter as a provincial nouveau riche. Here we may see Faulkner's imagination at work fusing onto the *Bovary* material his own interest in the social and economic developments of the postwar South. Whereas Charles never rises above the petit-bourgeoisie, Harry is financially successful: he first appears in "tight flannels and a white silk shirt and new ornate sport shoes that cost twenty dollars per pair" (TS, 296; FD, 174; S, 187), and shortly thereafter, he shows Horace a new repeating rifle and presses "upon him a package of cigarettes which he imported from South America" (TS, 305; FD, 178; S, 192). Yet despite his ostentatious dress and lack of taste, Harry is treated sympathetically by Faulkner because he has no pretensions. This highlights the petulant cruelty of Belle, for whom the author reserves his harshest anti-bourgeoisie scorn.

The transmutation that *Madame Bovary* underwent in Faulkner's imagination as he adapted it to his study of postwar alienation and deracination in *Flags in the Dust* is evident most of all in the superficial resemblance and fundamental dissimilarity between Léon and Horace Benbow. From the moment she meets him, Emma is much taken with the sensitive and bored clerk. Much given to fine talk and melancholy reverie, Léon's imagination is as conventionally romantic as Emma's: he prefers verse to prose because "it moves [the reader] far more easily to tears" (MB, 64). With his cultivated ennui and his aversion to the commonplace, Léon excites Emma's lust and her romantic yearnings.

In this description of Léon, we recognize the outer lineaments of Horace Benbow, Faulkner's bored and poetic lawyer. Like Léon's, Horace's affair with another man's wife is founded primarily upon his inability to resist her intense sexuality. Yet compared to Horace, Léon remains a shallow romantic poseur who breaks off his affair with Emma when his Rouen employer is about to promote him to head clerk: ". . . it was time to settle down. So he gave up his flute, exalted sentiments, and poetry; for every bourgeois in the flush of his youth, were it but for a day, a moment, has believed himself capable of immense occupations, of lofty enterprises" (MB, 226). Léon reveals his hard bourgeois nature when circumstances no longer flatter his exalted view of himself. And while Léon's imagination is as vulgar as Belle's, Horace possesses a poetic sensibility, even if it is that of an "arty," decadent, late nineteenth-century aesthete. Horace has far more intelligence, as well as imagination, than Léon; unlike the French clerk's initial infatuation with Emma, he never harbors any illusions about Belle: his pursuit of her is motivated solely by his lust.

Like Belle in comparison to Emma, Flaubert's Léon suffers when placed next to Faulkner's Horace. In Horace's relationship to Narcissa and to Belle and Harry Mitchell, Faulkner employed *Madame Bovary* to explore postwar enervation and his recurrent concern with the fate of the tormented Prufrockian idealist who simultaneously desires and recoils from life and from sexuality. A victim of repressed sexuality, like his sister Narcissa, Horace is excessively genteel and idealistic. Equating sex with filth, he divides women into two categories according to whether or not they refrain from sex: pure angels like Narcissa and prostitutes like Belle. He is a sexual innocent attracted to young girls like little Belle because of their virginal quality—much like Quentin Compson's befriending the little Italian girl in *The Sound and the Fury*. Horace's relationship with his sister is threatened and ultimately ended by his response to Belle's sexual allure. While his conscious intellect recoils in horror from Belle's corruption, his repressed sexuality drives him into her arms, into "shadowy shapes of dread and of delight not to be denied" (TS, 326; FD, 190; not in S). Initially trapped between the two opposed impulses of his sexuality, Horace is driven onward until he becomes Horace Benbow, "Carrier of Shrimp" (TS, 546; FD, 345; not in S). Because so few of Horace's interior meditations and actions appear in *Sartoris,* however, Faulkner's transformation of the *Bovary* material is obscured. The Horace of *Sartoris* seems little more than a conventional, world-weary figure of the fin-de-siècle tradition, little more than the pose which Léon assumes in *Madame Bovary.*[18]

Flaubert's influence on *Flags in the Dust* extends beyond Faulkner's use of elements of *Madame Bovary's* characters and plot. In *Madame Bovary,* Flaubert created one of the first great realistic novels, both in his painstaking attention to detail and in his ironic presentation of character. The novel has its romantic elements, which Faulkner would have found congenial, but frequently Flaubert's chilly irony provides a counterpoint to the shabby, often romantic illusions of his characters, revealing their genuine hypocrisy and avarice. This realism is often produced by juxtaposing an omniscient narrator's detached point of view with the more limited one of a character passionately giving voice convincingly and lyrically to his own dreams and desires with an astonishing lack of self-knowledge. If Faulkner early in his literary career was a late romantic poet of poses who frequently served up these personae without much irony and created landscapes more reminiscent of nineteenth-century England than of Mississippi, his fiction reveals a more realistic impulse which often exposes the illusions of his characters and roots them firmly in his own region. This development can be traced to Faulkner's reading of any number of authors—including specifically Balzac, Conrad, Joyce, Anderson—as well as to his growing personal maturity. Given the more specific influence of *Madame Bovary* on *Flags in the Dust* and *Sanctuary*, it is reasonable to suggest that Flaubert also played some role in Faulkner's developing use of irony in the interests of realism. *Flags in the Dust* is not as bitter a book as *Madame Bovary*—or *Sanctuary*—nor is Faulkner's narrative persona as impersonal as it is in *Sanctuary* or as Flaubert's is in his novel. Nevertheless, characters in *Flags in the Dust* frequently display a surprising amount of ignorance about themselves, and an omniscient narrator must supply the corrective of irony. That Faulkner borrowed from Flaubert's depiction of Emma his own juxtaposition of Belle's romantic illusions and her petulant cruelty to her child makes this suggestion all the more plausible.

As in *Sanctuary*, Flaubert's presence may also be detected in the anti-bourgeoisie sentiments of *Flags in the Dust*. A radical critique of the French provincial bourgeoisie, the small merchants and businessmen of Yonville, *Madame Bovary* portrays the lives of stunted characters who are all, in varying degrees, shallow, greedily materialistic, and self-important. Lacking any spiritual dimension and any genuine compassion, people like Rodolphe, Léon, the Abbé Bournisien, the tax-collector Binet, the pharmacist Homais, and Lheureux at times differ from each other only in the degree of their meanness. Despite Emma's scorn for them, she remains a member of her class. She at least possesses strong desires and a modicum of imagination, trashy as it may be; nevertheless, as the central figure of the novel, Emma outdoes all the others in mediocrity, vanity, and avarice.

A similar distrust of the bourgeoisie, especially of the bourgeoisie as capitalist, characterizes Faulkner's life and work, early and late. With his aristocratic, traditional leanings and his mixture of sympathy and admiration for the poor and the dispossessed, Faulkner frequently pilloried the middle classes in his fiction for their intolerant and hypocritical morality and their spiritual meanness: Jason Compson, Goodhue Coldfield, Flem Snopes all reveal their creator's antipathy for the petty-bourgeoisie especially. More than mere literary attitudinizing on his part, this stance stems not only from Faulkner's reading of nineteenth-century French novelists such as Balzac and Flaubert and of the English and French Symbolists, but also from his family heritage and from the literary climate of the time: such an attitude of *épatez le bourgeoisie* flourished among American artists and intellectuals during the 1920s.[19]

Still, Faulkner's debt to *Madame Bovary,* which I have sketched here, suggests that Flaubert's novel gave Faulkner a successful example to which he could refer in his own attempts to give his indictment of the middle classes artistic voice in *Flags in the Dust* and in *Sanctuary.* This is more clearly the case with *Sanctuary* than with *Flags in the Dust,* but the latter also deals with middle-class corruption. One thinks primarily of Faulkner's critical attitude towards Horace's futility and his overly-refined and repressed sister Narcissa, of his scathing portrait of Belle Mitchell, and of the new town to which Horace and Belle move after her divorce, a town unconnected to any sort of tradition and in which everything is an imitation of something else. Especially drawing out Faulkner's contempt is the town's courthouse building, "an edifice imposing as a theatre drop, flambuoyant [*sic*] and cheap and shoddy; obviously built without any definite plan by men without honesty or taste. It was a standing joke that it had cost $60,000, and the people who had paid for it retailed the story without anger, but on the contrary with a little frankly envious admiration" (TS, 541; FD, 341; not in S). Here "every fourth year the sheriff's office sold at public auction for the price of a Hollywood bungalow" and "the very air smelled of affluence and burning gasoline" (TS, 542; FD, 342; not in S). Doubtless, Faulkner's depiction of the new commercial class owes much to the great gallery of misers, bankers, and usurers created by Balzac, another novelist whom Faulkner especially admired, in novels such as *Les Paysans, Grandeur et Décadence de César Birotteau,* and *Eugénie Grandet,* and in novellas such as *La Maison Nucingen* and *M. Gobseck.*[20] Nevertheless, Faulkner's delineation of the crass, grasping bourgeoisie in the postwar wasteland of *Flags in the Dust* may be connected to his reading of *Madame Bovary.*

Madame Bovary may also have assisted Faulkner in turning toward the regional, toward his native Mississippi, in *Flags in the Dust.* A frequent critical position attributes Faulkner's discovery of his "own little postage stamp of soil" and his decision to create the cosmos of Yoknapatawpha by "sublimating the actual into the apocryphal"[21] to the example which Sherwood Anderson set in his work, most notably in *Winesburg, Ohio,* and to the advice which he gave the young Faulkner in New Orleans.[22] Faulkner himself inaugurated this view in his 1953 *Atlantic Monthly* essay on Sherwood Anderson. There Faulkner recalls a conversation with Anderson in which the older writer told him:

"You have to have somewhere to start from: then you begin to learn," he told me. "It dont matter where it was, just so you remember it and aint ashamed of it. Because one place to start from is just as important as any other. You're a country boy; all you know is that little patch up there in Mississippi where you started from. But that's all right too. It's America too; pull it out as little and unknown as it is, and the whole thing will collapse, like when you prize a brick out of a wall."[23]

Michael Millgate has been the most recent critic to suggest that Faulkner's third novel and the creation of Yoknapatawpha may owe much to Balzac. Millgate writes that Balzac's example "may still be discernible in the social structuring of *Sartoris/Flags in the Dust*" and that "the Balzacian concept of a systematically organized fictional world with novels of Parisian life, novels of provincial life, and so on, intertwined with a multiplicity of recurring characters, deliberately designed to demonstrate the complex interlocking of all the classes of society and the pervasiveness throughout them all of the same pattern of human folly" assisted Faulkner in attempting his own *Comédie Humaine* in the Yoknapatawpha cycle, even though Faulkner did not, in fact, adopt Balzac's scheme in full.[24]

That *Madame Bovary* as well as Balzac was on Faulkner's mind as he wrote both *Flags in the Dust* and *Sanctuary* leads to speculation about the role it may have played in the genesis of Faulkner's fictional cosmos. As early as his 1922 essay on O'Neill and despite his error about the setting of *Madame Bovary,* Faulkner was contemplating in Shakespeare, Balzac, and Flaubert the lesson that the path to the universal and the permanent in art runs through the regional and the transient. Although Faulkner never truly applied this lesson to his poetry, which remained restricted to capturing an ideal, pure essence in words, his achievement as a novelist rests on this principle. While apprentice fiction such as "Moonlight," "The Hill," and "Adolescence," which Faulkner wrote in the early 1920s, already reveals a shift from the imaginary pastoral landscapes of his poetry to recognizably southern settings, it is also worth remembering that the full title of Flaubert's novel is *Madame Bovary; moeurs de province* or, as Marx-Aveling translated it in 1886, *Madame Bovary; provincial manners,* a sub-title which could easily be applied to *Flags in the Dust* with equal accuracy.

I suspect that the young Faulkner admired Flaubert not only for his consummate style and artistic integrity but also for his regionalism, his realism, and his ability to construct a realm of the imagination out of the innumerable details and memories which Flaubert recalled from his childhood in Rouen, and that the novel may have been one of several determinants which conditioned, in *Flags in the Dust,* Faulkner's return to his own northern Mississippi with its possum hunts, sugar cane mills, and afternoons filled with slanting sunlight and corn whiskey. Granted, Flaubert deals almost exclusively with the provincial petty bourgeoisie in *Madame Bovary* whereas Faulkner, as a result of Balzac's tutelage and his own grander ambitions, examines the relationships among all the classes found in his rural society, from the southern aristocracy to the hill people. Yet *Madame Bovary,* like Balzac's novels of provincial and country life, also possesses along with *Flags in the Dust* a strong sense of place, displaying detailed attention to the rural society and land of a particular time and place, and exhibits a penchant for lyricism on its creator's part, although Faulkner's lyricism is more sympathetic towards his characters than Flaubert's. Furthermore, the incidents in both novels take place far from the turbulent developments of the respective periods in which they occur even though these developments impinge significantly on the two fictional worlds: in Flaubert's case, the rise of the French bourgeoisie; in Faulkner's case, the startling developments of the early twentieth century—the transition from a traditional, hierarchical society into a modern, democratic one, the change in the relative status of the various classes, and World War I—and the dislocation and disillusionment which followed in their wake. Both novels deal with a provincial "postage stamp of soil" wherein, nevertheless, the crucial social and cultural events of their respective ages are mirrored. In *Flags in the Dust,* Faulkner drew extensively for the first time upon the legends and history of his family and upon the region in which he was raised. As Richard P. Adams has noted, however, this move was not in itself responsible for Faulkner's literary achievement: "Anybody can look at the old home town, but not many people can write great fiction about it. That requires a highly developed technique because what a writer knows the most about is precisely what is hardest for him to render imaginatively."[25] Faulkner's use in *Flags in the Dust* of the familial and the regional on the one hand, and Eliot, Balzac, and Flaubert on the other, suggests that he was aware of this problem and searching for its solution, that he was developing a technique sophisticated enough to transmute the autobiographical and local material he was exploring. The greatest service which *Madame Bovary* performed for Faulkner at a crucial period of his artistic development may have been in providing an example of how a gifted talent could transform local color into universal art of the first magnitude.

In 1956, Faulkner told Jean Stein vanden Heuvel, as he repeatedly observed to other interviewers, that every writer is a thief, that "the writer's responsibility is to his art. He will be completely ruthless if he is a good one. . . . Everything goes by the board: honor, pride, decency, security, happiness, all, to get the book written. If a writer has to rob his mother he will not hesitate; the Ode on a Grecian Urn is worth any number of old ladies."[26] In his poetry, Faulkner's "thefts" from Swinburne, Housman, T. S. Eliot, and the French Symbolists are often put to use in skillful exercises which remain, nevertheless, derivative exercises. Even *Soldiers' Pay* and *Mosquitoes* remain self-consciously literary works. Faulkner's appropriation of *Madame Bovary* in *Flags in the Dust,* an appropriation which is not fully evident in *Sartoris,* attests to its creator's ability to master rather than be mastered by an influence, to his swift literary development which soon enabled him to write the novels of his first great creative period.

NOTES

1. William Faulkner, *Faulkner in the University,* ed. Frederick L. Gwynn and Joseph L. Blotner (Charlottesville: University of Virginia Press, 1959), 50; and *Lion in the Garden: Interviews with William Faulkner,* ed. James B. Meriwether and Michael Millgate (1968; reprint, Lincoln: University of Nebraska Press, Bison Books, 1978), 110, 217, 234, and 251.

2. See, for example, Joseph L. Blotner, *Faulkner: A Biography, Vol. I* (New York: Random House, 1974), 459; and Richard P. Adams, "The Apprenticeship of William Faulkner," *Tulane Studies in English* 12 (1962); reprint in *William Faulkner: Four Decades of Criticism,* ed. Linda Welshimer Wagner (East Lansing: Michigan State University Press, 1973), 30. Adams mentions Faulkner's respect for Flaubert's style but admits that he has not "been able to make out that Faulkner used Flaubert directly to any great extent in his own fiction" (30). In "Faulkner's Masters," *Tulane Studies in English* 23 (1978), Michael Millgate writes that Faulkner "saw Flaubert as a type of the complete artist, absolutely dedicated to his craft, absolutely in control of every aspect of his work" (153). Faulkner himself initiated this view of his attitude towards Flaubert when he said, "Well, in Bovary I saw or thought I saw a man who wasted nothing, who was— whose approach toward his language was almost the lapidary's" *(Faulkner in the University,* 55).

3. Cleanth Brooks, *William Faulkner: Toward Yoknapatawpha and Beyond* (New Haven: Yale

University Press, 1978), 127, 210; and Caroline Gordon, "Notes on Faulkner and Flaubert," *Hudson Review* l:222–31. *Elmer* was recently edited by Dianne L. Cox and published in *Mississippi Quarterly*, [referred to hereafter as *MissQ*) 36 (summer 1983): 337–460.

4. Guerard suggests that Flaubert's creation of art out of the boring and the commonplace by means of a relatively impersonal narrative technique and a spare prose style which create aesthetic distance lies behind Faulkner's attempt to wring art from a brutal and ugly reality in the same manner. See Albert J. Guerard, *The Triumph of the Novel: Dickens, Dostoevsky, and Faulkner* (1976; reprint, Chicago: University of Chicago Press, Phoenix, 1982), 120, 123, and 125–31, passim. In "Faulkner and Flaubert" (*JML* 6 [1977]: 222–47), Arthur F. Kinney explores the influence of Flaubert's narrative technique upon Faulkner's own narrative strategies, of *Madame Bovary* upon *Sanctuary,* and of the *Temptation of Saint Anthony* upon *Requiem for a Nun.*

5. Random House published Douglas Day's edition of *Flags in the Dust* in 1973. Because of the textual unreliability of this edition of *Flags in the Dust* (see Thomas L. McHaney's "The Text of *Flags in the Dust,"* *Faulkner Concordance Newsletter* no. 2 [November 1973]: 7–8; and George F. Hayhoe's review-essay "William Faulkner's *Flags in the Dust,"* *MissQ* 28 [summer 1975]: 368–86), 1 have drawn my quotations in this article from the typescript of *Flags in the Dust,* which is on deposit at the William Faulkner Collection at the University of Virginia Library in Charlottesville. I am grateful to Mrs. Jill Faulkner Summers for permission to quote from this typescript. I have also used the Random House edition of *Sartoris* (New York, 1961) which reproduces by offset the 1929 Harcourt, Brace edition. Subsequent references to the *Flags in the Dust* typescript, to the Random House *Flags in the Dust,* and to *Sartoris* will be cited parenthetically in the text.

6. Horace's elegant futility in *Flags in the Dust* was shaped by Faulkner's reading of Eliot's poetry and by his friendships with Phil Stone and Ben Wasson more than it was by *Madame Bovary.* In "'The Germ of My Apocrypha': *Sartoris* and the Search for Form" *Mosaic* 7 (fall 1973): 27, James Gray Watson argues on the basis of some direct and some extremely oblique allusions to "The Love Song of J. Alfred Prufrock" and *The Waste Land* that "Faulkner drew heavily on Eliot for his portrait of Horace and in particular for Horace's relationship with Belle Mitchell." For the influence of Phil Stone and Ben Wasson on Horace Benbow, see Emily Whitehurst Stone's "How A Writer Finds His Material," *Harper's Magazine* 231 (November 1965): 158; and Blotner's *Faulkner,* 1:546. In Horace's passive aestheticism, Faulkner was probably also exploring critically a tendency in his own nature: like Faulkner himself, Horace smokes a pipe, plays tennis, and likes to wear his wartime uniform around Jefferson even though he was a noncombatant. In two recent notes, Linda E. McDaniel argues that in *Flags in the Dust* Faulkner borrowed from Keats's *Endymion* for his characterization of Horace and from Keats's *Hyperion* and *The Fall of Hyperion: A Dream* for his creation of the Sartoris myth (see "Horace Benbow: Faulkner's *Endymion,"* *MissQ* 33 [1980] : 363–70 and "Keats's Hyperion Myth: A Source for the

Sartoris Myth," *MissQ* 34 [summer 1981]: 325–33). McDaniel's argument, however, makes use of many tenuous verbal parallels, and she ignores entirely Faulkner's exploitation of familial and the regional sources in *Flags in the Dust.*

7. In his presentation of Horace's illicit affair with the discontented wife of a prosperous cotton speculator in *Flags in the Dust,* Faulkner was also returning to and drawing upon a similar triangle in his unfinished novel *Elmer.* In *Elmer,* Elmer Hodge, a would-be painter, is a sensitive young man who idealizes women, like Horace, as a result of a platonically incestuous childhood relationship with his sister Jo-Addie who provides him with the love his parents fail to offer. Like Horace, Elmer also has an affair with a voluptuous, corrupt female. When Ethel becomes pregnant by Elmer, he offers to marry her. In order to live the life of a prosperous bourgeoisie, however, Ethel instead marries a successful, insincere businessman named Grover and suggests that Elmer leave town. Many differences exist between these two triangular relationships, but the essential similarities arc striking. While the number of specific plot and character parallels between the Benbow triangle and Flaubert's novel suggests that Faulkner had *Madame Bovary* in mind when he wrote *Flags in the Dust,* it is conceivable that his portrayal of Ethel in *Elmer is* also indebted to Flaubert's novel. Years later, Faulkner created another similar triangular relationship in *The Wild Palms,* where Harry Wilbourne takes Charlotte Rittenmeyer away from her husband, Bradley, who is also a successful businessman. Thomas L. McHaney notes echoes of *Elmer* in *The Wild Palms* in "The Elmer Papers: Faulkner's Comic Portraits of the Artist," *MissQ* 26 (summer 1973); reprint in *A Faulkner Miscellany,* ed. James B. Meriwether (Jackson: University Press of Mississippi, 1974), 45–48, and in *William Faulkner's "The Wild Palms": A Study* (Jackson: University Press of Mississippi, 1975), 21–22n. 46.

8. William Faulkner, *Sanctuary: The Original Text,* ed. Noel Polk (New York: Random House, 1981), 16. Subsequent references to this edition will be cited parenthetically as "OS" in the text.

9. Gustave Flaubert, *Madame Bovary,* trans. Eleanor Marx-Aveling (New York: Boni & Liveright, 1918), 67. All subsequent references to *Madame Bovary* will be to this edition and will be cited parenthetically in the text.

10. That *Sanctuary* is Faulkner's bitterest novel is a critical commonplace. In its tone and in its exploration of the hypocrisy and meanness lurking beneath bourgeois respectability, *Sanctuary* was doubtless also shaped somewhat by Faulkner's reading of *Madame Bovary,* a novel populated with a gallery of despicable petty bourgeois characters. Joseph Blotner hints at this connection when he writes that Faulkner conceived the original text of *Sanctuary* as "a spectacular mystery-detective-gangster story, a commercially successful novel, and a work of art which would mirror the corruption of society at large in the lives of a small number of people from different levels of society. (There had been something of this in that novel Faulkner so admired, Flaubert's *Madame Bovary.)*" See Blotner, *Faulkner,* 1:606.

11. See Loic Bouvard's 1952 interview with Faulkner in *Lion in the Garden,* 72. Other references to Flaubert and *Madame Bovary* in *Lion in the Garden* may be found on pages 135 and 157. For Faulkner's comments on the same at the University of Virginia, see *Faulkner in the University,* 55–56, 150, and 160. Providing no answer to the question of when Faulkner first encountered *Madame Bovary* are the two uninscribed volumes by Flaubert which were in Faulkner's cottage at Knole, the estate of Mr. and Mrs. Summers in Charlottesville, Virginia, when he died: Frances Steegmuller's 1957 Random House translation of *Madame Bovary* in a Modern Library edition and an undated *Complete Unabridged Novels: "Madame Bovary," "The Temptation of Saint Anthony"*—it also includes *Salammbo* published by Greystone Press of New York. See Joseph L. Blotner, comp., *William Faulkner's Library—A Catalogue* (Charlottesville: University Press of Virginia, 1964), 94. So far, my efforts to find the exact publication date of the Greystone Press volume have been unsuccessful, but the firm first began publishing in 1936 (See *Publishers Weekly* 132 [16 January 1937]: 232).

12. William Faulkner, *Lion in the Garden,* 135.

13. William Faulkner, *William Faulkner: Early Prose and Poetry,* ed. Carvel Collins (Boston: Little Brown, 1962), 86. The essay entitled "American Drama: Eugene O'Neill" appeared in the "Books & Things" column of the University of Mississippi's newspaper *The Mississippian.*

14. Carvel Collins has recently offered the tantalizingly undocumented assertion that in 1925, while in France, Faulkner wrote in a French copy of *The Temptation of Saint Anthony* "an angry attack, accusing it of shaming *Madame Bovary.* He ended his paragraph of vituperation by thanking God that Flaubert had died" (See Carvel Collins, "Biographical Background for Faulkner's Helen," in *Helen: A Courtship and Mississippi Poems,* by William Faulkner [Oxford, Miss. and New Orleans: Yoknapatawpha Press and Tulane University Press, 1981] , 56.) Collins also notes Faulkner's use of *The Temptation of Saint Anthony* in *Elmer* and in *Mosquitoes* (30).

15. Because *Flags in the Dust* borrows elements of character and plot rather than specific passages from *Madame Bovary,* I have not been able to tie Faulkner's allusions to a particular text of Flaubert's novel. Since they were Faulkner's first publishers, I have referred to Boni and Liveright's 1918 edition of the novel, which uses the popular Eleanor Marx-Aveling translation first published in 1886 (London: Vizetelly).

16. In his memoir *Count No 'Count: Flashbacks to Faulkner* (Jackson: University Press of Mississippi, 1983), the late Ben Wasson writes that this scene was based upon an incident which occurred at the Oldhams's house and which he later related to Faulkner. Sometime before Faulkner wrote *Flags in the Dust,* Estelle Franklin returned to Oxford from Honolulu with her daughter Victoria for a short visit. Wasson recalls a spontaneous romantic encounter with Estelle in the Oldham music room after she finished playing the piano, an encounter which Victoria's sudden appearance in the room interrupted. Later that night Wasson told Faulkner about the incident. Wasson does not date his account, but he says that Estelle was still living in Honolulu

and brought only Victoria with her. Malcolm Argyle Franklin was born on December 3, 1923, in Shanghai, so Estelle's visit no doubt preceded Malcolm's birth. Blotner records that in May of 1921, Estelle and Victoria visited Oxford for a month, and that later that year the Franklins moved from Honolulu to Shanghai *(Faulkner,* 1:306, 315). Since the Oldhams visited the Franklins in Honolulu during the summer of 1920, it would seem that the incident Wasson relates occurred during the summer of 1921 (see *Count No 'Count,* 81, 84).

17. In Horace's weekly trips to fetch the shrimp which Belle so ardently craves, Faulkner presents a summation of her essential nature which was lost during the cutting of *Flags in the Dust.* Before the days of refrigeration and deep-freezing, shrimp were a delicacy. Because shrimp are highly perishable, decaying rapidly after they die, only those who lived within a few miles of where the shrimp were taken could enjoy them. That Belle prefers shrimp above all other foods thus becomes significant in several ways. By the time Horace picks them up, the shrimp have already begun to decay, and their rank smell merging with Belle's own heavy scent acts as an emblem of her corruption, as well as that of the town to which she has brought him. Furthermore, having shrimp regularly shipped in on ice from Gulfport must be costly, given Horace's difficulty in making ends meet, and so reveals Belle's expensive tastes and selfishness. Finally, her demanding such a delicacy reflects her bourgeois desire for gentility. Horace's fetching of Belle's shrimp is one of the more memorable scenes in *Flags in the Dust*—Faulkner made use of the same material though not the same passages in *Sanctuary*—and perhaps the inspiration for the scene may stem from Rodolphe's musings about one of his mistresses in *Madame Bovary* as well as from Faulkner's own experiences in New Orleans and Pascagoula: "Virginie is decidedly beginning to grow fat. She is so finikin with her pleasures; and besides, she has a mania for prawns" (MB, 101). (Patricia A. O'Hara of Rutgers University pointed this passage out to me.)

18. By portraying Horace passively drifting with open eyes towards his fate, Faulkner broadened his treatment of the "special problems of the twenties and a good deal of the waste land . . . in a small southern town" in *Flags in the Dust* (Cleanth Brooks, *William Faulkner. The Yoknapatawpha Country* [1963; reprint, New Haven: Yale University Press, 1966], 114). Horace, whose problems clearly do not stem from the war, is just as doomed as young Bayard Sartoris, the returned aviator who violently seeks and finally attains release in death from his anguish over the war and the death of his twin brother, John. Numerous critics have recognized that the complementary and parallel relationships between Bayard and Horace in *Flags in the Dust* are blurred by the absence in *Sartoris* of some of the narrative material dealing with Horace. See, for example, Michael Millgate's *The Achievement of William Faulkner* (1966; reprint, Lincoln: University of Nebraska Press, Bison Books, 1978), 84–85; Cleanth Brooks, *William Faulkner: The Yoknapatawpha Country,* 103–6; Panthea Reid Broughton's "Faulkner's Fancywork," review of the Random House *Flags in the Dust, Saturday Review/World* 1 (26

January 1974): 44; and Andre Bleikastern's *That Most Splendid Failure: Faulkner's "The Sound and the Fury"* (Bloomington: Indiana University Press, 1976), 75.

19. For a detailed discussion of this phenomenon, see Frederick J. Hoffman's *The Twenties: American Writing in the Postwar Decade* (New York: The Viking Press, 1955), 304–70.

20. See my article "Balzac and Faulkner: The Influence of *La Comedie humaine* on *Flags in the Dust* and the Snopes Trilogy," *MissQ* 37 (summer 1984): 325–51.

21. William Faulkner, *Lion in the Garden*, 255.

22. See, for example, Adams, 17–18; H. Edward Richardson, "Anderson and Faulkner," *AL*, 36 (November 1964): 312; and Brooks, *William Faulkner: Toward Yoknapatawpha and Beyond*, 20. In "Faulkner's Essays on Anderson," in *Faulkner: Fifty Years After "The Marble Faun,"* ed. George H. Wolfe (University: University of Alabama Press, 1976), James B. Meriwether offers a persuasive rebuttal to this view, claiming that Phil Stone and Faulkner himself deserve as much credit as Anderson in this matter (174–75).

23. William Faulkner, "A Note on Sherwood Anderson," *The Atlantic Monthly* (June 1953), reprint in *Essays, Speeches & Public Letters*, ed. James B. Meriwether (New York: Random House, 1965), 8.

24. Michael Millgate, "'A Cosmos of My Own': The Evolution of Yoknapatawpha," in *Fifty Years of Yoknapatawpha: Faulkner and Yoknapatawpha, 1979*, ed. Doreen Fowler and Ann J. Abadic (Jackson: University Press of Mississippi, 1980), 28. In his essay "William Faulkner's Human Comedy" (*New York Times Book Review*, 29 October 1944), Malcolm Cowley was the first critic to suggest that Faulkner's Yoknapatawpha saga was "perhaps inspired by his early reading of Balzac" (4). Other notable treatments of Balzac's influence on Faulkner include Claude-Edmonde Magny's "Faulkner ou l'Inversion Theologique," in *L'Age du Roman americaine* (Paris: Editions du Seuil, 1948), 196–243 (a condensed translation of this essay appears in *Faulkner: A Collection of Critical Essavs*, ed. Robert Penn Warren [Englewood Cliffs, N.J.: Prentice-Hall, 1966], 66–78); Michel Mohrt's "William Faulkner ou Demesure du souvenir," *Preuves* 4 (April 1954): 8–14, and his *Le Nouveau roman americaine* (Paris: Gallimard, 1955), 80–123; Roxandra V. Antoniadis's "Faulkner and Balzac: The Poetic Web," *CLS* 9 (September 1972): 303–26, and her "The Dream as Design in Balzac and Faulkner," *Zagadnienia Rodzajow Literackich* 17 (1974): 45–57; Percy G. Adams's "Faulkner, French Literature, and 'Eternal Verities,'" in *William Faulkner: Prevailing Verities and World Literature*, ed. Wolodymyr T. Zyla and Wendell M. Aycock (Lubbock: Interdepartmental Committee on Comparative Literature, Texas Tech University, 1973), 10–12; and my "Balzac and Faulkner."

25. Richard P. Adams, "At Long Last, *Flags in the Dust*," review of the Random House *Flags in the Dust, Southern Review* 10 (autumn 1974): 883.

26. William Faulkner, *Lion in the Garden*, 239.

From Oxford: The Novels
of William Faulkner

RICHARD GRAY

Willliam Faulkner was born, brought up, and spent most of his life in the American South, a region which he claimed he could simultaneously love and hate—and which, he declared in later years, 'I will still defend . . . even if I hate it.'[1] Just what he felt he might be defending was not always clear. 'In the South,' Faulkner said once in an interview, 'there is still a common acceptance of the world, a common view of life, a common morality.'[2] Unfortunately, he did not go on to say what he thought that morality was. Or, again, in *Intruder in the Dust* Gavin Stevens declaims (on behalf of Southerners faced with the possibility of enforced desegregation),

> We are defending not actually our politics or beliefs or even our way of life, but simply our homogeneity. . . . only from homogeneity comes anything of a people or for a people of durable and lasting value.[3]

Reprinted with permission of the author from *American Fictions: New Readings,* ed. Richard Gray (Totowa, N.J.: Barnes and Noble, 1983): 165–83.

That still left the question unanswered, however. If, as Faulkner appeared to believe, a region or community is 'the indigenous dream of any given collection of men having something in common, be it only geography and climate,'[4] then what exactly was the dream that had given his own homeplace identity? And in what ways, more specifically, was he himself not only from but of the South?

> *Tell me about the South* [says Shreve in *Absalom, Absalom!*]
>   *What's it like there. What do they do there. Why do they live there. Why do they live at all.*[5]

In a sense, Faulkner never stopped 'telling,' since the Yoknapatawpha novels as a whole constitute an imaginative recovery of the South, an attempt to know it as a region. These novels not only tell, however, they show: much of their power derives from the fact that, in drawing us a map of his imaginary county, Faulkner is also charting his own spiritual geography. The dreams and obsessions which so startle and fascinate Shreve are his, the novelist's, and not just an aspect of described behaviour. They profoundly affect his fiction, feeding into the substance of each narrative: so that when, for instance, Quentin Compson is described in *Absalom, Absalom!* as 'a barracks filled with stubborn backlooking ghosts'[6] the reader feels that the description could equally well apply to the story itself—and to Faulkner, the master storyteller, as well as Quentin, his apprentice.

What are the dreams and obsessions that help shape the novels in this way? What intrigues Shreve, the Canadian, and compels Gavin Stevens to see the South as a homogeneous place? Perhaps the first thing that strikes anyone new to the South, Southern writing, or indeed to Faulkner, is simply that: the sense of place which hovers behind the remarks of Shreve, Stevens, and their creator—because that sense is so strong, obvious even to the outsider, and in certain ways quite unusual, even strange. As one fairly minor Southern writer has put it, 'More than any other people of the world, the Southerners have that where-do-you-come-from sense'[7]; and, with a few qualifications, one would have to agree. The environment seems to be as much a part of the Southern character as any moral, emotional, or intellectual quality is: so much so, in fact, that W. J. Cash in *The Mind of the South* comes close to making the environment—and the sultry, stormy climate that goes with it— actively responsible for the character. One need not go as far as this, however, in order to see that for Southerners a sense of belonging to what Faulkner called a 'little postage stamp of native soil'[8] is absolutely essential, if only because (to quote another Southern writer, Eudora Welty) '*feelings* are bound up in place. . . . It is by knowing where you started that you grow able to judge where you are.'[9]

To some extent, this sense of place is a widespread characteristic, to be found—if one looks only at the literature of the past hundred years—in writers as otherwise different as Hardy and Joyce, Yeats and Lawrence. And yet there is a difference, I think, between the notion of place that characterizes most Southern books, including Faulkner's, and the notion of place as it reveals itself in other writing. In English fiction, for instance in a novel like *Tess of the D'Urbervilles,* the place, wherever it may be, seems to be already established and identified, a prepared landscape structured by countless previous activities and perceptions; it is there, the impression is, for the writer to record and for the characters to enter and be defined by. In Southern writing, by comparison, there is a far more conscious, more open and deliberate sense of the landscape being structured: tamed by the particular eye that confronts it, given shape and substance by the particular imagination that comes to grapple with it in the text. So, in *Absalom, Absalom!* the landscape of Sutpen's Hundred is made by the major characters and narrators, imaginatively and sometimes also literally; each of them creates a place that gives their inner lives geographical location, a local habitation and a name. Equally, the people Faulkner describes in the inter-chapters of *Requiem for a Nun* seem to will Jefferson into being: in order, like the girl who scratches her name on a window-pane in the town jail, to leave some 'fragile and indelible' evidence of themselves on the physical universe—something that says, '*Listen, stranger: this was myself: this was I.*'[10]

Character, narrator, and also the author: in scenes like the one, say, that opens *Light in August,* a sense of place seems to be created by the seeing eye of the writer—as he observes the land over which Lena Grove travels and gradually attaches to it the notions of ceremony and permanence. Like the setting on the banks of the Mississippi River in John Crowe Ransom's poem, 'Antique Harvesters,' what appeared at first anonymous and meagre assumes a heroic significance. The calculated and, to some extent, 'high profile' language is partly responsible for this: the mules pulling the wagon on which Lena rides, for instance, are said to 'plod in steady and unflagging hypnosis,' while Lena herself is compared to 'something moving forever and without

progress across an urn.' But just as important is the emphasis Faulkner puts
on the active perception and, in effect, reinvention of this scene. Watching
the wagon, we are told,

> . . . the eye loses it as sight and sense drowsily merge and blend, like the road
> itself, with all the peaceful and monotonous changes between darkness and day,
> like already measured thread being rewound onto a spool. So that at last, as
> though out of some trivial and unimportant region beyond even distance, the
> sound of it seems to come slow and terrific and without meaning as though it
> were a ghost travelling a half mile ahead of its own shape.[11]

Here, as elsewhere in his landscapes, Faulkner seems to be inhabiting a space
that would otherwise be empty: clearing a wilderness, in his own way, and
filling 'a kind of vacuum'—as Shreve describes the South, at one point, in
Absalom, Absalom!—with solidity and spiritual presence.[12]

Of course, this difference as far as the sense of place is concerned between
Faulkner and someone like Hardy is partly a matter of impression and degree.
Ultimately, Hardy is just as much making a landscape by writing about it as
Faulkner is. But in Hardy's work, I think, the language refers us to something
that is supposed to be objectively there, more or less in its entirety, its essential patterns established and requiring only a frame: in the Yoknapatawpha
novels the writer is very much more his own explorer and topographer. Place
is far more ambiguous and fluid because, like the settings in many of Wallace
Stevens's poems, it is clearly and indeed sometimes ostentatiously (thanks to
the obtrusively figurative, oratorical idiom) the product of an interchange
between language and environment, the mind and its surroundings. It is constantly created and then re-created out of a feeling of personal need.

This is also the case with that sense of the past for which Southern writers, and again most notably Faulkner, are famous. Southern literature is, as
Allen Tate put it once, 'a literature conscious of the past in the present.'[13] At
first sight, that may not make it seem very different from other literature: an
awareness of history is not, after all, a Southern monopoly—nor was it a
Southerner who said that those who forget the past are condemned to repeat
it all the time. Here, however, as with the sense of place, there is a difference
between Southern and most other writing, because in Southern books memories are nurtured in a way that can only be described as heroic; yesterday is
much more of a living and even obtrusive presence, much more available to

recreation and change. Just as, in a way, many earlier Southerners tried to involve themselves with a tradition by consciously imitating the manners and habits of an inherited aristocracy—by living as one of them, William Byrd of Westover, put it, 'like . . . the patriarchs'[14]—so modern Southern writers have tried actively to reconstruct the past, to make a tolerable inheritance for themselves. Even more important, they have made the actual attempt to do this one of their leading subjects.

Not that every involvement with the past in the Yoknapatawpha novels takes this deliberate form: Old 'Colonel' Bayard Sartoris is introduced to us, in *Flags in the Dust,* as a man haunted whether he likes it or not, while some of the characters in *Sanctuary* and *Light in August* appear to behave like sleepwalkers, so tied to another time that they can hardly begin to function. For such people, the phrase associated with Joe Christmas in *Light in August* might serve as an appropriate epitaph—'Memory believes before knowing remembers'[15]—since they rarely seem aware that their minds have been shaped by ghosts. These characters are counterpointed, however, by others who are consciously trying to recollect and reinterpret the past: like the Southern boys described by Gavin Stevens in *Intruder in the Dust,* for whom 'yesterday won't be over until tomorrow'[16] and who feel, consequently, that it can be changed—not merely remembered but reinvented.

It is an indication, perhaps, of just how deeply embedded in Faulkner's work this idea of actively recovering the past is that it is adumbrated in his very first novel. At the center of *Soldiers' Pay* is Donald Mahon, a living corpse, badly wounded in the First World War, who has been cut off from his past by the loss of memory. He appears to be in a state of suspension, waiting for something as one of the characters observes,

> Something he has begun, but not completed, something he has carried over from his former life that he does not remember consciously.[17]

Just what that something is eventually becomes clear: towards the end of the novel Mahon remembers in detail the day on which he was wounded, and then he dies. His past has been reimagined, apparently, and since it has he can have a present; the story has been recovered, re-told, and can now be ended.

A comparable but infinitely more complicated process occurs in *Absalom, Absalom!* where character after character appears to be reinventing the past in order to create a sense of identity. A narrative that links yesterday to today is something that people like Quentin Compson and Shreve clearly yearn for, as they work together,

> creating . . . out of the rag-tag and bob-ends of old tales and talking, people who perhaps had never existed at all anywhere, who, shadows, were shadows not of flesh and blood which had lived and died but shadows in turn of what were . . . shades too, quiet as the visible murmur of their vaporizing breath.[18]

With the past as with place, the reality seems to be a kind of vacuum which the observer must populate with his own imagined inhabitants; or, if not that exactly, it is at any rate an uncharted territory containing a few clues, one or two hints and guesses, to tease even the least curious or speculative of minds. The speculations, as several critics have pointed out,[19] are the author's and reader's as well as the characters': Faulkner throws himself furiously into the process of reconstructing the Sutpen story, and the reader is so required to fill in the gaps, compare versions, and discover inconsistencies that he too becomes a historian and storyteller, actively engaged in reimagining the past. Nor is this process confined to the one novel. 'I am telling the same story over and over,' Faulkner admitted once, 'which is myself and the world.'[20] The entire Yoknapatawpha series—with its recurring characters, its repetition and revision of familiar stories, and its gradual accumulation of incident— ends up by offering us a microcosm of history in which 'nothing ever happens once and is finished'[21] either for the author or for the reader.

Quite often, one consequence of emphasizing and exploring past experience is a radical sense of human limitations. People, seen in terms of what they have done rather than what they might do, seem no longer free and perfectible but deeply flawed, weighed down by the burden of inherited failure. This, it seems, is what has happened in Southern thought and writing: a preoccupation with the past (and, of course, the fact that the South has had to suffer failure, defeat, and humiliation) has encouraged Southerners to believe that, to quote one of them, 'evil . . . is the common lot of the race.'[22] More particularly, it has prompted Southern authors to replace the Adamic hero of American legend with characters who dramatize, express, or explore the idea that 'Man is conceived in sin and born in corruption and he passeth from the stink of the didie to the stench of the shroud.'[23] Of course, outside of the American context this would not be a remarkable notion (the South did not, after all, invent the idea of Original Sin) were it not for the fact that it is usually associated with one thing in particular—the potent, if often shadowy, figure of the black. For the black brings with him, whether as slave, half-breed, or more simply as a member of an oppressed race, an unnerving reminder of inherited guilt. To the white Southerner he becomes, simply by being there on the scene, an emblem of sin, the reminder of a crime committed not so very long ago by some mythic, communal ancestor.

To the white Southerner, that is, and to the white Southern writer: it is worth emphasizing that writers like Faulkner have had some experience of the guilt they are talking about in their books. That guilt is part of their structure of thought and feeling as Southerners of a particular race, and so it invariably becomes ingrained in the texture of their work. When they come to explore evil, in fact, that exploration becomes a peculiarly self-conscious activity: which is to say self-aware, self-dramatizing, and self-critical. This comes out, I think, in a book like *Go Down, Moses:* when for instance, one of the characters Roth Edmonds feels that he can no longer sleep in the same bed as Henry Beauchamp, the black boy who has been his closest friend and constant companion up until then. There is no specific reason why Roth feels this, Faulkner tells us. It is just that

> . . . one day the old curse of his fathers, the old haughty ancestral pride based not on any value but on an accident of geography, stemmed not from courage and honour but from wrong and shame, descended to him.[24]

In effect, Roth inherits the racial bias and guilt of his ancestors and re-enacts their Original Sin. The fact that he and Henry are related, since they share the same (white) great-great-great grandfather simply compounds the sin: Roth is denying his 'brother' in a double sense, Faulkner implies, and repressing his humanity in a way that must remind the reader of both Thomas and Henry Sutpen. One could go on discussing the further reverberations of this episode: the way in which, for instance, it illustrates Faulkner's tendency to dwell on miscegenation rather than slavery as the repressed myth of the Southern past. What I want to emphasize here, however, is that the power of this incident depends on the fact that it echoes a feeling provoked by the entire narrative. The idea of the black as the bearer of a curse is at once a preoccupation of the various characters, something that helps to give them a definable identity, and part of the mythological framework of the novel in which they appear. We are invited to observe and examine the sense of doom, and we are also made to share it. And this, quite simply, is because it is an obsession of the *writer's*, not just a facet of the behaviour he describes. It is something which, having inherited, he cannot ignore or suppress—and which he is now inviting us to explore.

Self-conscious: it may be an inadequate term, but it is perhaps the best shorthand way of referring to a certain quality or set of qualities that Faulkner shares with many Southerners, especially Southern writers. The deliberate construction of a landscape, a sense of place; an urgent, dramatized recreation of the past; and the rediscovery, and the very personal and self-critical exploration, of an inherited name for evil—these can all be absorbed into the idea of self-consciousness, as long as that idea is interpreted in a fairly generous fashion. It is perhaps significant, too, that Southern history and literature constantly present us with people who are self-conscious in a more straightforward sense, and whose self-consciousness leads them into a concern with manners, ritual, and self-dramatization. Life, under the pressure of this concern, is transformed into a kind of heroic art or, less grandly, into a carefully controlled game. One thinks, in Southern history, of the sheer theatricality of so many local heroes—in fairly recent times, people like Cotton Ed Smith, Pitchfork Ben Tillman, and Huey Long. Or one thinks of that love of rhetoric, gorgeously contrived, self-aggrandizing speech, which has long been a regional characteristic. As W. J. Cash remarked, rhetoric flourished in the South,

> far beyond even its American average; it early became a passion—and not only a passion but a primary standard of judgement. . . . The greatest man would be the man who could best wield it.[25]

In Southern literature, this same interest in self-dramatization, ceremony and oratory can be found everywhere—for example, in those characters of Caroline Gordon and Eudora Welty who tend to treat life as a game or dance; in that concern with manners and ritual shown equally by John Crowe Ransom and Allen Tate; and in the abundant, apparently inexhaustible language of a writer like Thomas Wolfe.

To some extent, Faulkner's participation in all this is obvious. Of the great modern American novelists he is easily the most rhetorical and *oral,* and the one most interested in the theatrics of living. He shares with many of his characters a love of language that is nothing less than passionate—a love which is registered, among other things, in his long, labyrinthine or elaborately balanced, sentences; his metaphors that startle the reader with their bravado; his sonorous word melodies, his syntactical fluidity, and his startling juxtapositions of image and sound. Coming from a culture of the spoken word, he and people like Gavin Stevens and V. K. Ratliff (*The Hamlet, The Town, The Mansion*) are always willing to spin out a story or repeat a familiar tale, adding colour with the products of their own verbal wit and inventiveness. Both author and characters seem clearly aware, too, that this inventiveness can be applied to living as well as storytelling: which is perhaps why one of the narrators in *Absalom, Absalom!* remembers the protagonist Thomas Sutpen as a kind of actor or dancer, who willed himself into the part of gentleman. Sutpen, we are told,

> was like John L. Sullivan having taught himself painfully and tediously to do the schottische, having drilled and drilled himself in secret, until he . . . believed it no longer necessary to count the music's beat.[26]

Sutpen has his own design; he is the keystone of his own self-appointed drama. In turn, each of those trying to re-tell his story (including, of course, the reader) is firmly placed as someone attempting to write a new play built around his or her individual consciousness.

What all this tends to leave out of account, however, is the sheer slipperiness of Faulkner's attitude to language and just how far his self-consciousness could take him. Certainly, he was not averse to role-playing in the simple sense or even to playing parts himself—the plain farmer was a favourite one in later life just as 'Count Nocount,' the careless bohemian, had been in his youth—and he could be as easily seduced by words as Cash's notional Southerner. Even during the period of his greatest work, from about 1929 until 1936, he was not above committing such verbal atrocities as this, in the apparent belief that he was producing powerful rhetoric:

> Now they could cross Grandlieu Street. There was traffic in it now; to crash and clang of light and bell, trolley and automobile crashed and glared across the intersection, rushing in a light kerb-channelled spindrift of tortured and draggled serpentine and trodden confetti pending the dawn's white wings—spent tinsel dung of Momus' Nile barge clatterfalque.[27]

But most of the time that very self-awareness which prompted him to play roles, or emphasize the theatricality of his characters' behaviour, also made him acutely conscious of the dangers of words and the fictive process—made him suspect, in fact, that they might end up by disguising the subject rather than exposing it. Quite frequently, this distrust of artifice in general and the artificial structures of language in particular is attributed to a woman. 'Women,' we are told in Faulkner's first novel, 'know more about words than men ever will. And they know how little they can ever possibly mean.'[28] This is a sentiment echoed by a character in *Mosquitoes* ('They don't care anything about words except as little things to pass the time with'[29]), and either illustrated or expressed by such otherwise diverse figures as Addie Bundren in *As I Lay Dying*, Laverne Schumann in *Pylon*, Charlotte Rittenmeyer in *The Wild Palms*, and Eula Varner in *The Hamlet* and *The Town*. Even if it is not associated with a woman (occasionally, for instance, Faulkner prefers the silent figure of the sculptor or craftsman), this suspicion that 'words are no good'[30] is invariably there thickening the texture of Faulkner's writing—adding a further dimension of self-consciousness by implicitly questioning the scope and success of his own verbal constructs.

Exactly how this thickening process works can best be indicated by looking briefly at one novel; and perhaps as good an example as any in this respect is offered by *The Sound and the Fury*, the book most intimately related to Faulkner's own experience ('. . . I am Quentin in *The Sound and the Fury*,'[31] he once admitted) and the one that remained his favourite throughout his life. At the centre of *The Sound and the Fury* is Caddy Compson. She is its source and inspiration: the book began, Faulkner tells us, with the 'mental picture . . . of the muddy seat of a little girl's drawers in a pear tree where she could see through a window where her grandmother's funeral was taking place.'[32] She is also its subject: 'To me she was the beautiful one,' Faulkner said later,

> she was my heart's darling. That's what I wrote the book about and I used the tools which seemed to me the proper tools to try to tell, try to draw the picture of Caddy.[33]

She could perhaps be seen as the book's ideal audience—that is, if we accept the proposition put forward by a character in *Mosquitoes* that 'every word a writing man writes is put down with the intention of impressing some woman.' [34] It is certainly her story from which Faulkner tries to 'extract some ultimate distillation' by telling it four or five times; and in trying to capture her essence he seems to have experienced an 'emotion definite and physical and yet nebulous'[35] which, at the very least, matches the feelings he attributes to the Compson brothers Quentin and Benjy—in its intensity, that is, its ephemerality, and not least in its sexual connotations.

In short, Caddy Compson is the novel's beginning, middle, and end, the reason why it exists ('I who had never had a sister,' he declared, 'and was fated to lose my daughter in infancy, set out to make myself a beautiful and tragic little girl'[36]); and yet she seems somehow to exist apart from it or beyond it, to escape from Faulkner and all the other storytellers. To some extent, this is because she is the absent presence familiar from many of Faulkner's other novels: a figure like Donald Mahon, say, or Thomas Sutpen who obsesses the other characters but very rarely speaks with his or her own voice. Even more important, though, is the fact that she is female, and so by definition someone who tends to exist for her creator outside the parameters of language: Faulkner has adopted here the archetypal image (for the male imagination, at least) of a woman who is at once mother, sister, daughter, and lover, Eve and Lilith, virgin and whore, to describe what Wallace Stevens once referred to as 'the inconceivable idea of the sun'[37]—that is, the Other, the world outside the Self. And while she is *there* to the extent that she is the focal point, the eventual object of each narrator's meditations, she is *not there* in the sense that she remains elusive, intangible—as transparent as the water, or as invisible as the odours of trees and honeysuckle, with which she is constantly associated. It is as if, just as each narrator tries to focus her in his camera lens, she slips away leaving little more than the memory of her name and image.

Not that Faulkner ever stops trying to bring her into focus—for himself, his narrators, and of course for us. Each section of the book, in fact, represents a different strategy, another attempt to know her. Essentially, the difference in each section is a matter of rhetoric: in the sense that each time the tale is told another language is devised and a different series of relationships between author, narrator, subject and reader. The Jason section, for instance, is marked by a much greater sense of distance than the other sections. Faulkner is clearly out of sympathy with this Compson brother, even if he is amused by him (he once said that Jason was the character of his that he disliked most). Jason, in turn, while clearly obsessed with his sister and her daughter, never claims any intimacy with either of them. And the reader is kept at some remove by the specifically public mode of speech Jason uses, full of swagger, exaggeration, saloon-bar prejudice, and desperate attempts to bolster his image of himself:

> Once a bitch always a bitch, what I say. . . .
>
> I never promise a woman anything nor let her know what I'm going to give her. That's the only way to manage them. Always keep them guessing. If you can't think of any other way to surprise them, give them a bust in the jaw.[38]

By contrast, Faulkner tends to identify with Caddy's oldest brother, Quentin, to the point where the second section can become almost impenetrably private. Quentin, for his part, tries to abolish the distance between Caddy and himself—although, of course, not being insane he is less successful at this than Benjy. And he tends sometimes to address the reader like Jason—or, at least, try to address him—and sometimes like Benjy to forget him. Whether addressing the reader or not, however, his language remains intensely claustrophobic: based not on a logic of the senses as Benjy's is, nor on the appearance of rational logic as is Jason's, but on a tortuous and convoluted series of personal associations. The style is intense and disjointed, ranging between attempts at orderly narration and uncontrolled stream-of-consciousness: Quentin, it seems, is always trying to place things within conventional linguistic structures only to find those structures slide away or dissolve.

> I found the gasoline in Shreve's room and spread the vest on the table, where it would be flat, and opened the gasoline.
>
> *The first car in town a girl Girl that's what Jason couldn't bear smell of gasoline making him sick then got madder than ever because a girl Girl had no sister but Benjamin Benjamin the child of my sorrowful if I'd just had a mother so I could say Mother Mother*[39]

The disintegration of syntax in passages like this one finds its analogue, in the second section as a whole, in Quentin's failure to tell his story in an orderly manner. Quentin cannot quite subdue the object to the word; equally, he cannot quite construct a coherent narrative for himself because, in losing Caddy, he has lost what Henry James would call the 'germ'[40] of his narrative—the person, that is, who made sense of all the disparate elements of life for him by providing them with an emotional centre.

As I have suggested already, Quentin's idiot younger brother Benjy is very like Quentin as far as intentions are concerned but quite unlike him in terms of achievement. Benjy, too, wants to ignore the otherness of his sister; for him, however, this leads to very few problems since, according to his own radically limited perception of things, otherness simply does not exist. There is nothing 'out there,' as he sees it, everything is merely an extension, an adjunct of his own being. The whole purpose of Benjy's language is, in fact, to deny the irreducible reality and particularity of the objective world and to absorb every experience, each person or thing that confronts him, into a strictly closed and subjective system:

> I opened the gate and they stopped, turning. I was trying to say, and I caught her, trying to say, and she screamed and I was trying to say and trying and the bright shapes began to stop and I tried to get out. I tried to get off of my face, but the bright shapes were going again.[41]

Vocabulary is kept to a minimum; the sentences are simple, declarative, and repetitive; and the presence of an audience of any kind never even begins to be acknowledged. Benjy's 'trying to say' really involves little more than an attempt to simplify by identifying knowing with being—an effort, not to communicate, but to reduce everything to a private code; and, in response to it, the reader is likely to fluctuate between feelings of strangeness or what the formalists call 'defamiliarisation'[42] and a more radical, less pleasurable sense of alienation.

And what of Dilsey, and the final section of the novel? Here, of course, the reader is addressed directly and with consideration, in an attempt to communicate that scrupulously avoids the self-conscious swaggering of Jason's monologue. Caddy, in turn, is recalled with understanding and warmth—but with the acknowledgement that she is a separate person whose separateness needs to be remembered and respected. And Faulkner himself—or, to be more accurate, a third-person narrator who bears a close resemblance to the author[43]—appears for the first time as a distinct voice and a distinctive presence, ready to embrace Dilsey and her point of view even while describing them strictly from the outside. In effect, all the relationships here between author, narrator, subject, and reader are characterized by a combination of sympathy and detachment; while the language carries us into a world where significant contact between quite separate individuals does at least appear to be possible.

> The day dawned bleak and chill, a moving wall of grey light out of the north-east which, instead of dissolving into moisture, seemed to disintegrate into minute and venomous particles, like dust that, when Dilsey opened the door of the cabin and emerged, needled laterally into her flesh, precipitating not so much a moisture as a substance partaking of the quality of thin, not quite congealed oil. She wore a stiff black straw hat perched upon her turban, and a maroon velvet cape with a border of mangy and anonymous fur above a dress of purple silk. . . . [44]

For once, the closed circle of the interior monologue is broken, the sense of the concrete world is firm, the visible outlines of things finely and even harshly etched, the rhythms exact, evocative, and sure. And yet, and yet . . . : here, as in the passage from *Light in August* discussed earlier, the language is intricately figurative, insistently, almost obsessively artificial; and the emphasis throughout is on appearance and impression, on what *seems* to be the case rather than what is. We are still not being told the whole truth, the implication is, there remain limits to what we can know; despite every effort, in fact, even this last section of the novel does not entirely succeed in naming Caddy. So it is not entirely surprising that, like the three Compson brothers, Dilsey (who, as the passage just quoted indicates, tends to dominate this section) is eventually tempted to discard language altogether. In this respect, Quentin's suicide, Benjy's howling, and Jason's moments of impotent, speechless fury find their equivalent in the mindless chant that the Compson's black housekeeper and cook shares with the congregation at the Easter Day service: in ways that are, certainly, very different all four characters place a question mark over their attempts to turn experience into speech by turning aside from words, seeking deliverance and redress in a non-verbal world.

These are only the crudest of distinctions, of course, for there is a great deal more than I have indicated to the rhetoric of *The Sound and the Fury:* but perhaps I have said enough to make the point. At times, Faulkner felt that experience, life 'out there,' existed beyond the compass of language: a feeling that would prompt him to claim that all he really liked was '. . . silence. Silence and horses. And trees.' [45] But at other times, he seemed to believe that he could and should try to inscribe his own scratchings on the surface of the earth, that he should at least attempt the impossible and tell Caddy's story, using all the tools—all the different voices and idioms—available to him. As Faulkner himself put it once, 'Sometimes I think of doing what Rimbaud did—yet I will certainly keep on writing as long as I live.' [46] And at all times, no matter what his mood, Faulkner was effectively drawing on his Southern heritage: that self-consciousness, and more specifically that acute sense of both the possibilities and the limits of language, which was part of the 'common view of life' given to him by his region.

• • •

It is often said that Faulkner is a modernist writer.[47] In a way, this is undeniable. His is a literature of the edge, marked by a sense of disorientation and experiment, unafraid to explore the fundamentals of expression: as such, it has much in common with, say, the writings of Joyce, Eliot, and Pound, or in other arts with the work of Stravinsky or the post-Impressionists. But it would be wrong to assume that, because of this, Faulkner was not also a literary regionalist or that his regionalism was invariably at odds with his modernism. Sometimes it was, perhaps. More often than not, however, those characteristics which might in another writer be termed specifically modernist were in any case a part of Faulkner's regional inheritance. He did not have to turn to Eliot, for instance, to discover the importance of a tradition: all around him he could find examples of people trying to recreate the past, to forge a valid inheritance for themselves. Nor did he have to refer to Joyce in order to become aware of the fictive process, the difficulties of naming and telling: that awareness was inherent in the Southern preoccupation with artifice, role-playing, and rhetoric. All of this is not to say that Faulkner did not know of writers like Eliot and Joyce, and was not influenced by them. Of course he knew of them—although he was sometimes misleading about the amount he knew—and was affected by them—although perhaps less than is commonly imagined. But it is to say that, for the most part, what Faulkner responded to in those writers, and in modernism generally, were forms of knowledge and speech that he could also find in his regional tradition; what he absorbed from the crisis of his own times tended merely to confirm, comment upon, or develop that dream (to use his own word), that system of inherited argument and metaphor, that was the special gift of the South. 'You know,' Faulkner said once in an interview, sometimes I think there must be a sort of pollen of ideas floating in the air, which fertilizes similarly minds here and there which have not had direct contact.[48]

For Faulkner, that 'pollen of ideas' was primarily Southern in origin; with its help, he managed to produce fiction that was regional in the best sense— something that could speak from Oxford, Mississippi, and the land he loved and hated to anyone anywhere willing to attend.

NOTES

1. Robert A. Jeliffe, ed. *Faulkner at Nagano* (Tokyo: The Kenkyusha Press, 1956), 26.

2. James B. Meriwether and Michael Millgate, eds., *Lion in the Garden: Interviews with William Faulkner 1926–62* (New York: Random House, 1968), 72.

3. *Intruder in the Dust* (1948; reprint, London: Chatto and Windus, 1949), 155. The extensive quotations from Faulkner's work in this essay are reproduced by permission of the Author's Literary Estate, Chatto and Windus Ltd., Curtis Brown, and Random House, Inc.

4. 'An Introduction to *The Sound and the Fury,*' ed. James B. Meriwether, *Mississippi Quarterly* 26 (summer 1973): 411.

5. *Absalom, Absalom!* (1936; reprint, London: Chatto and Windus, 1937), 174.

6. Ibid., 12.

7. Eugene Walter, *Untidy Pilgrim* (New York, 1954), 21.

8. *Lion in the Garden,* 255. For Cash's remarks on the Southern environment, see *The Mind of the South* (1942; reprint, New York: Vintage Books, 1957, 48–49).

9. 'Place in Fiction,' in *Three Papers on Fiction* (Northampton, Mass, 1962), 11. For a fuller discussion of the sense of place, see Lewis P. Simpson, *The Dispossessed Garden: Pastoral and History in Southern Literature* (Athens, Ga., 1975).

10. *Requiem for a Nun* (1951; reprint, London, Chatto and Windus, 1953), 231. See also page 230.

11. *Light in August* (1932; reprint, London: Chatto and Windus, 1933), 6.

12. Page 361.

13. *Essays of Four Decades* (New York, 1967), 545. For a fuller discussion of the sense of the past, see Thomas D. Young, *The Past in the Present: A Thematic Study of Modern Southern Fiction* (Baton Rouge, La., 1981).

14. Letter to Charles Boyle, Earl of Orrery, 5 July 1726, cited in *The London Diary and Other Writings,* ed. Louis B. Wright and Marion Tinling (New York, 1958), 37.

15. Page 111.

16. Page 194.

17. *Soldiers' Pay* (1926; reprint, London: Chatto and Windus, 1930), 152.

18. Page 303.

19. See, for example, John T. Irwin, *Doubling and Incest/Repetition and Revenge: A Speculative Reading of Faulkner* (Baltimore, Md., 1975), 20, 157; Estella Schoenberg, *Old Tales and Talking: Quentin Compson in William Faulkner's Absalom, Absalom!' and Related Works* (Jackson, Miss., 1977), 135, 140; Joanna V. Creighton, *William Faulkner's Craft of Revision* (Detroit, Mich., 1977), 12.

20. Cited in David Minter, *William Faulkner: His Life and Work* (Baltimore, Md., 1980), 34.

21. *Absalom, Absalom!*, 261.

22. Allen Tate, 'Remarks on the Southern Religion,' in *I'll Take My Stand: The South and the Agrarian Tradition* by Twelve Southerners (1930; reprint, New York: Harper Torchbooks, 1962), 159.

23. Robert Penn Warren, *All the King's Men* (New York, 1942), 180. For a fuller discussion of the sense of evil, see C. Van Woodward, *The Burden of Southern History* (Baton Rouge, La., 1966).

24. *Go Down, Moses and Other Stories* (1942; reprint, London: Chatto and Windus, 1942), 83.

25. *Mind of the South*, 53.

26. Page 46

27. *Pylon* (1935; reprint, London: Chatto and Windus, 1935), 57.

28. *Soldiers' Pay*, 252.

29. *Mosquitoes* (1927; reprint, London: Chatto and Windus, 1964), 96.

30. *As I Lay Dying* (1930; reprint, London: Chatto and Windus, 1935), 136. Examples of the sculptor or craftsman figure include Gordon in *Mosquitoes* and Cash Bundren in *As I Lay Dying*.

31. Cited in Joseph Blotner, *Faulkner: A Biography* (New York, 1974), 1522.

32. *Lion in the Garden*, 245.

33. Frederick L. Gwynn and Joseph L. Blotner, eds., *Faulkner in the University: Class Conferences at the University of Virginia 1957–58* (Charlottesville: University of Virginia Press, 1959), 6.

34. Page 208.

35. 'An Introduction to *The Sound and the Fury*,' ed. James B. Meriwether, *Southern Review* 8 (autumn 1972): 709; 'Introduction to *the Sound and the Fury*,' *Mississippi Quarterly*, 414.

36. 'Introduction to *The Sound and the Fury*,' *Southern Review*, 710.

37. *Notes Toward A Supreme Fiction*, 'It Must Be Abstract,' poem 1. For a fuller discussion of Caddy, see André Bleikasten, *The Most Splendid Failure: Faulkner's 'The Sound and the Fury'* (Bloomington, Ind., 1976).

38. *The Sound and the Fury* (1929; reprint, London: Chatto and Windus, 1931), 179, 192.

39. Ibid., 171.

40. See Henry James, *The Art of the Novel*, ed. R. P. Blackmur (New York, 1934), 42.

41. *The Sound and the Fury*, 64.

42. See the introduction to this volume.

43. The 'implied author,' to use Wayne Booth's term in *the Rhetoric of Fiction* (Chicago, 1961).

44. *The Sound and the Fury,* 330.

45. *Lion in the Garden,* 64.

46. Ibid., 71.

47. The tendency to describe Faulkner as a modernist dates back at least as far as 1929. See Winfield Townley Scott's review of *The Sound and the Fury* (Providence *Sunday Journal,* 20 October 1929), in John Bassett, ed., *William Faulkner: The Critical Heritage* (London, 1975). See also Michael Millgate, *The Achievement of William Faulkner* (London, 1965) and Donald M. Kartiganer, *The Fragile Thread: The Meaning of Form in Faulkner's Novels* (Amherst, Mass., 1979) for, respectively, one of the most effective and one of the more recent developments of the same idea.

48. *Lion in the Garden,* 30–31.

Index